ALICE BABER

ALICE BABER

AN ARTIST'S TRIUMPH OVER TRAGEDY

GAIL LEVIN

PEGASUS BOOKS
NEW YORK LONDON

ALICE BABER

Pegasus Books, Ltd.
148 West 37th Street, 13th Floor
New York, NY 10018

First Pegasus Books cloth edition February 2026

Interior design by Maria Fernandez

Library of Congress Cataloging-in-Publication Data is available.

ISBN: 979-8-89710-040-8

10 9 8 7 6 5 4 3 2 1

Printed in the United States of America
Distributed by Simon & Schuster
www.pegasusbooks.com

For John as always
and in honor of Alice Baber and all women artists
whose works have remained hidden in museum storage for decades.
May they see the light of day.

Contents

INTRODUCTION

A lice Baber (1928–1982) produced exquisite abstract paintings of vibrantly colored shapes that sometimes create an illusion of floating light. Upon her premature death on October 2, 1982, Baber, just fifty-four years old, was hailed by *The New York Times* as an "artist of lyrical abstractions."[1] In New York, her work had already entered the permanent collections of the Museum of Modern Art, the Metropolitan Museum of Art, the Solomon R. Guggenheim Museum, and the Whitney Museum of American Art. Yet, how could such an accomplished body of paintings have since fallen into near obscurity?

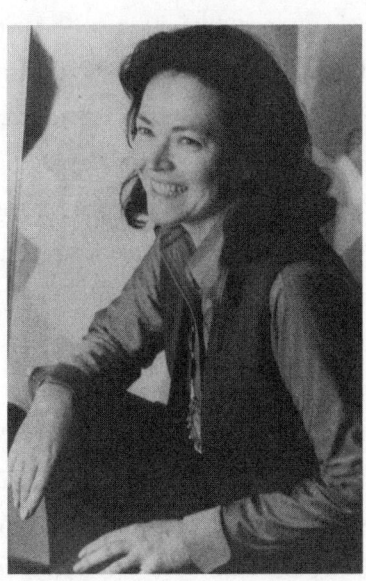

At the time of Baber's passing, the New York art world had shifted its focus to neo-expressionism and young male artists like Jean-Michel Basquiat, who was just then meeting Andy Warhol, with whom he would collaborate. But, even among women artists, attention was elsewhere, ignoring so-called lyrical abstractionists like Baber. In the wake of activism by feminist artists like Judy Chicago and Miriam Schapiro throughout the 1970s, by the early 1980s, when Baber died, younger conceptual artists, like Barbara Kruger or Jenny Holzer, were attracting attention for political art containing provocative texts.

Baber died just a few years before the founding in New York in 1985 of the Guerrilla Girls, an anonymous group of women artists, initially formed to protest the Museum of Modern Art's *An International Survey of Recent Painting and Sculpture* exhibition in the summer of 1984, which, out of 165 artists, included only thirteen women. The activist group worked to highlight gender and racial bias in museums and elsewhere in the art world, injustice that Baber herself had tried to correct.

Baber became one of the activists who worked to find ways to advance not only their own careers but also those of others—despite the bias that stood in their way. In the late 1970s, Baber spoke out on a public panel against discrimination in the art world that limited opportunities not only for women but also for Black people, immigrants, and veterans. At the time, few were speaking out for the disenfranchised.

In fact, we can thank feminist activism for raising the current consciousness that some very talented women artists, like Alice Baber, deserve our attention and await rediscovery. Despite finding early acceptance, Baber left no spouse, nor children, nor a dealer dedicated to marketing her surviving work. Thus, she fell from public awareness.

Born in Charleston, Illinois, Baber arrived in New York City in 1951, still in her early twenties. Ambitious, she met with early success, even after she began, from 1959 to 1968, to divide her time between New York and Paris. She did so to share her life with fellow Midwestern painter Paul Jenkins, whom she married in 1964. After their divorce in 1970, however, the marriage was not listed in chronologies in Baber's catalogues. Eventually, especially after her death, Baber's name disappeared from Jenkins's chronologies too, further erasing her.[2] As a couple for just over a decade, Baber and Jenkins had occasionally exhibited together, painted watercolors on the beach together, traveled extensively, and shared a passion for Asia and collecting Asian art.

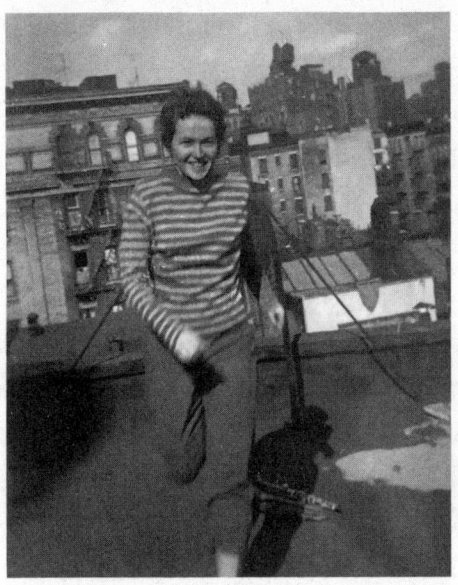

By the time I first researched and wrote about Jenkins, whom I had interviewed while working on my biography of Lee Krasner, Baber was long dead and remained unmentioned and forgotten. I know now that Jenkins's widow, the late Suzanne Donnelly Jenkins, whom he met in 1977 and married on July 20, 1979, omitted her late husband's previous two marriages from all the chronologies that she controlled and misled anyone who asked about Baber.[3] Two of the major obituaries for Paul

Jenkins—in *The Guardian* in London and in *The New York Times*, omit any mention of his first two marriages, although his daughter, a product of his first marriage, is listed.[4] Only one obituary, in *The Independent* in London, did divulge the two earlier marriages.[5]

Dozens of Baber's paintings remained in the possession of Jenkins, then in his estate, hidden from view.[6] Of course, the couple must have exchanged art works during their time together. One 1958 canvas by Jenkins, *Lunar Moth*, was included in a major 1975 monograph on his work, listed as owned by Alice Baber.[7] After Jenkins's death, his widow started selling some of Baber's artworks, but she required that at least one of the art dealers purchasing them, Berry Campbell Gallery in New York, agree to refrain from organizing a show of Alice Baber's work, a request that the gallery honored during Suzanne Jenkins's lifetime.

None of these works by Alice Baber were inscribed to Paul Jenkins, so it is possible that one of her many traveling shows was returned to the Paris home that the couple had shared until mid-1968, when they broke up, instead of to Baber in New York. Although the reason that this body of Baber's work ended up in Jenkins's custody no longer matters, the fact is that these works, along with the couple's live-in relationship and eventual marriage, were hidden by Jenkins and his widow for decades.

The implications of their strategy can be seen in the catalogue essay on Baber that Eliza Gregory, associate director of Ronchini Gallery in London, published in late 2024, where she appears to have unwittingly based her narrative about Alice Baber and Paul Jenkins on a deceptive account purposefully fabricated by Paul's widow, Suzanne, who never met Alice. Gregory thus writes of Baber and Jenkins: "They met in Paris, which at the time was a melting pot of American expat artists, many of whom took advantage of the GI Bill enacted after World War II . . . It was under this artistic landscape that Baber completed a brief stint at the École des Beaux-Arts, having moved to Paris in 1951."[8] In fact, it is well documented that Baber moved with Jenkins from New York to Paris in 1959, so that she could live with him. Baber's only earlier residence in France was attending summer school in Fontainebleau in 1951, during which time she was residing more than an hour outside of Paris.[9]

The intentional omission of Baber's name in literature on Paul Jenkins helps to explain how she could be left out of the recent book and exhibition, *Americans in Paris: Artists Working in Postwar France, 1946–1962*, which devotes attention to Jenkins.[10] While it is true that Baber did not begin to live in Paris until 1959, she was already showing her art there in important group shows in 1959 and 1960.[11]

Yet in 2021, Baber was included in a similar exhibition and book project in France, *United States of Abstraction: Artistes américains en France 1946–1964*.[12] This exhibition included Baber's 1962 canvas, *Before Songs*, borrowed from a private collector in Belgium, and a canvas by Paul Jenkins borrowed from a museum in Grenoble. As such, the organizers did not need to rely on Jenkins's widow for loans of Baber's artwork and were spared distortions of Baber's story.

When Suzanne Jenkins commissioned me to write catalogue essays about the work of Paul Jenkins, she never mentioned Alice Baber. Yet long before I discovered Alice Baber's art, her name was already known to me, but not as Jenkins's second wife. I recall that while I was working on Lee Krasner and abstract expressionism, I knew Baber's name from the Alice Baber Memorial Art Library, established through her estate and by her friends and supporters for the Guild Hall Museum in East Hampton, New York.

A book on the history of Guild Hall by former director Enez Whipple states, "It was in 1983 that Guild Hall first learned it would be the recipient of a gift from the estate of the artist Alice Baber amounting to $138,000 and used to establish the Alice Baber Library in the Leidy Gallery. It opened in 1986 with the artist's fine collection of art books as its core."[13] By now, that book collection and even the room that housed it have vanished without a trace.[14] I also learned that Baber had lived nearby in Sag Harbor.

The subject of Alice Baber never came up in discussions with my late friends, the sculptor Ibram Lassaw and his wife, Ernestine, whom I have since learned were close friends with Baber with whom Ibram sometimes participated in group shows.[15] After Ibram's death, his daughter, Denise, knowing of my interest in India, shared with me some books on Indian art, which, she told me, Alice Baber had given to Ibram.[16]

For my 2011 article about the history of the 1975 feminist show *Women Here and Now*, where Carolee Schneemann debuted her performance of *Interior Scroll*, a landmark event in feminist art history, I tried to interview all the women still alive who had participated in this exhibition, curated by Joyce Kozloff and Joan Semmel and held at Ashawagh Hall, long a venue for the community of artists who congregated in The Springs, a hamlet in East Hampton, New York.[17] While I was able to speak with the organizers and several of the other artists who took part, I was decades too late to contact Alice Baber, whose name I merely recorded in the list of participants of this exhibition.[18]

Recalling these early missed clues, I was intrigued to take on the task of putting together the puzzle of Baber's life, finding that the enduring power of her art presents a challenge well worth pursuing. I began my research using Alice Baber's papers at the Archives of American Art, since no biography of her exists; indeed, no definitive chronology, nor any catalogue raisonné of her work. For me—an art historian long interested in women artists, color, and abstraction—Baber had remained a curious question mark.

While Baber does appear in some books on women artists, she does not appear in books on abstract expressionists, despite having been the exact contemporary of Helen Frankenthaler and having met and shown with her and several of the other abstract expressionists.[19] The omission of Baber underscores that her art represents a new kind of abstraction.

Perhaps it is this sense of "newness" in Baber's art that has resulted in a surprising plethora of Baber merchandise online. I was amazed to find her images available for sale not only as reproductions suitable for hanging on the wall, but also as tank tops, T-shirts, pillows, blankets, bath mats, bath towels, aprons, mugs, jigsaw puzzles, magnets, notecards, spiral notebook covers, iPad cases, and coasters. Finding at once such recognition for and exploitation of Baber's art that she will never know, I could not decide whether to cry or to cheer. But I tell myself, that as more and more museums, galleries, and private collectors are beginning to show interest in Baber's work, at least some of the people who are attracted to Baber's designs will want to know who she was.

But this story is also an exposé of some of those who conspired to write Alice Baber out of history, including powerful male art historians and critics, curators, and the widow of Paul Jenkins, Baber's former companion and spouse for over a decade. In this sense, Baber becomes paradigmatic of women artists of her generation and earlier, who had to face incredible bias just to be taken seriously.

Researching Baber's life and art has sometimes seemed like an archaeological excavation with plenty of exciting surprises along the way. What a revelation to view Baber's monumental 1979 painting, *The Path of the Grey Falcon of the Dawn*, in pristine condition, languishing in an off-site storage warehouse of the Metropolitan Museum of Art. But what a puzzle that the Met has neither exhibited nor loaned this beautiful painting for more than forty-five years (CP #46).

The pale palette of this canvas is challenging to photograph well; when I began this project the Met's website showed Baber's painting, which depends on its subtle coloration and large size for impact, only as a tiny black-and-white reproduction. From my experience as a curator, I am also aware that unsolicited gifts to museums are often less valued than works the museum has had to purchase.

Baber's painting, buried for decades, evokes the fairy tale *Sleeping Beauty*, or the story of the tomb of King Tutankhamun, who became world-famous only after the British archaeologist and Egyptologist Howard Carter discovered his intact tomb in 1922. Like such tales, Alice Baber's forgotten art and her story await our discovery. For me, putting together the record of Baber's art and life has involved reconstructing her history by unearthing tiny fragments and then facing the challenge of piecing them together—evidence like shattered shards of a buried, broken pot. Only by putting together the pieces of this puzzle can we begin to interpret her singular art and understand its lasting significance.

Since the process has been so much more challenging than my previous biographies—where my subjects Edward Hopper, Lee Krasner, or Judy Chicago were so much better known—I include in my narrative a few stories of how I happened to discover some of the personal relationships that the rather private Baber developed but tried to keep to herself. Indeed, it is part of Baber's story that she intentionally omitted such personal documents from her extensive professional papers, which she bequeathed to the Smithsonian Institution's Archives of American Art. In fact, missing from her papers are documents that would illuminate her marriage and her other romantic relationships. Fortunately, some evidence remains, including letters Baber wrote, some of which were preserved by their recipients.

Alice Baber's story is that of a bright, beautiful, personable, and educated middle-class young woman from rural Illinois, who ventured alone to New York City in the early 1950s, an era when few single women had the courage or the means to take on such a challenge. Yet, Baber was dedicated, energetic, and determined to become a professional artist. Despite her considerable talent and abilities, she had to overcome many obstacles, some which all artists face, but many specifically aimed at women. How Baber maneuvered and managed to succeed is a tale worth knowing and still useful for artists today.

CHAPTER I

Taking the Plunge: New York City (1951–1954)

Alice Baber arrived in New York City on her return from studying art in Europe during the summer of 1951. She recounted how, on the ship, she had the good luck to meet Colette [Levy] Roberts, an artist and art critic, who became her first acquaintance in the New York art world. It was Roberts who invited Baber to attend her first ever New York gallery opening—a show at John Heller's gallery on East 57th Street.[1]

Roberts, a Frenchwoman born to a Jewish family, was a graduate of the University of Paris. She had also studied art in Paris with the abstract painter Roger Bissière at the Académie Ranson, and with the medievalist art historian and theorist Henry Focillon at the École du Louvre. She had fled to New York in 1939 as World War II began in Europe. Before Baber met her, Roberts had served, from 1947 to 1949, as gallery director of the Argent Galleries of the National Association of Women Artists, located at 42 West 57th Street, in the heart of the New York art world.[2] Thus, Roberts was familiar with the immense challenges women artists faced. She also had an insider's view of museums, having worked from

1950 to 1951 as secretary for Alan Priest, curator of Far Eastern Art at the Metropolitan Museum of Art.[3]

Beginning in 1953, Roberts was the art editor for *France Amérique*, the French-language newspaper in New York. She directed the gallery Grand Central Moderns from 1952 to 1968, and brought attention to previously unknown artists, such as the sculptor Louise Nevelson. Thus, for Baber, a twenty-three-year-old art student from a small Midwestern town, meeting Roberts, who was teaching drawing on the ship on which she returned home from Europe, was the perfect introduction to New York's art scene.

Baber responded to this unexpected opportunity with enthusiasm, finding in Roberts a role model for a successful woman managing to work in the New York art world. Taking courage from the example of her new friend, Baber began making the rounds of the galleries, looking for employment. At one gallery, she heard about someone wanting to share costs with a roommate. That woman turned out to be living at the bohemian Chelsea Hotel, a kind of urban artists' colony on West 23rd Street. Thus, Baber landed in New York City and temporarily moved into the Chelsea, which Dylan Thomas once described as a place "where cockroaches have teeth."[4] The adaptable Baber lived there for about eight months.

By the late spring, Baber found a place to live on her own in a mews at 73 Bedford Street in the West Village, a place she held onto until the late 1970s.[5] With her love of poetry, she might well have discovered that a neighboring house at 75 ½ Bedford Street was where the poet Edna St. Vincent Millay had briefly lived from 1923 to 1924, followed later by the actor John Barrymore.[6] Baber's neighborhood, situated in the West Village hangout of Bohemia and Beat poets, would become legendary after June 1969, when the Stonewall Inn, located around the corner on Christopher Street, became the site of its homosexual patrons' resistance to a police raid that gave birth to the gay liberation movement.[7] Although she moved there in the less turbulent days of the early 1950s, Baber was clearly not looking for a quiet puritan corner of New York in which to set up her home.

Living alone was a radical social choice for a single young woman at the time that Baber moved on from the Chelsea Hotel to her own space in the spring of 1952. Her goal was to live an independent life as an artist and her means to achieve this was through writing for a living. From early childhood, Baber enjoyed writing and recalled that she had elected to study journalism in college because "I thought I could use it to make money. . . . When I came to New York I did get jobs, writing jobs, so it was something that I planned and that worked for me."[8] In fact, while Baber was at Indiana University, *Vogue* magazine's search "for talent" was reported in the student newspaper, raising awareness that there was the possibility of women earning a living by working for such popular publications in New York.[9]

Baber later explained, "I used my journalism by writing publicity for a home furnishing place, where my knowledge of art was useful, and I have done the same thing for designers. I also worked for a magazine for four years."[10] Baber referred to the year or two that she spent working as a publicist for the noted American industrial designer George Nelson, considered a pioneer of American modernism. He ran his own firm and employed a roster of accomplished designers.

Trained in architecture, Nelson designed interiors, furniture, exhibitions, and products for industry. He published interviews in *Architectural Forum* with major European designers, such as the architects Walter Gropius, Ludwig Mies van der Rohe, and Le Corbusier. From 1945, Nelson became the director of design for Herman Miller, the prestigious furniture company that produced some of the era's classic pieces of furniture, including the Noguchi table, the Eames

Lounge Chair, and the Marshmallow sofa.[11] Baber's work in Nelson's firm offered her an insider's view of a successful modern designer.

Nelson's company projects ranged from kitchen design to company logos.[12] A note on Christmas Day 1954 from Baber's father, Adin, to his sister-in-law, Alice's beloved Aunt Bonnie, states: "If you haven't discarded it. Save Dec. 13 *Life*. The kitchen by Gco. Nelson is Alice's but no one knows it, and, of course no employee would get credit (CP #22). [Her sister] Nan's very efficient and Southern exposure. Alice and I came down from NYC yesterday p.m."[13] Adin and Alice were visiting Nancy in the new home that she and her husband had recently purchased in Bethesda, Maryland.

The *Life* feature story to which Adin referred was titled "Beauty in a Busy Place." Subtitled "The Kitchen Gets Its First Full Array of Colored Appliances," the article begins, "Piecemeal attempts to get color in the kitchen, now that it has become a gathering place for family and friends, have taken away some of the room's antiseptic look."[14] The very colorful eat-in "bright new kitchen" that Adin Baber said was Alice's was credited as "designed by George Nelson for General Electric," and the article boasted "teams up colors with white . . . Storage cabinets are painted in the new G. E. colors and are specially installed in the kitchen to make a flat wall."[15] In fact, this kitchen features a lively palette of yellow, pink, and blue with touches of orange, reminiscent of Baber's 1963 canvas, *Where They Meet*, which, after all, is the purpose of a colorful, cheerful, eat-in kitchen.

Adin Baber later explained to a friend that Alice had spent two years working as a publicist for George Nelson, and that she had then worked for *McCall's* magazine for four years, initially in kitchen design.[16] Alice described her four years working at *McCall's* as having been its "art editor." Her work as an "art editor" could have entailed graphic design or editorial content; however, the magazine had no features on visual arts. The name Alice Baber, for example, appears on the *McCall's* masthead as an unspecified editor in December 1955; there are sections on food, house and home, fashions, and features such as the "Ten-Year-Old Toymaker" and "What Children Teach Us About Christmas."[17]

One of Baber's assignments for *McCall's* we know about from Denise Lassaw, the daughter of Baber's close friends Ibram and Ernestine Lassaw. Denise recalls that in the mid-1950s, Alice had her produce two pictures on paper to hang on the wall displayed in a feature story, which shows two small children making art at a built-in desk.[18] Denise remembers being delighted that Alice paid for her pictures and gave her a copy of them reproduced in the *McCall's* story (CP #6). The copy that Baber wrote for this feature, in the October 1958 issue, states, "A play area when the children are small, this long counter also serves as a desk and a place for Mother to spread her sewing or sort laundry (the gas washer-dryer is conveniently next to it)."

Baber worked for longtime editor and publisher Otis Lee Wiese, who, fighting stiff competition from other women's magazines in the 1950s, tried unsuccessfully to reposition *McCall's* as a magazine for the entire family, a focus far from Baber's interests. By January 1957, Alice Baber is listed with three others as an editor on the *McCall's* masthead underneath the art director and the art coordinator. At the time, *McCall's* had a regular column by Eleanor Roosevelt, as well as cooking, fashion, and home features. *McCall's* also published patterns for sewing clothes, but the magazine paid scant attention to the visual arts.

Kitchen appliance brochures that survive in Baber's family suggest the kinds of texts that she would be employed to write during the 1950s. Indicative of the mentality of the postwar era, one such brochure is headlined HOW TO STAY IN LOVE FOR YEARS AND YEARS AND YEARS.[19]

The next page continues: "Introducing . . . two nice people," and the accompanying illustration shows a masculine "Frigidaire electric range" with a smiling face, bowing with his top hat in his hand. The gesture of the new anthropomorphic stove is directed toward a young housewife, dressed in a perky print dress, high heels, and apron, who responds to his bow with a curtsy.

The accompanying text describes the new electric range as a "handsome and handy helper as ever stood by to assist a fair lady at mealtime. We know that he'll capture your heart, and predict that you'll stay in love for years and years and years . . . But lasting affection, as we know, is based on understanding. And the woman whose love lasts longest is the woman who knows best how to handle her man. So we're suggesting, Mrs. Housewife—strangely suggesting—that you learn how to handle the new man in your life *now*." Such advertising messages might well have been intended to discourage ambitious young women who dreamed of having their own careers.

Women, who had entered the workforce to take the places of men who were serving in the Armed Forces during World War II, were encouraged by the US government, following the end of the war, to return to domestic life as wives and mothers. Advertising supported the government's need to influence gender roles. The iconic image of Rosie the Riveter had to give way as soldiers returned home and needed their jobs back.[20] It was at this transitional moment that Baber entered college. Her future career would be affected by the new opportunities for women that emerged during the war.

While Alice Baber wrote for a living, she lived to paint. Thus, she led a double life, working a 9:00–5:00 day job, while pursuing a nighttime passion—making art. Baber later admitted: "I worked for a magazine. And I tried not to let people know that I did. I didn't make a big point of it because it was considered very unprofessional to have a job. But I figured you had to survive, you had to do something and there weren't any teaching jobs. That was—it's very hard in New York to get some teaching jobs until you've had some shows."[21] At the time, it was also much more difficult for women to land full-time teaching positions in universities or at art schools. As a result, the highly motivated Baber produced her paintings on weekends or at night.

Baber's work as a journalist or editor by day is not so different from previous generations of male painters, including John Sloan, Edward Hopper, Arthur Dove, and Mark Rothko, all of whom worked for a time as illustrators for magazines, newspapers, or books.[22] An earlier generation of American women, often less famous as fine artists, also worked successfully as illustrators, including Peggy Bacon, Djuna Barnes, Esphyr Slobodkina, and Clara Tice. Even more artists moonlighted by writing articles about art—for example, John Sloan, Edward Hopper, Marsden Hartley, Barnett Newman, Elaine de Kooning, Fairfield Porter, and Don Judd.

Despite the day jobs writing and editing, Baber recalled "doing a series of figures when I first came to New York, when my friends and I used to pose for each other, and we all would be tired, so that by the time you get around to posing, usually we would be in a sleeping position. So, I painted a friend of mine, which I called *Ursula Sleeping* (CP #6), because of my admiration for the Carpaccio. And the only connection with the Carpaccio that has anything to do with composition was that it was a recumbent figure."[23] Referring to the figure of Vittore Carpaccio's *Dream of Saint Ursula* (1495), Baber explained how she now sees that reclining figure as "a mountainscape," making a pointed comment about what she sometimes called metaphor, or something that seems representative or symbolic of something else, especially something abstract: "So you see everything for me is not one thing, but a dozen other things."[24]

At least two canvases of recumbent figures by Baber are known to have survived. She painted one in tones of blue that recalls both the palette of Pablo Picasso's Blue period and the theme of Berthe Morisot's painting of a *Young Girl Reclining on a Sofa*. Yet, when Baber focused on the peaks and valleys of her model's body, the bold outline of the figure's contour that she emphasized does recall "a mountainscape."

On the other hand, Baber depicted another extant recumbent figure amongst a variety of geometric patterns, colors, and ornamentation that seem to predict a direction that her painting would take in its evolution to abstraction (CP #7). This second recumbent figure was surely Baber's response to seeing the large show of Henri Matisse's work, organized at the Museum of Modern Art by Alfred H. Barr Jr., which opened on November 14, 1951, shortly after she had moved to New York. Barr's book, *Matisse: His Art and His Public*, accompanied this important show, giving Baber plenty to study.

One of Baber's paintings of a recumbent woman with its ornamental background recalls Matisse's painting *Odalisque au coffret rouge* (1927), which was not in the show.[25] However, Baber has adopted her own combination of Matisse mannerisms; even her checkered background repeats the backdrop of Matisse's *The Hindu Pose* (1923) (CP #7), which was included in the show and would have appealed to Baber because of its theme and her developing interest in Asian religions and culture.[26]

Remaining focused on painting the figure, Baber wanted to have a model to work from life, so she dropped by Hans Hofmann's art school, located at 52 West 8th Street. She came close to enrolling to study with this popular German émigré artist and teacher, an abstract expressionist, who was known to be a huge enthusiast of Matisse's art. But when Baber looked in on a class, she heard Hofmann critiquing a student and saw him working on another student's drawing, causing her to reject the idea of studying with him.

Baber rejecting the idea of a teacher working on student's drawing echoes actual protest by Lee Krasner, who earlier did study with Hofmann and resented his intervening with her drawings in progress, especially when he once ripped up one to make a point.[27] Baber, who had already developed a direction she was pursuing, was not incorrect when she viewed Hofmann as teaching "a kind of cubism, kind of a dynamic cubism," which led to a "certain look," which also did not interest her.[28]

Still searching for access to a life model, Baber went over to the Art Students League on West 57th Street.[29] She enrolled in a class there but found that she disliked the noisy instruction offered by the artist Bernard Klonis, so she dropped out, even forfeiting her tuition. Finally, in 1954 she took anatomy at the Art Students League with the venerable Robert Beverly Hale, which she thought was unobjectionable. Hale, who taught observation from life and the principles of chiaroscuro, inspired his students to see and draw forms in the geometric "mass conceptions" of cylinders, cubes, or spheres.[30] Baber must also have noticed that Hale was then the Met's first curator of the newly established Department of Contemporary American Art; in 1957 he would become known for championing the Met's purchase of Jackson Pollock's monumental abstraction, *Autumn Rhythm*.

Baber continued her education at New York University, where in 1955 she enrolled in a graduate course in Hellenistic art history at the Institute for Fine Arts. Although Baber was intellectually curious and industrious, she never completed enough graduate credits to earn a master's degree, which would likely have helped her obtain a regular teaching position, a secure income, and enabled a less peripatetic life.[31] The other graduate course she took at this time, which hints at her later passion for exotic travel, was in cultural anthropology, focusing on the study of human societies and their development, taught at NYU's downtown campus in Greenwich Village.

It was in Greenwich Village that Baber found inspiration for one of her figurative pictures, which she referred to as depicting Bleecker Street New York City (CP #8). A vertical-format canvas, this undated composition from the early 1950s is bright and lively. It depicts six people visible at an outdoor produce market with a green hanging scale in the foreground. This was a typical scene during the 1950s, when Italian-speaking vendors sold their wares in open carts in Greenwich Village on the north side of Bleecker Street, in an outdoor market that extended from Jones Street to Cornelia Street. At the time that Baber painted her canvas, however, Italian immigrants had already begun moving out to other boroughs and musicians and Beat poets, like Allen Ginsberg, had started to move in.

Baber, the sheltered girl from the Midwest, was fascinated by both the vanishing immigrant life and the vanguard artists experimenting with new styles in art and life. For *Bleecker Street New York City*, she created her composition by referencing several black-and-white photographs that she took on Bleecker Street. When she mailed these snapshots to her father (who already had the painting) in 1965, she commented that she had just found them and recalled: "The one with the XXX in corner was probably the picture I used but I must have added the old lady on right from another (CP #8). I might find another with everything in it but I remember I did make some changes."[32]

Baber included only one female figure—"the old lady"—who sports a bright red scarf and a boldly printed garment. In both the flattened shapes of the fruit and the patterned garment, one sees hints of Baber's future abstractions with their biomorphic shapes and vivid colors. Later she would explain: "I think about the color consciously. I must add what is needed. The right darks, the right lights have to be there and I must know the forms which have been created by the colors' work as forms."[33]

Another surviving figurative painting from her first experience of the city, Baber called *New York City Scene* (CP #9). The canvas is an outdoor scene with figures among trees in a park that recalls her paintings of trees from the time of her studies at Indiana University. This picture appears to depict Hasidic Jews wearing their signature black broad-brimmed hats and women with their heads covered, maintaining strict clothing traditions held over from eighteenth-century Europe. The scene Baber depicted was most likely on the Lower East Side. She even included a wrought-iron fence typical of the city. In painting such an exotic New York City scene as if it were from another time and place, Baber might have been inspired by the course she took in cultural anthropology.

Baber might also have been emulating Arshile Gorky's pre-abstract paintings, painted in reminiscence of his childhood in Armenia. "When I went to New York City in 1951," Baber recalled years later, "everyone seemed to be involved with memories of Gorky. Even today [1975] I dare not look at his work too closely. Unlike many artists, Gorky takes over the mind, and those hard-won spectacular forms of Gorky become like a poem that you think you once wrote."[34] Gorky's admirers were numerous, from male painters like Jackson Pollock, Mark Rothko, Willem de Kooning, and Milton Resnick to Ethel Schwabacher, a woman painter who met Gorky in 1927 and studied independently with him from 1934 to 1936. It was Schwabacher who organized Gorky's memorial retrospective exhibition for the Whitney Museum, which took place from January 5 to February 18, 1951, just months before Baber's arrival in New York in September.[35]

No doubt that Baber would have studied the exhibition's substantial catalogue for the Gorky show in which Schwabacher wrote, according to *The New York Times*, "a deeply sympathetic commentary."[36] Gorky's "quest was to embody the soul of the image in form. Into his imagery, he has distilled the experiences of a poet, a poet-in-paint whose range extended from an intuitive lyrical poetry of nature to a tragic daemonic poetry of human emotion," Schwabacher concluded.[37] Her interpretation of Gorky's art fit perfectly Baber's love of both painting and poetry.

Baber developed her interest in Gorky's later work around this time, when she began experimenting with some of her own earliest abstractions. Some of her surviving early paintings are already nonobjective (CP #10). One is untitled, but through its lines and shapes, relates to Gorky's abstraction, such as his lithograph from 1931, *Painter and Model*. Another painting from this era is titled *Frieda Fromm-Reichmann* (CP #11), after the Jewish psychotherapist who fled Nazi Germany and immigrated to the United States in 1934, a story of seeking refuge that echoes Gorky's journey. (Baber misspelled the therapist's name as "Freda From Reishman.") Fromm-Reichmann published a book in English in 1951, *Principles of Intensive Psychotherapy*, and saw patients in New York City through the William Alanson White Institute.

Baber, who left pages of notes about her dreams, could have been one of Fromm-Reichmann's patients. If so, Baber was much more fortunate than Jackson Pollock and Lee Krasner, who sought therapists through the same William Alanson White Institute where Fromm-Reichmann worked, but they ended up with renegade therapists associated with a radical breakaway Sullivanian cult.[38] Frieda Fromm-Reichmann might not have been Baber's own therapist; instead, another therapist might have encouraged Baber to read Fromm-Reichmann's book. In Baber's handwritten notes, she mentions both a "Dr. G" and a "Dr. C," but the identity of these doctors remains unknown.[39]

Baber, who was eager to absorb new ideas for her art, also remembered spending a lot of time in New York's museums. In the Met, for example, Baber spent time studying various artists, especially the seventeenth-century Baroque painter Peter Paul Rubens, whose paintings she had first discovered as a child visiting the Ringling Museum in Florida. She now felt about the Flemish master that there was "a great deal about drawing that I could learn from looking."[40] She told how much she admired "Baroque space," commenting, "I do like this idea of space doing all kinds of crazy things . . . The unexpected."[41] Another time, she emphasized, "I'm not interested in flat space: I'm interested in a kind of 'Baroque' space, and I like undulating forms across the canvas."[42]

From New York's Frick Collection, Baber reported studying "Fragonard"; however, it was not the Frick's murals of *The Progress of Love* by Jean-Honoré Fragonard that held her attention, but instead the French Rococo artist's most famous painting, *The Swing* (CP #33), in the Wallace Collection in London, about which she exclaimed, "I just love. I like the idea of something swinging through space. I don't think that's such a great painting anyway [with] that particular shoe, and the whole thing but I like the idea of the swing, and I have made paintings with swings."[43]

Baber had known this Fragonard in reproduction since her adolescence, when she had received the gift of Rockwell Kent's 1939 book, *World Famous Paintings*, which includes *The Swing*.[44] Baber's *Swing, Green Swing* (CP #33), *Orange Swing*, and *Yellow Swing* are several examples of the titles she gave to lyrical abstract canvases that she painted in 1966; in 1969, *Wayward Swing* (CP #33); in 1970 she painted a canvas she called *The Swing and the Bridge*. Baber continued to embrace the idea of conveying movement through space. She expressed her emotions through imagined shapes and colors arranged in a meaningful, yet abstract manner.

In the Frick Collection, Baber focused on *The Forge* (ca 1817) by the Spanish Romantic master Francisco Goya, which depicts three blacksmiths toiling over an anvil. She called this work "probably the most complete painting of the figure that's ever been done—the combination of a leg silhouetted against the red fire, the black lines, which are created both by the costume and also the artist just deciding to use a black line. In other words, I looked at that painting when I was trying to decide: Do you use line or don't you use line?"[45]

Baber also remembered spending "hours and hours at New York's Museum of Modern Art. The painting that was the biggest problem for me when I came is the Klee painting of the fish."[46] She was fascinated by Paul Klee's *Around the Fish* (1926), a garnished platter of fish surrounded by seemingly disparate signs and symbols—a cross, full and crescent moons, an exclamation point, a forked red flag—all floating against a dark abyss (CP #12). Speaking about Klee's *Around the Fish*, Baber told how she asked herself, "What happens on the other side of those forms? They're fairly flat and so I went home and thought and thought and I remember asking [the American Surrealist artist] David Hare, I said, 'What do you think happens on the other side of shape in paintings floating in space?' And he said, 'I don't know.' I don't think he was too interested. It haunted me, it still does."[47]

Baber appears to have responded to her expressed admiration of Klee's picture in her untitled abstraction with a bright red background, which can also be read as a still life of a fish. Her composition (CP #12) repeats the bottom curve of the platter in Klee's image and her cross-hatches create a sense of scales on her fish, which like Klee's fish is surrounded by abstract shapes and marks. The chartreuse color from Klee's lower left, which resembles a melon, is repeated by three circles on the lower left of Baber's painting. Baber's early attraction to this painting by Klee, which is often described as "cryptic" or resistant to interpretation, predicts her development as a painter of abstraction compositions that evoke, but never depict or illustrate.

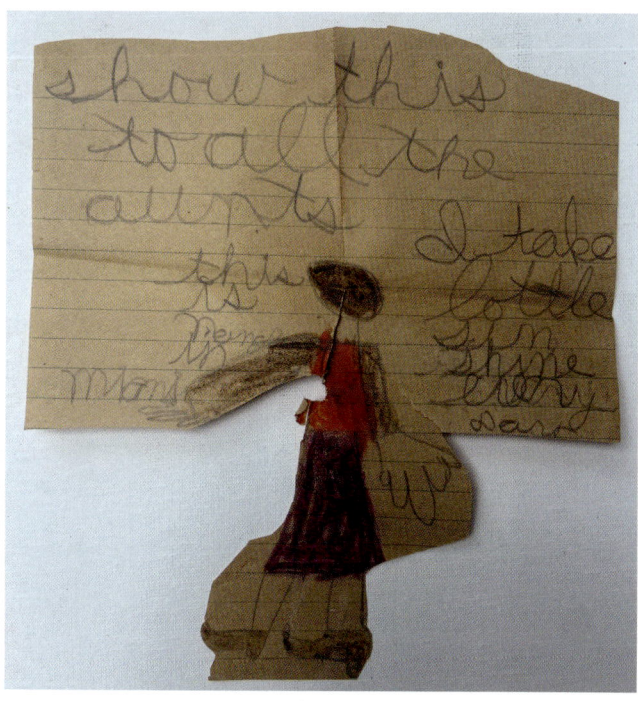

Alice Baber, *Self-Portrait in Florida*, ca 1933, watercolor and pencil on paper, 9 x 11 inches, private collection. "Show this to all the aunts. This is me in Miami. I take a little sunshine every day."

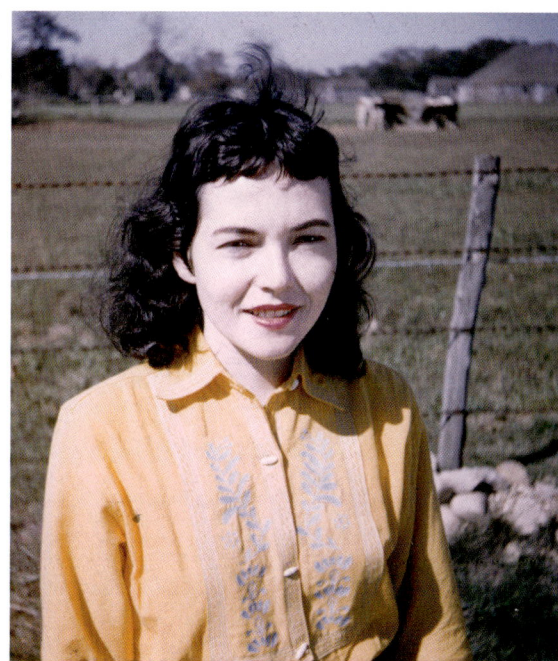

Ibram Lassaw, *Alice Baber in Springs*, 1955, stereo slide. Possibly taken at the old Miller's farm, once on Fireplace Road, The Springs, East Hampton, NY.

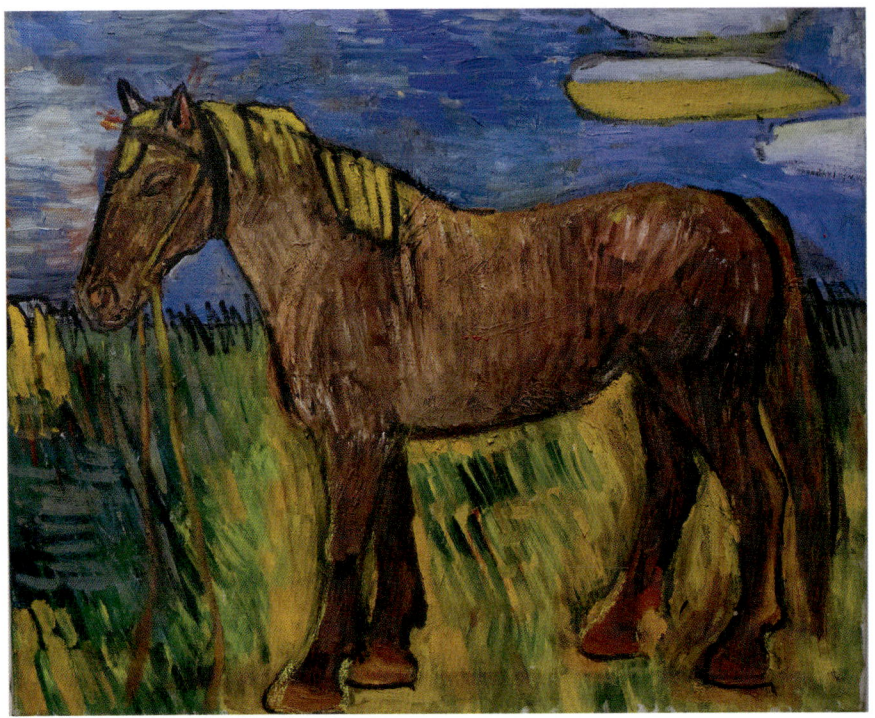

Alice Baber, *Untitled* [horse] ca 1941, oil on canvas, 24 x 30 inches,
Link Art Gallery, Paris, IL.

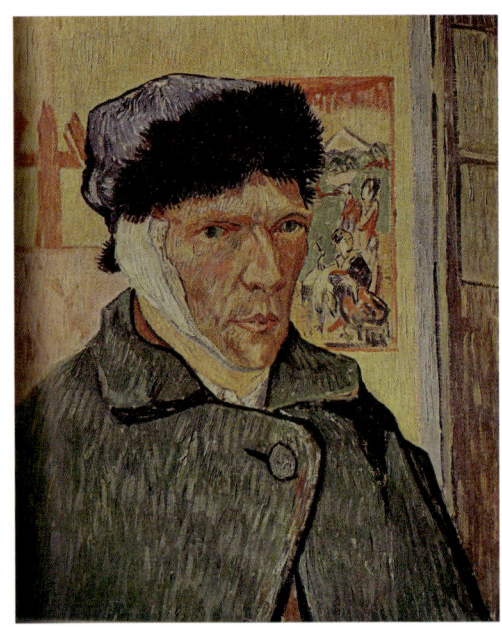

Vincent Van Gogh,
Self-Portrait with Bandaged Ear
[and Japanese print],1889,
from the Courtauld Gallery in London,
reproduced in Rockwell Kent's
World Famous Paintings, 1939,
owned by Alice Baber.

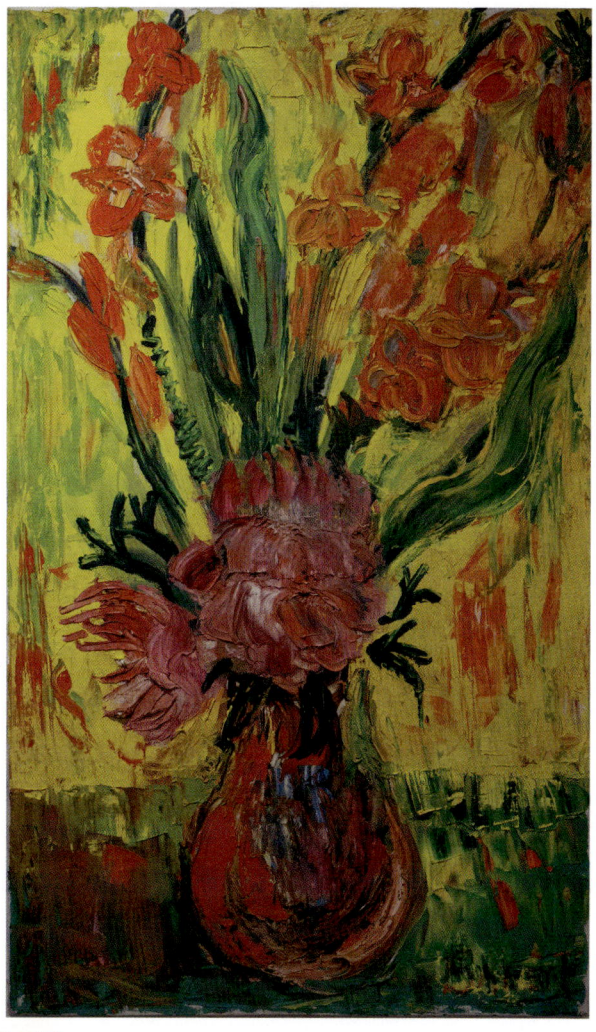

Alice Baber, *Untitled* [still life red vase and flowers], ca 1941–45, oil on canvas, 40 x 24 inches, Link Art Gallery, Paris, IL.

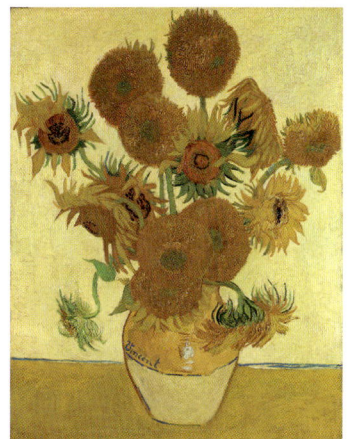

Vincent Van Gogh, *Sunflowers*, 1888, reproduced in Rockwell Kent's *World Famous Paintings*, 1939, owned by Alice Baber.

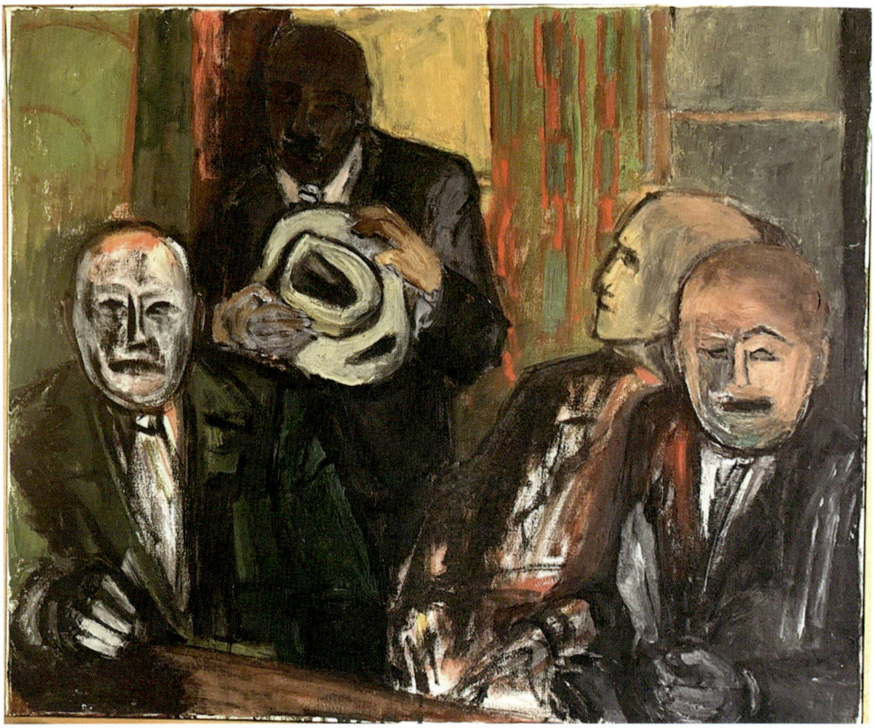

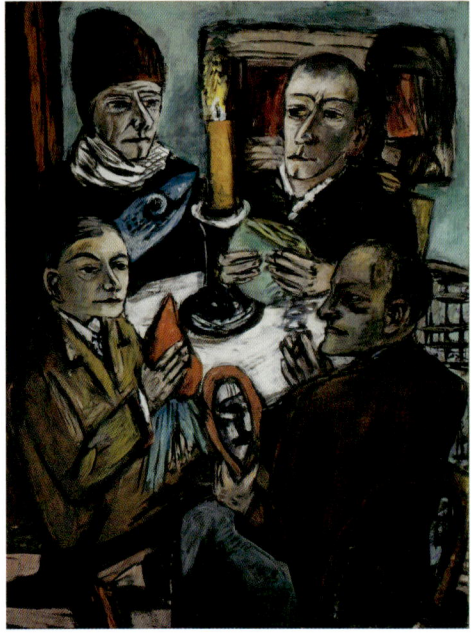

Alice Baber, *Untitled* [Four Men after Max Beckmann],1946–49,
oil on canvas, 25 ¾ x 31 ¾ inches, private collection.

Max Beckmann,
Les Artistes mit Gemüse
[Artists with Vegetable], 1943,
oil on canvas, 58 ⅞ x 45 ¼ inches,
Mildred Lane Kemper Art Museum,
St. Louis, MO. University purchase,
Kende Sale Fund, 1946.

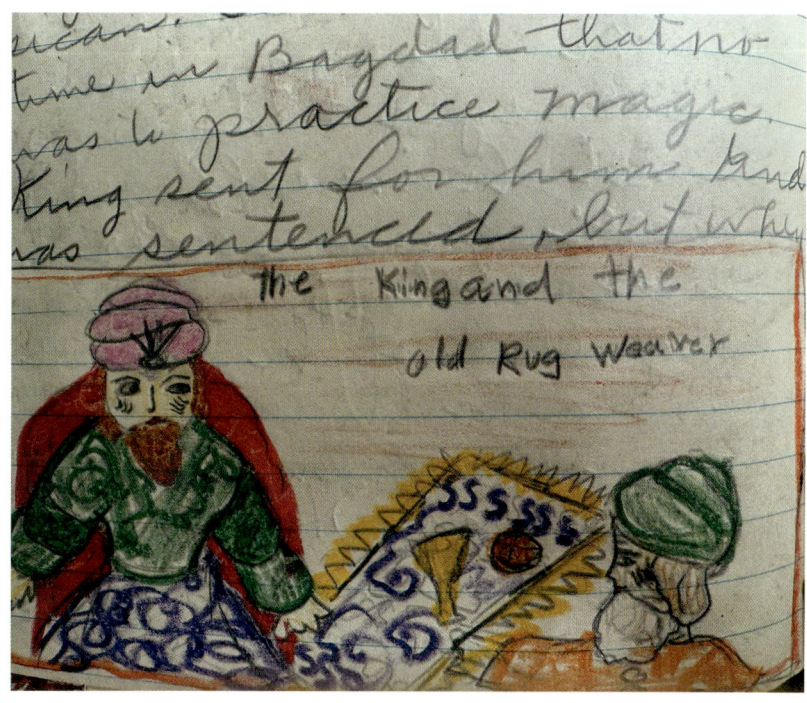

Alice Baber, *The King and the Old Rug Weaver*, July 5, 1939, colored pencil on paper, 3 x 6 ½ inches, on page 8 ½ x 6 ¾ inches, from notebook entitled *My Poems and Stories by Alice Baber*, Baber Family Archives.

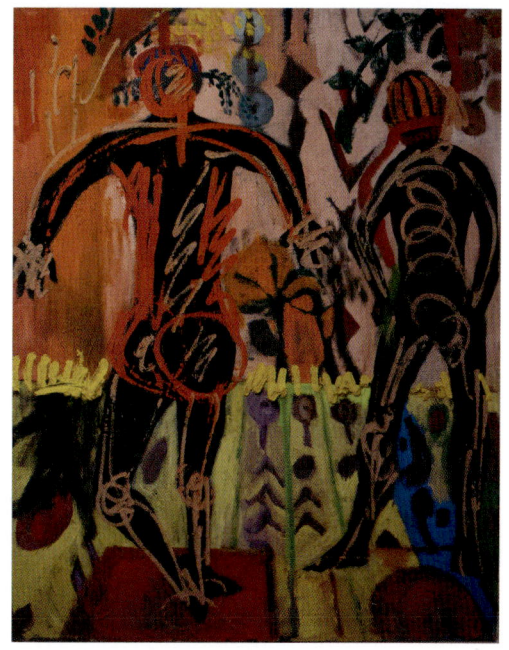

Alice Baber,
Untitled [two abstract male figures],
ca 1950, oil on canvas, 30 x 24 inches,
Link Art Gallery, Paris, IL.

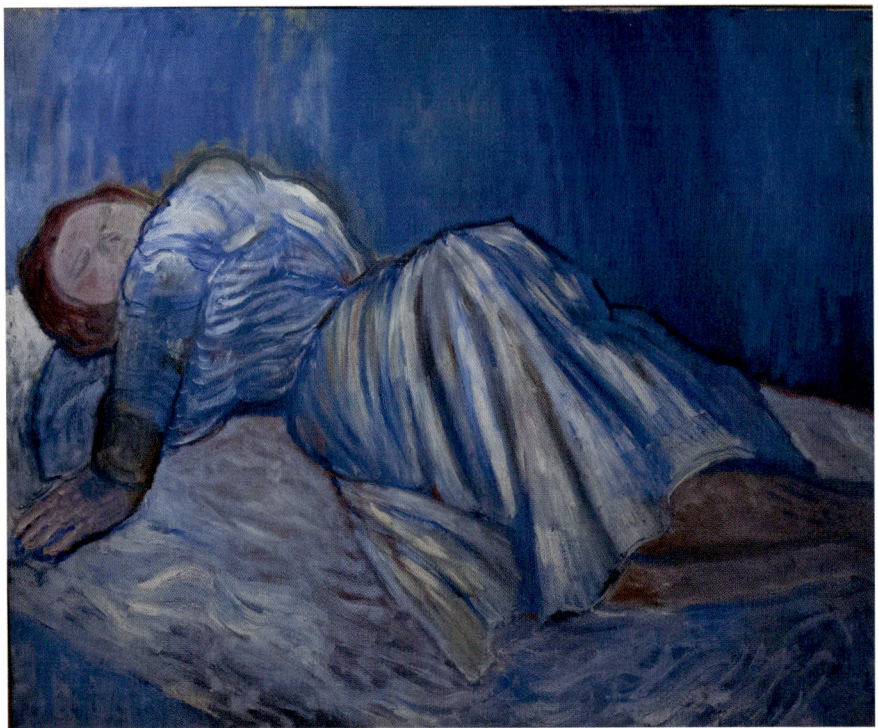

Alice Baber, *Ursula Sleeping* [Woman in Blue in Repose], ca 1952–55, oil on canvas, 40 x 50 inches, Link Art Gallery, Paris, IL.

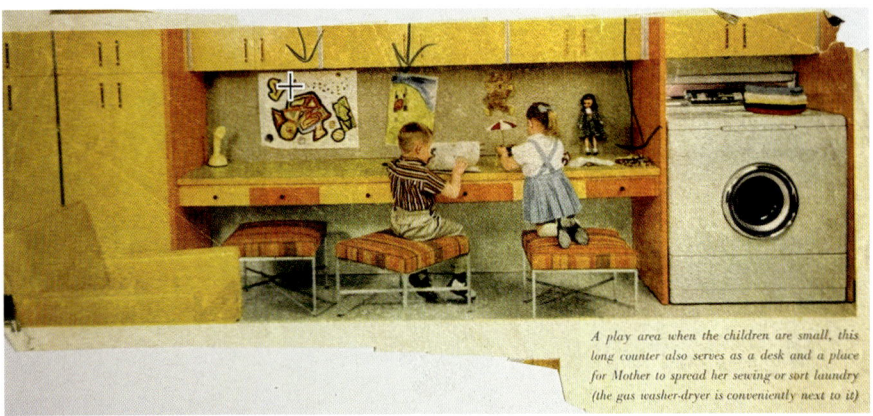

A play area when the children are small, this long counter also serves as a desk and a place for Mother to spread her sewing or sort laundry (the gas washer-dryer is conveniently next to it)

McCall's magazine, October 1958 (vol. 86, no. 1), with drawings Alice Baber commissioned from 12-year-old Denise Lassaw for feature article, "High, Wood and Handsome." Detail from page 132, captioned: "A play area when the children are small, this long counter also serves as a desk and a place for Mother to spread her sewing or sort laundry."

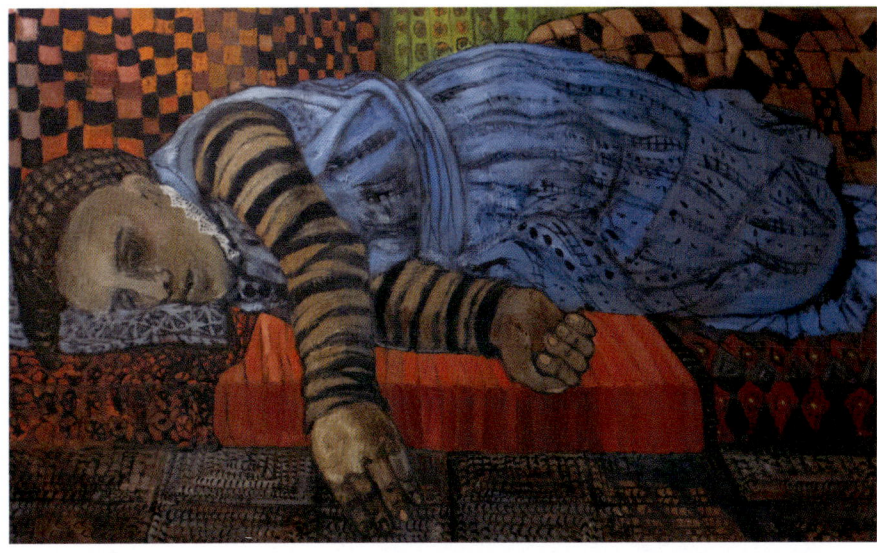

Alice Baber, *Untitled* [woman in blue on side before checked background], ca 1952–53, oil on canvas, 24 x 40 inches, Link Art Gallery, Paris, IL.

Henri Matisse,
The Hindu Pose, 1923,
oil on canvas,
32 $^{11}/_{16}$ x 23 $^{5}/_{8}$ inches,
private collection.

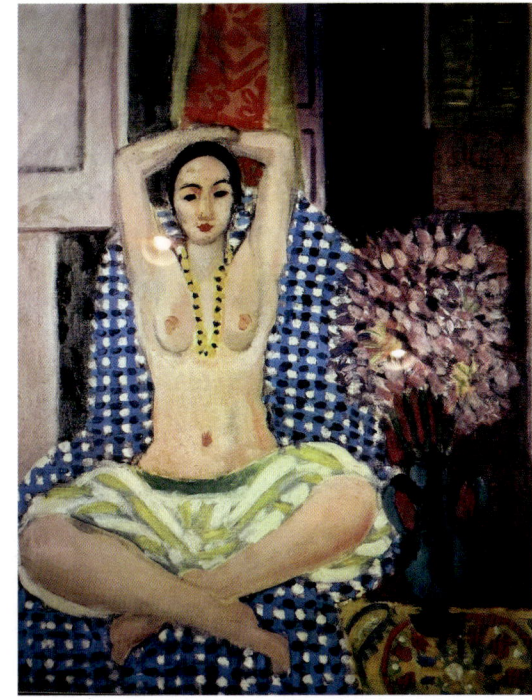

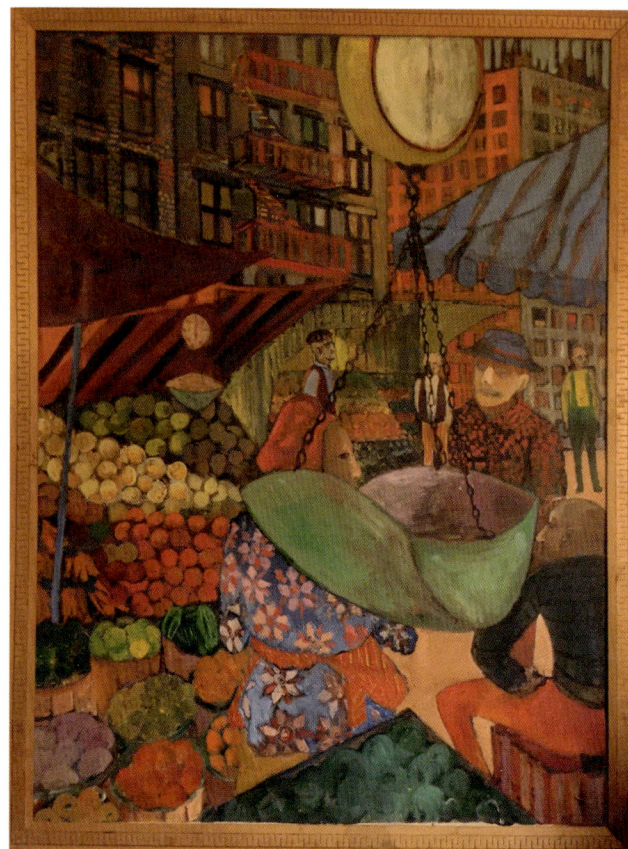

Alice Baber,
*Bleecker Street New
York City*,
ca 1952–53,
oil on canvas,
40 x 30 inches,
private collection.

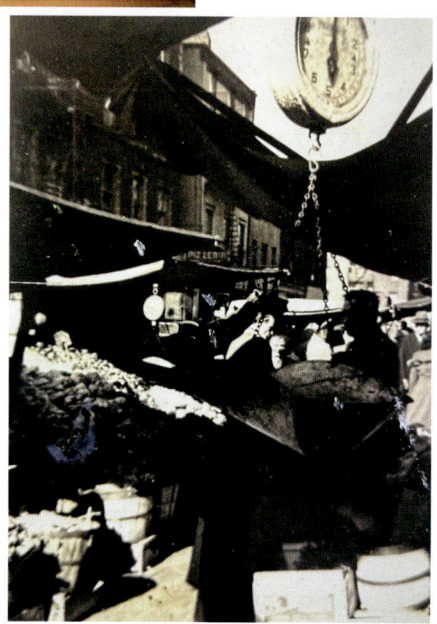

Alice Baber, *Bleecker Street New York City*,
ca 1952–53, black-and-white photograph,
Baber Family Archives.

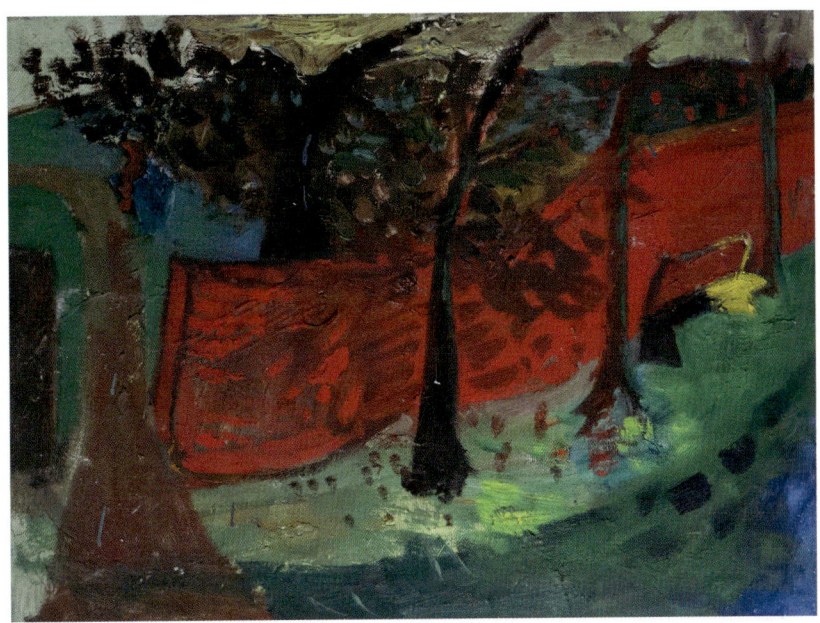

Alice Baber, *Untitled* [landscape with red wall], ca 1950, oil on canvas, 18 x 24 inches, Link Art Gallery, Paris, IL.

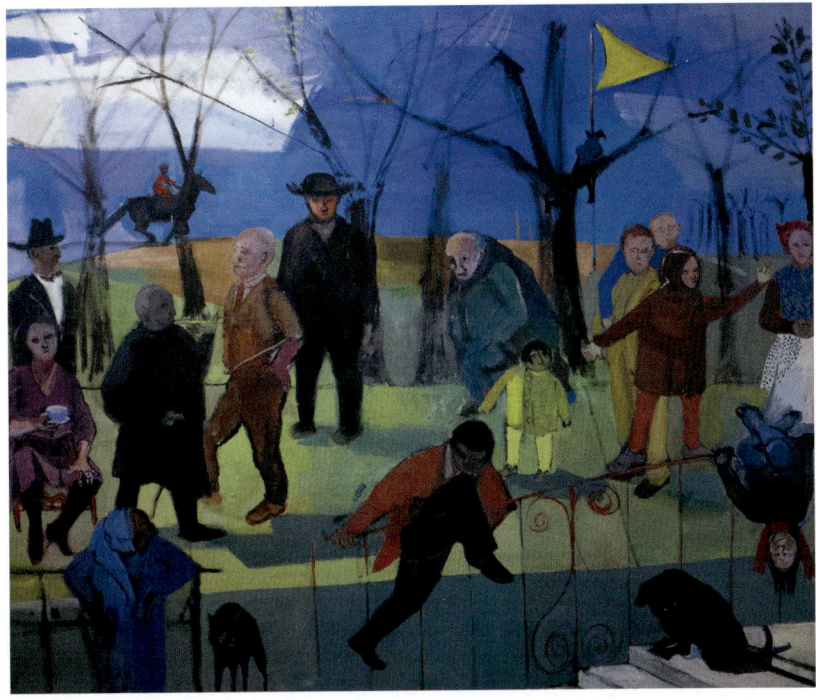

Alice Baber, *New York City Scene*, ca 1952–53, oil on canvas, 40 x 48 inches, Link Art Gallery, Paris, IL.

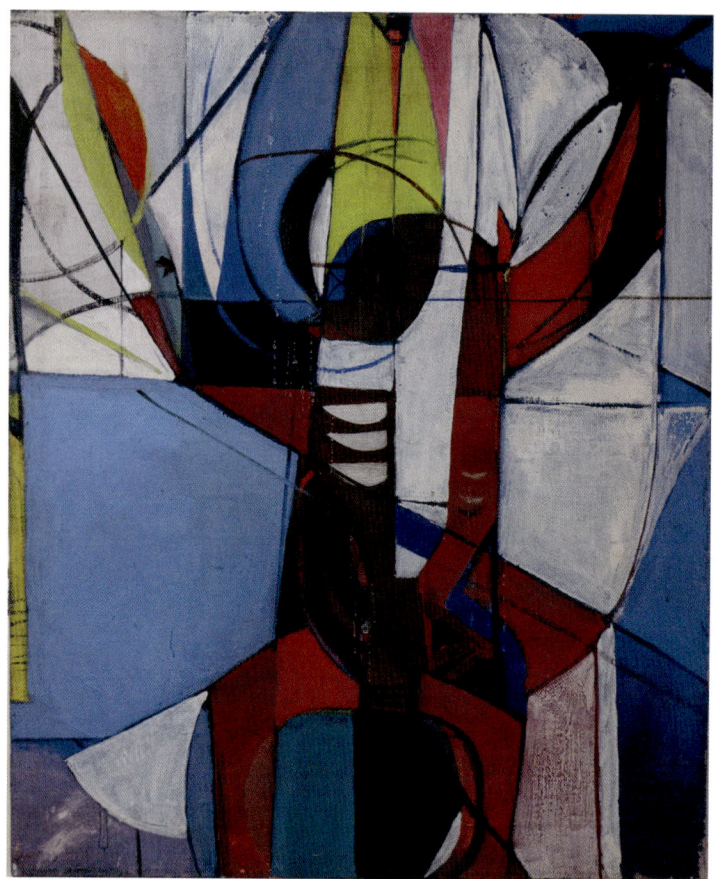

Alice Baber,
Untitled [after Gorky], ca 1952–55,
oil on canvas, 34 x 20 inches,
Link Art Gallery, Paris, IL.

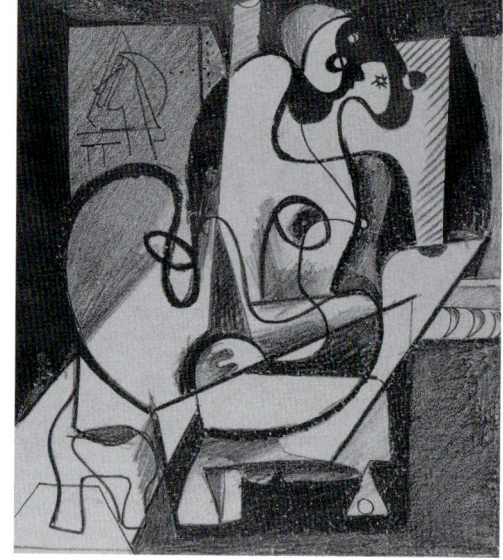

Arshile Gorky,
Painter and Model, 1931,
lithograph on wove paper,
11 7/8 x 9 13/16 inches,
Brooklyn Museum, Brooklyn, NY.

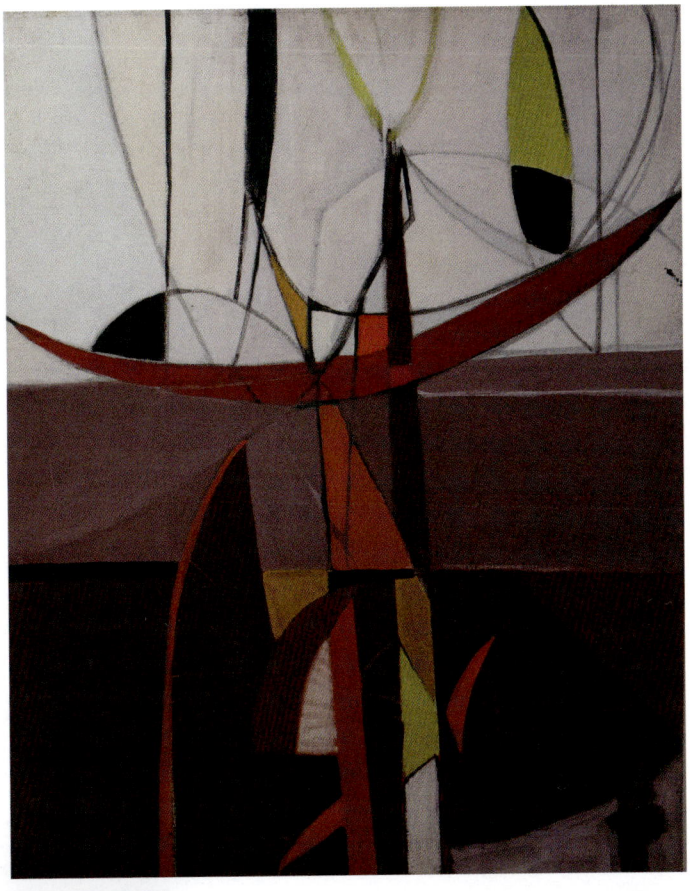

Alice Baber,
Frieda Fromm-Reichmann,
ca 1952–55, oil on canvas,
30 x 24 inches,
Link Art Gallery, Paris, IL.

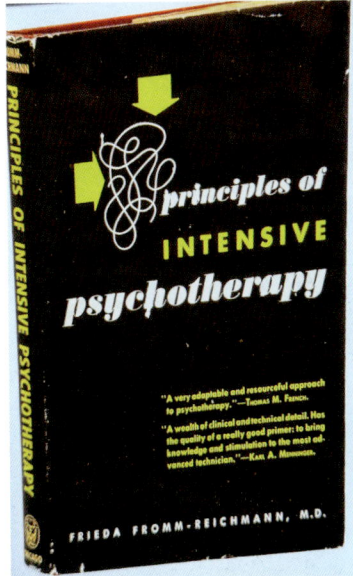

Cover of 1951 book,
Principles of Intensive Psychotherapy
by Frieda Fromm-Reichmann.

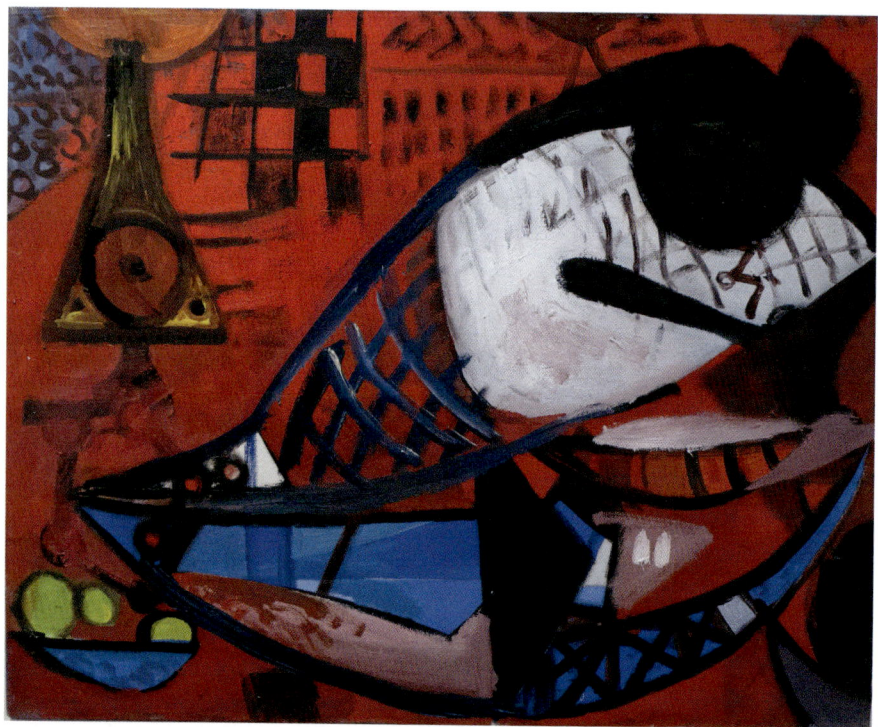

Alice Baber, *Untitled* [abstract with central figure on red ground], 1952–55, oil on canvas, 24 x 30 inches, Link Art Gallery, Paris, IL.

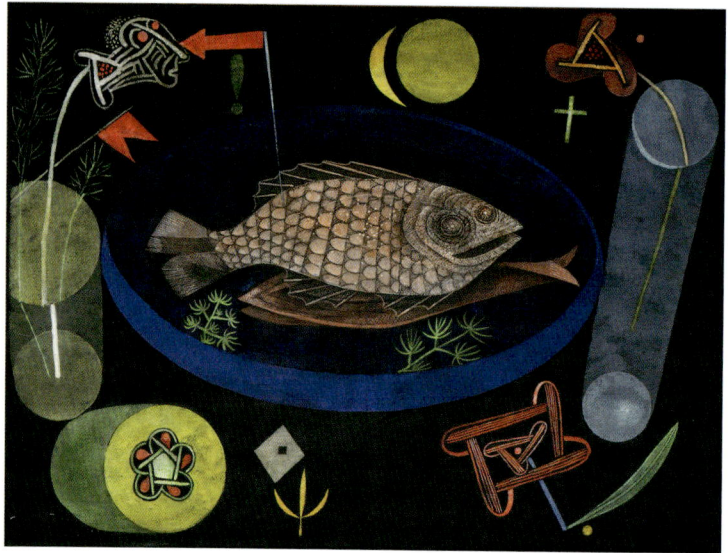

Paul Klee, *Around the Fish*, 1926, oil and tempera on canvas, 18 3/8 x 25 1/8 inches, Museum of Modern Art, NY, Abby Aldrich Rockefeller Fund, 271.1939, image copyright © The Museum of Modern Art/Licensed by SCALA/Art Resource, NY.

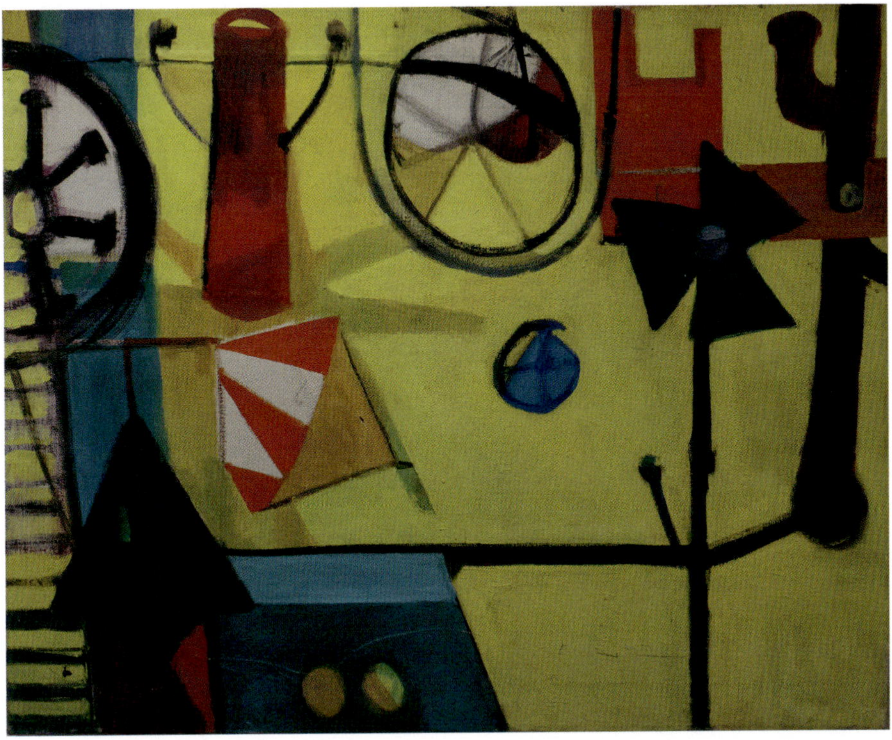

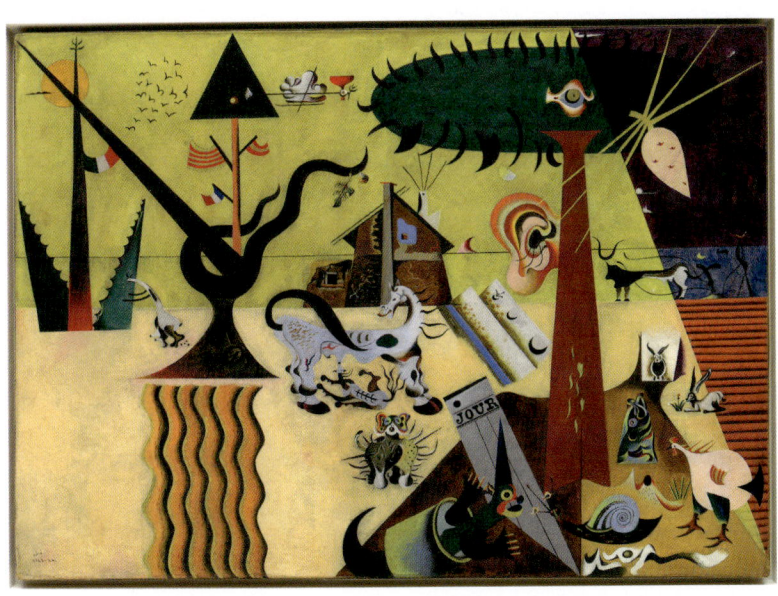

Alice Baber, *The Wheel*, 1952–55, oil on canvas, 24 x 30 inches, Link Art Gallery, Paris, IL.

Joan Miró, *The Tilled Field*, 1923–24, oil on canvas, 26 x 36 ½ inches,
Solomon R. Guggenheim Museum, NY.

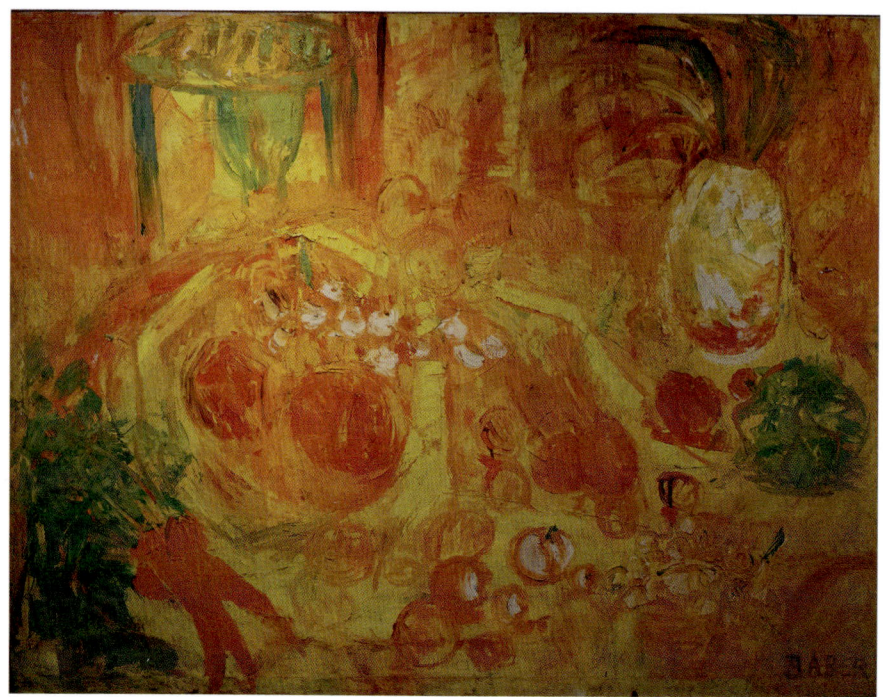

Alice Baber, *Still Life (Orange)*, 1957, oil on canvas, 50 x 65 inches, Link Art Gallery, Paris, IL.

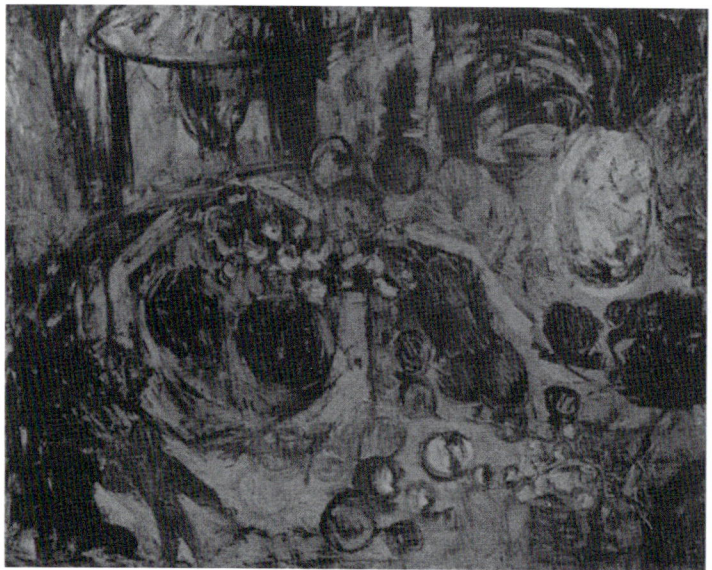

Alice Baber, *Still Life (Orange)*, 1957, as tiny black-and-white reproduced in *Art News*, April 1957.

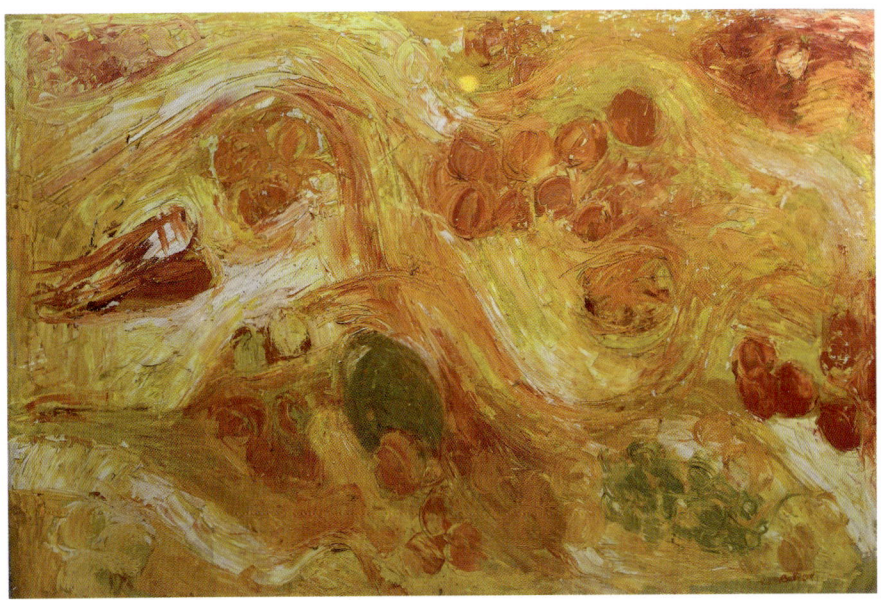

Alice Baber, *Battle of the Oranges*, 1958, oil on canvas, 40 x 60 inches, private collection.

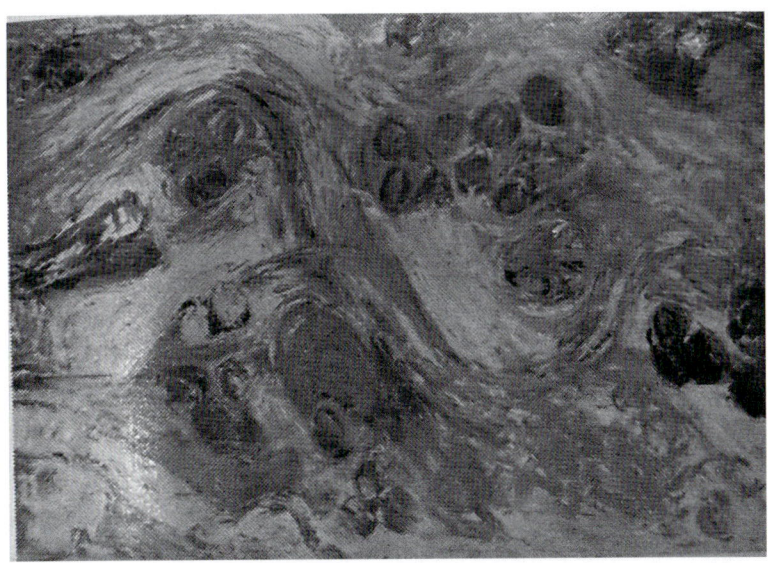

Alice Baber, *Battle of the Oranges*, 1958, as a tiny black-and-white reproduction from *Arts Magazine* of November 1958.

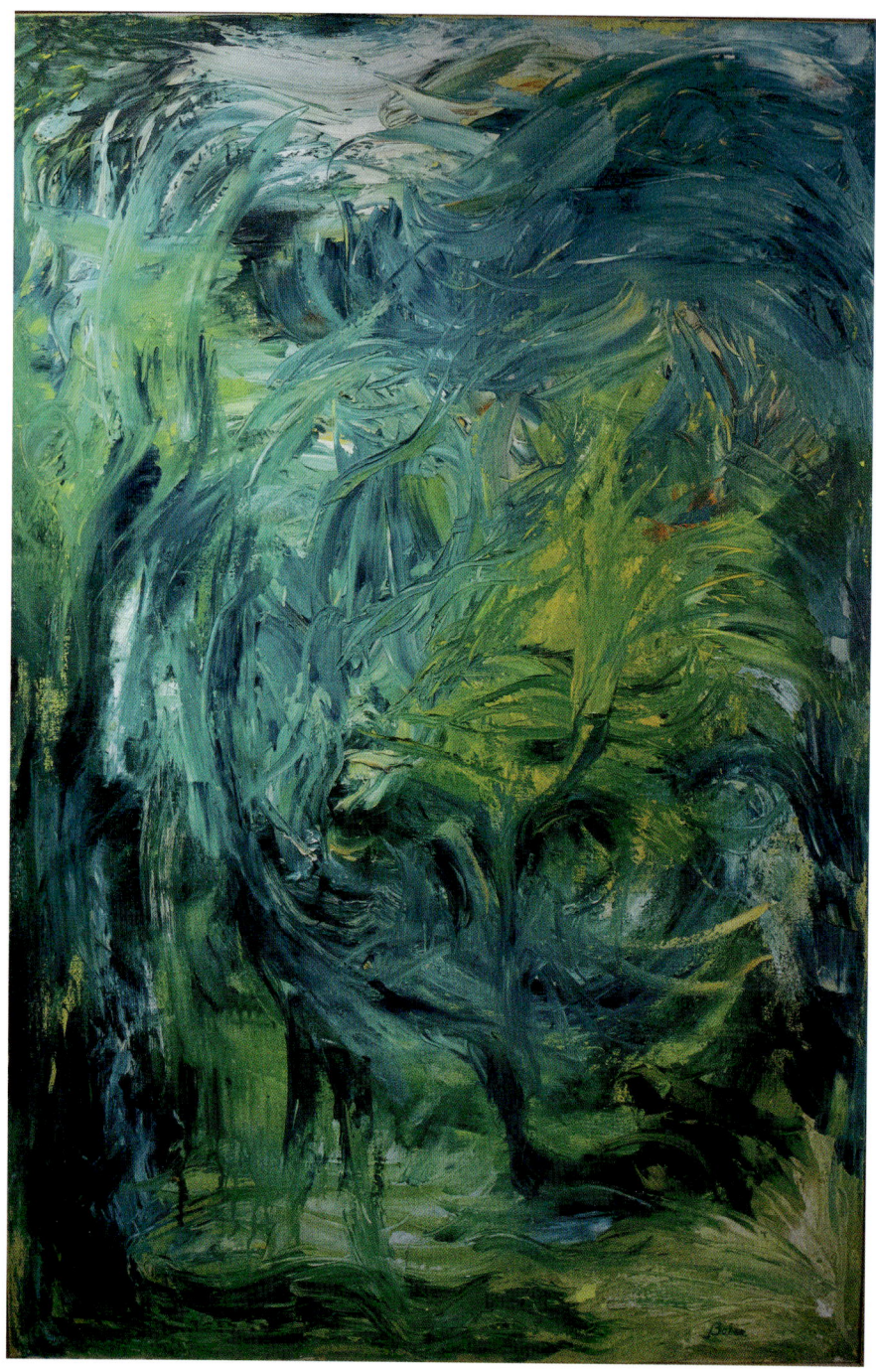

Alice Baber, *The Everglades*, ca 1958, oil on canvas, 60 x 40 inches,
Link Art Gallery, Paris, IL.

CHAPTER 2

The Scene: Cedar Bar to the Club (1953–1958)

A lice Baber not only absorbed art in New York's museums, she also threw herself into the city's art scene. She recalled the unavoidable sexism at the raucous Cedar Bar, located at 24 University Place, near 8th Street in Greenwich Village, which was then New York's premier gathering place for vanguard artists: "If you walked in the door . . . Like you made your grand entrance, complete with remarks. Friends had to come to your aid, your enemies hitting [on] you, and whatever. But it was . . . Because of one night I was brave enough to go and sit in the Cedar Bar, and sort of take my medicine by making myself sit there. . . . that was the night that Felix [Pasilis, March Gallery founder] sort of went round and asked all the people that he saw and knew if they'd like to be in the March Gallery. And I was very pleased [to be invited]."[1]

The March Gallery, located at 95 East 10th Street, opened in March 1957, and became one of several cooperative galleries concentrated on 10th Street, each supported by their member artists' dues. Baber remembered "rent was thirty dollars a month, or something like that," and that she soon volunteered to be the treasurer, which she said she preferred to sweeping the floor.[2]

When Baber wrote up this history for the 1977 exhibition *Tenth Street Days: The Co-Ops of the 50's*, she gave more details: "I went to the Cedar Bar one evening in the spring of 1957. Felix Pasilis came over to my table and asked if I wanted to help start a co-operative gallery—he had found that the basement of his building was available for a very low rent. I was pleased to be invited and went to the founder's meeting. We called ourselves 'March' because we got together that month."[3] She also told how when others proposed names of artists for the gallery, she suggested Wilfrid Zogbaum and Elaine de Kooning.[4]

Not even curatorial work could mask the need to clean up and renovate the space: "We swept the floor and painted the space white. When we didn't remember to sweep or to pound nails into the walls, Felix called us a 'Bunch of intellectuals.' I said I would be treasurer instead of a sweeper. My treasurer's notes show that we paid dues of $2.50 a month. The 24 original members were all in our first show."[5]

Present from its inception, Baber was proud to be one of the March Gallery's founding members. The group she joined included artists Robert Beauchamp, Lester Johnson, Matsumi "Mike" Kanemitsu, and Patricia "Pat" Passlof. The two friends that she promoted, Elaine de Kooning and Wilfrid Zogbaum, she had met through Ibram Lassaw and his wife, Ernestine. Baber and Passlof were among the youngest members. Other prominent artists who later joined and showed at the March Gallery included the sculptors Anne Arnold and Mark di Suvero. For Baber, joining the March Gallery was a major step forward as she struggled to make her way as a young woman artist in 1950s New York.

With Richard Ireland from her cohort at the March Gallery, in February 1957 Baber worked on creating stage sets for two experimental productions at the Tempo Playhouse.[6] The Tempo was a nonprofit off-off-Broadway theater located on St. Mark's Place during the time when the East Village was becoming a significant place for avant-garde productions, sometimes by avant-garde authors like Jean Genet and Gertrude Stein, both associated with gay and lesbian culture.

Baber participated in a group show held at the March Gallery in April 1957. Her painting caught the attention of the influential critic Thomas B. Hess, who related to it as abstract art. Her entry, *Still Life (Orange)*, a dazzling oil on canvas, 50 x 66 inches, had a vivid—almost electric—palette made up of dominating oranges, reds, and yellows with accents of green (CP #14). She achieved the illusion of a brilliant yellow light and used a very warm palette to transcend her ordinary subject matter: a kind of kitchen still life with carrots, beets, and other produce arranged on a table contrasted with a luminous green lamp in the background and green leafy tops of carrot bunches.

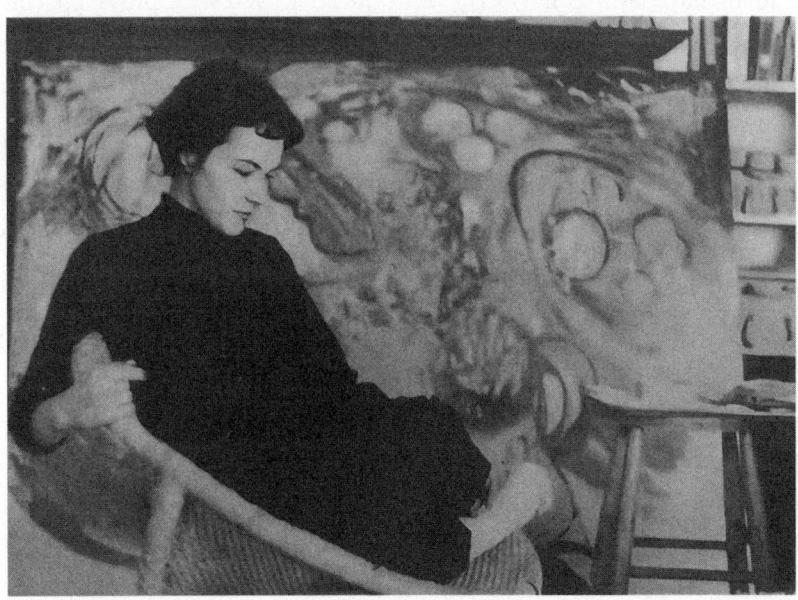

Hess discussed the show for *Artnews* in the essay "Younger Artists and the Unforgivable Crime," about the next generation of artists displacing the abstract expressionists and what he saw as the staying power of abstract art. After explaining that the March Gallery was a co-op, organized by the participating artists, he noted, "The situation here is tentative—one is convinced of a smoldering abstraction from Patricia Passloff [*sic*], Alice Baber's still life seems headed to Style."[7]

As an editor, Hess won praise from the abstract expressionist sculptor Philip Pavia, who in his journal wrote, "Hess's sharp eye for choosing artists, year after year, made the new art clearer. Hess had a great eye for format. He didn't consider format just another element of style. He focused especially on the format as the new invention in the new art. Not being a great admirer of the First Wave painters and not being prejudiced by the style-lover Greenberg, Hess helped to save the savages from the uptown redcoats."[8]

For Baber to elicit an early comment from a major critic like Hess and to have *Still Life* (1957) reproduced in *Artnews* provided the young artist, who was still working a day job as an editor at *McCall's* magazine, the first published confirmation reinforcing the value of her efforts.[9] Unfortunately for Baber, the small black-and-white illustration reproduced in *Artnews* could not convey any of the visual excitement generated by her ambitious painting (CP #14), which depended upon its lively palette and large scale for its impact.

Baber admitted that she was surprised by the successful reception in the press: "Rocco [Armento] and I were reviewed in *Artnews* by Tom Hess. We discovered that *Artnews* would write reviews of Tenth Street shows, also *Arts*."[10] She also noted that while many co-op galleries made artists mind the galleries during the hours the space was open, the March Gallery hired Deborah Sperberg (without pay), Enid Furlonger, and then Janet Keyishian.[11]

Baber participated in another large group show at the March Gallery from September 27 to October 18, 1957.[12] While not all the artists of this show's roster are well-known today, several are, especially Elaine de Kooning, Pat Passlof, Lester Johnson, Boris Lurie, Robert Beauchamp, and Wilfrid Zogbaum.

Even before March Gallery was founded, Baber had begun to attend the regular panel discussions about modern art that took place at "the Club," a meeting place at 39 East 8th Street founded in October 1949 by Philip Pavia with colleagues who included fellow sculptors Peter Grippe, Ibram Lassaw, and James Rosati, and painters like Bill and Elaine de Kooning, Philip Guston, Franz Kline, Mercedes Matter, and Milton Resnick, among others.

Pavia's wife, the painter and critic Natalie Edgar, recollected years later in her notes to an edition of her husband's published journal: "As the expatriates who had lived and worked in Paris after the war gravitated back to New York in the mid-fifties, artists like Norman Bluhm, Paul Jenkins and Alice Baber brought a sophisticated international style to the mix that was the Club membership."[13]

The problem with Edgar's statement is that Baber, except for her brief visit during the summer months of 1951, which she spent studying in Fontainebleau and touring Europe, did not live in or visit France until 1959, but even then she spent about half of each year in New York. Her initial experience at the Club was much earlier and unrelated to her later relationship with Paul Jenkins and their time spent together as a couple in Paris.

Baber recalled in an interview that "within about a year, one of my teachers came to New York and gave a party and invited some other artists whom I got to know, and through them I got to the Artists' Club. So, I immediately met all the people in the art world at that time—it was smaller then: there were only five hundred, as opposed to the two or three thousand you could find now—and I just kept painting away."[14] Baber's teacher who traveled to New York was probably Alton Pickens, who participated in a group show at the Curt Valentin Gallery in May 1953.[15]

Baber told an interviewer that she met the sculptor Peter Grippe, and that she asked him, "Would I be allowed to come to The Club?" She reported that Grippe responded, "Sure, you come to The Club and give my name. So I went once but I felt very strange 'cause I didn't know anyone and Peter wasn't there that night. I didn't know him all that well either. I walked in and there [was] some kind of program, a discussion with poets. It was interesting but, of course, rather strange and I found out later that a lot of the discussions at The Club were wonderfully way-out."[16]

Although Baber left few records of her social life, evidence has survived to document a few of the friendships that she made at "The Club." The older abstract painter, Ilya Bolotowsky, shot a very short film called "Wolf Kahn Paints a Picture" around 1955. The subject of Kahn's picture was a portrait of Alice Baber, which he produced on a piece of glass as she posed at the Club (see page 39). Kahn was Baber's contemporary and a close friend, and, for a time in the early 1950s, the loftmate of Felix Pasilis with whom Baber showed at the March Gallery. This filming likely took place close in time to the 1954 portrait of Tom Hess, for which, Kahn recounted, the critic posed simultane-ously for both him and Elaine de Kooning at the Club.[17] Bolotowsky's son, Andrew, who was only about five years old at the time, remembers Kahn and Baber as a couple and his special affection for Baber, whom he recalls as giving him a nickel to buy his favorite chewing gum.[18]

Baber explained her history at the Club: "I didn't know anyone so I didn't go back for another year and when I did go back, I had met David Hare at a party and David Hare knew the Lassaws and the Lassaws went to The Club every Friday, so Ernestine would take me sometimes, Ibram would too. Ernestine was marvelous because she introduced me to everyone at The Club so I didn't feel strange and I must've met Philip immediately."[19] Once Baber met Philip Pavia, the organization's founder, whom she found "very welcoming," she said she felt comfortable going to the Club. Thus, the Lassaws were instrumental in helping Baber adjust to art world life (CP #1).

Baber later recalled that during the 1950s, when Ibram was building the Lassaws' house, located on Fireplace Road, not far from Jackson Pollock and Lee Krasner's farmhouse in East Hampton: "I came out in the summer, almost every weekend. I'd call up Ernestine the same way I call her in New York, and she'd say, 'Do you want to come out?' She was marvelous. Then I started meeting everyone . . . I remember we were walking on the beach and we ran into Lee and Jackson, which was one of the few times that I saw him and since he didn't talk very much, the times that I did see him I didn't have a conversation with him."[20]

In daybooks Ernestine kept, she noted on Saturday, August 11, 1956, that she and Ibram were spending time with Alice, who traveled out from the city to spend the weekend with them in East Hampton.[21] They took her to a dinner party at the home of the abstract expressionist painters Jim and Charlotte Brooks, who lived in Montauk, at the eastern tip of Long Island. Baber already knew Brooks by reputation since she remembered that the designers at the George Nelson studio had admired his work.

As they were returning to the Lassaws' home, the couple quipped that the unusual traffic suggested "someone was having a big party and didn't invite us." Upon arriving home, however, a phone call spread the shocking news that Jackson Pollock was dead at age forty-four, having lost control of his car while driving under the influence of alcohol. His action cost the life of one of his two passengers.

The next day, Sunday August 12, Ernestine recorded that their friends Duchamp and his wife Teeny (Alexina "Teeny" Duchamp had been the wife of Pierre Matisse, the daughter-in-law of Henri Matisse, and was now the second wife of Marcel Duchamp) came over, that it rained, and that she and Alice went to the beach before Alice returned to the city. The Lassaws were friends with Duchamp and Teeny, their neighbors in the city, whom they also saw on Long Island.[22] This was possibly Alice's first or only encounter with Marcel Duchamp, the legendary French artist whose work is associated with cubism, Dadaism, futurism, and conceptual art. Even if Baber felt intimidated by Duchamp's celebrity, she would have appreciated meeting the older controversial figure with the Lassaws.

At the time Baber recalls, "I felt very young . . . I was terribly shy," explaining why she initially felt so restrained when visiting the Club: "It would be absolutely marvelous to have the presence to stand up and make a comment, etc. . . . I never did."[23] She explained, "Some of the boys were rather rude and I felt that you had to be on your toes a little bit at The Club. . . . the men didn't like it if the women wore jeans. And since a lot of the women wanted to wear blue jeans, some women did, and some didn't. There were these kind of pressures that were in the air. But there were much, much more important pressures like, was your work abstract, did you understand what was happening . . . the meaning of gesture."[24] "The women's movement was born in the Club," Philip Pavia quipped. "They would get up there and tell us off—aggressive, and the joke was that we'd make monsters out of these women and got even the wives to talk. They did, too."[25]

Not wanting to call attention to herself, Baber did not wear blue jeans at the Club. Lucy Freeman Sandler, the art historian and widow of the art critic Irving Sandler, recalls Baber from the time that they all spent there: "I have a clear picture of the way she looked probably around 1960 when Irving was running The Club, because I thought she was exceptionally beautiful with pitch black hair and red high heels, and I do remember that she was with Paul Jenkins."[26]

Baber, who gradually gained more confidence, remembered that in 1955, a year when John Ferren was presiding at the Club, she suggested the topic of color for a series of panels. She recalled, "I had been brooding since 1953 about green. I told Ray Parker that year that I had heard somewhere that green was not to be used."[27] Yet for Baber, green was a beloved color from her childhood in rural Illinois. In June, flat vast green fields of crops stretch as far as the eye can see. She once recalled a time when everything was "raining green," which she recorded in one of her early poems, "Colors of the Rainbow." She knew from her childhood that green symbolizes growth and renewal. Baber explained that she and Parker were still using green, but explained, "Later I traced the dictum to Landès Lewitin and Mondrian."[28]

Landès Lewitin was a famous curmudgeon participating at the Club when Baber began to network. She referred to a dictum by Piet Mondrian, the Dutch *De Stijl* artist, whom many then in the New York art world knew from his participation in the group American Abstract Artists, where he found a wartime welcome while taking refuge in the United States. Mondrian had long since made the decision to limit the palette of his mature abstractions to primary colors—red, blue, and yellow—combined with black and white.

The abstract expressionist painter Milton Resnick complained about the garrulous Lewitin's preoccupation with color, which Baber had also heard about and attributed to this older artist, whom Resnick, the child of wealthy Jewish immigrants fleeing the Bolsheviks' victory, had dismissed as "an Egyptian, a Jew but he denied it."[29] Resnick lamented Lewitin's repetitious "color theory talk," griping, "He'd go on and on, and the whole idea was that if no one had anything to say, he was going to talk about color; unless you could stop him somehow."[30] Baber, on the other hand, paid polite attention to Lewitin's pronouncements, especially, because to her, such talk seemed much more novel, and, significant, since she focused on color herself. Unlike Resnick, she had no investment in whether or not Lewitin was concealing his Jewish identity.

Several other members of the Club offered exciting new ideas that appealed to Baber's budding passion for Japanese culture. These artists were fascinated by Zen, a form of Mahayana Buddhism that developed in China and spread to Vietnam, Korea, and Japan. Baber was active at the Club in time to hear a three-panel series on Zen, organized by Philip Pavia in November 1954. A speaker for the November 5 session on Hasegawa Zen was Matsumi Kanemitsu, who, like Baber, was a founding member of the March Gallery.

The panel, Zen II, took place on November 19 and was presented by Ibram Lassaw, moderated by Harry Holtzman, the American artist who had helped Mondrian take refuge in New York during World War II.[31] By 1954, Baber had become close friends with Ernestine and Ibram Lassaw, who were regulars at the Club. "Alice and Ernestine were buddies, going to drawing classes, studying French together, roaming galleries or museums, finding magical rocks," recalled the Lassaws' daughter, Denise.[32]

Alice's father, Adin Baber, was so pleased to hear about his daughter's supportive friend that from his prized library he sent Ernestine, who liked to garden, a book, *Just Weeds* by Edward Rollin Spencer, inscribed, "Adin Baber June 14, 1943 [when he acquired the book] Now presented to the friend of Alice Baber; Ernestine Lassaw by Adin Baber 1958."[33] Adin accompanied his gift with a two-page letter of gardening and botanical advice.

In addition to encouragement from Ernestine, Baber recalled that she had had "thousands of talks with Ibram [Lassaw] . . . about such things—Suzuki and that sort of thing, as much as talking about art."[34] Baber referred to Daisetsu Teitaro Suzuki, the Japanese essayist, philosopher, religious scholar, and author of books and essays on Buddhism, Zen, and Eastern philosophy that influenced many American artists in the twentieth century, including Ibram Lassaw, who attended his classes at Columbia University.[35]

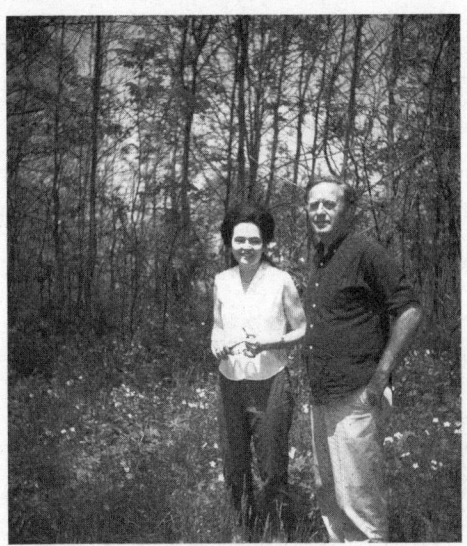

Ernestine Lassaw's photo of Ibram with Alice.

The fascination with Japanese culture that Baber and Lassaw shared subsequently led Baber to organize at the Club a panel on *Noh* drama, classical Japanese performance dating from the fourteenth century, which she recalled that she "enjoyed enormously and some people did and some didn't. To this day [1973], they still complain. It was a demonstration of a *Noh* play done in brown *kimono*, which is, you know, tuxedo for Japanese, with what [the] gestures mean and with an interpreter from the Japan Society. And naturally this was too far afield for some artists, and others remember it well."[36] She recalled working hard on this event, even helping with the mailings and encouraging people to come. For interpretation, Baber had called upon New York's Japan Society, an organization founded in 1907 to promote friendly relations between the United States and Japan. After a suspension of activities during World War II, John D. Rockefeller III led Japan Society's postwar expansion.

Baber's genuine intellectual passions and her vivacious presence at the Club prompted the artist David Hare, a well-established player in the avant-garde art scene in New York, to take an interest in her. The Lassaws' daybook for Thanksgiving Day 1954 records that Baber was a guest for their holiday meal, together with her companion, David Hare.[37] The Lassaws knew Hare, who was more than a decade older than Baber, from Provincetown at least as early as the summer of 1947.[38]

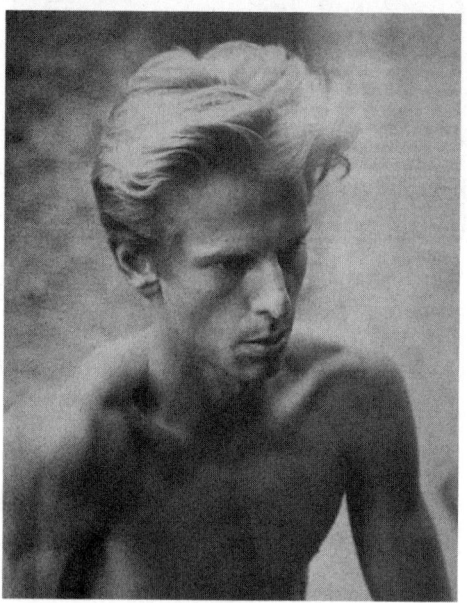

David Hare

Closely associated with surrealism in New York, David was the son of Meredith Hare, a wealthy New York lawyer, and his wife, Elizabeth Sage Goodwin, an art collector and supporter of the 1913 Armory Show, which first introduced European modern art to the American public. Through his cousin, the painter Kay Sage, the wife of the French surrealist painter Yves Tanguy, David Hare had met most of the surrealist artists who had taken refuge in the United States during World War II. He collaborated with these surrealist émigrés on the surrealist journal *VVV*, which he cofounded and edited from 1941 to 1944 with the poet and writer André Breton, and the artists Max Ernst and Marcel Duchamp. Thus, Hare was both wealthy and well-connected.

Before Baber met Hare, he was married to Susanna Winslow Wilson, the daughter of Frances Perkins, whom he divorced in 1945. He took up with Breton's artist-wife, Jacqueline Lamba, who with her seven-year-old daughter, Aube, began living with Hare.[39] Hare, through his connection to his mother-in-law, Frances Perkins, who served as the secretary of labor for President Franklin D. Roosevelt, had been able to assist Breton and Lamba in their efforts to take refuge in New York during the war. In fact, it was Hare's wife, Susanna, who had written an affidavit for Lamba to expedite her immigration papers.[40]

Lamba got to know Hare while she was working as the main translator at *VVV*. After Lamba left Breton in 1942 for Hare, Breton wrote a book of poems in lamentation, *How to Protect Young Cherry Trees from Hares*, illustrated by Arshile Gorky.[41] Hare and Lamba married and had a son, Meredith Merlin Hare, born in 1948. According to some sources, Lamba's marriage to Hare ended in 1951, when she returned to France; they divorced in 1955.[42] In fact, Baber's romance with Hare suffered from hidden ambiguity in Hare's earlier relationship with Lamba. To Baber, Hare the surrealist, a major player in the art world, looked like he was available. But he was also like an iceberg, with most of the peril concealed beneath the surface.

Denise Lassaw recalls, for example, that she and her parents spent the summer of 1954 in New Mexico with Hare and Lamba and their son Merlin before Lamba returned permanently to France.[43] Ernestine Lassaw, after visiting Lamba in France in 1962, reported, "Jacqueline never gave up on David."[44] In fact, her biographer reports that Hare visited Lamba once a year, or they met in New York, and, despite the acrimony of his third wife, he sent her monthly checks for the next forty-two years.[45] Of Lamba, Hare told his fourth wife: "I will always love her."[46]

Ernestine Lassaw recalled in an interview that Hare had "many girl friends" and that "he wasn't a very good husband to any of his wives. He was too egocentric. I don't know if he loved anybody. He liked people, but he was a very mixed-up person. He fooled with drugs; he enjoyed his life; he had lots of money and did whatever he wanted. He was unique, fascinating, he had a great sense of humor and laughed a great deal. He was fun to be with; he sang and played the ukulele. Women were crazy about him."[47] Alice Baber appears to have been just one of his many girlfriends. At the time, however, Baber—the trusting, ambitious, small-town girl—probably believed from their first encounter that Hare was separated with a divorce imminent. "David Hare," Baber recounted, "talked to me about the Surrealists."[48]

"Hare is a surrealist," wrote the eminent art historian Robert Goldwater, husband of the French American sculptor Louise Bourgeois: "One can agree with Clement Greenberg, who, ten years ago [ca 1948–1949], wrote: 'Hare's is the most intensely surrealist art I have ever seen—in the sense that it goes all the way in the direction of surrealism and even beyond, developing surrealism's premises with a consistency and boldness the surrealist doctrinaires themselves have hardly envisioned.'"[49]

Baber's enthusiasm for surrealists like Joan Miró (who visited New York from February to October 1947) was surely encouraged by Hare. Several of Baber's abstract canvases surviving from her earliest years in New York, especially three with yellow backgrounds, recall three well-known works by Miró: *The Tilled Field* (1923), *Catalan Landscape (The Hunter)* (1924), and *The Hermitage* (1924). Baber's canvas *The Wheel* (CP #13) relates to Miró's *The Tilled Field*, setting bold black forms against a yellow ground. Her *Composition in Yellow* recalls Miró's *Catalan Landscape (The Hunter)*, including a stick figure and other forms that reveal influence by Miró's painting. An untitled canvas by Baber recalls Miró's *Hermitage* with its bright yellow ground, heavy black forms, and the red circle floating toward the top of her picture, echoing the earlier Miró.

Baber also painted at least two canvases with exotic birds, which recall early surrealist images by Max Ernst, such as his *Birds Also Birds, Fish Snake and Scarecrow* (ca 1921). One of Baber's birds is shown against a blue ground in profile recalling this painting by Ernst, with whom Hare had collaborated on *VVV* during the period when Ernst, with the help of the art dealer Peggy Guggenheim (whom he briefly married), took refuge in New York.

Hare's introduction of Baber to surrealism and the American art world in New York would not continue. The Lassaws' 1956 daybook shows Baber and Hare as frequent guests together in the first half of the year, then suddenly, after June 24, Alice appears regularly, but without David. The daybook entry for Thanksgiving Day 1956 records "Jacqueline and David, Merlin [their son], Alice, David Young and Eve?; Nogouchi [*sic*] and friend? Over early except for David Young and Eve." Then, the 1957 daybook lists on July 3, "Alice and Herb late to nite" and on July 6, "Sat 2:30 Alice and Herb left," suggesting that the new couple spent the extended Fourth of July holiday with the Lassaws. Since Denise Lassaw did not recall Herb, we are left to speculate on his identity, although he was for a time romantically involved with Baber.[50]

Further research makes clear that Herb was the novelist Herbert Gold. Baber left a page of notes describing a dream, reporting: "Herb Gold is there & ruins the party for me almost."[51] Baber, with her passion for literature, especially poetry, would have been interested in Herbert Gold. His marriage to the writer and professor Edith Zubrin from 1948 until 1956 had ended, so he was free to be with Baber in 1957.

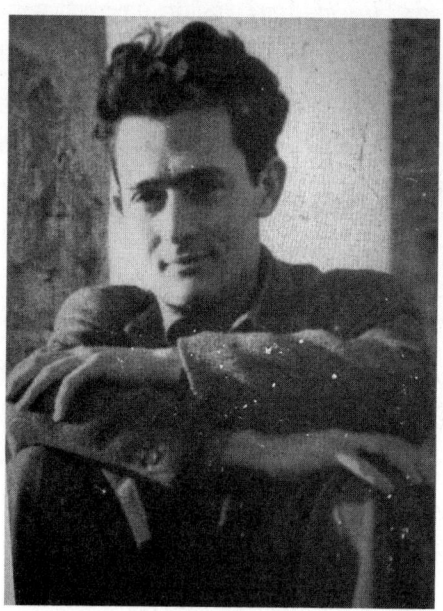

Herb Gold

In February 1958, Baber had Herb Gold write a letter of recommendation for her application for an artist's residency at Yaddo. Thus, Baber met Gold around the same time that James Jones recalled first meeting her.[52] Since the two novelists knew each other, it's possible that

James recalled meeting Alice in New York, before their more significant meeting in Paris, which led him to write about her painting.[53] Baber's acquaintance with Gold, however, was much more fleeting.

Despite Gold's letter of recommendation to Yaddo, the exact nature of Baber's relationship to him remained a mystery to me. Then, I attended the annual luncheon of a seminar to which I have belonged for many years, "Women Writing Women's Lives," on June 3, 2024. As I arrived, I spotted the novelist and memoirist Alix Kates Shulman, like me a long-time seminar member. I immediately intuited that she would have known Alice Baber, imagining that they would have met through feminist circles in the 1970s. When I posed the question, she immediately responded, "Yes, I knew her, but I haven't thought about her for years." As we spoke, Shulman suddenly recalled: "We met when she came to a dinner at my home with Herbert Gold. It was just the two of them and my first husband, Marcus Klein [then a graduate student in the English Department at Columbia, teaching at Barnard College]."[54] Alix explained that she knew Herb Gold from Cleveland, where she grew up, and that she once took a course he taught at Case Western Reserve University.

The moment when Alix met Alice—in the late 1950s, just before Alice went to Yaddo, in part after Gold's letter on her behalf—turned out to be much earlier than I had imagined. At the time, Gold was known for his 1951 novel, *Birth of a Hero*, which was seen to have insights into young American men who suffered early divorce and too-early fatherhood, described, according to one reviewer, in "embarrassingly familiar detail."[55] What this same reviewer described as permitting "his flair for farce to erupt into a full-scale novelistic realization of that acerbic humor most of his readers call 'sick,'" must have been off-putting for Alice.

Alix recalled Alice as very beautiful and intelligent. She remembered that Alice then invited Alix and her husband to her home for dinner, but that she did not include Herb Gold. Having gone to Alice's dinner party at her home on Bedford Street, Alix remembers being amazed that Alice was a single woman living alone in her own place in New York. This, she insists, just wasn't done in the 1950s. Alice, though, at least tried to protect herself from such young men who made the rounds, while chuckling "with adolescent glee" over their "conquests," as portrayed by Gold and described by his reviewer.[56]

Alix Kates Shulman has written about how Beat culture of the 1950s, despite the new jazz and poetry being "stimulating and exciting," was actually quite "oppressive to women" and dominated by "outright misogyny."[57] Herb Gold fits this pattern. Years later in his memoir, Gold commented about his own behavior in New York City in the 1950s: "When disappointed, I sought to be abusive . . . When I was abusive, I was really nasty."[58] He also boasted: "We were sexist pigs, that is, lonely floaters on the sea. We looked for a community of shared girls. We sought pride and fellowship through the bodies of women. We sought revenge against women through revenge against women. . . . We made jokes. We told tales."[59]

Only after my discovery of Alix's recollection of Alice did I realize that, well into his nineties, the indiscreet Gold had given Helen Frankenthaler's biographer several interviews in which he discussed at length his sequential affairs with both Helen and Alice.[60] Gold, who told how he was "attracted to all these pretty young women," was introduced to Frankenthaler by the critic Harold Rosenberg and his wife, the writer Natalie Tabak, whom he met at Yaddo in the summer of 1956. He recalled Frankenthaler, who had just ended her five-year relationship with the critic Clement Greenberg, as ambitious, generous, but "kind of plain," claiming, "I didn't find her attractive physically." He complained that he was turned off by her habit of playing Frank Sinatra records when they were in bed: "Sometimes she would croon along."

Gold dismissed Frankenthaler's painting, later admitting that his taste was then "very conventional. I liked the French Impressionists." Yet, he insisted that he preferred the company of painters more than writers, so he "hung out at the Cedar Tavern with Al Leslie." "A lot of the action at the Cedar Tavern," he recalled, "was about men looking for women, or discussing their victories, or meeting buyers."

The Cedar Tavern is likely where Gold first met Baber, about whom he emphasized, "When I met Alice, I didn't deceive Helen. The affair ended rapidly." For him, this liaison with Helen of just a few months was inconsequential, but as for Alice, Gold had turned her into an enemy, the rival woman that stole Helen's man. And not just a woman, but another ambitious painter whom Frankenthaler would exclude from the guest lists for the many parties she gave, where people in the arts mingled. Gold recalled meeting the writer Ralph Ellison, whose novel *Invisible Man* was published in 1952. Gold was skeptical about Frankenthaler: "She had a party for [the longtime critic for the *San Francisco Chronicle*] Alfred Frankenstein, I felt she was sucking up to him. He was the biggest deal in San Francisco."

Excluded from Frankthaler's entertainments and the opportunities to mingle was Baber, whom Gold recalled as "very pretty," "dark-haired, slim; from the Midwest; studied art at one of those universities." "She had wonderful bangs. . . . the bangs fell over her eyes and she did this rapid blinking because she was trying to keep the hair out of her eyes; it was very sexy. I was willing to put up with her smoking."

Gold contrasted Frankenthaler's space for hosting lavish parties on West End Avenue with Alice's place in Greenwich Village, "On the ground floor; it faced on a courtyard; it was small." "It was a poor artist's apartment. . . . a mews off Commerce Street." Her voice was "girlish," he recalled. "The sex was great. She dressed in bohemian, beatnik style of the '50s; skirts; she had no money." "She was not highly read," he judged, concluding, "She was not questing intellectually; she wanted to be an artist." "She came to New York to be an artist." He insisted, "I liked her. I even liked her painting," adding, "Alice Baber later married a deep-voiced second-rate abstract expressionist." Gold also volunteered that before he met Baber, she had "had an affair with Matta," the Chilean-born artist. More than sixty years later, Gold confused two well-known surrealists: David Hare with Roberto Matta, who lived in the United States only from 1938 to 1948, and then divided his life between Europe and South America during the 1950s and 1960s.

Herb Gold's own recollections and his published descriptions of his own bad behavior connect to Baber's notes that she had a bad dream about Herbert Gold almost ruining a party for her. This makes us wonder what she must have dreamed about her relationship with the equally problematic David Hare. Baber might have initially overlooked Hare's unpredictable behavior because he was so well-connected in the art world.

From his early engagement with experimental photography, Hare had moved on to make surrealist sculpture, which he managed to exhibit widely, including at Art of This Century, Peggy Guggenheim's New York gallery. Hare was also a founder of the short-lived (1948–1949) Subjects of the Artist School at 35 East 8th Street along with the painters Barnett Newman, William Baziotes, Mark Rothko, and Robert Motherwell. The school's philosophy, which encouraged experimentation, was that each artist had within themselves personal subjects waiting to be released in their paintings. The school rejected traditional subject matter, excluding landscape, still life, or figures. Hare explained that the artist's subject should "grab me. I don't want it to look like something I've ever seen before in my life."[61] Hare might have impressed Baber with this idea since she later insisted how much she wanted her own art to be unlike anyone else's work.

From 1954 to 1957 Hare participated in the invitational New York Painting and Sculpture Annuals held at the Stable Gallery, which was established in 1953 by Eleanor Ward in what was once a livery stable on Seventh Avenue at West 58th Street. Baber recalled in an interview that she was first selected for the Stable Gallery Annual exhibition by the sculptor David Hare, and that each of the artists in the previous show could select an artist for the next show; however, she gave no indication that she had ever been personally involved with Hare.[62] Among the other invited artists, Audrey Flack recalled that the show was "strictly for Abstract Expressionist painters. Nick Marsicano [with whom she had studied at Cooper Union] recommended my work, and I was thrilled to participate in the 1956 Annual."[63]

On an unrelated application form, Baber listed the Stable Gallery Annual and noted that she was "Invited by artist jury to show with group," so Hare and Marsicano were possibly both members of the artist jury for the Stable Gallery Annual.[64] Baber exhibited in both the fifth Stable Annual, which took place May 22–June 16, 1956, and again in the sixth Stable Annual, held May 7–June 1, 1957, which was the last year this particular show took place. Drawn to Baber's talent as well as her energy, beauty, and winning personality, it is not surprising that Hare chose her work for the show.

In the fifth Stable Annual in 1956, most of the artists were men; however, Baber showed with other accomplished women, including Janice Biala, Elaine de Kooning, Perle Fine, Audrey Flack, Helen Frankenthaler, Grace Hartigan, Sally Hazelet Drummond, Lee Krasner, Joan Mitchell, Louise Nevelson, Miriam Schapiro, and Yvonne Thomas. Getting to participate in this prestigious group show was a major milestone for Baber.

Although Baber does not seem to have gotten any mention in the press for the 1956 Stable Annual, her work, when shown with just four men in a group show at the March Gallery in April 1957, did elicit a comment from Dore Ashton, who wrote, "Alice Baber shows full-blown, brightly expressionist interiors with still lifes."[65] "The second show had 4 painters," Baber recalled of the March Gallery: "Bill Gambini, Burt Hasen, Boris Lurie and myself and one sculptor, Rocco Armento."[66]

In contrast with these lesser-known men, the men who made up most of the 115 artists in the sixth Stable Annual in 1957 included the prominent known figures Robert Motherwell, Hans Hofmann, Alfred Leslie, William Baziotes, Ad Reinhardt, John Graham, Charles Seliger, Esteban Vicente, Ibram Lassaw, and Philip Guston, all of whom except Graham were considered abstract expressionists at the time and all likely to overshadow a young woman still searching for her own style.

Determining decades later just who was an abstract expressionist often seems very arbitrary. For example, the tiny collages of Anne Ryan have been categorized as abstract expressionist, while Baber's paintings, some of which are large-scale abstractions, are not included in a recent study of abstract expressionism among the other women with whom she showed in the Stable Annual in 1957, including Mary Abbott, Ruth Abrams, Elaine de Kooning, Perle Fine, Grace Hartigan, Joan Mitchell, Charlotte Park, Pat Passlof, and Yvonne Thomas.[67]

Reviewing the 1957 show for *The New York Times*, Dore Ashton focused on the male artists, including Adja Yunkers (although that he was Ashton's husband at this time went unacknowledged), but mentioned just four of the women in the show—Miriam Schapiro, Louise Nevelson, Nell Blaine, and Joan Mitchell—when the women in this show not only included Baber, "one of the artists just getting under way with their public careers," but also such notables as Lee Krasner, Elaine de Kooning, Grace Hartigan, Louise Bourgeois, Lois Dodd, and Marisol (Escobar).[68] Baber was a longtime friend of both Elaine de Kooning and Joan Mitchell.

Nor were all the artists abstract—for example, Nell Blaine, Lois Dodd, and Marisol are all known for representation—Blaine and Dodd for painting landscape and Marisol for figurative sculpture. Their work created a context for Baber, who described her painting in the sixth Stable Gallery Annual as "a red man, so I would say that the first work that people saw [of mine] was figurative."[69] She was reported to have painted these brilliant red male figures after visiting Gary, Indiana, where she "observed sweaty steel workers bowed over their furnaces."[70] Working in thick paint, she caught the rawness of their physical labor.

Baber's painting teacher at Indiana University, Alton Pickens, must have provoked Baber's interest in depicting steelworkers, since he had already published in leftist periodicals like *New Masses*, and by 1955 would show his own figurative paintings with social realist artists such as Philip Evergood and William Gropper at the ACA Galleries in New York, going against advice he received from the art historian Robert Goldwater.[71]

When Baber explained how she produced all-blue or all-red paintings, however, what she focused on reflects formalism not social realism: "I started doing these red men, they were all red and I found [the] male figure more interesting in the point of view of straight lines so that when I would go and draw from the figure, I would draw the male model and work that out. These figures were influenced by Cézanne, although Cézanne wouldn't claim them. But what excited me in the quality of drawing in Cézanne was the nervous line. And I guess I worked towards a kind of nervous edge in these things."[72]

Baber participated in another group show, *Looking Back: Exhibition of Older and Present Work by 13 Artists*, which took place May 2–21, 1958, at the Marino Art Galleries at 46 West 56th Street in New York.

Among those showing with Baber were Paul Georges, Boris Lurie, Lester Johnson, Matsumi Kanemitsu, Felix Pasilis, and Dorothy G. Voss, who wrote an essay for the show's flyer.[73] Several of the participants were members of the March Gallery. Baber recalled: "From the downtown shows in those days you often got an offer to show uptown, or to show in the group shows uptown."[74]

Baber was clearly continuing to network. Her generosity in social situations was recorded by the painter Jules Olitski, who wrote a memoir that tells of Baber's role in sharing with him how the critic Clement Greenberg, unbeknownst to Olitski, had admired his work in his first solo show, held in the spring of 1958 at the Zodiac Room of the New York dealer Alexander Iolas. Olitski heard indirectly from a young artist, Fred Schneider, a mutual friend, who had heard from Baber, who had just called him and told him what she had heard Greenberg say at a cocktail party downtown: "Clement Greenberg is there holding forth on the art scene and how low it has sunk, and someone asked him whether there is anyone around he thinks is any good, and he said, 'Yes I saw some paintings today by a guy I never heard of. He's good . . . I didn't want to go for his paintings, they looked kind of "Frenchy." But they're good. What's his name? Olitski. Yeah, that's it.'"[75]

That same spring, Olitski and Greenberg participated in a large group show of life drawings, which also included Baber. It was the first show ever at the short-lived Workshop Gallery, located in Manhattan at 332 East 51st Street. The show, which opened on May 6, 1958, was organized by the gallery's owner, Connie Levene, (later known as Constance Kane), who was then the wife of Sam Levene, a prominent American actor and Broadway director.[76] Baber showed an image of a male figure in ink that she priced at $85; Pat Adams offered a drawing for $15; Greenberg asked $50 for each of his two pencil drawings; and John Ferren asked $200 and $350 for his works on paper.[77] In addition to work by the owner herself, some of the other participants were Elaine de Kooning, Paul Georges, Alex Katz, Fay Lansner, Theodoros Stamos, and Paul Jenkins. Thus, this show is the first documented encounter between Alice Baber and Paul Jenkins and further confirms that she knew Clement Greenberg.[78] Baber's work was well enough regarded that the Workshop Gallery included her pen-and-ink drawing of a forest in its summer show.

Baber had now launched herself as a painter in New York. Although she considered herself to be shy, her networking skills had resulted in membership in a co-op gallery, participation in several group shows, and she got accepted into a residency at a prestigious artist's colony. What remained unsettled was her need to find stability in her romantic life, which would enable her to socialize in the art world, while focusing on creating and promoting her own artwork.

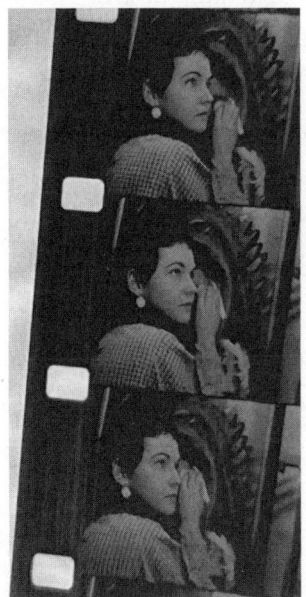

Alice Baber in Ilya Bolotowsky's film
Wolf Kahn Paints a Picture, ca 1956, shot at The Club.

CHAPTER 3

Finding a Partner
(1958)

B y the spring of 1958, Alice Baber, not yet thirty years old, had
established herself in the New York art world. So much so that she
applied for a residency at Yaddo, the artist colony in upstate New York,
set on a four-hundred-acre estate in Saratoga Springs, where the mission was "to nurture the creative process" by offering artists a supportive
place to work without interruption.[1] It was the second year in a row
that Baber had applied, but this time she was accepted. Asked to state
her goal for her stay at Yaddo, she wrote that she planned "to complete
a series of paintings dealing with natural forms in formal terms."[2]

To get into Yaddo was an accomplishment for any young artist,
whether pursuing the visual arts, literature, or music and the performing arts. It was also an opportunity to meet creative people who
worked in other disciplines. Baber asked her former Indiana University
art history professor, Henry Hope, to "sponsor" her by writing a letter
of reference. She also asked for letters from the painter Hyde Solomon
and the novelist and poet Herbert Gold, whom she had dated.

Gold, who had twice been a guest at Yaddo, wrote that Baber was
"emotionally stable with considerable self-possession and charm"

and answered affirmatively Yaddo's question of whether she was self-sufficient enough and if she could live harmoniously with others. Gold described her as "a gifted and serious painter" and said that he perceived "a rapidly maturing personal expressiveness."[3] While Baber had brought along Gold on a visit with the Lassaws over the Fourth of July weekend in 1957, by the time she got to Yaddo, she was no longer involved with him.[4]

Henry Hope, chair of the Fine Arts Department at Indiana University, reported that he remembered Baber well and gave her high grades "in scholarship, artistic ability, and character." He recommended her highly, adding that she had done well at the summer School of Fontainebleau. Her last reference, Hyde Solomon, Baber might have met through her day job. He mentioned that a Yaddo residence would be of great benefit to her since "she holds a fulltime job most of the year," something about which she rarely spoke. Solomon, a confirmed homosexual, was beloved for producing charcoal portrait studies of his fellow residents at Yaddo.[5] He was on a first-name basis with Yaddo director Elizabeth Ames, so that must have helped Baber's chances.[6]

Notified of her acceptance with a letter from Ames written on April 7, 1958, Baber began her stay at Yaddo on Friday, May 30, 1958, and remained until Saturday, June 28.[7] Her sociability would allow her to thrive in such a communal setting among other visual artists, writers, and those in the performing arts, from composers to choreographers.

By May 6, 1958, Baber had gotten to know the painter Paul Jenkins, while both artists were exhibiting in the Workshop Gallery's show of life drawings. Five years older than she, Jenkins had also grown up in the Midwest, in his case in Missouri and Ohio. The two might have met earlier, but their encounter was surely after Baber's weekend of July 4, 1957, with the Lassaws, when she was accompanied by Herbert Gold.

Jenkins had been living in Paris, where he had established a network of friends, a close relationship with a supportive art critic, and found several galleries willing to show his art; he exuded much more charm than Gold. Although Jenkins was still married, separated from his wife and young daughter, he seemed much more appealing than Gold.

Beginning in July 1955, Jenkins had spent a year living in New York when he met Willem de Kooning, Franz Kline, Robert Motherwell, Ad Reinhardt, Jackson Pollock, and Lee Krasner. Before they met, Jenkins and Alice Baber did know several people in common, among them Clement Greenberg and the artist Mike Kanemitsu.

It might have been through Kanemitsu, a fellow founding member at the March Gallery, that Baber first met Jenkins. Though Kanemitsu was born in 1922 to Japanese parents living in Ogden, Utah, he was taken to Japan and grew up living with his grandparents, near Hiroshima, speaking only Japanese. Returning to the United States in 1940, he enlisted in the US Army in 1941, at which point he renounced his Japanese citizenship and became a US citizen.

Despite this choice and his birthplace, Kanemitsu was arrested after the attack on Pearl Harbor and interned by the US government. It was then that he took up drawing. Once released, Kanemitsu rejoined the US Army and served as a hospital assistant in Europe. Discharged in 1946, he studied with the modernist painter Fernand Léger in Paris, before ending up in 1951 at the Art Students League of New York, where he studied together with Jenkins in the painting class taught by the popular Yasuo Kuniyoshi, who had arrived alone from Okayama, Japan, in 1906 at the age of sixteen.

Kanemitsu, who was very close to Jenkins, later recalled how he and Jenkins had met as students in Kuniyoshi's class and how Jenkins had helped him out by purchasing his artwork when he was unknown and struggling to survive: "It's a help to me to, you know, pay my rent." Kanemitsu remarked on how much of his art Jenkins had purchased in order to help him. It was a generosity with colleagues that distinguished his character.[8]

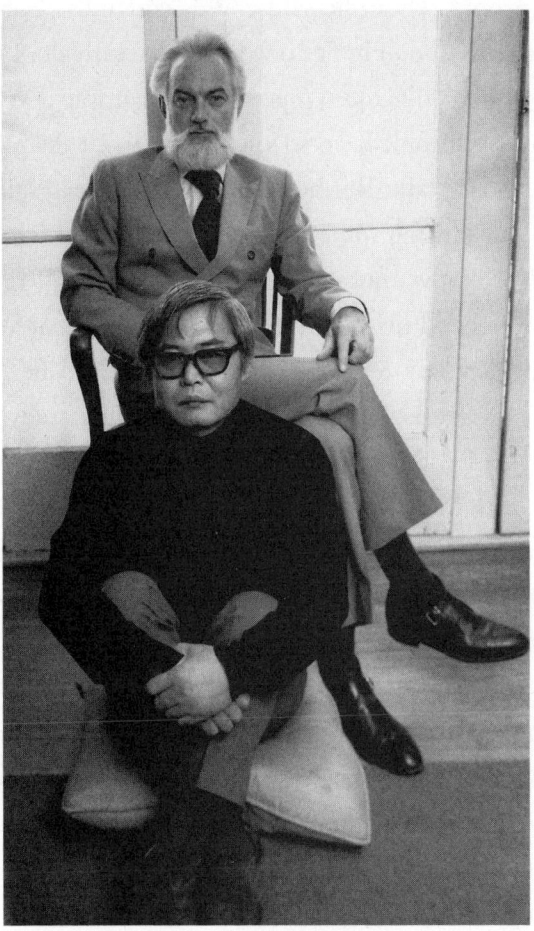

Paul Jenkins with Mike Kanemitsu

In fact, Kanemitsu's analysis helps to shed light on what Baber fell in love with and then rejected. Kanemitsu insisted what a hard worker Jenkins was, but also emphasized how much he loved to party. Kanemitsu also admired how industrious Jenkins was: "If he don't paint, he editing for his biography or he write[s]. He's a very good writer, too; he write play. . . . And he have [*sic*] most talent to observe people."[9]

Kanemitsu was an insightful observer about Jenkins's interactions with people, whom he said could "convince them to respect his knowledge—kind of hypnotize idea. He really do. I saw how he operate, and I don't like to say 'operate' but that way that he talk into men and women. People have no knowledge about abstract painting, but he sell, and he talk. But he don't talk like cheap salesman type of talk. He was talking something else, and people fascinate about him. And Paul know almost any subject. He's a well-read man."[10]

With enormous admiration, Kanemitsu declared that Jenkins could speak about most any topic: "About writing. (And he know about astronomy and astrology, many mysticisms. He'll study.) And only knowledge that he lack is probably music. He don't know very well much music. But the rest of fields, he know everything."[11]

Yet, Kanemitsu saw Jenkins as little appreciated by other artists, whom he saw as jealous of his friend and supporter: "And most artists, they don't like him, personally, because I think that the reason they don't like him, Paul, is that he's so elegant—well dressed and well spoken. That kind of artists want to be like Paul, but they can't be. . . . So they call him a phony or all this kind of thing. But there is no such thing as phoniness in Paul Jenkins."[12]

Kanemitsu sensed what others including the painter Archie Rand, observed of Jenkins, whom he considered "a bit of the charlatan," recalling: "Paul was a charming egoist and the kind of borderline faux-spiritualist that populated a lot of the second waves of beatnikism . . . He was smart." Rand observed that Jenkins's "woo-woo was counter-pointed by his tailored suits and distinguished tone of voice, making him, in his mind, all things to all people. He wanted to be seen as inscrutable and therefore to be admired for not being 'understood,' above their heads—a control freak emitting his own legend. A slick, urbanized Zen guru. Far out but so sophisticated."[13]

In fact, Jenkins was a trained actor. He met his first wife, Esther Ebenhoe, while both were working in an open-air theater in Cleveland Heights, Ohio; he was then acting. They married on May 19, 1945. He served in the US Maritime Service and enlisted in the US Naval Air Corps during World War II. After his military service, he studied playwriting at Carnegie Tech (now known as Carnegie Mellon University) in Pittsburgh. He was painting and drawing independently before he moved to New York City in 1948 and began to study painting on the GI Bill at the Art Students League, where he developed a deep admiration for his teacher, Yasuo Kuniyoshi.

After several temporary separations, Paul and Esther Jenkins conceived in Paris their only child—a daughter, Hilarie Paula Jenkins—who was born there in 1954. Hilarie recalls that the family returned from Paris after her mother's sister-in-law, Ida Hancock, died suddenly, leaving behind three children. Esther's mother, Hilarie's grandmother, implored her daughter to come home from Paris to help her brother's family in Pittsburgh. Paul stayed in New York, and it was during this temporary separation that his infidelity took its toll, ultimately ending his marriage.[14]

During the previous year, while Paul was alone in New York, it was at Clement Greenberg's place on Bank Street in the early spring of 1956 that Jenkins first encountered a disturbed Jackson Pollock and encouraged him to travel to Paris to see him and his wife, only to have the forty-four-year-old painter protest, "It's too late for that."[15] In April, Greenberg arranged for Jenkins and two other abstract painters—the German-born Friedel Dzubas and Alan Davie (then visiting from Scotland for his show in New York)—to go and see Pollock in East Hampton, where Jenkins recalled that Pollock's wife, the artist Lee Krasner, prepared lunch.

After witnessing a disturbed Pollock shoot an arrow into the wall of the kitchen in his East Hampton home in front of the tormented Krasner, Jenkins sent the couple a gift of the book *Zen and the Art of Archery*, written by the German philosopher Eugen Herrigel, and first translated into English in 1953. Jenkins inscribed the book: "Again many good thoughts for the weekend spent with you both. Here is the archery book and Esther [Ebenhoe Jenkins, his wife] & I hope you enjoy reading it. Before returning to Paris, I hope we will [have] another chance to talk—if we don't however it has been a real joy to have visited and will remember always your generosity."[16]

Jenkins's gift to Pollock and Krasner reflects his interest in Zen, which he would also share with Baber, whom he would soon meet.[17] Lee Krasner's visit to Paris, however, where she stayed with Paul and Esther, documents that Jenkins's first marriage was still intact on August 12, 1956.[18] The couple were legally separated in 1957, although their divorce would follow later.[19]

Jenkins, after having his first solo show at the Martha Jackson Gallery in New York in 1956, arranged to exchange, for two years beginning in early 1957, his Paris studio, located in Montparnasse, where many famous artists and writers lived earlier in the twentieth century, for the New York studio of the American artist Joan Mitchell, which was located on St. Marks Place in Greenwich Village.[20] Thus, Jenkins was living in New York in 1957, but we can only speculate if he had made this move from Paris because he wanted to make arrangements for ending his marriage.

Meanwhile, Alice Baber continued to network in the art world. She recalled that she first met the painter Ray Parker, whom she saw at the Club, through some friends from Indiana University. Baber remembered spending an evening at Parker's with the artist Robert Motherwell, noting, "It was an absolutely wild evening because he was fighting with Betty [Little], the wife he would soon divorce, before marrying Helen Frankenthaler the next year."[21]

By June 1958, Paul Jenkins seemed so attractive to Baber that she was eager to write to him from Yaddo. Lacking a pen or a normal pencil, she wrote him a short note with an eyebrow pencil.[22] Once she got hold of a pen, something of Baber's experience at Yaddo, as well as clues about the couple's developing relationship, are recorded in a letter she wrote to Jenkins, thanking him for his "nice funny letter" and telling him, "I think it is *fine* for you to go out with Lee [Krasner, Pollock's widow, who at nearly fifty, was twenty years older than Baber]. It is warm tonight for a change. The window is open and I can hear the loud speaker from the race track, the baying of foxes and the batting of moths. Almost as noisy as New York. I sketched this morning and got one good drawing, rescraped a painting this afternoon, took nap & read Henry James. I feel adjusted to room, studio, and people."[23]

Yaddo offered many other guests for diversion, but Baber focused her attention and her comments to Jenkins on the figurative painter Shirley Dreyfus (who showed at ACA Galleries); the composer Ben Johnston, who taught at the University of Illinois at Urbana–Champaign, was "au currant [*sic*] and seems to be on all the arts" and told her, "Merce Cunningham will be out next year"; and the poet Donald Petersen, who "doesn't know anything about modern art, thinks artists should do portraits, because he spent 5 years on the sonnet form for discipline."

Baber then tells Jenkins: "Everyone here is married & devoted to wives and children (2, 3, & 4 children the average) so you can see that I am being good while you are out with Lee." She signs her letter: "Til Sunday, Love, Alice."[24] Clearly, however, they both knew that Jenkins was no longer "devoted" to his wife and daughter. After experiencing the divided loyalties of David Hare, as well as the self-proclaimed abuser Herbert Gold, Jenkins's situation seemed acceptable.

Apparently, he was legally separated from Esther and their daughter, Hilarie, then not quite four years old.

Baber wrote Jenkins several letters from Yaddo, suggesting that she really missed him. She wrote: "My room is very basic, and so is the studio which is down a winding road, a row of three studios with high ceilings, not too large, and with someone else at the far end. The whole place seems deserted because it is so large. There is the mansion, the W. house (also large with an enormous receiving room done in burnt orange oriental carpet & chairs which gives off a strange unreal light), and many outer buildings."[25] She reported that after dinner many guests listened "to music in the quiet room which must have been a chapel, also Tudor style."[26] She wrote that there were "wonderful things to draw here. Large trees of all shapes, very baroque."[27]

Baber added, "Lots of gossip from Hilton on the way up."[28] It seems that her visit coincided with that of her contemporary, the art critic Hilton Kramer, whom she noted in an earlier letter, drove up with Leslie George Katz, a writer on art and literature, who later founded the Eakins Press Foundation and was a longtime member of the board of the Yaddo artists' colony.[29] Baber knew Kramer, who had done some graduate studies at Indiana University, through mutual friends from her alma mater.[30] Baber was hoping to get a ride back to the city with Kramer and Katz. She tells Jenkins that she has had an evening conversation with about eight others but that she misses him.[31]

In another letter to Jenkins, Baber asks him, "What do you think of this line: 'He demanded too much of art because he hoped for so much from life,' this from a book on Blake. Blake believed in 4 levels of inspiration or fantasy. I am investigating them. The author also uses a term which interests me but which I do not understand called empsychotic but which has to do 'with representing objects as emotion & as attitudes' and the opposite. This carried to extreme becomes surrealism says the author."[32] The book she was reading, but failed to name, was *William Blake: The Politics of Vision* by Mark Schorer, published in 1946.[33] Sharing William Blake's love of both poetry and painting, Baber's interest in Blake's visionary imagination in these two creative arenas does not surprise.

Having conveyed her intellectual investigation into Blake, Baber switches to the personal, telling Jenkins how much she had just enjoyed seeing him in New York City. Now back at Yaddo, busy drawing, she expresses her hope to return to the city to see him the following weekend. Her focus on her still-new relationship with Jenkins certainly preempted her getting better acquainted with other Yaddo guests.

The intimacy of this new relationship is documented by Baber's casual but focused pencil sketch of Jenkins asleep, with his face etched in profile, his rumpled pajama top open. Baber's rare surviving figurative sketch is signed ALICE BABER, NEW YORK 1958.[34] The style seems to be the "nervous" line that she said was inspired by Paul Cézanne.

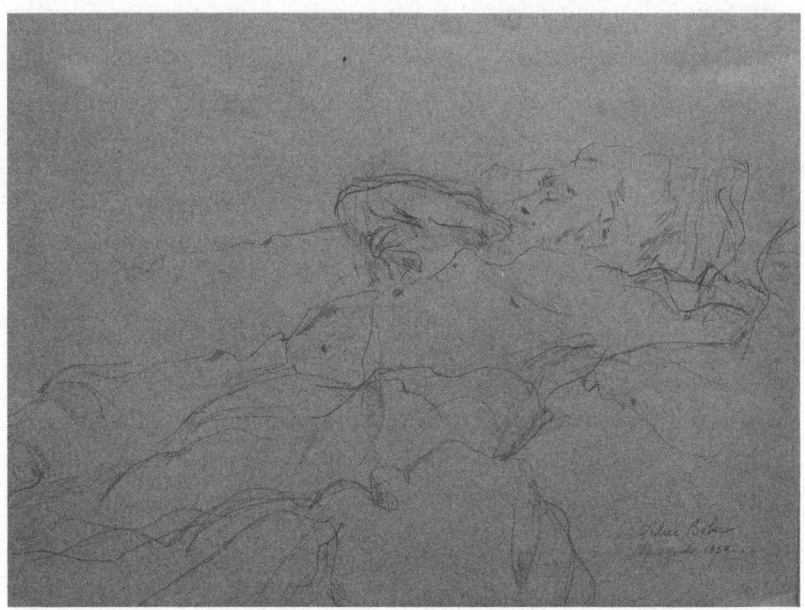

It also was in 1958, in the first flush of their romance, that Baber gave Jenkins what they then called an ivory "Eskimo" knife (which today we can more properly identify as Inuit), made by a member of an Indigenous people living in northern Canada and parts of Greenland and Alaska. Baber had intended to add the knife to Jenkins's collection of ivory objects, but her thoughtful gift also suggested a new technique to him. In a kind of performative action painting, Jenkins began to use the ivory knife to help direct the flow of poured acrylic paint onto his canvases, sensing that he could gain greater control: "With the smooth organic surface of the ivory I could use great pressure against the sensitive tooth of the canvas. It wouldn't abrade, like a metal knife would."[35] Baber's gift eventually resulted in a 1966 film on Jenkins's technique directed by Jules Engle, produced by his dealer Martha Jackson, *The Ivory Knife: Paul Jenkins at Work*, which was shown at the Museum of Modern Art and received the Golden Eagle Award at the Venice Film Festival in 1966. In the film Jenkins mentions that the ivory knife was a gift from Alice Baber, but he neither identifies her, nor explains that she was both an artist and, at that time the film was shot, his wife.

In contrast to Jenkins's technique, or to that of her contemporary Helen Frankenthaler, there is no pouring of paint in Baber's abstract work. She wanted nothing accidental. "She applies the paint with her finger, thinned to make the shapes transparent," the painter and critic Ann McCoy observed of her friend Baber's technique. "The paint is scrubbed into the canvas. Every hue is individually mixed and applied with a definite effect in mind."[36] Baber was trying to paint light.

Neither Baber nor Jenkins, however, poured paint onto raw or unprimed canvas like Helen Frankenthaler or Morris Louis, both of whom were influenced by Clement Greenberg's intervention. Neither Baber nor Jenkins wanted the paint to be absorbed into the surface of the canvas, which they primed to avoid absorption. Baber worked mostly in oils on a white acrylic gesso ground.[37] One critic who knew Baber well stated that she disliked the chalky look of acrylic and continued to use oil as she has had since her early still lifes.[38] Baber explained of the stained and poured-paint artists that she and Jenkins worked in the "same territory, but we don't get together and, among other things, we use different methods."[39] Since Baber sought a much greater sense of control in her painting process, she rejected the notion of pouring paint.

Both Baber and Jenkins were drawn to Asian art and culture. Baber's interest goes back much before she took a course in college. In a snapshot of Alice and her sister as young girls, Nancy holds a doll, but Alice displays her folding fan. Such fans originated in Japan around the seventh to eighth century before they were adopted in China and elsewhere. Such an Asian artifact might well have reflected the broad intellectual interests of Adin Baber and the many books he had at home. The exoticism of Alice's Japanese fan reverberated years later, when she enrolled in a course at Indiana University taught by a well-known Asian art curator. Remembering her professor, she said, "I think my favorite art history course was from Theodore Bowie who taught Oriental art. And I think it was the only class I ever made A+ in. I really enjoyed it enormously."[40]

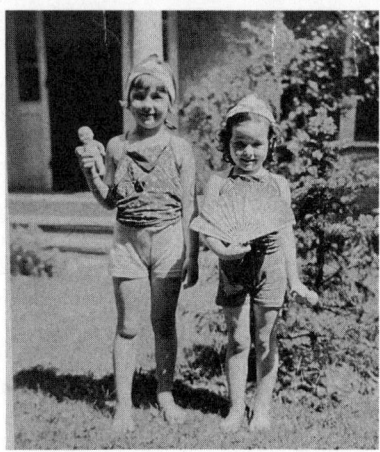

As for Jenkins, he discovered Asian art as a child in his hometown of Kansas City, Missouri, at the Nelson Gallery (now the Nelson-Atkins Museum of Art), which opened in 1933 to much fanfare and with the beginnings of its now famous collection of Asian art. Through his great-uncle, Jenkins also got to meet the celebrated American architect Frank Lloyd Wright, who collected Japanese prints. Jenkins later commented on one of his favorite Japanese artists: "Hokusai's particular structures and grid compositions laid down laws as much for Frank Lloyd Wright as for Vincent van Gogh."[41]

Jenkins's interest in Hokusai, Japanese art, and Vincent van Gogh recalls Baber's own early admiration for van Gogh, whose *Self-Portrait with a Bandaged Ear* before a Japanese print that the Dutch painter had collected was reproduced in color in *World Famous Paintings*, the 1939 book Baber had owned since adolescence (CP #2). Jenkins, after having spent four years in New York at the Art Students League studying painting with Yasuo Kuniyoshi, considered the Japanese émigré artist his mentor.

Both Jenkins and Baber titled their paintings with a specific poetic association for each work, often citing the name of a particular color. From late 1959, Jenkins used the preface *Phenomena* for his titles, which he might have borrowed from Goethe.[42] Jenkins explained his choice of the plural of phenomenon: "We see one thing but are never one. We are many things but gravitate toward the single point. It is an acknowledgment of the variables which make the plural [of *Phenomenon*] ever present."[43] Baber, however, instead of choosing just one theme for her titles, repeated a few favorite references like ladders, jaguars, paths, pipers, or other variations on sound, often combining more than one of these favorite references in her enigmatic titles.

"The Interrelation of Sounds and Colors" was an essay later given to the couple by its Indian author, who inscribed the offprint, FOR MR. AND MRS. PAUL JENKINS WITH BEST REGARDS, LAXMI SIHARE,

AUGUST 26, 1968.[44] Sihare focused on "the concept of the matching of sounds and colors," writing about the Asian origins of the idea that had been popularized in the West by modernist artists such as Wassily Kandinsky and František Kupka, and musicians such as Alexander Scriabin and Thomas Wilfred.[45]

While, as Mike Kanemitsu hinted, Baber was much more likely than Jenkins to connect sound and music with color, both Baber and Jenkins put a priority on painting light. Jenkins cited Claude Monet's statement, "Light is the real person in the picture," as an early influence on his own development, as he explained, "What is most important to me is what I can't see—and that is what I must paint. Paint the invisible which you know is there. Paint its astral colors and light and substance."[46]

Even while painting abstractions, Baber explained one of her sources in 1973: "I like the feeling of light or wind flowing on an uneven surface, like the golden surface of a reliquary, so that here you see the saint's leg, there you don't," explaining how much she appreciated icons.[47] "I like the idea of the hermit in the cave, of course leading to El Greco figures and so forth, or the curved space behind the shape. So, you have the figure, and the space comes around it. So, in that the hermit is the dark shape, the cave itself is a light cave, and the rocks are sort of floating in the air. I mean, they're not underfoot; they're all over the place sort of defying gravity. But it does have a definite reference to me."[48]

Baber's comment underlines how she intentionally tried to paint light to create shapes in her paintings that appear to float and to defy gravity. She would play with the thought of such imagery in her *Dance of the Wind Cave* (1973) (CP #40) and in her *Hermit in the Cave of Light* (1976) (CP #42). In *Dance of the Wind Cave*, we see that the white light resembles that in the depiction of divine light in the sky in the upper left corner of El Greco's *St. Jerome Penitent* (1610) (CP #40). She later commented, "Light is nearly always mystical. I mean it would be hard to keep light from being mystical. You'd have to work very hard."[49] What Baber felt was that spiritual truth was attainable through her subjective experience and that she could convey such insight through her artwork.

Where Baber and Jenkins differed, however, was in their estimates of the validity of psychotherapy in attempting to approve one's ability to function in life. We know that Baber painted an early abstraction she named after Frieda Fromm-Reichmann, the psychoanalyst and author. The introspective Baber also recorded and kept many notes about her dreams.

In contrast, Jenkins seems to have considered psychoanalysis frivolous, even a joke. He left evidence by posing with the fellow painter John Hultberg for two black-and-white photographs taken in New York by Walter Silver in 1957. In one photograph, Jenkins assumes the role of the analyst taking notes, while Hultberg, playing the role of the analysand, lies on the bed beside him. In the other photograph of the pair, their roles are reversed and Jenkins is lying down with a cigarette between his lips, while Hultberg pretends to take notes. At the time of their spoof of psychoanalysis, both men were represented by the New York dealer Martha Jackson.

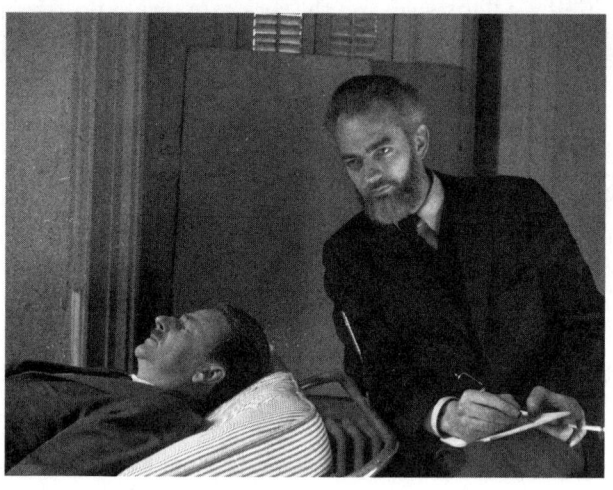

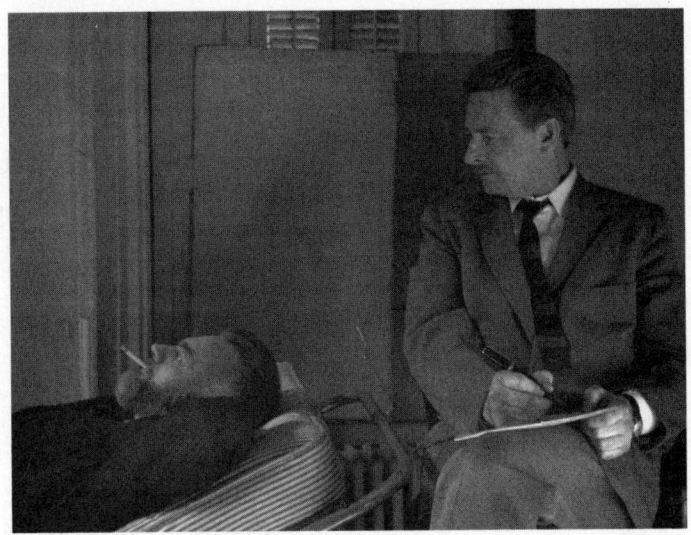

Neither Jenkins nor Hultberg turned out to have much control over their drives and desires. The two men both drank to excess and were repeatedly unfaithful to their several wives. Both men and Alice Baber were exposed to the surrealist movement, which was influenced by Freud and psychoanalytic theory, but which intended to liberate desire and sexuality by breaking down rationality. At the time that Baber met Jenkins, his charm was so captivating that she paid little heed to his excesses. Focusing instead on their shared obsession with light and with color, as well as their mutual enthusiasm for Asian art and Buddhism, Baber wanted to be with Jenkins. In early 1959, when Jenkins returned to occupy his Paris studio, Baber chose to join him in France. Although this is well documented by extant correspondence and interviews, at least two recent studies mistakenly claim that Jenkins returned to Paris only in 1961, reflecting intentional misinformation from the late Suzanne Donnelly Jenkins, the artist's widow.[50] While Jenkins was legally separated from his first wife in 1957, it is not clear when their divorce was finalized.[51]

To financially support herself, Baber was helped by her father, who was continually very generous, in marked contrast to parents who fear that their children will fail in a career in the arts. Adin, believing in Alice's talent, encouraged her to abandon her day job so that she could focus on her own art full-time.[52] Adin later justified his support of Alice's artistic career to her older sister: "It was my suggestion that she take a leave of one year absence to spend all her time painting. But she said she couldn't afford the expense. I promised to pay her studio rent and expenses for canvas and paints (I did not realize that one tube of pigment costs so much.)"[53] A prescient Adin then reflected, "Good paintings do not sell for much money until 100 years after the deaths of the artist and then the more perceptive collectors collect the profits. Alice's paintings now sell for, depending on sizes, from $500.00 to $1,500.00."[54] (More than four decades after Baber's death, her auction prices reached nearly $700,000.)[55]

Alice Baber described her work experience as including five years on the editorial and creative staff of *McCall's*, including becoming its art editor, all of which she claimed enabled her to "bring a diversity of experiences to bear in panel discussions concerning women."[56]

Further evidence of her father's remarkable support was recorded on March 24, 1962, when Adin wrote a letter to a Mrs. D. M. (Hester) Rhodes in Chicago, telling her about Alice's artwork and asking if she might take an interest in his daughter. He wrote that Alice was then "developing murals."[57] No murals have since come to light, but perhaps he simply referred to her large-scale paintings on canvas.

Adin Baber's belief in Alice's talent and the encouragement he offered supported her ambition to become a professional artist and prepare to have her first solo exhibition.

CHAPTER 4

First Solo Show
(1958)

S ome critics identified Alice Baber in the 1950s as "a young second-generation Abstract-Expressionist painter."[1] Baber, however, differentiated the focus of her work from that of many of the abstract expressionists: "I was certainly a part of a whole movement of artists who were interested in abstraction, but my particular direction was not involved with their canons. For example, I'm interested in movement, but not gesture or dirty color. I wanted pure color. That was more important to me than some type of gesture or attack."[2]

In fact, Baber, born in 1928, was the exact contemporary of Helen Frankenthaler and Pat Passlof, who are both considered abstract expressionists. Although Baber knew both women, she had more in common with Passlof, with whom she showed from 1957 on Tenth Street at their co-op, the March Gallery, than with Frankenthaler, who had her first solo show in the fall of 1951 at the Tibor de Nagy Gallery, just as Baber was first arriving in New York City. Frankenthaler was born the daughter of a wealthy and influential Manhattan family; her father was Alfred Frankenthaler, a New York State Supreme Court judge. Frankenthaler jump-started her career in 1950, when she met the powerful art critic Clement Greenberg, with whom she had a five-year-long romantic relationship.[3]

In contrast, Passlof and Baber struggled to make it in New York. Baber grew up in Illinois, while Passlof's family moved from Georgia to middle-class Queens, still a long way from Frankenthaler's privilege. Passlof's career got a boost when she studied with Willem de Kooning in 1948 at Black Mountain College in North Carolina. It is possible that Alice's close friendship with Elaine de Kooning distanced her from Pat Passlof since Pat's relationship with Milton Resnick followed his affair with Elaine. Pat continued her study with Willem de Kooning privately in New York, when he introduced her to Resnick, with whom she began to live in the mid-1950s and married in 1961.[4]

Alice was much closer to Elaine, who was a decade older than she. The two women, who shared a close friendship with the supportive couple Ibram and Ernestine Lassaw, both showed at the March Gallery, and remained lifelong friends. Elaine Marie Catherine Fried grew up in suburban New York, raised by a problematic mother, who took her to museums and encouraged her interest in art. She studied art in New York, including privately with Willem de Kooning, whom she married in 1943. Through a tumultuous marriage, the couple struggled with alcoholism, infidelity, and a nearly twenty-year-long separation, reuniting in 1976.[5]

Thus, the routes to sustained success for women artists coming of age in the 1940s and 1950s were full of potholes, hurdles, and unseen traps that could derail the best-laid plans, the most dedicated creative worker. With so many entrenched obstacles for women artists, those who succeeded were often the intimate partners of male artists, who were often somewhat older than their female partners.

As for Baber, she arrived on the New York art scene when her cohort at the March Gallery hosted her first solo show, which took place there from October 24 to November 13, 1958. After the show opened, Baber's friend Anne Alpert threw a party for her at her home, located nearby at

107 West 11th Street.[6] Alpert, the first ex-wife of Chilean-born surrealist artist Roberto Matta, was an American artist who was also the mother of twin boys (born in 1943), both of whom became artists: Sebastian Matta and Gordon Matta-Clark, a well-regarded site-specific artist in the 1970s. For Baber, the March Gallery show was a huge success.

The staff photographer at *The Village Voice*, Fred W. McDarrah, photographed Baber and Jenkins together less than two weeks after her first solo show closed on November 13—she now had a new show, a new beau, and was sitting on top of the art world. McDarrah got his photograph of Baber and Jenkins together at the opening party for a Sam Francis show at the Martha Jackson Gallery in New York, on November 25, 1958. The glamorous couple posed spontaneously for the photographer while attending their friend's opening party, held at what was also Paul's gallery. One has to look closely to see that Jenkins, elegantly dressed in a dark suit, holds a drink in his right hand and clasps the hand of a smiling Baber in his left; the sleeve of Baber's fashionable lighter-colored suit is just barely visible beneath Jenkins's darker sleeve. McDarrah captured Jenkins leaning toward Baber, who smiles with pleasure.

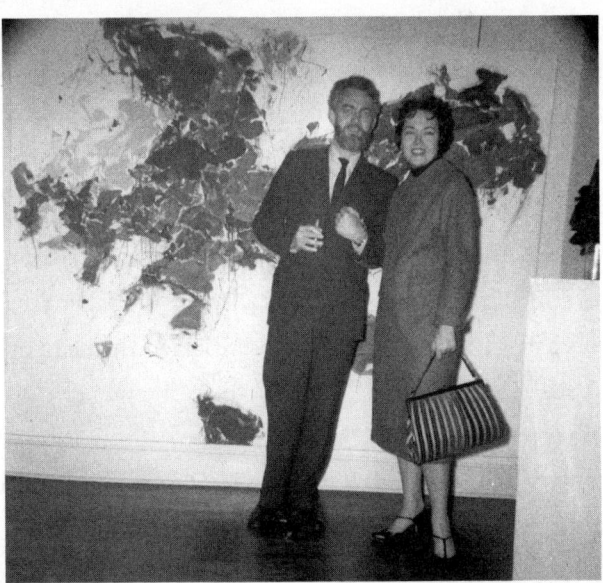

Jenkins knew the internationally prominent Sam Francis from Paris, where the Californian had lived and exhibited during the 1950s, before coming to New York in 1957 and moving back to California in 1961. Among the critics who championed Francis was Michel Tapié, whom Jenkins sought out and befriended in Paris.[7]

Francis's interest in color set against large areas of whiteness relates to compositional concerns and portraying light, which Baber often considered in her own paintings. Jenkins, Baber, and Francis also shared an interest in Asian culture and Buddhism, all of which suggests why the new couple was present at this event and were willing to pose in front a painting by Francis.[8]

In her own exhibition, Baber's abstractions grew out of the colorful pictures of still life that she had been producing, "sort of floating in space."[9] She wrote, "My early work was still life and from it came the tree of life, the celestial garden, the rivers, the mystical ladders, colored wind and rain, plants made of jewels, mythical springs, and the final rim of the universe."[10] Hers was not a mundane sensibility.

Another time, Baber said that she had been looking at the still life paintings by the seventeenth-century Dutch baroque artist Judith Leyster, who had been one of the most prominent women artists of her day.[11] Baber told an interviewer in 1980: "I started doing still life in about 1957—somewhere like that and I worked and worked with still life. And as the still life became abstract, it started to float, which I let it do and those, those shapes are somehow—I'm still making a kind of floating still-life, which becomes landscape."[12] Baber recalled that the abstract artist Landès Lewitin had criticized the head of a cow in one of her still life paintings.[13] But, by then, she was already moving away from representation.

In a canvas Baber called *Battle of the Oranges*, painted in 1958, just months before her solo show, she transformed the shape of

citrus—oranges—suddenly turning them into diaphanous circles
(CP #15). She produced translucency instead of Cézannesque weight,
perhaps recalling the crop and the vivid colors seen in bright sunlight
that she must have observed while spending winters in Florida as a
child. The pictures, she recalled, were "without a kind of gravity. And
the colors were reds and yellows and oranges. . . . The paint was still
fairly heavy. In places. It would be thin and then it would be thick."[14]
Here, as the artist Ann McCoy pointed out, Baber began to disassociate
form from color, enabling color to float in space.[15]

It could be mere coincidence, but Grace Hartigan, whom Baber
knew from the Club, had painted and exhibited a series of pictures
inspired by collaborating with the poet Frank O'Hara. Hartigan began
her series in November 1952, responding to O'Hara's suite of poems
called *Oranges: 12 Pastorals*. But neither Hartigan's paintings, with their
somber palette of black and grays and elements of text, nor O'Hara's
poems were about fruit or still life, nor had either imbibed the citrus
groves during a childhood spent in Florida as Baber had.[16]

Baber later stated: "In 1958, I painted a still life so wildly that
I called it the 'Battle of the Oranges.' From orange to cloud to
Jacob's ladder—ambiguity and simile and metaphor." "Ambiguity,"
she explained, "means getting a varied response from myself and from
other viewers. It is the path away from cliché. Many people respond
to a given color in three ways and to a form in about the same number.
It is not enough. It is the problem of stereotyping."[17]

Battle of the Oranges was also reproduced in black-and-white
(CP #15) alongside a brief review in *Arts Magazine* in its "In the
Galleries" section, which opened with a description of lively pictures:
"Large, brilliantly colored canvases of curling, flaming and feathery
strokes of paint have each their special éclat—the glowing *Suttee* with
its mounting flames of scarlet, rose, and pink, or the more thinly

painted *Sirenidae* with its stained cherry reds embroidered with arabesques of white and orange (CP #17)."[18] The critic James R. Mellow, who signed his review only as J. R. M., went on to declare: "Miss Baber's most impressive group of works are the Vanitas series, with their suggestions of still life—writhing, draped and folded forms in whited yellow and orange in which clusters of rounded shapes in bright orange or red nestle like ripe and burning fruit. In that series, particularly in *Battle of the Oranges*, she seems to be infusing into the still life something like exuberance and passion which Soutine let loose upon his landscapes."[19] By seeing Baber's paintings as a Vanitas series, Mellow refers to works of art that contain symbols of mortality or the impermanence of material things; for example, some seventeenth-century Dutch still life paintings. He perhaps senses what James Jones will later articulate as the "tragedy of light."

That first solo show of Baber's in 1958 was also inscribed into history in a comprehensive review written by the poet James Schuyler, who was born in Chicago, but raised in upstate New York. His estimate of Baber's show, published in *Artnews*, commented that "her pictures speak with a New York accent, though impersonally so," which was a rather remarkable accomplishment given the bias that people from the provinces who manage to enter the cultural scene in New York sometimes experience.[20]

Schuyler's review is especially important since it documents Baber's early paintings, some of which have remained unidentified or lost: "In her free abstractions, she paints a world in which everything is gloriously falling. There is *Cibola*, a feathered and imaginative flight in orange and reds, hued with white and magenta, that seeks a childhood image of golden cities."[21]

Here Schuyler referred to Baber's *Cibola*, a Spanish transliteration of the name for Cevola (sometimes Sevola), the native name for a

Zuni pueblo (Hawikuh Ruins). The mission of Francisco Vázquez de Coronado's sixteenth-century expedition was to search for the legendary Seven Cities of Gold, the great wealth early Spanish explorers believed existed in the southwestern United States.[22] Years later, Baber told an interviewer, "I like the idea of the space itself being a kind of—as I call it—a sacred space, because it's a chosen space. And I was reading about how in ancient cities there's part of a space considered sacred and that interested me."[23]

Both Alice Baber's wide-ranging intellect and her interest in ancient cities and Spanish explorers in the Americas links to her father's writing on Hernando de Soto. While Francisco Vázquez de Coronado was seeking the mythical Seven Cities of Cíbola in the Southwest, Hernando de Soto was searching for treasure in the Southeast, having landed on present-day Tampa Bay in the spring of 1539.[24]

Another Florida theme—*The Everglades*—was an important focus among Baber's paintings that caught Schuyler's attention in his review of Baber's first show. He singled it out as an eye-catching canvas, 60 x 40 inches, that had a "bending yellow light into blue-green strokes" and remarked how that picture (CP #16), which harkened back to Baber's childhood spent in Florida, "expounds her grasp of the intricacy of surface, a restless movement that coils and lilts upon itself."[25] Baber's surface in *Everglades* was produced with thick textured paint, likely applied with a palette knife rather than a brush alone.

Alice's father recalled to her sister Nancy how when he encountered *Everglades*, exhibited in Alice's first solo show in New York, he "knew then even with my little knowledge of art that Alice was an artist."[26] He said that he recognized at once that her canvas depicted a "bald-cypress hammock," a particular phenomenon of nature found in Florida swamps and marshes. This hammock, which has nothing to do with the sleeping accommodation made by rope mesh and suspended between two trees, is where a dense stand of broad-leafed hardwood trees grow on a natural rise of limestone only a few inches in elevation, turning that drier land into a contrasting ecosystem.[27]

The power of Adin's recognition depended on his recall of an experience in one such hammock from Alice's childhood, which he shared in a letter to Alice's older sister, Nancy. The girls' mother had heard about a hammock located on the way to Homestead, Florida, to which she took her entire family to explore. "There was a pathway, but through it for we weaker tourists. About midway I felt Alice's hand hunting mine and she said, 'Pappy can't we go back out—I feel smothery. So we went out and you and mother went on. This is the origin of your painting. . . . Alice painted another and larger one for me."[28] Thus, Baber managed to convey a sense of movement, of threatening chaos, of the fear that she perceived as a small child, venturing into unfamiliar dark tropical surroundings.

Another of Baber's paintings, *The Edge of the Trees*, Schuyler found to be "a close-up of a distant detail, with a shaft of blue bisected off-center that is both sky and water, and the depths of distance." Recalling, despite its small scale, Claude Monet's large paintings of the sky and clouds reflected in a pond of waterlilies, it appears that Baber's early abstract composition (or a study for it) has survived and is closely linked to the abstract paintings that followed it.

Schuyler also wrote, "*Sirenidae* changes the stroke to white and golds on a rose madder ground that is abstract and sensual, undulating and under sea."[29] Here he refers to Baber's canvas *Sirenidae* (CP #17), which is the scientific name for four species of eel-like aquatic salamanders found in the southeastern United States, including Florida. This bright red painting survives.[30] It depicts a bold curvilinear form that suggests Baber's reference to the sea creature, which she knew about from her tropical Florida childhood.

Other titles take us further afield. Schuyler noted, *"Bar-le-Duc caps the show in a freedom of fresh blues and a shattered rose."*[31] This French title, *Bar-le-Duc*, recalls Baber's experience in the summer of 1951, when she was painting in classes at Fontainebleau and then immediately afterward toured France. She named her canvas *Bar-le Duc* for the well-preserved town in northeast France with memorable architectural splendor from the Renaissance.

Whatever Baber wanted to convey in her art, she did so with a joy for experimentation. Her move from still life to abstraction was helped by her trying new techniques in watercolor. The critic Alexandra de Lallier observed Baber working and reported how "in the middle of a watercolor Baber had used paper tissues to quickly draw several small shapes inside a larger shape. The paint was still wet and it looked as though she had painted in a lighter color. The remaining color was not only lighter, it had taken on a 'softness and resonance of light.'"[32] Eventually Baber realized that she could transfer this technique, which she called "sinking" and "lifting," to her oil paintings.[33]

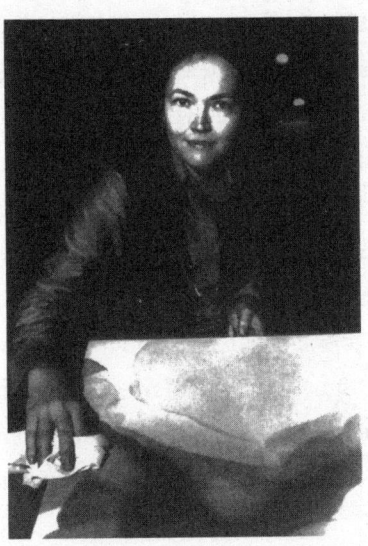

Baber explained her early painting to the novelist James Jones, telling him that she was searching for "a way to get the light moving across the whole thing."[34] Jones understood that in *Battle of the Oranges* (CP #15), "the spatial relationships between the oranges became agitated, somehow no longer fixed, hence the title. It was for her the painting in which she departed from subject matter and moved toward a more personal image, personal metaphor."[35] It seems that Jones saw Baber's agitation of space as a metaphor for the inner agitation of her psyche.

Baber's interest in metaphor began to develop early in her career. Already in 1958 at Yaddo, she was reading Mark Schorer's book on William Blake, in which chapter 4 is titled, "Source and Use of Metaphor." Schorer's discussion of mysticism and metaphor were two themes that spoke to Baber. Her deep interest in literature prepared her for her continuing intellectual dialogue with James Jones.

Jones was the first to interpret Baber's art on a new level beyond aesthetics when he explained that he understood the bright colors in her paintings to be evidence of her tragic vision.[36] Jones reads Baber's use of bright colors to convey tragedy or loss: "She could not tolerate the triteness of painting sorrow in the conventional way: that she wanted more than that; that she wanted to paint sorrow in light gay colours, as nature does. This may sound strange looking at all these lovely, laughing brilliant colours she uses." The meaning Jones perceives in Baber's use of vivid colors is reminiscent of how Lee Krasner described painting brightly hued abstractions even as she was grieving, immediately following the sudden death of her husband, Jackson Pollock, in 1956: "I can remember when I was painting *Listen* [1957], which is so high-keyed in color—I've seen it many times since and it looks like such a happy painting—I can remember that when I was painting it I almost didn't see it, because tears were literally pouring down."[37]

Perceiving pain in Baber, who at fifteen years old had suffered the sudden loss of her mother, Jones argued, "In looking closer one can see and feel an almost terrifying poignancy, a near weeping sadness and sorrow in these delicately gay and summer-bright colors. It is as if she is trying to tell us about her native Illinois, with its brilliant blinding sun, its dust, its summer-deep greens, that Summer itself will not stay. School must begin again. Grandmothers and oldsters will not last the Winter."[38]

Late in life, Baber commented on this article by Jones in which "he described the nostalgia of the green of the trees in summer and the sadness of color. And I agreed completely that color was not a totally joyous experience, but had other elements. And that article was called 'The Tragedy of Color.'"[39]

The perceptive Jones writes about losing "grandmothers and old-sters," yet when Baber lost her mother, she lost the first person who encouraged her to work in visual arts. Baber's doting father, who had first urged his younger daughter to write poetry, did step up and try to fill the gap left by his wife's untimely death. He appreciated his daughter's fragility.

Baber compensated for the premature loss of her mother by developing a close friendship with Ernestine Lassaw, who was almost a generation older than she, knew the art world well, and was very nurturing. The Lassaws' home became a haven for Baber, where she brought her boyfriends to meet her close friends, and received advice and enthusiastic encouragement. Ibram Lassaw photographed their group of friends at Christmas dinner in 1958 at the Lassaws' New York City loft, recording Ernestine, the hostess, seated by the window; together (clockwise) with Paul Jenkins, Philip Pavia and his then-wife Marcia, Alice Baber, and the painter and filmmaker Alfred Leslie.[40]

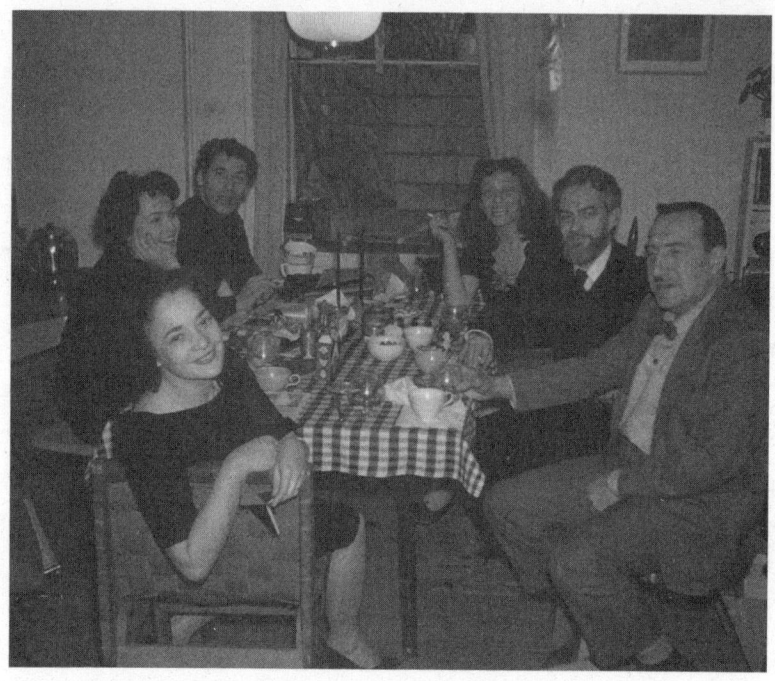

Christmas dinner at the Lassaws, 1958

Baber's presence at such holiday gatherings suggests a sense of family life reinvented for her in the home of the Lassaws. What Baber had experienced as a young child, however, turns out to have been much more complicated than the teenager's loss of her nurturing mother. Living in New York, at a long distance from her devoted father, Baber found in the Lassaws the loving mentors that she needed.

CHAPTER 5

Flashback to Child of Tragic Vision
(1928–1946)

I t is the first time (and so far, the only time) I have had the opportunity to study the development of a serious, good painter from almost the moment of new inception," the novelist James Jones asserted about Alice Baber's art.[1] He had watched her, he said, "with a close eye and a closer intellectual interest over a period of about eight years."[2] However, eight years back from his September 1965 *Studio International* article would point to 1957, when Baber was just beginning to put her work on view in group shows in New York.

Yet, a letter that Baber wrote to her father from Paris in May 1959 suggests that Jones was not exact when he calculated the number of years since he had first met Alice. She wrote: "Have met the best seller author James Jones & his wife who come from Palestine, Ill. They are very nice tho I think Palestine wasn't sure. They have been helpful about critics & are going to buy a painting. They have a collection started."[3] When Baber and Jones met in Paris, it was an unexpected encounter of two creative souls recognizing that they came from rural communities in the same remote region of eastern Illinois.[4]

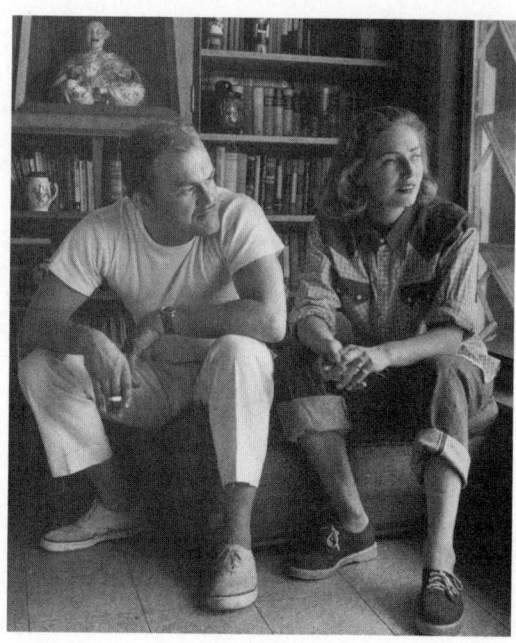

James and Gloria Jones, ca 1959

Baber's bright colors struck Jones as evidence of a "tragic vision," an effort to "paint sorrow."[5] As for the sorrow about which Jones wrote, he was no stranger to sorrow in his own life, having suffered an alcoholic father who died by suicide and a violent mother.[6] To understand Baber and her art, it would be useful to find and explore the cause of her "tragic vision," as identified by the author of the National Book Award-winning debut novel, *From Here to Eternity* (1951), which deals with personal tragedies among American soldiers serving in Hawaii, just before the attack on Pearl Harbor on December 7, 1941. Since we know that Jones and Baber knew each other well, it's imperative to explore what was behind his judgment. He seems to have perceived some discomfort in Baber's psychology, her point of view, and in her personal experience. Later, her father would tell her husband that she was sensitive. Thus, it is necessary to try and understand her reality and the events that helped shape her psyche.

Jones's insight into Baber and her art was unique. The validity of his interpretation is confirmed by her positive response to his essay about her, sustained over many years, during which she often had it reprinted, translated, or excerpted in her catalogues. Her steadfast response sharpens and focuses the usual inquiries into an artist's life.

On the surface, Baber's origins seem ordinary enough. We know that Alice Baber, daughter of Lois Mary Shoot and Adin B. Baber, was born on August 22, 1928, in Charleston, Illinois, her mother's birthplace, as well as the site of Abraham Lincoln's fourth debate on September 18, 1858. Lincoln faced off against Stephen Douglas in a series of debates focused on slavery, as they competed for a US Senate seat representing Illinois. Lincoln became the subject of several books written by Alice Baber's father, Adin, who was proud of being the great-grandson of William Hanks, a first cousin of Abraham Lincoln, through Lincoln's mother, Nancy Hanks.[7]

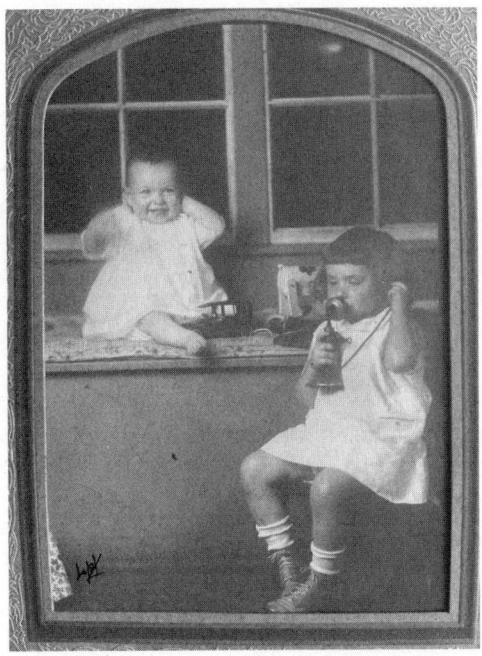

Alice and Nancy Baber, summer 1929

When Alice's mother, Lois Mary Shoot, was born on December 24, 1892, her father, Tilford Taylor Shoot, was forty-four years old, and her mother, Mary Elizabeth Wilhoit Shoot, was forty-one. Lois, who was the youngest of eight children, married Adin B. Baber on September 27, 1924, in her hometown of Coles, Illinois, some thirty miles away from his hometown.[8] Alice's sociability might reflect growing up with such a large extended family with many cousins, aunts, and uncles. Lois and her four older sisters were especially close, as is documented in a photograph of their gathering in Charleston, Illinois during the early 1930s.[9] Compared to the rural home of Adin Baber, Lois's family came from a small city, offering the resources of Eastern Illinois University, which in 1895 began to train teachers. For his education, Adin B. Baber had left his home in rural Edgar County and gone east to upstate New York, where he studied civil engineering at Syracuse University. He told his daughters that he had "fired a furnace and waited on tables at Syracuse University—I never told it. Mama sent me from her meager 'pin-money.' I do not know the origin of that name but it was sure appropriate in those times."[10] During World War I, Adin volunteered as an ambulance driver in France with the American Field Service; in 1919 he drove US treaty negotiators daily to Versailles from Paris. Returning from Europe, Adin married and settled down to raise his family in his forebears' fertile farming region in Illinois, near the Indiana border. But living in Paris, Illinois, the memory of French culture stayed with him. For his honeymoon, he drove his bride all the way to French-speaking Montreal and Quebec City in Canada.[11] Later, he supported his daughter's study of art in France.

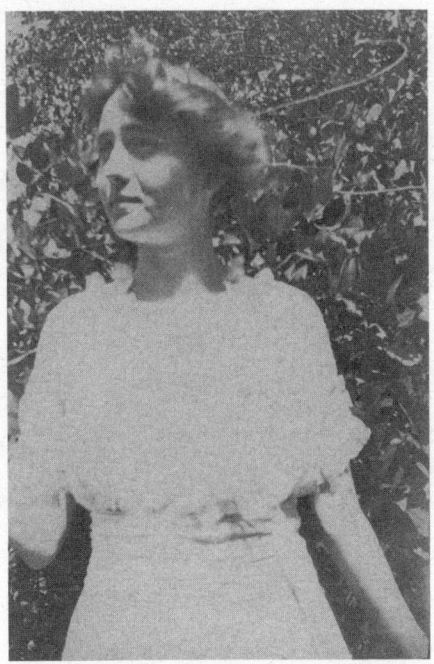

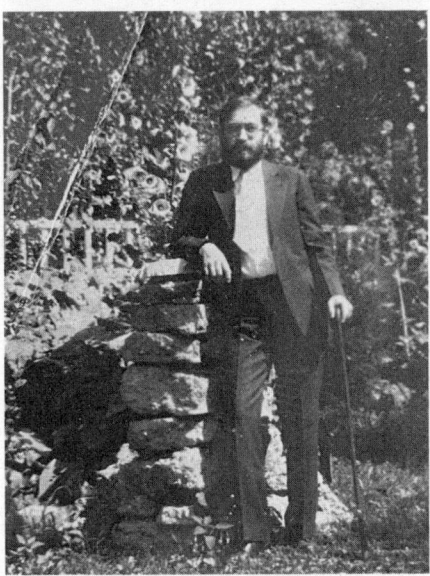

Lois Mary Shoot and Adin B. Baber around the time
of their marriage on September 27, 1924.

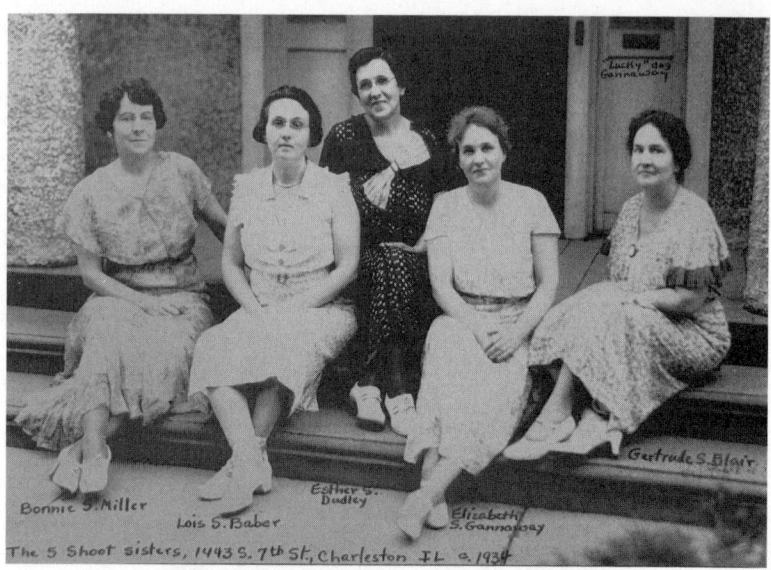

Lois Shoot Baber (2nd from the left) with her sisters, 1934

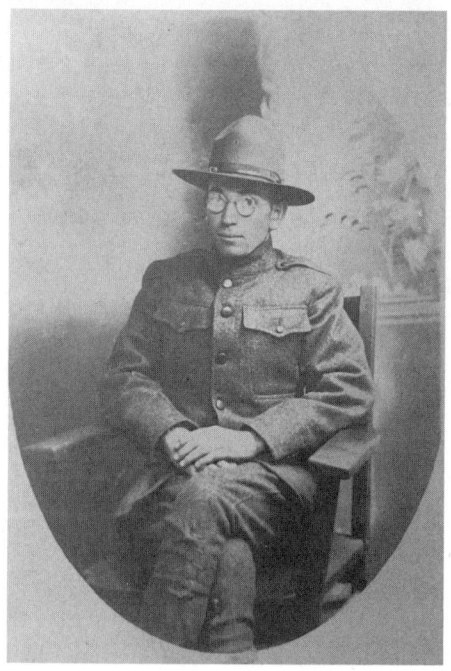

Adin Baber as an ambulance driver in France, ca 1918

Adin's father, Dexter Dole "Deck" Baber, Alice's paternal grandfather, was born and raised in this same area and attended North Central College in Danville, Indiana, before working as a cattle and grain merchant.[12] He was the son of Adin Baber and Mary Ellen Hanks, a cousin of Abraham Lincoln.[13] At his death at the age of ninety-eight in 1965, Dexter left Adin a great deal of Illinois farmland, some of which had to be sold to pay the estate taxes.[14] Adin, the executor of his father's estate, auctioned off 62.35 acres on January 21, 1967.[15]

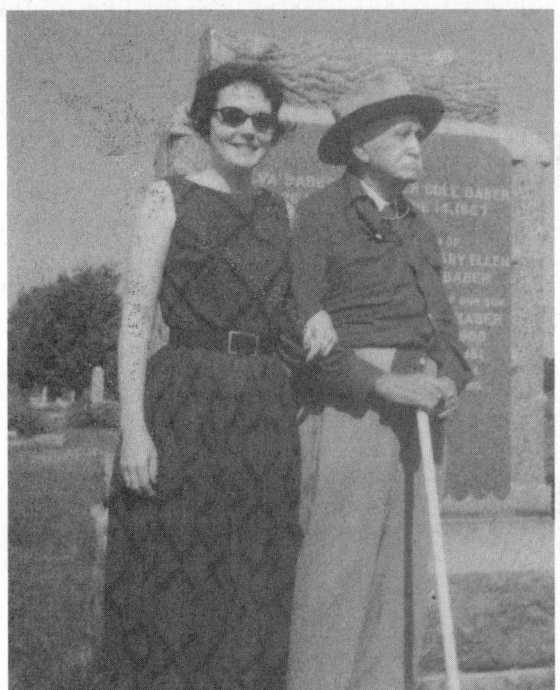

Alice and her grandfather Dexter Baber

The serious distress, which spoiled little Alice's childhood and traumatized her family, began with Dexter's uncle, Asa Baber, the great-uncle of Alice's father, who was elected treasurer of Edgar County, Illinois, in 1859. In 1865 Asa assisted with the organization of the

First National Bank of Paris, the county seat of Edgar County, and was made its first cashier, a post he held until 1870, when he was elected the bank's president, an office that he would hold for forty-five years.[16] At Asa's death in 1915, his son, Frederick Baber, who had served as the mayor of the town of Paris, was elected the bank's president until he resigned to resume farming. At that time, by 1924, the grandnephew of one of the bank's founders, Adin B. Baber, Alice's father, who had worked as the bank's cashier, became the bank's president.[17]

PARIS BANKER TO MARRY read the local headline for the article in which his future mother-in-law, Mrs. Tilford P. Shoot of Charleston, Illinois, announced on September 9, 1924, Adin B. Baber's engagement to her daughter Lois. Before too long, their growing family, including Alice's older sister, Nancy, lived comfortably in a house at 525 Prairie Street in Paris, employing (according to the 1930 US Census) Kate Hornbrook, a fifty-five-year-old local widow and immigrant from Germany, as a live-in servant.

Yet, just over a year after Alice's birth, the stock market crashed and the Great Depression ensued—not an easy moment for her father to be responsible for a bank, which eventually failed.[18] The local economy in Paris and the surrounding counties then depended on corn and cattle agriculture, as well as coal mining, which the community's bank was expected to help facilitate. Having made loans to farmers, who were expanding during the national economic boom of the 1920s, the bank, now led by Adin Baber, was forced to cope with local people who could no longer pay their debts.

At the beginning of the 1930s, prices for a bushel of corn fell to just eight or ten cents, making it cheaper than coal to burn as fuel.[19] With the depressed prices for farm products, the value of land also collapsed, so that farmers lost their farms when they turned out to be worth less than they owed to the bank, which had to foreclose on their mortgages.

Across the nation, there were a half million farm foreclosures a day.[20] At the same time, thousands of banks failed during the first four years of the Depression.

Although the exact story has not come down in the Baber family, Adin Baber as the bank's president had to carry out the stressful task of foreclosing on his friends and neighbors. He had to deal with the pain of his embattled community and frustration at his inability to fix the enormous problems. The Paris city directory for 1930 lists Adin Baber as both president of the First National Bank & Trust Company and vice president of the T. A. Foley Lumber Company, which suggests that a change took place in his employment.

Adin Baber's grandson, John M. Kern (Alice's nephew), recalls family stories that his grandfather had suffered a "nervous disorder" or a mental breakdown around the time of the stock market crash of 1929 and the ensuing Great Depression. A fragmentary but undocumented story tells of Adin attending a banquet for the bank and imagining that the wine had been poisoned. According to family lore, this delusional belief is why Adin left the bank, and, with Lois, took their two children and moved from their house on Prairie Street in Paris, Illinois, to live in south Florida. The immediate result, however, was that Adin initially spent time hospitalized because of mental illness.[21]

Adin Baber's treatment took place around 1931, just after new legislation—the Mental Treatment Act (MTA) of 1930—amended the Lunacy Act of 1890. As a result, "lunatics" officially became *patients*, and "asylums" *mental hospitals*.[22] Now mental illness could be viewed more like physical illness and admission for treatment could be negotiated between the doctor and the patient. Some psychiatrists established separate programs—often called psychopathic hospitals—within general hospitals to treat patients suffering from acute mental illnesses.

It is not clear which hospital first treated Adin Baber, but by February 23, 1931, he was in treatment at St. Francis Hospital in Miami Beach. This institution was run by the Franciscan Sisters of Allegany, New York, who traveled to Florida in 1927 to staff the failing Allison Hospital, which they renamed St. Francis Hospital. In a letter (written on hospital stationery) to his father in Dudley, Illinois, Adin wrote: "I had to come here again but for only a few days I think. I continue to have attacks but I throw them off more quickly, and am stronger physically all time."[23]

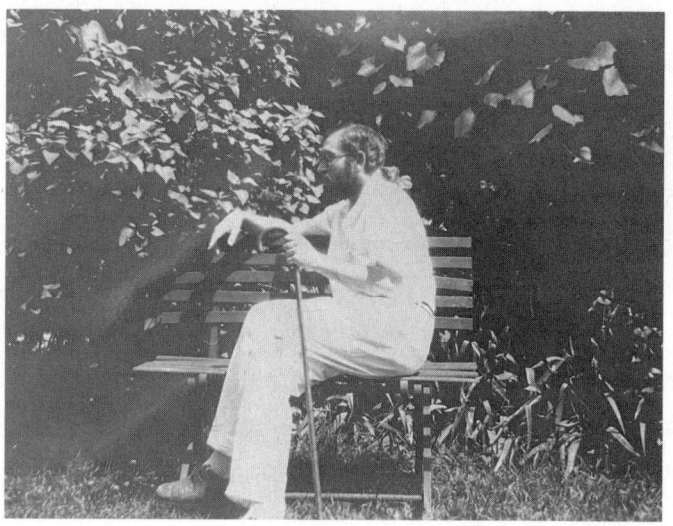

Adin's concern in the letter is to get his father to help Lois, who was forced to sell their house in Paris, Illinois. Coping with the turbulence of the Great Depression as well as his own demons, Adin writes, "I think that crowd of blackguards [an eighteenth-century term for scoundrels or villains] will sell us out at minimum legal time." He gave specific instructions how to protect the house up to $5500. As for the furniture, he requested "just claim everything & put up a fight until I get well and can cope with them, advise you to say nothing." He explains that he understands the power and the damage that various individuals can do, but laments that "Lois worries all time, and some of her sisters keep her upset, and that doesn't help." Adin concludes, "Yes indeed I shall get well and show up like Banquo's Ghost to some in Paris." His bitter reference to William Shakespeare's *Macbeth* while hospitalized for mental illness is ironic since in the play, Macbeth sees Banquo's ghost sitting in his chair at a banquet, yet only he and the ghost can see it, and the other guests think Macbeth is going insane.[24]

Although the process of getting help for mental distress had recently become less stigmatized, it was still nothing to discuss in public. The stock market crash had caused a lot of panic. Anecdotal discussion of the suffering that ensued nationwide identified temporary mental illness and even spikes in suicide. For example, in a 1931 essay, "The Jumping-Off Place," the literary critic Edmund Wilson described a seaside hotel on the West Coast where "the suicide rate is twice that of the Mid-Atlantic coast."[25]

No one in the Baber family ever discussed publicly their initial period in Florida, during which Adin spent time in a hospital recuperating from his mental breakdown. Perhaps his hospitalizations were brief enough and his two children were too young to understand, so they weren't told the reason for their father's absence. When the Baber family first departed for Florida, Alice was around three years old and her older sister and only sibling, Nancy Shirley Baber, around five. Nancy's eldest son, Alice's nephew, John M. Kern, recalls that his mother told him that she and Alice once visited their father in the hospital.[26]

Publicly, however, Baber's family stated that their move to Florida was so that the warmer winter climate would protect Alice, a precocious and creative child, who suffered poor health, including "severe bouts of bronchitis."[27] Documents suggest that Alice might have suffered from such an ailment. A letter to Lois Baber from Nancy's Sunday School teacher, dated March 25, 1930, thanks her for sharing a little Easter song, praises Nancy, and reads, "I am glad to hear you baby is improving and shall welcome her to Sunday School when you return."[28]

Yet, while the Baber family's precarious situation involved many other factors, this was the only reason for retreating to Florida that they were willing to discuss publicly. Explaining why the Babers first departed for Florida, Alice later repeated this simpler statement in official accounts. Yet, since the physical health of Alice's mother was also said to have been fragile, stress must have had some impact on the entire family, however unacknowledged. A surviving photograph of Lois reveals a haggard mother with her two young daughters, suggesting a woman suffering emotional and financial stress during the Great Depression.

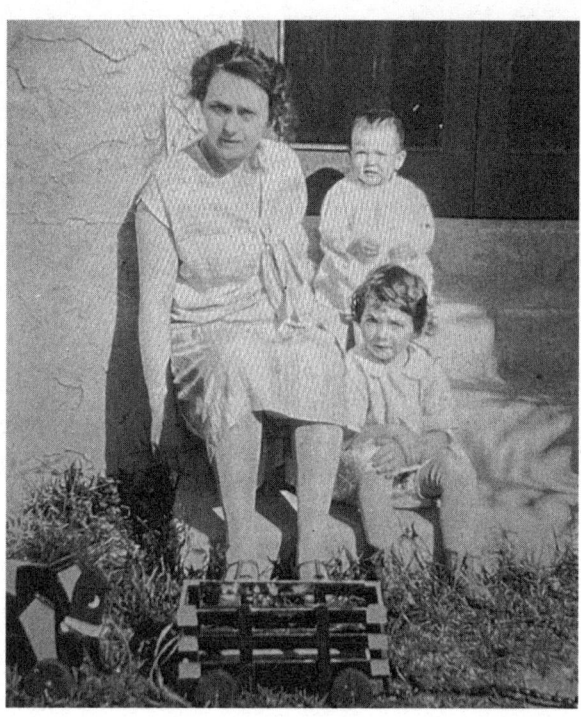

We get something of Lois's perception of three-year-old Alice in her January 15, 1932, letter, sent to her sister Gertrude from Kansas, Illinois, where they had spent Christmas: "Nancy just loves her sewing outfit that you sent her for Christmas and so does that naughty Alice. She wants to do all that Nancy does & insists."[29] Since they were forced to sell their home in Paris after Adin's breakdown, Lois and the children were staying in the rustic Kansas farmhouse, a mile north and a mile east of the town of Kansas, Illinois, built by Adin's grandparents on land first purchased by his forebears in 1865.

How much Alice later knew about what had transpired in her father's period of mental crisis remains unclear, but Adin never again ran a bank. From a surviving Christmas card from Lois's sister, the girls' Aunt Bonnie, postmarked December 22, 1932, we know that the girls were then at the Baber ancestral farm in Kansas, Illinois, probably spending the holiday with Lois's family while Adin was in the hospital in Florida.[30]

Apparently, Adin Baber's family used the rustic family farmhouse in the immediate period after he left his employment as bank president. In an undated typed letter many years later, Adin wrote to his daughters, recalling to Alice "the stair well where the gate from the bottom of stairway of the Paris house was hung here to keep you from falling downstairs the years of 1931–2, that we lived or camped here. Such a short time so long ago!"[31]

In another of his letters to his two daughters, Adin Baber years later recommended advice, telling them how to maintain their health: "In all things be moderate. Do not un-necessarily expose yourself. Get plenty of sleep and a balanced diet. There is a history of nervousness in past members of our family so do not 'Burn the candle at both ends.' Extreme fatigue or toxins may cause it to crop out. Guard against it. This is not a mental aberration but probably is due to overactive mentality in times of stress. I have experienced it, it has been my cross, so I know whereof I speak."[32]

The extreme stress, which Adin Baber experienced from the stock market crash and the contracting economy, caused him to write to both his daughters another undated letter of advice, which was only to be read after his death. In this letter, he gave them advice about how to hold on to ownership of the family farmlands: "SAFEGUARD ITS TITLE by not mortgaging except in dire emergency such as illness or invalidism . . . Should you be operating your farm yourselves and times become hard do not try to maintain your income by expanding the operations. Retract. Cut down expense and live frugally until the emergency is over. When times are prosperous buy quality things. When times are bad do without."[33] Adin Baber never got over the traumatic experience of having to foreclose on struggling farmers in his community.

Sometime in the early 1930s, Adin had recovered enough that he "opened a store" at Little River, Florida (in Miami), where he worked as a grain merchant, selling feed for farm animals as had his father.[34] By 1934, the Miami city directory lists "Plantation Supply Co. (Adin Baber) feeds" at 104 NW 79th St."[35] A letter from Adin to Nancy on stationary from this store asks: "How are you? Is Alice quite grown up? Does she put on airs?" He also spoke of moving and packing, suggesting the family's unsettled state.[36] The stationary indicates that Plantation Supply Co. sold poultry feeds, dairy rations, grain, fertilizers, insecticides, and seeds.

Also from this era, a photo taken outside Plantation Supply Co. survives showing Alice and her sister Nancy posing next to the store's sidewalk sign cut out in the shape of a rooster, announcing FEED. Posing dressed in her shiny Mary Jane shoes, little Alice, who looks to be about five years old, manages to offer up a smile, while her older sister, who perhaps understood much more of the family's recent trauma, appears glum. Even as the girls' father began his new business with which he knew that he could support his family, it would never satisfy him.

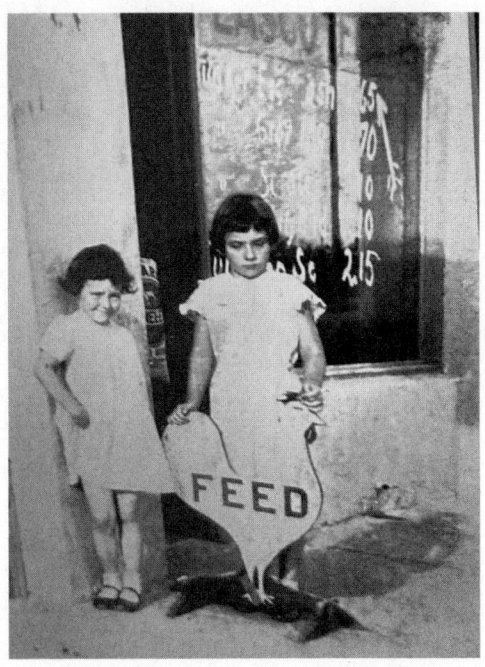

Eventually, Adin would also work as a writer, exploring history and natural history, a pursuit that gave him more satisfaction, if not much income. This might explain his later willingness to support Alice's efforts to become a professional artist. For the winters, Adin, his wife, and children all lived in Miami, but during the hot and humid summers, Lois brought their two children back to see their extended families in Illinois. Evidence indicates that some years Lois, Nancy, and Alice stayed in Kansas, where the girls attended the local school.

A November 12, 1937, letter from nine-year-old Alice to her older cousin, Gerry Jane, asks if she liked school when she was little. Alice describes a day of presentation of plays that her school had with another school: "Our play was about a little girl and how she was lonely and her book case came alive." Each of the pupils portrayed a book: "The Pied Piper of Hamlin town came first. I was last. I was Peter Pan."[37] She comments, "We aren't doing much at home except being sick"; then, she writes, "I will tell you a poem I made up":

Oh the moon is a round round lantern, that hands [*sic for hangs*] in the western sky,
    And the little stars are matches, that past him go floating by.
    But how do these stars get lighted, way up there in the sky,
    Why old mother cloud she strikes them as they go floating by.
    And then old blusters north wind, when day brake [*sic*] is coming nigh,
    He blows out the old lantern and matches,
    As they go floating by.[38]

This poem is remarkable not only for a nine-year-old to have written, but because it foretells the adult Alice Baber's obsession with light and the heavens.

A composition book, dated July 5, 1939, titled "My Poems and Stories by Alice Baber," survives, and demonstrates that more than one of Baber's enthusiasms was formed in childhood. One story from her tenth year is titled "The Old Rug Weaver" and is set in "far away India," where she would travel several times as an adult and collect rugs and other textiles. Her collection was notable enough that it was featured in a book about rugs.[39] She writes, "His rugs were once known far and wide for their beauty and fine weave but now as he had grown old other weavers took his place in making the finest rugs." She tells how he goes on to make "a magic rug," and flies off to Baghdad, where he is summoned to the king, a scene which she illustrates in a lively color pencil drawing (CP #5).

Not as exotic as Baghdad, the Baber family's annual migration south to Florida clearly stoked the imagination of Alice. Their adventure usually involved camping out in a tent along the way, a practice then called motor camping. They continued this until World War II began and required gas rationing from December 1, 1942.[40] A snapshot taken of Alice and Nancy sitting on the running board of the family's truck, which appears to be a 1930s Dodge with a canvas cover over the truck bed that might have been used for sleeping or for transporting a tent. The photograph is labeled on the verso: "In Cumberland Presbyterian church yard north of Nashville Tenn. June 1936."

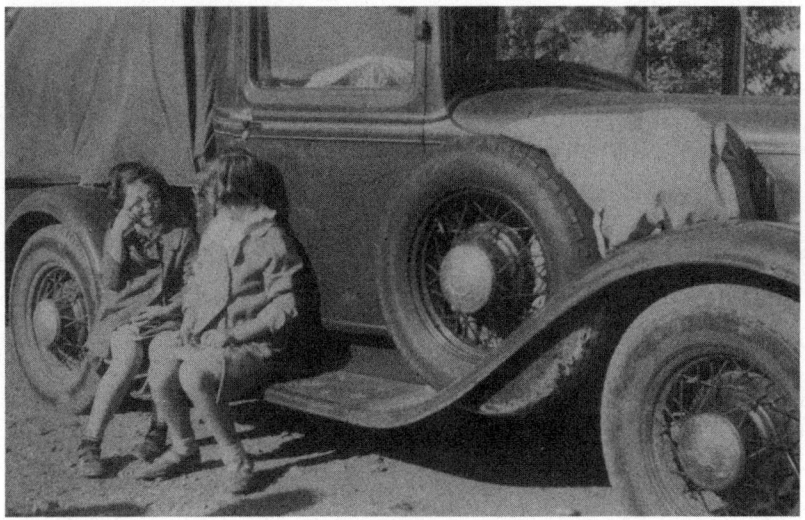

"From the point of view of my painting, the memory that I have of the Everglades and the tropical gardens and everything are wonderful . . . sort of a bank, a memory bank for painting. So, I wouldn't want to have missed out on that, but I also feel very strongly in my roots in Central Illinois," Baber reflected late in life.[41] "The color that I found in Florida," Baber asserted, "was absolutely wonderful and I still seek tropical situations whenever I can because I find that particularly in watercolors, I can paint better when I am very near the water, and getting a reflection of light from the sand and the water itself."[42]

While his family traveled, Adin Baber, remaining in south Florida, got his business, the feed store, established, and developed his interest in natural history. He became active in the South Florida Historical Society, Everglades Natural History Association, and Fairchild Tropical Garden. During Alice's adolescence, the last years of the family's residence in Florida, her father researched and published in 1941 an article about native plants, "The Foodstuff of the DeSoto Expedition."[43]

Adin no doubt shared his interest in natural history with his daughter, Alice, as attested by her poem, "Ancient Palm Tree," dated May 12, 1940, and written out on the stationary of her father's business, "Plantation Supply Co. A Quality Feed Store, 104 N. W. 79th Street, Miami, Florida,"[44] when she was in sixth grade:

> Oh palm tree in the silver moonlight
> Tell your tales to me
> Have you seen pirate ships
> Out on yonder sea?
> Have you heard their booty twinkle
> As times twas buried in the sand
> Have men broken off your leaves
> So that rulers could be fanned?
> Oh palm trees in the silver moonlight

Tell your tale to me
As you rustle your wise old leaves
And look out upon the sea.

Once again, the child who would become the artist Alice Baber is already obsessed with light, especially the light in the heavens, whether it be moonlight or starlight.

Some of the titles for Alice Baber's artworks, like *The Everglades*, also relate to her experience in Florida and the influence of her father. For example, in his article focused on the sixteenth-century Spanish explorer Hernando de Soto, he mentions the native plant "Persimmons, *Diospyros virginiana*, which dried made into a kind of bread."[45] The name, persimmon, and the image of dark red fruit that grows on trees in commercial production in Florida persisted in Alice Baber's imagination long enough that in 1959, she named one of her early colorful abstract oil paintings with a lot of dark red *Persimmon* (CP #18).

Adin Baber's interest in pursuing stories of Native American history, including details of their diet and the de Soto expedition, could be linked to family stories of hidden ancestry. According to her estate, Alice "proudly claimed some Cherokee blood," although both sides of Alice's family appear to have descended from early European immigrants, mostly English with some German ancestry on her mother's side.[46] The ancestry of Adin Baber's mother, Eva Effie Parker, however, can be traced back to parents in Guilford, North Carolina, a state where members of the Cherokee Nation still live.[47] Alice's sister, Nancy, who worked to update her father's book on the Hanks family, left careful notes and correspondence discussing applications for admittance as "Choctaw" by Lydia Harper and Fielden Hanks and other Baber relatives. She noted that there "was a bill presented in the U.S. House of Representatives to support their applications which died in committee and the applications were all rejected for lack of proof, but it is very interesting."[48] The Choctaw people were originally located in the Southeastern Woodlands, in what is now Mississippi and Alabama.[49]

Alice Baber's interest in Native Americans reflect family stories of which Adin, with his intensive study of Hanks genealogy, would have been aware. This theme appears in a childhood poem she wrote, "The Indian Dance," which was later published by her father who identified it as coming from her fifth year:

> "Chee hi hi" sing the Indian warriors
> as they dance around the campfire.
> "Chee hi hi Chee hi hi" as the Indian warriors go to battle.

This Native American theme also suggests what will be Baber's lifetime fascination with peoples and cultures from distant places, many of which she visited. Although she would later express empathy with people of ethnicities other than her own, she was said to have been proud to have some Native American ancestry.[50]

Baber's father, who long pursued his interest in Native American history, was also active in the Illinois State Historical Society. When Alice was not yet four years old, he published an article, "Early Trails of Eastern Illinois," in which he wrote about how the Native American trails followed watersheds and water courses and became the basis for future highways.[51] The time that Adin Baber was writing this article coincides with the approximate period that he was suffering mental illness from stress. Perhaps he got his mind off his own troubles by discussing various battles and the "unfriendly Iroquois."[52]

Hundreds of years ago, Illinois was home to many different Native Americans, including the Sauk, Meskwaki, Potawatomi, Kickapoo, and Winnebago. The state is named after the Illiniwek Nation. Besides other place names, Illinois has other cultural markers of its Native American history, including archaeological sites and public sculptures such as Lorado Taft's colossal figure of *Black Hawk* (1911) in Oregon, Illinois, or James Earle Fraser's *The End of the Trail* (1918) at the Art Institute of Chicago. Adin Baber's interest combined with the presence of such cultural artifacts contributed to inscribing an awareness of Native American heritage into the collective memory of a sensitive and intellectually curious child such as Alice.

When back in Illinois for their summers, Adin Baber's family lived in the simple 1873 farmhouse built by his grandparents. The house, which was enlarged and improved over time, did not have electricity and running water until "the FDR era" or at least not before 1933. During World War II, Adin's family moved back from Florida to live in the farmhouse full-time. Adin Baber, who was rather attached to this somewhat rundown place, continued to live there until his death in 1974. After his daughters left home, however, he stopped modernizing the old house and "instead preserved older ways of living such as cooking over coals in the fireplace with his grandparents' cast iron 'spiders,' Dutch ovens and pots hung from the crane."[53]

Adin's grandson and Alice's nephew, John M. Kern, recalled that Adin Baber was "a bit eccentric and sensitive, ideally suited for living alone. He was a sweet and smart and frequent correspondent . . . got very devoted to writing, mostly genealogy and self-published about seven books."[54] For income, he established the Kansas Cattle Loan Corporation, through which he worked writing cattle loans for banks in Chicago and St. Louis. Devoted to nature and passionate about botany, Adin Baber preserved woods near the house that he called West Grove. Thus, this family's deep roots in rural Illinois nurtured the artistic development of Alice, the younger of his two daughters.

Alice Baber never forgot her powerful visual memories of nature nor the region's characteristic craft tradition: "When I was a child I was surrounded by quilts. They had been made two generations before and were unsigned. . . . The quilts gave color to my life, and poetry—Fire on the Mountain, Bird-of-Paradise. There was the color of the light as it came through the window blinds and spread gold over the colors of the quilt."[55] Alice also remembered seeing her aunt's neighbor with a quilting rack set up for a quilting bee, though she felt that such communal creative events were "long over."[56]

Alice Baber recalled that the house of her grandparents and great-grandparents contained lots of quilts, signed by her ancestors—Lucy, Amos, Callie—who had moved westward to central Illinois via the Daniel Boone Highway, the "Wilderness Road" blazed through Virginia and Kentucky by Daniel Boone in 1775, to open the Western Frontier to settlement.[57] Alice remembered that as a child, she had lessons in both sewing and embroidery, and used these skills to make clothes and quilts for the marionettes that she played with.[58]

Alice is said to have been "always imaginative."[59] She later spoke about "color memory, that anything that you remember well you remember in very vivid color, and anything that's particularly sort of gloomy becomes very gray. . . . My most interesting memories are in very brilliant color. I remember a day when I was four that it rained and it was green, everything. The rain was green, everything was green. And I remember looking at a sea shell when I was about three and everything was yellow. The whole world."[60] Her father wrote to her sister Nancy that Alice's first recorded memory was "a yellow sea shell we used for [a] butter dish."[61]

Another time, Baber recalled, "I'd stand on the front porch of the farmhouse looking out at the fluffy asparagus and say it was *raining green*."[62] Baber told one interviewer that nowhere were sunsets "more spectacular" than in Illinois, where "they'd be 'blue, with great streams of light shot with reds and pinks and yellows.'"[63] Her early recollections of color suggest not only rural Illinois but also the contrasting and complementary environment of semitropical rain, plants, and seashells that she experienced while living in south Florida.

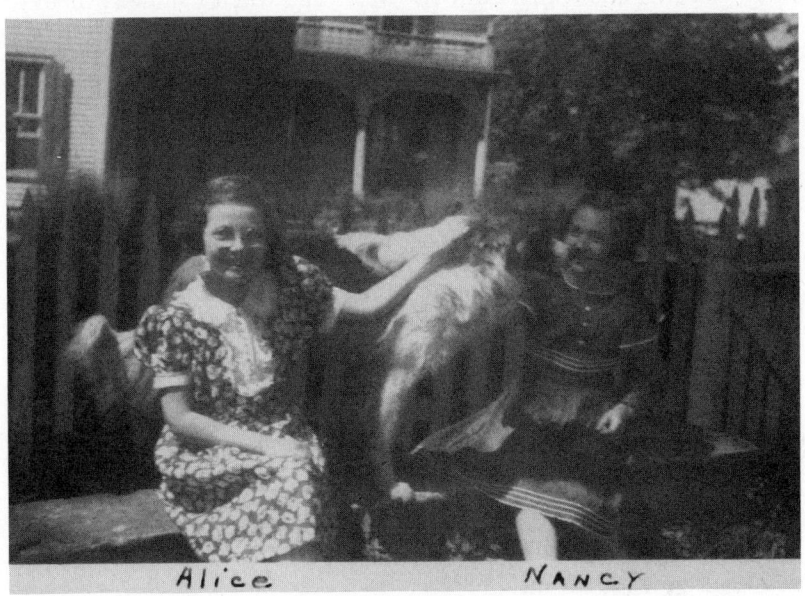

Alice and Nancy in front of the farmhouse porch

The effect of the family's moving about stimulated Alice, who, by the age of five, wrote poems regularly. Her proud father later recalled that Alice "began to see flowers and colors and make verses of nice poetry about them at age five. She discarded them into the waste basket but her mother collected them and she never learned that they were saved until a few years ago [when] I had a selection published."[64]

Alice's father elaborated on the story behind the poems' eventual publication: "Her mother and I first heard her humming little rymmes [*sic*] when she was four years of age. At six, learning to write, she scribbled many attempts on scraps of paper, and discarded them into the waste basket, owing to lack of satisfaction with them."[65]

Adin Baber recalled that Alice's mother "salvaged many but Alice was furious to have them discovered and read. Thereafter, her mother and I surreptitiously searched for them and kept them hidden. She knew nothing about this until two years ago when I showed them to her husband, Paul Jenkins. At his request the scraps were typed and six copies made. One copy was shown to Miss Aileen Fisher, the noted poet and author of children's books of verses."[66] Fisher selected out of around a hundred poems, fourteen to be published, and came up with the title *Thoughts of a Little Girl*. Adin Baber sent out the little booklet of Alice's juvenilia for Christmas in 1968.

One of the first poems that her mother saved from that era was called "Colors".[67]

> Colors of the rainbow
> Colors of the sea
> Colors of the garden
> But green is for me.

Published as written when she was only five years old, her poem "Beauty," Alice thought she wrote in 1935, when she was already six or seven. This poem reflects her childhood appreciation of the environment she knew in Florida:

> Flowers of the sunshine
> Moss is on the tree
> White caps on the ocean
> Rolling in to me.[68]

Baber recalled, "When I was five years old, I decided that I would be either a poet or a painter. And I remember the day that I decided, and I'm sure that I really didn't know what it meant to be either one of those."[69] What Baber clearly needed was a means to express her emotions, many of which she could not yet comprehend.

Baber reflected: "I was very good at art. I could copy things. . . . And then, as far as poetry was concerned, I wrote it all the time and was encouraged mostly from my father, I think. In a way, I think my mother encouraged the painting more and my father the writing, but I think that was just because it happened to fall into their interests a little more."[70] She reflected, "Well, my mother, I think, looking back, must have taken art history in college."[71] Recalling that several framed reproductions of famous artists hung in the family home, Alice revealed her interest in her own history.

Several of Alice Baber's early creative endeavors survive. She was probably no more than five years old when she invented *The Fairy Book* featuring her own text and illustrations. The book's cover is labeled and decorated in crayon. The frontispiece of *The Fairy Book* presents, beneath the sun, a tiny pencil sketch of a fairy holding a magic wand. Another opening shows a view of the sun above a sailboat across from the dedication: A BOOK OF FAIRY STORIES BY ALICE BABER TO HER FATHER.[72] As a child, it is said that Alice "transformed the rings of morning dew behind the farmhouse into 'fairy rings' where she firmly believed fairies had danced the night before."[73]

The Babers had plenty of books at home to stimulate their daughters' imaginations and creative endeavors. A few of them survive. One example, *Poems for the Very Young Child*, was a gift to her older sister, inscribed to Nancy Shirley Baber "From the Horsewoman"—Marian.[74] These rhyming poems emphasize observations of nature, the seasons, birds, flowers, and fairies, some of little Alice's favorite themes.

Contemporaneous with her poems, Alice's very early watercolor
Self-Portrait in Florida also survives, which appears to date from when
she was around six or seven years old. She wrote in pencil on an accompanying page "Baber Alice to Aunt Bonnie," next to a red heart (CP #1).
Bonnie was one of her mother's four sisters.[75] Alice wrote in pencil around
a standing frontal figure, depicting herself with oversized arms and high-
heeled shoes, shown in profile: "show this to all the aunts \ this is me in
Miami \ I take a little sunshine every Day." Taking sunshine in Florida for
its vitamin D against Alice's chronic bronchitis might seem like an innocent comment, sent as a child to her aunt; however, it sounds paradoxical
as a health practice since we know that Baber's life would be cut short by
melanoma, for which childhood exposure to sunlight is now considered a
major contributing factor for the development of this often fatal skin cancer
later in life.[76] Ironically, Baber's fascination with light—the sunlight that
would cause her early death—began as a preoccupation in her childhood.

Yet, exposure to sunlight in Florida is both expected and unavoidable.
Alice also absorbed sunlight whenever she sought out nature, an arena
that her father encouraged. Her early affection for plants and animals in
the wild is reflected in another of her poems, "The Robin":

> "Yo ho," cried a Robin. Glad spring time has come.
> With ever a laff.
> And ever a hum.
> The little chicks
> A-hatching now,
> Out of pure white eggs
> At first a little wobuly,
> Upon their frail legs.
> "Autumn now is coming,"
> Cryed the robin in dismay,

"Good By all yee
Boys and girls,
I now must fly away."

For the sake of credibility, one is relieved to see that the five-year-old Alice not only made spelling mistakes, but she missed the actual color of the eggshells, which should be robin's egg blue. Yet Baber's childhood poems nonetheless reveal her acute visual perception and her love of color, light, and movement, all of which are already evident.[77] This poem also takes as its theme the dramatic need to go south as the weather turns colder, just as Alice and her sister did every winter. Yet another of Alice's poems from age six evokes her time in Florida:

The sun smiled on the ocean,
The waves came out to see,
They had a race opean [*sic*] the sand,
And the sun fell in the sea.

How sophisticated if she already comprehended the difference between the meaning of *see* and *sea*.[78]

By the age of seven, she penned "Alice's Kitten":

Fluffy is our little cat,
She never cared about a rat,
She chooses always our best chair,
And where you sit she does not care.

Alice's love of cats was evident even earlier in a photograph, apparently taken during a summer visit to the farmhouse in Illinois, in which both she and her sister each cuddle a kitten.

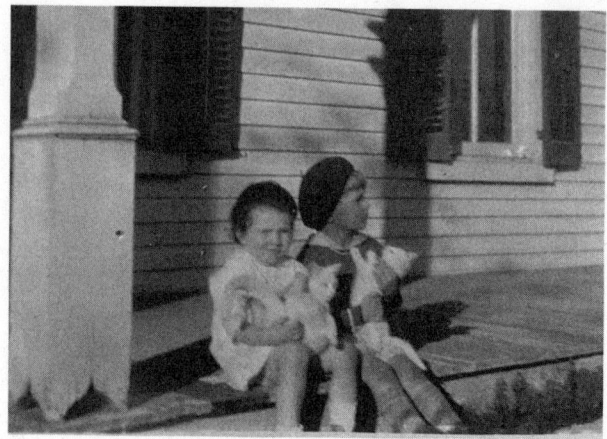

The penultimate poem in the published book, written before she turned nine, is inscribed, "To Daddy on Father's Day 1937: The White Lilies that Blow":

> Down by a sparkling stream,
> Some pearl white lilies blow
> Dawn opeans [*sic*] them first so
> They might see,
> And shine of her golden glow
> Sir Night will not scatter their
> Pedals afar
> Lady Noon will not let the sun
> Scorch the white lilies
> That blow in the breeze.

Alice's sophistication beyond her years is such that one is grateful to see "pedals" for "petals" and other spelling errors. This poem makes clear that she understood her father's passion for plants.[79] Inspired by her experience of Florida's environment, Alice wrote "End of a Day in the Tropics" in 1937, when only eight or nine years old; however, it was not chosen for inclusion in the booklet:

> A cool breeze rippled the ocean
> And a red glow fell beneath
> While the waves made a sort of rumble
> As if to never cease
>
> Then pale pink and orange
> Swept over the lovely sky
> While the palm trees bending to the sun
> Sang a whisper of good-by.[80]

Alice's eighth birthday party, held outdoors at the family farm in Illinois on August 22, 1936, is documented with a group of surviving snapshots. Seven girls celebrated together with Alice and her sister Nancy, posing in the back of a dump truck, perhaps being treated to a hayride. In another photograph, each girl held her doll, posing much like new mothers with their infants. Alice was the only one who wore glasses.

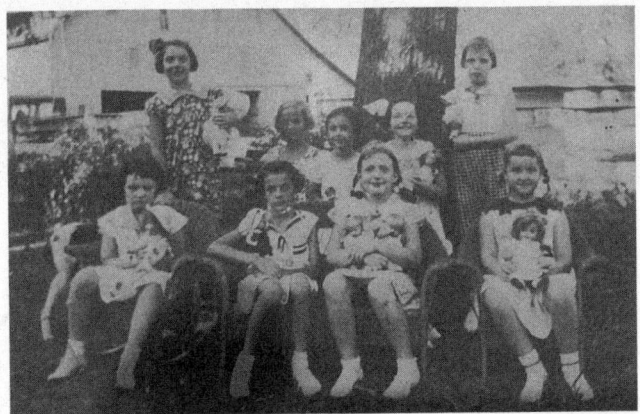

Alice is in front of the tree, 2nd from the right, back row

Not just the spectacles, but her sophisticated creative efforts to paint and to write poetry made Alice Baber stand out early. Yet as a nine- or ten-year-old girl, she still enjoyed playing with her doll, which we see her holding, standing beside a palm tree in Miami with a plump woman in a hat identified on the back of the 1938 photograph as Nelle Nelson, who was probably the family's nanny or housekeeper.

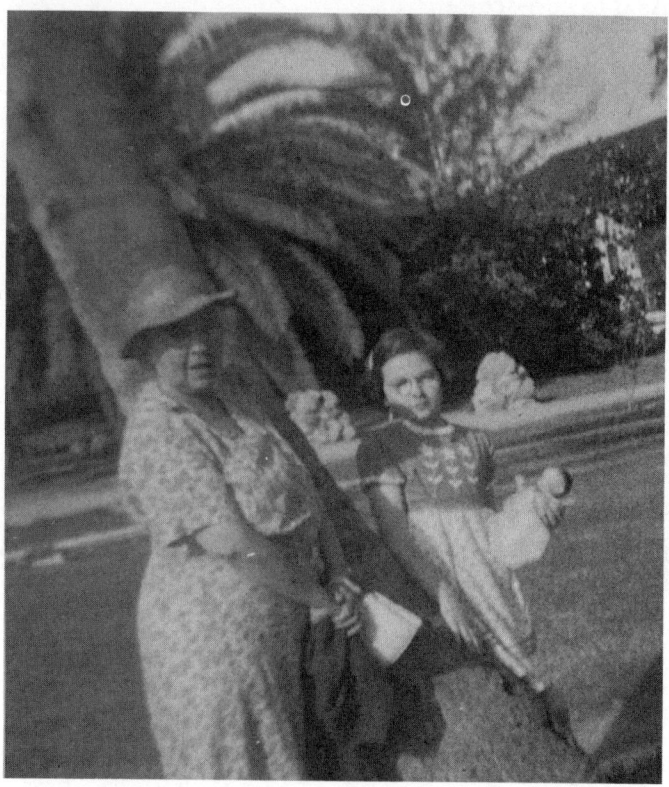

The dolls that Baber and her friends held were important for encouraging emotional, social, and cognitive skills through imaginative play, role-playing, and for learning language skills and empathy. By the time she turned eight, however, the focus of the precocious Baber was already diverted to studying painting in private lessons. She was also writing poems and putting them in hand-bound paper books. One she made of blue construction paper, ornamented by small drawings and initial letters, as a gift for her father, inscribed, "To Daddy Xmas 1939," when she was eleven years old. Baber's first poem in this "book," titled "My Beautiful Maiden," anticipates some of her later interests in her paintings. She writes in part:

> Her cheeks were like peach blossoms,
> Her eyes like turquoise stone,
> When she laughed 'twas like twinkling of silver bells,
> And velvet chimes in tone.

The emphasis on color and sound in Baber's painting is already evident. In this book's second poem, "The Mighty Wind," the second stanza begins:

> When storms at sea, makes waves fly high
> Sinks ships and roars & clangs

Once again, we see that Baber emphasizes sound attached to visual spectacle. She also made a drawing of a male head in profile as a personification of "The Mighty Wind."

At twelve, Alice began taking college-level summer painting classes outdoors at Eastern Illinois State Teachers College in nearby Charleston.[81] Her sister also enrolled in this class.[82] The lessons included still life and landscape painting in oil. Alice loved her teacher, the Illinois landscape artist and outdoorsman Paul Turner Sargent, who was a cousin on her mother's side of the family.[83] Sargent also painted images of nature from his travels, including to Florida, where Alice's family had been living in "a part of Miami that was near the Everglades . . . in the middle of the avocados"[84] Alice recalled of south Florida: "It was very flat, so what I got a sense of was the color of the sky."[85]

Alice enthused decades later: "He was our local famous painter, Paul Sargent. And he was really quite good. Looking back now, his painting was a combination of sort of Courbet, impressionism, and so forth. But enormously talented and very much, say, a product of some other time, some other place. But he taught me perspective and I adored it and I was eight years old and I took a lot of lessons and I practiced."[86]

Baber never forgot her first art teacher—with good reason. Her studies with him resulted in 1941 her winning, at age thirteen, a blue ribbon in the juvenile department of art at the Illinois State Fair in Springfield. Alice was heralded as the youngest member of the summer painting class at Eastern Illinois State Teachers College.[87]

The type of bold, repetitive brushstrokes and thick impasto paint that Baber was using in her surviving painting of a horse (CP #2) in field of yellow and green grass suggests that she had already been looking at reproductions of paintings by Vincent van Gogh. Two paintings by van Gogh—his *Sunflowers* (CP #3) and a *Self-Portrait with Bandaged Ear* (CP #2)—appear as full-page color plates in Rockwell Kent's 1939 book, *World Famous Paintings*. This was the book of which Alice recalled receiving two copies as Christmas gifts. Her painting of a horse that she saved all her life could be the image that won her the blue ribbon at the state fair.

Baber's surviving still life of red gladiolas and other flowers in a red vase (CP #3) is probably her response to seeing the reproduction of van Gogh's *Sunflowers*. Her background is yellow like van Gogh's, and her paint handling is a thick impasto, recalling the work of the post-impressionist. Baber also duplicates other aspects of the Dutch painter's composition: both the horizontal line across the canvas representing a table edge as well as the centrality of the vase's placement on a vertical canvas. Baber's spiky red bloom on the lower left side of her composition also echoes the outline of van Gogh's spiky sunflowers.

That Baber was attracted to emulate art by the emotive van Gogh, who is said to have expressed his anxiety through the thickness of his paint, could echo Baber's own anxiety.[88] She had, after all, survived a sickly childhood, while observing both parents' fragile health. It seems likely that the tragic vision, to which James Jones referred in his 1965 article, occurred early in Baber's life and influenced her to reject the typical path in life for a woman coming of age in the 1950s. Baber did not seek an early marriage and children and determined instead to pursue a career as an artist, even if that meant living alone.

An undated page of Baber's handwritten notes reads: "I was born into guilt by association. I was born a woman, I was lucky because my family didn't make the usual distinction and until I hit art history, I didn't know there was a problem."[89] She could not have missed, however, that in her book, *World Famous Paintings*, there were no women artists, no female role models to inspire a young girl to become an artist.

When Baber recalled *World Famous Paintings*, however, she was not thinking about gender, but remembering that her favorite painting was Jean-Antoine Watteau's *The Embarkation for Cythera* (1717) because she "liked the shimmering of the cloth . . . at the time, I felt like that's what painting is, being able to get that."[90] Another time, she remarked, "The first thing I loved in painting was being able to get the sheen of silk."[91] Just as she wrote about light in her poems, Baber's particular focus on painting light was evident very early.

Baber reported that the first art museum she visited was the John and Mable Ringling Museum of Art in Sarasota, Florida, where she would have seen the founders' collection of European paint-ings, intended to promote art appreciation among young people.[92] For Baber as a child, one of the highlights could have been the large French canvas *Plowing in Nivernais*, painted in 1850 by Rosa Bonheur, one of the most famous woman artists of her time, who was considered a leading animal painter. Baber, coming from rural Illinois, might have appreciated Bonheur's depiction of a fertile land-scape, recalling familiar farm scenes.

The Ringling Museum's original collection featured baroque mas-terpieces: paintings by the seventeenth-century Flemish baroque artist Peter Paul Rubens and the Italian baroque artist Guercino, among other European masters. Guercino's immense *Annunciation* of 1628–29, with its colossal figures, roughly four times life size, presents the Archangel Gabriel floating through clouds, gesturing toward the Madonna, set against divine illumination, which brings to mind Baber's lifelong obsession with the drama of light.

By May 4, 1940, Adin Baber was visiting the family farm in Kansas, Illinois. An unsigned letter to him from Lois reads, "Alice is delighted with this & wants you to see it. She went to Venetian pool this A.M." The Venetian Pool is a historic public swimming pool in Coral Gables, Florida, completed in 1924.[93] All such excursions were curtailed, however, when the imposition of gas rationing during World War II kept Baber's family isolated in rural Illinois, living in her great-grandfather's house just outside of the small town of Kansas (in Edgar County, Illinois), where Alice attended Kansas Community High School.[94] A photograph, revealing her black hair and pale complexion, taken of her there at age thirteen on February 28, 1942, shows her wearing an elaborate floral head-dress as if for a pageant or perhaps marking her as the winner of a competition.

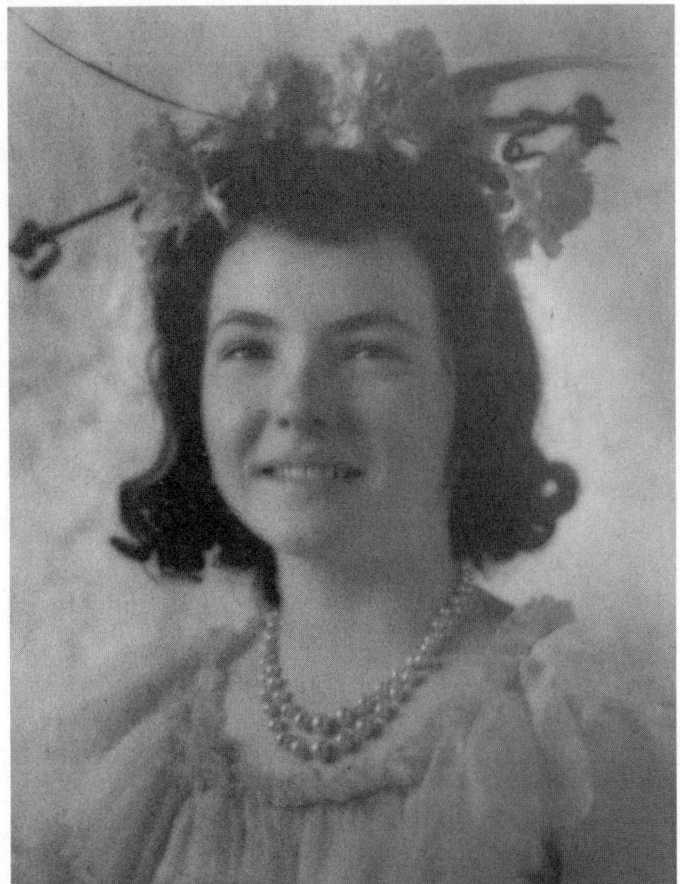

Baber remarked years later "about growing up in the Midwest and what I experienced that's in my work. I think one thing you develop in the Midwest is color hunger. There is a greyness here. You don't really see brilliant color, so it's in your head."[95] Baber, having gone back and forth between Florida and Illinois for so many years, was especially sensitive to regional difference in climate, color, and light.

Not long after the Baber family's routine had been forced to change, their serenity was shattered on August 2, 1943, when just before Alice's fifteenth birthday, her mother, only fifty years old, died suddenly.[96] Lois Shoot Baber died from a cerebral hemorrhage, also known as a hemorrhagic stroke, commonly caused by high blood pressure.[97] Alice's nephew, John M. Kern, remembers hearing from his mother how unexpected his grandmother's death was and what a heartbreak this was for the entire family.[98] He recalls evidence of the immensity of his grandfather's loss: "On August 3rd he wrote 'Lois died' on the calendar and never turned the page. It hung [for years] on the end of a pie safe by the kitchen door, where you would see it as you went out."[99]

A memorial book kept by Adin Baber recording the moment of his wife's funeral includes poignant poetry that poured out of him. His anguish was mirrored in the adolescent Alice, for whom losing her mother was traumatic. The entire family's intense grief is palpable in the documents that survive. A page printed with two roses, which records flowers sent in Lois Baber's memory, contains an entry that appears to have been inscribed by Alice herself: "From Alice, Nancy, & daddy—beautiful spray of blue delphinium, pink carnations, and pink roses, with mother's shrimp plant blossom & a stalk of pink gladioli from North Miami garden club."[100]

The funeral for Lois Mary Shoot Baber took place on August 4, 1943, at the Baber farmstead. Officiating were three local clergymen from the Kansas Presbyterian Church, the Kansas Methodist Church, and the Wesley Foundation. On August 17, 1943, Adin Baber recorded in the memorial book his poem, which, he noted, he "Dreamed":

> My lover has gone in her early fall
> To live in a land so fair
> She's gone to her friends beyond the wall
> She'll plan a garden there
> And I go on but the chill's here

And all the world is gray

I walk alone but not for long

She'll be waiting for me in her garden that day.

Another page in the memorial book, which is also inscribed "A. B.,"
is Adin's note "To Nancy and Alice." Its second stanza states:

The rain will patter on our attic roof,

    And the snow will swirl o'erhead,

But, safe within our little cribs, we'll sleep

    In peace. God rests the dead.

    Mother and Daddy

Adin's concern for his daughters is evident but also his profound
influence in shaping his youngest daughter's creative bent. Alice will
later echo her father's association of gloom with things appearing "gray."
His attention to the sound of rain pattering on the roof also evokes
Alice's own sensitivity to sounds.

For Alice, accepting her mother's untimely death was all the more
difficult since she later wrote that she considered her sister Nancy
"treacherous because she was jealous of me."[101] On the same page of
unpublished notes, Alice wrote, "In my dream when I realized I could
never trust this person I knew it would be like my sister & I was very
disturbed"[102] It is easy to imagine that a sibling would find it difficult
to compete with such a talented and creative younger sister, especially
one who merited and received much more parental attention because
she was an unhealthy child.[103]

John M. Kern reflected on the relationship of his mother and
his aunt: "I didn't think they were competitive, but I do think they
found each other's choice of lifestyle (very different!) irresponsible and

criticized it a bit. My mom tended to find fault in general and her sister's choices were not excepted."[104] Yet despite their differences, years later, after Nancy survived her sister's death, evidence suggests that she was very proud of Alice's accomplishments.

Despite coping with her grief after her mother's early and sudden death, Alice was a model student at Kansas Community High School. She was on the staff of the school newspaper, *The Kourier.* She was a member of several clubs and served as her class president during her sophomore year. Not surprisingly, Alice earned A's in English and world history, which predicts her love for world travel and writing. She also earned high marks in chemistry and received a mix of A's and B's in algebra.[105]

Alice also sang in the Girl's Glee Club and played oboe in the high school band, a link to the titles with auditory names that she later gave pictures such as *The Ringing and the Ringing* (1967) (CP #29), *Day of Sounds* (1971), *Sound of the Wind* (1975), *Swirls of Sounds—Wind, Rock and Sun* (1975), *Swirls of Sounds—The Ghost in the Banyan Tree* (1976) (CP #43), *Pink Sound* (1977), *Night Drum* (1977) (CP #45), *The Voice of the Yellow Ladder* (1979), *The Many Songs of the Mountain* (1980), *Sound of the Blue Dance of the Jaguar* (1980), and *Pink Flute of the Jaguar* (1982) (CP #48). Baber said, "There have been periods in my life when I painted to music."[106] She told how she liked "drum rhythms," which she considered "abstract sound."[107]

Baber told an interviewer how she wanted to play an instrument in high school, a "mysterious esoteric instrument, and my idea of that (a sort of romantic idea) was the pipes of Pan. And I thought, why don't I play the flute. Well the high school music director said we already have someone playing the flute, so why don't you play the oboe."[108] She found the oboe "extremely difficult . . . you really have to learn to do your own reeds."[109] But the image of "the pipes of Pan" had been in her imagination at least since the poem she wrote the summer she turned twelve.[110] The image of Pan is linked to nature and to the sounds of nature.

"Alice Baber appears to believe that all sensory phenomena can be 'rendered visible' (to use Paul Klee's wonderful phase). She gives many of her paintings auditory names, such as 'Sounds of the Piper's Ladder,' 'The Bridge of Sounds,' or 'The Key of Sound and Light,' as if they, too, like those mysterious paintings of the Himalayas [Tantric art] might depict 'luminous sound,'" wrote art historian Virginia Pitts Rembert, who met Baber.[111] Rembert noted Baber's "deep sensitivity to color."[112]

Baber's close connection to music and sounds suggests that she was synesthetic—individuals able to see their specific visions by paying attention not only to what they can see but also to what is set off for them by their other senses: hearing, smell, touch, or taste.[113] Scientists label such responses "photisms."[114] Such sensory crossovers result from synesthesia, but while they are symptomatic of a particular condition in the brain, synesthesia is not a disease.

The sound-to-color trigger is often inspirational to painters and it appears to have been especially significant for Baber's creative process. Only recently, however, scientists have linked synesthesia to anxiety, which Baber seems to have suffered from throughout her adult life.[115] Some people with synesthesia find dealing with the effects "overwhelming."[116]

Baber explained how she conceived a painting and how she used all her senses, which indicates the sensory crossovers that identify her synesthesia: "I must feel a certain color. I see it everywhere, I feel it, I hear it, I taste it, and I want to eat it. I start from the driving force of the color. I feel one color (color hunger); then comes a second color to provide light, luminous light. It will be the glow to reinforce the first color. I then discover the need of one, two, three, or more colors, which will indicate and make movement."[117]

Synesthetic artists' visual experiences often also involve movement, and Baber fits that pattern too. In the 1920s, the experimental psychologist Heinrich Klüver came up with a pictorial list of types of movement observed through synesthetic perceptions. "Shapes can radiate, rotate, morph, kaleidoscope, drift, spiral, and reduplicate. Shapes experienced by synesthetes also show movement and can appear suddenly, permutate, magnify, repeat, dart quickly, and change colors abruptly and (seemingly) arbitrarily."[118]

To take just a few examples: Baber's canvas *The Turning Door* (1969) (CP #32) demonstrates her synesthetic perception and depiction of movement.[119] As documented in others with synesthetic perception, Baber's painting resembles a kaleidoscope, where forms appear to drift and reduplicate. Baber's *Lavender High* (1968) (CP #30) shows the implicit movement of various blue-and-purple-toned shapes that permutate, magnify, and repeat, while bright yellow shapes pop out to convey light. Baber often utilized such oval shapes, *x* configurations, and implicit movement of those shapes—for example, in both *Lavender Ways to the Seasons* (1968) (CP #31) and in *Floating Crossing* (1970) (CP #34).

In an undated essay, Baber wrote, "I think that color should be intense to a point beyond purity, be passionate as well as rational, and that each color should have many *voices*. And I believe that light should come from many sources in the painting including inside the colors so that the forms are bathed all over in it," explaining that to describe herself, she had "chosen the term 'Chromatic Illuminist.' By this I mean being involved in clear color and light."[120]

As we have seen, Baber's preoccupation with light goes back to her early childhood. Another of her childhood poems predicts her intense lifetime focus on light and movement. It is also said to have been composed when she was just five years old. It creates a remarkable image for a future painter and is aptly called "A Picture":

The moon through [*sic*] a beem [*sic*] ore the water,
Twas a dream on that beautiful night,
The water reflected it shivering,
The stars made a twinkling light.

Baber's engagement with both light and sound figured in a 1977 essay on her art by G. S. Wittet, who had been years earlier the editor of *The Studio*, an English art magazine, and then worked at *Studio International*. He noted that Baber's early canvases employ "the light to provide dramatic contrasts. They also laid the basis for the later paintings in which a bright palette had a greater range of chromatic tones to perform in. Though broadly speaking Baber is an abstract colourist, there has always been a penetrative quality to her laid surface that went far beyond the flat two dimensions of pure colour field applications."[121]

Given Baber's early fixations and special sensitivities, it's interesting how normal she seemed to her classmates. For example, the blurb next to her photograph in her high school yearbook reads: "Not all artistic people are Bohemian; Alice proves it." Not being perceived as "socially unconventional in an artistic way" would later prove useful.[122] Baber's sociable personality would serve her well as she set her ambition on becoming an artist. At five feet five inches tall with thick, jet-black hair described as "a leonine mane," contrasted with her pale complexion, hazel eyes, and a winning smile, Alice was also rather attractive.[123]

Alice's father, who believed in her talent, saw to it that both Alice and Nancy were sent away to study at proper women's colleges. Given Baber's perception of sibling rivalry, it is not surprising that she chose to attend a different college from her sister.

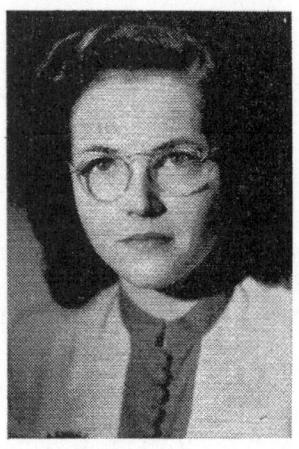

ALICE BABER

"Not all artistic people are Bo-
hemian; Alice proves it."

Girls' Glee Club 2, 3, Secretary 3; Band
1, 2, 3, 4; F.H.A. 1, 2, 3, 4, Vice-presi-
dent 4; Commercial Club 4; G.A.A. 1,
4; Class President 2; Student Council 1.

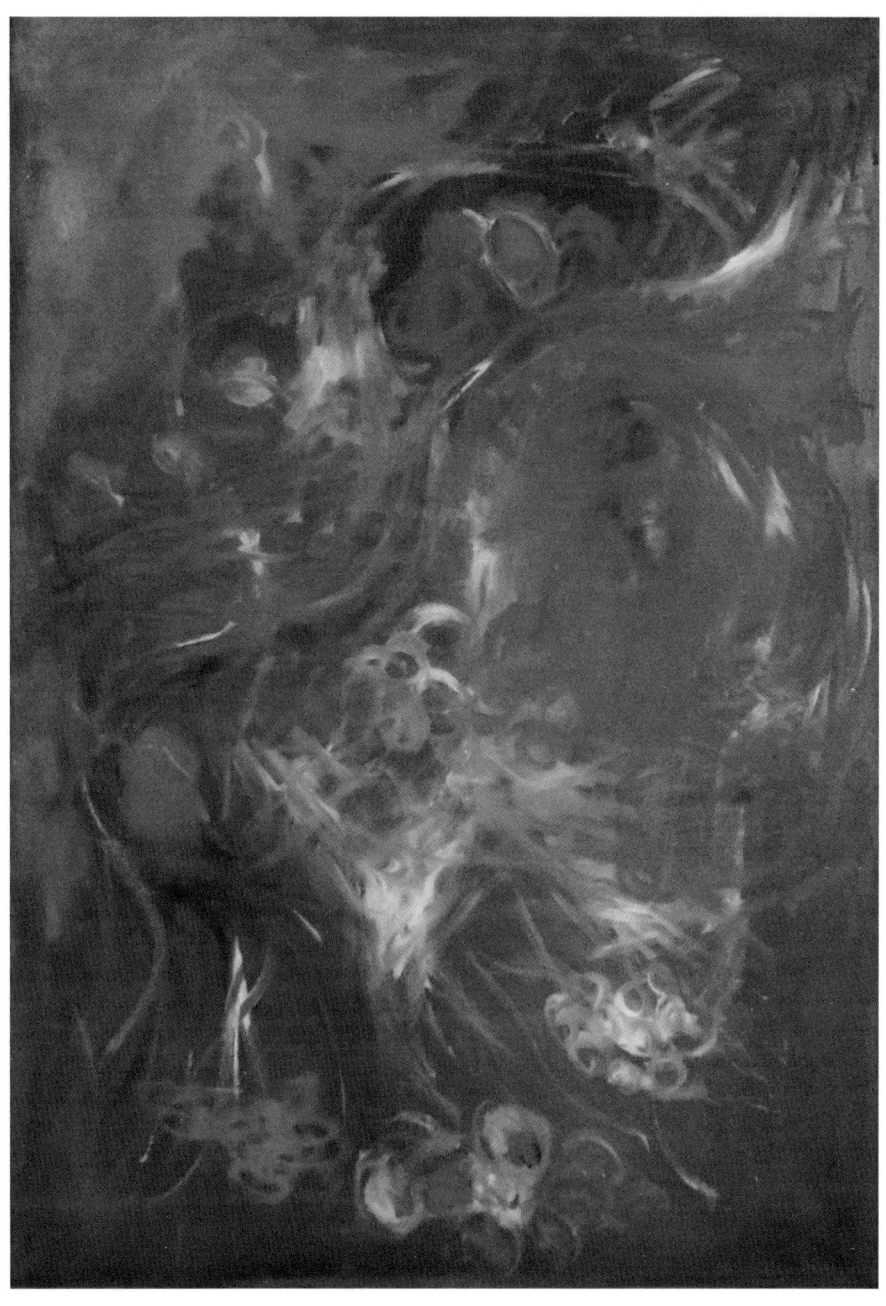

Alice Baber, *Sirenidae*, 1958, oil on canvas, 70 x 50 inches,
private collection.

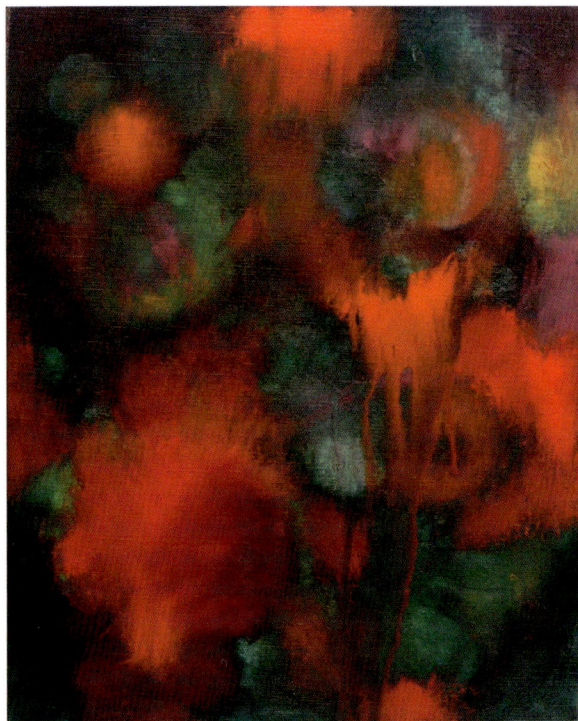

Alice Baber,
Persimmon, 1959,
oil on canvas,
29 ½ x 24 ½ inches,
private collection.

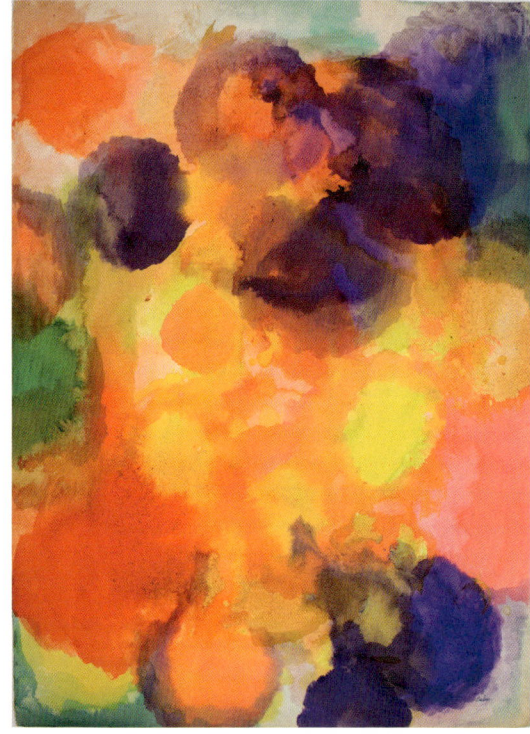

Alice Baber,
I Saw It Once, 1959,
watercolor on paper,
29 ⅞ x 22 inches,
private collection, courtesy
Jody Klotz Fine Art, Abilene, TX.

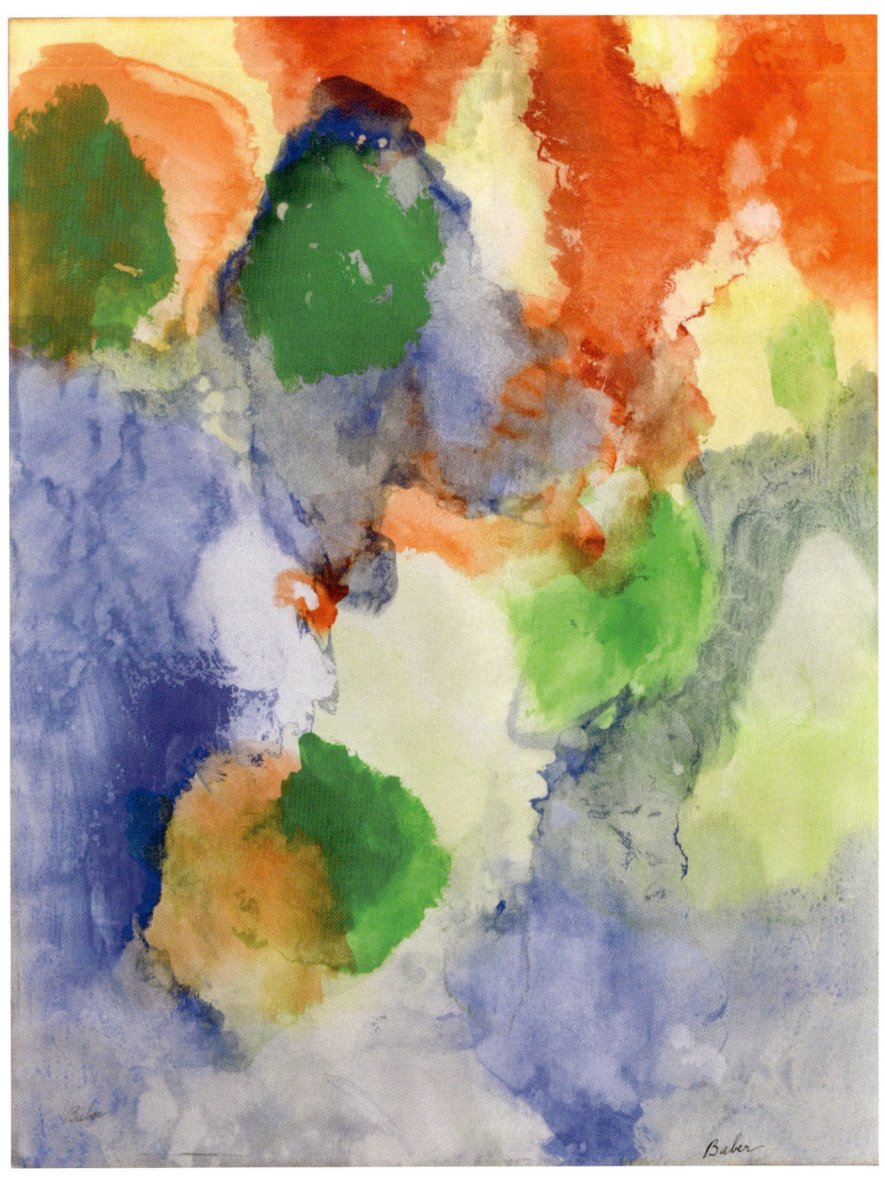

Alice Baber, *Porto de la Selva*, 1960, watercolor on paper, 25 x 20 inches,
Robert and Christina Tonti, Dallas, Texas.

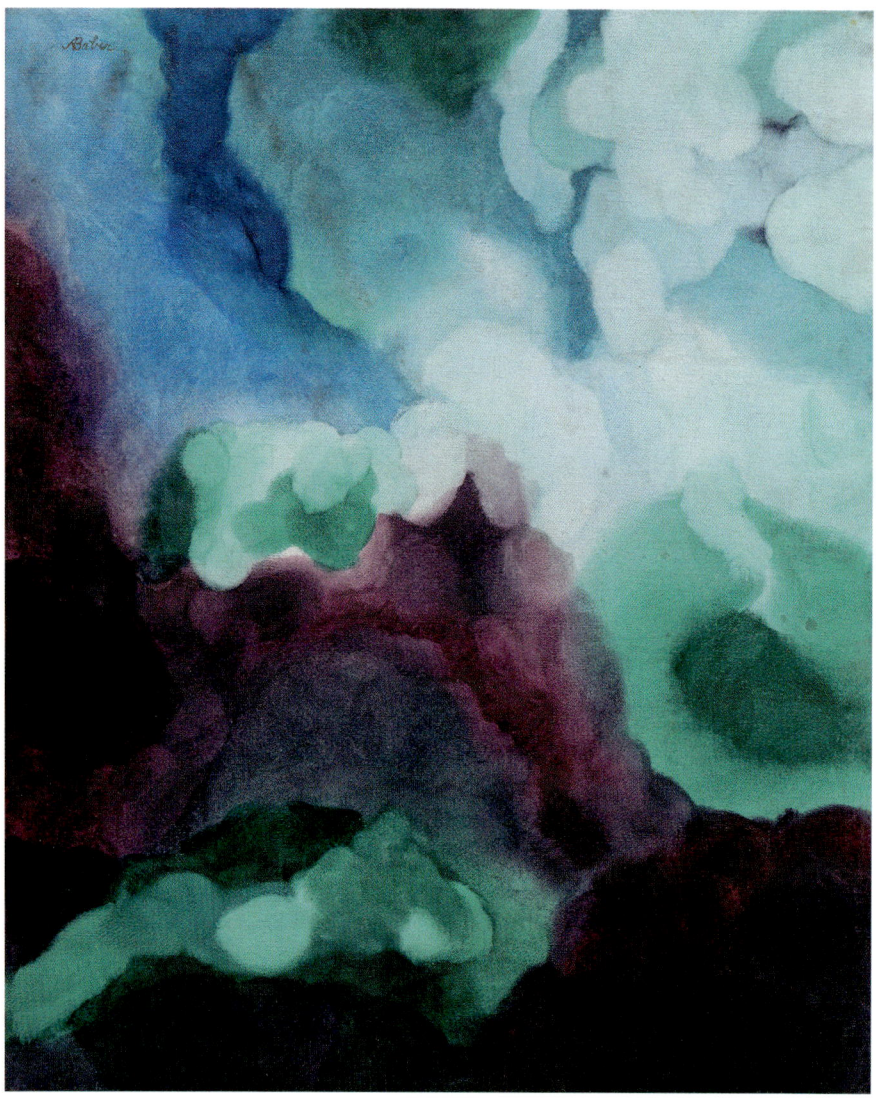

Alice Baber, *Piper's Message*, 1962, oil on canvas, 28 ½ x 23 ½ inches, courtesy Jody Klotz Fine Art, Abilene, TX.

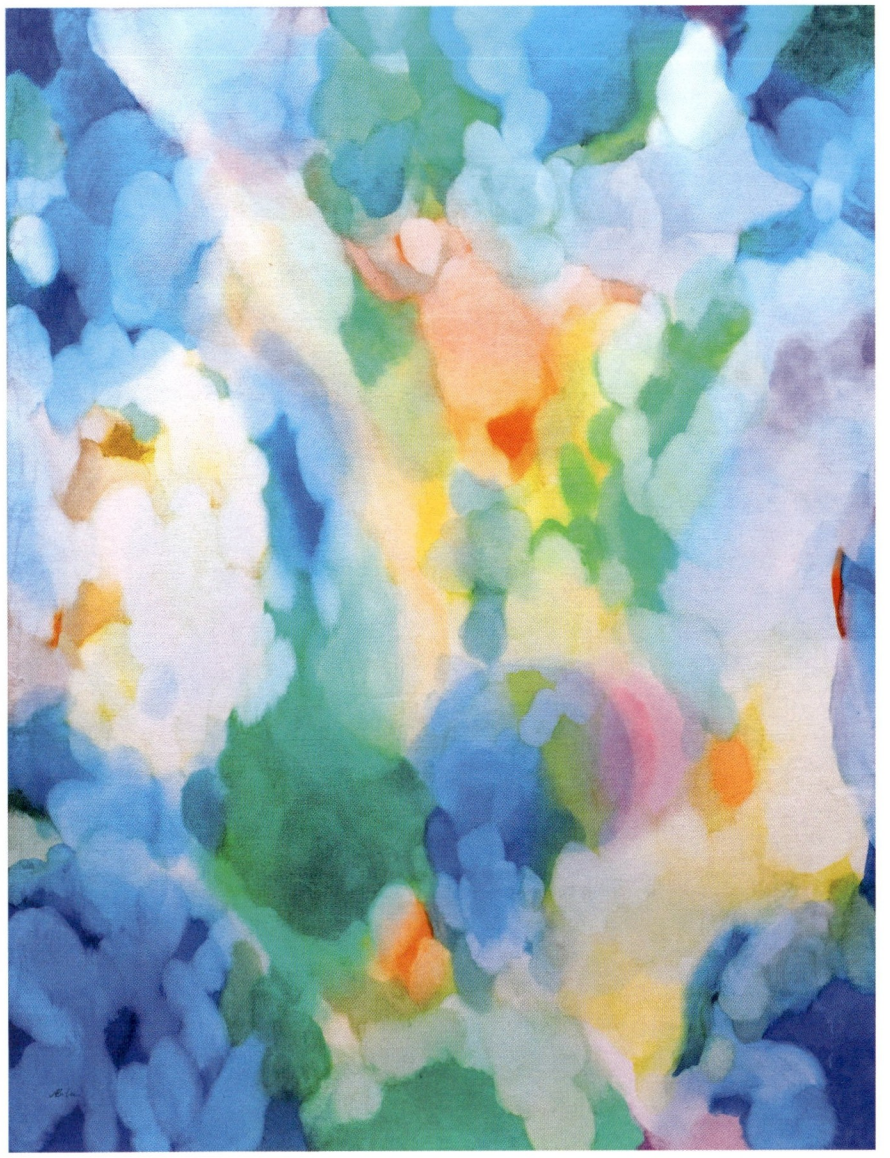

Alice Baber, *Just Arrived*, 1962, oil on linen, 57 x 44 ½ inches, collection of Jim Carrey.

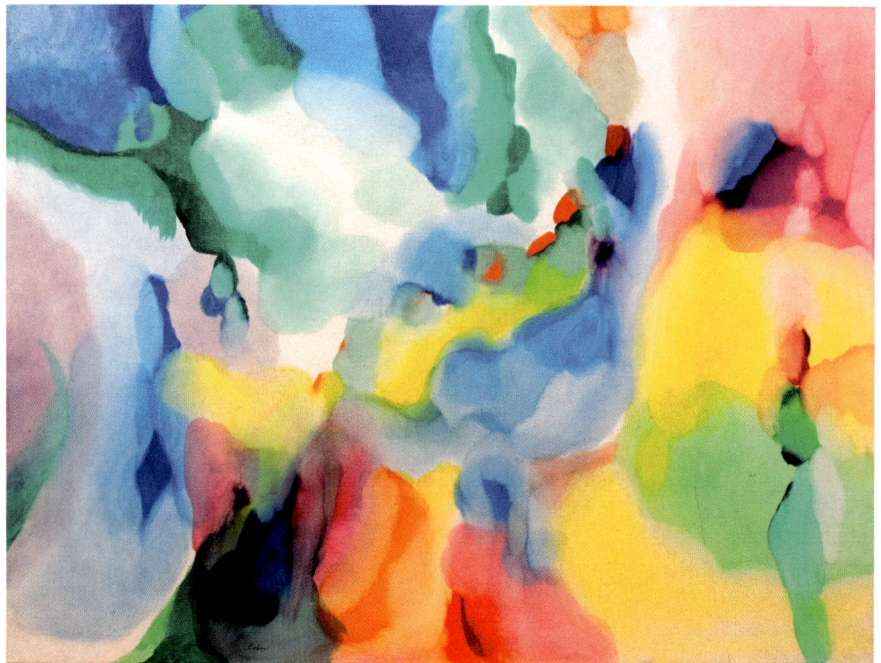

Alice Baber, *Where They Meet*, 1963, oil on linen, 37 ¾ x 51 inches, courtesy Jody Klotz Fine Art, Abilene, TX.

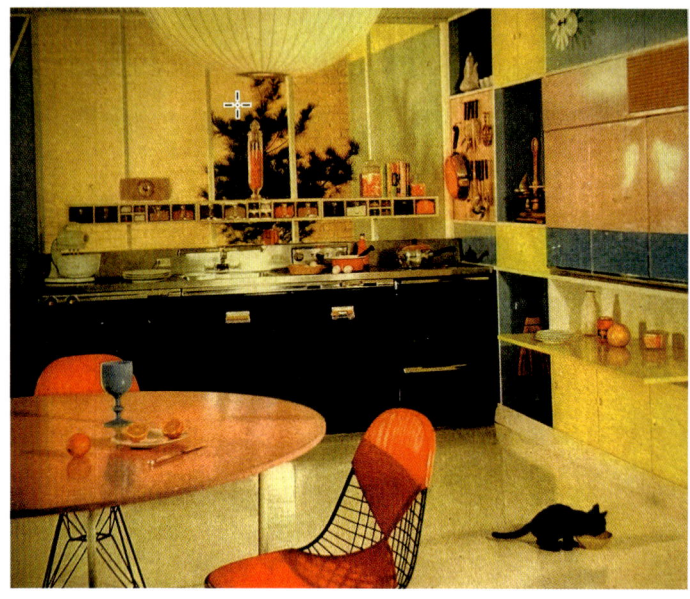

Alice Baber kitchen design for George Nelson, *Life Magazine*, December 13, 1954, page 114, detail.

Alice Baber,
*Across the Wide,
Tokyo*,1964,
collage and watercolor
on paperboard,
10 ½ x 9 ½ inches,
courtesy
Lincoln Glenn Gallery, NY.

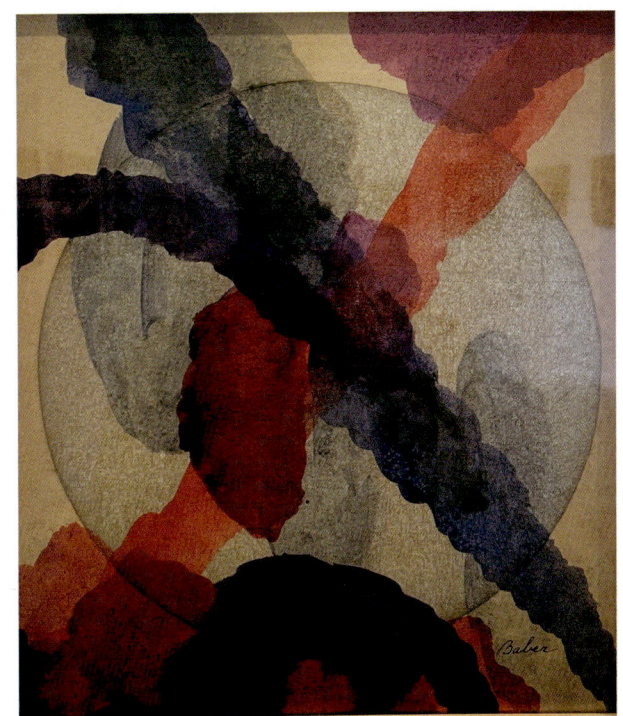

Alice Baber,
Shakespeare Used It, 1964,
collage and watercolor
on paperboard,
10 ½ x 9 ½ inches,
private collection.

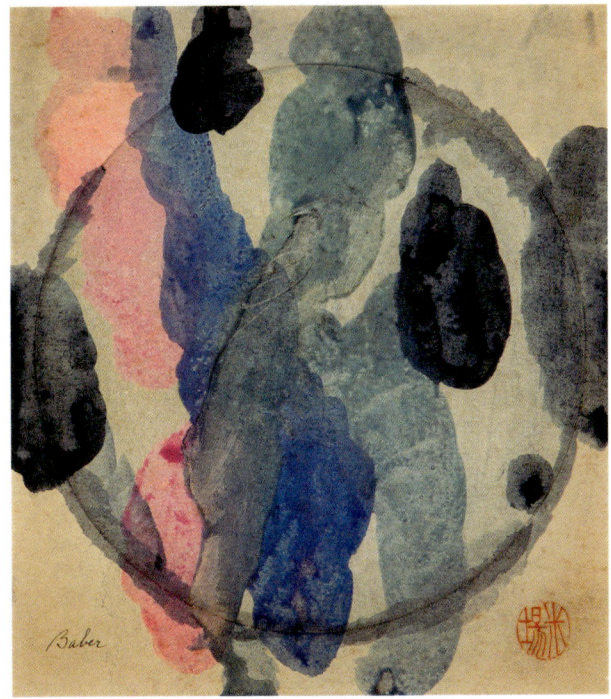

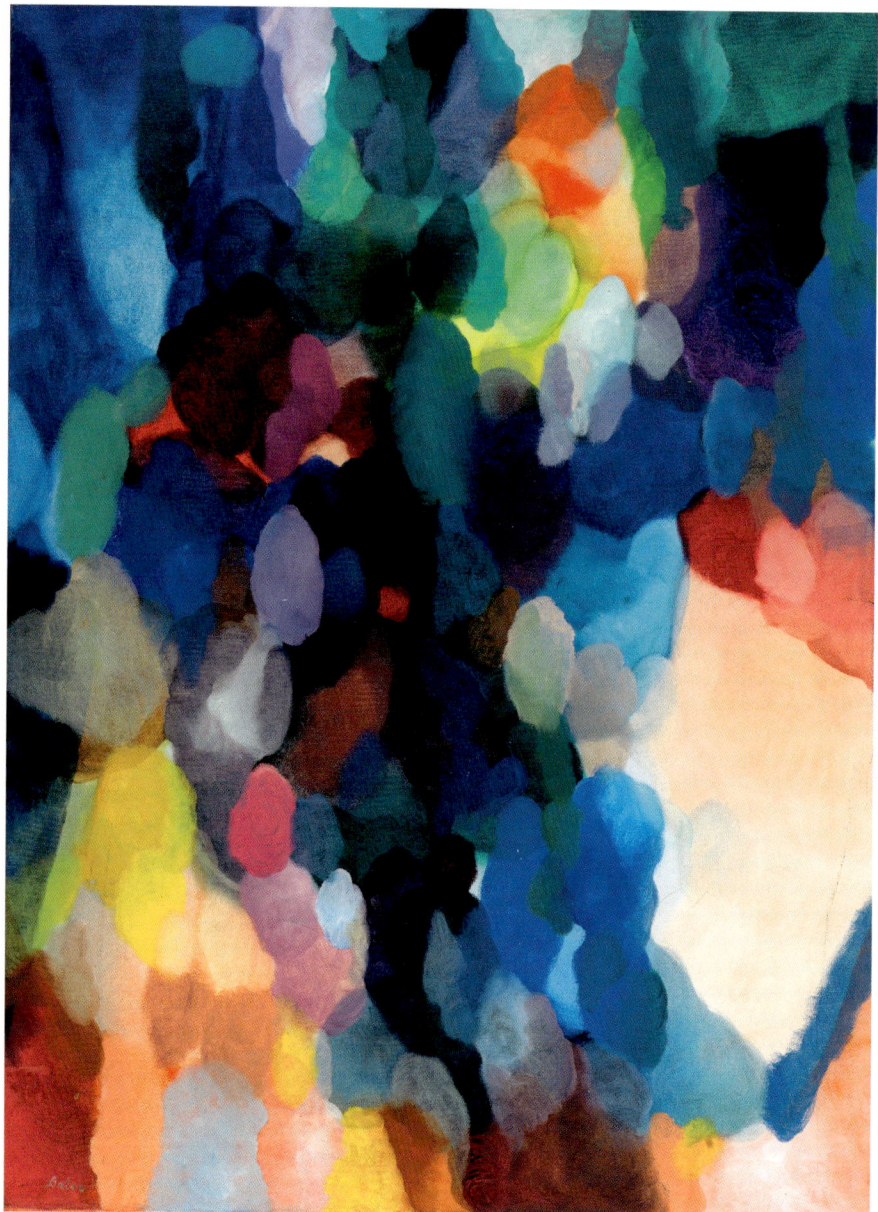

Alice Baber, *Noble Numbers*, 1964–65, acrylic on canvas, 50 7/8 x 38 inches, Smithsonian American Art Museum, Washington, D.C., gift of the artist.

Alice Baber,
Pink Change, 1965,
oil on canvas,
18 x 14 ¾ inches,
collection of
Russell and Lou Light,
Fort Worth, TX.

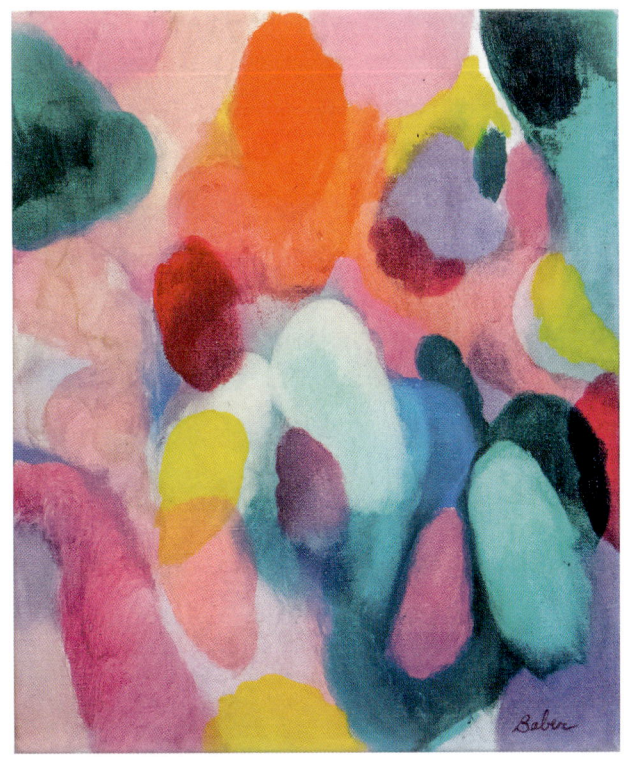

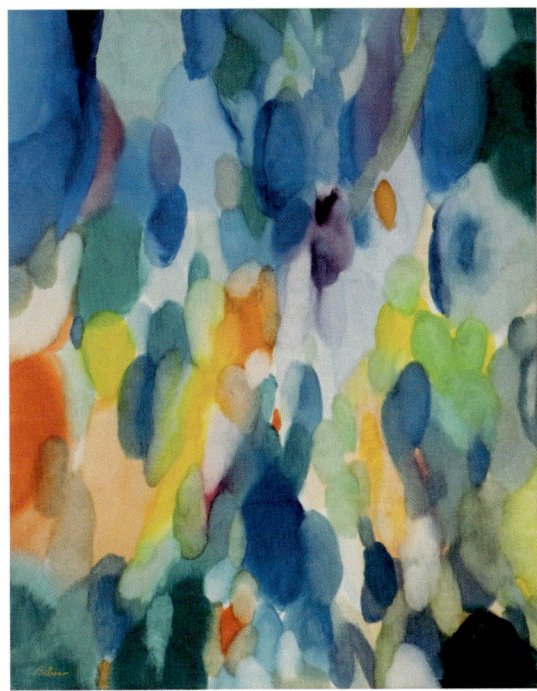

Alice Baber, *Bright Safe*, 1965,
oil on canvas, 39 x 31 ½ inches,
courtesy Emily Friedman Fine Art,
Los Angeles, CA.

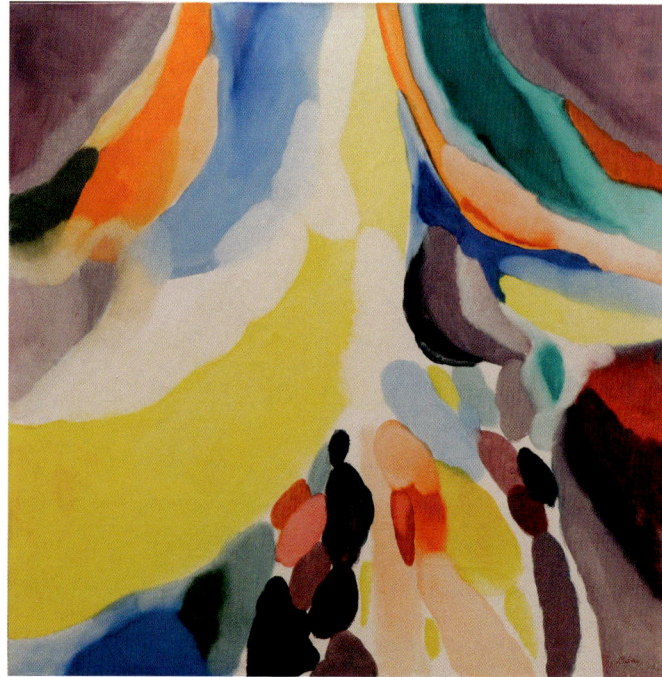

Alice Baber,
Seven Wonders,
1966, oil on canvas,
40 x 40 inches,
private collection.

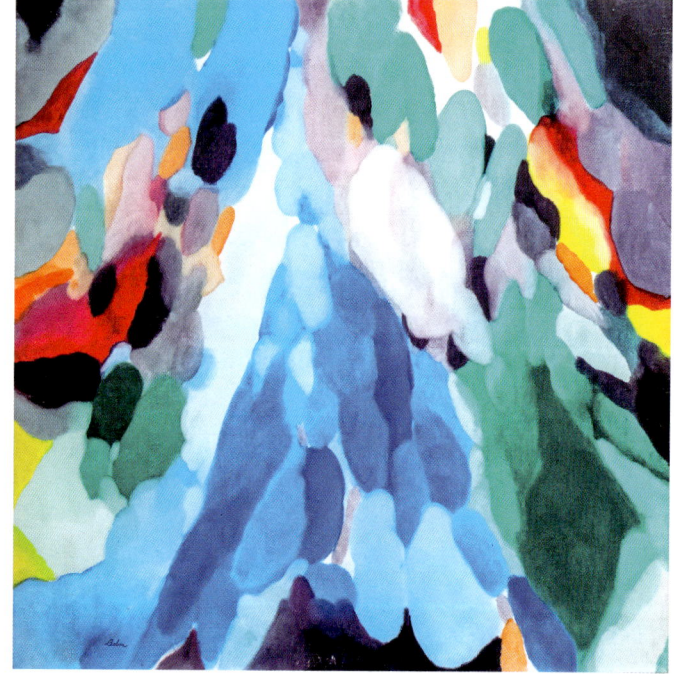

Alice Baber,
Ladder Forest, 1966,
oil on canvas,
40 x 40 inches,
collection of Robert
& Ana Greene.

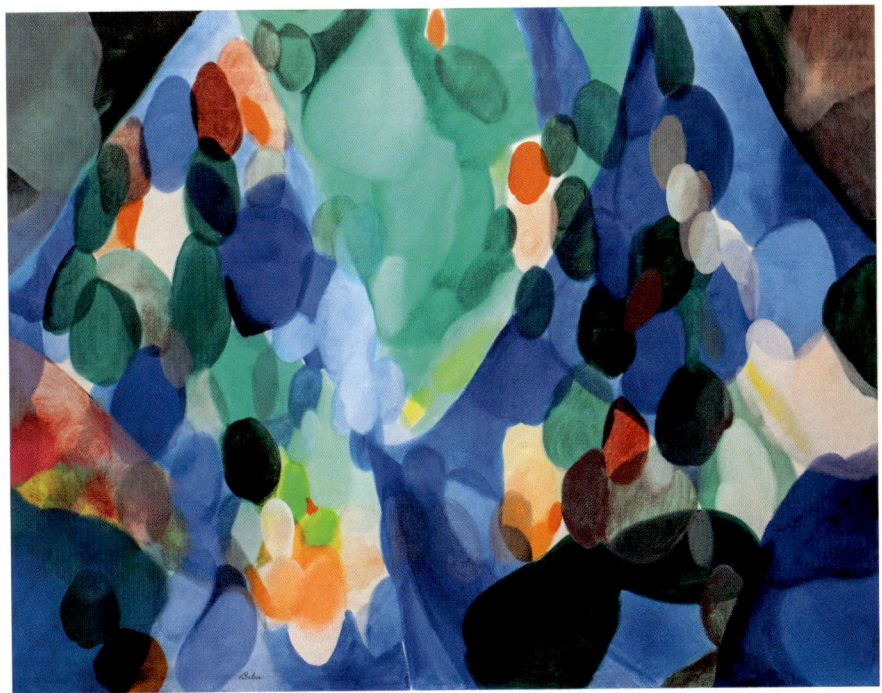

Alice Baber, *Axe in the Grove*, 1966, oil on canvas, 48 x 64 inches,
courtesy Jody Klotz Fine Art, Abilene, TX.

"For me the process of painting begins in color hunger,
light hunger, and dark hunger, the need to find form
and space. The experience of looking, turning, moving,
changing, then, sorting, shifting, and grinding the
thoughts of the hand onto the 'sacred space.'"
—Alice Baber, 1979

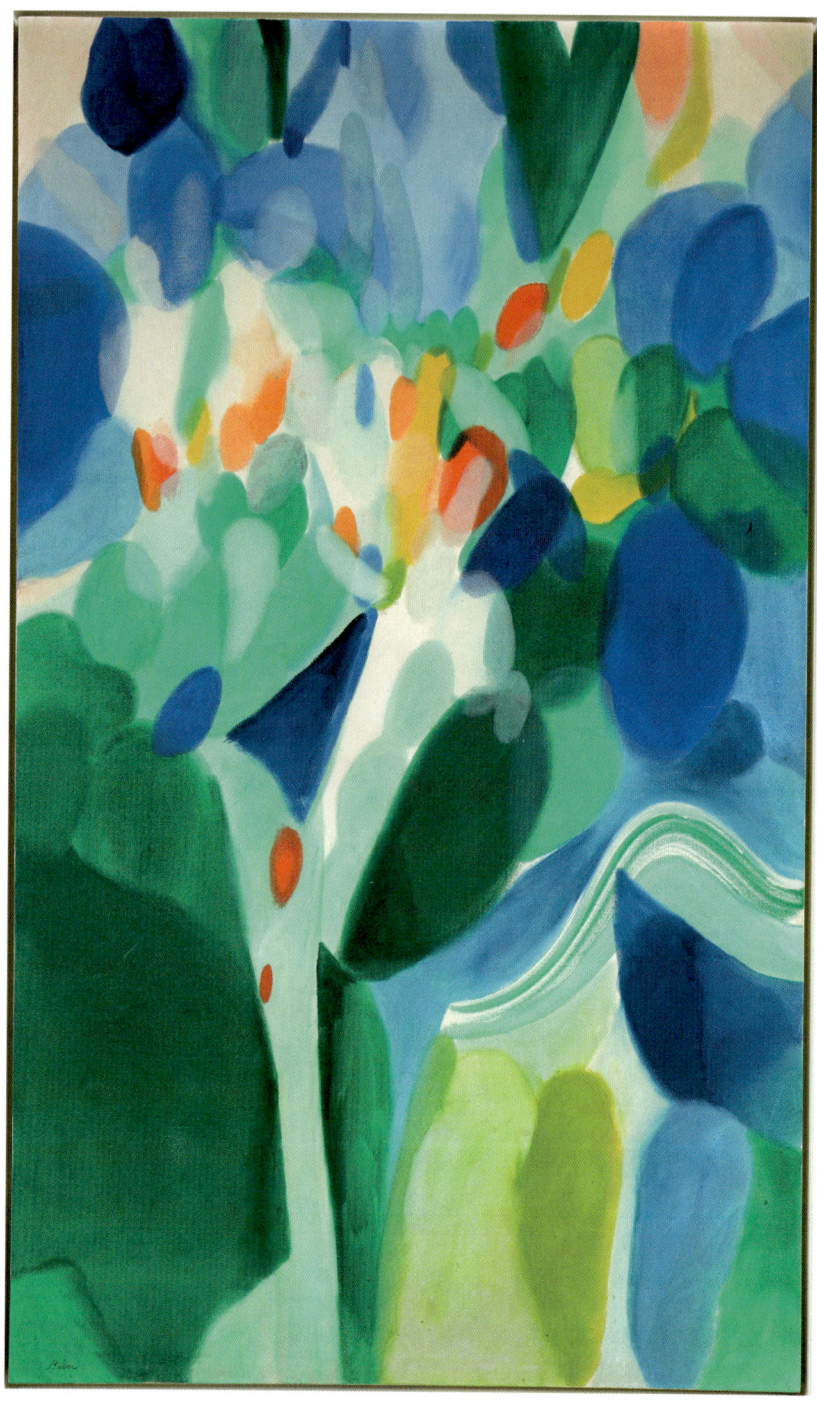

Alice Baber, *The Green Reed*, 1966, oil on canvas, 64 × 38 inches,
courtesy Berry Campbell Gallery, NY.

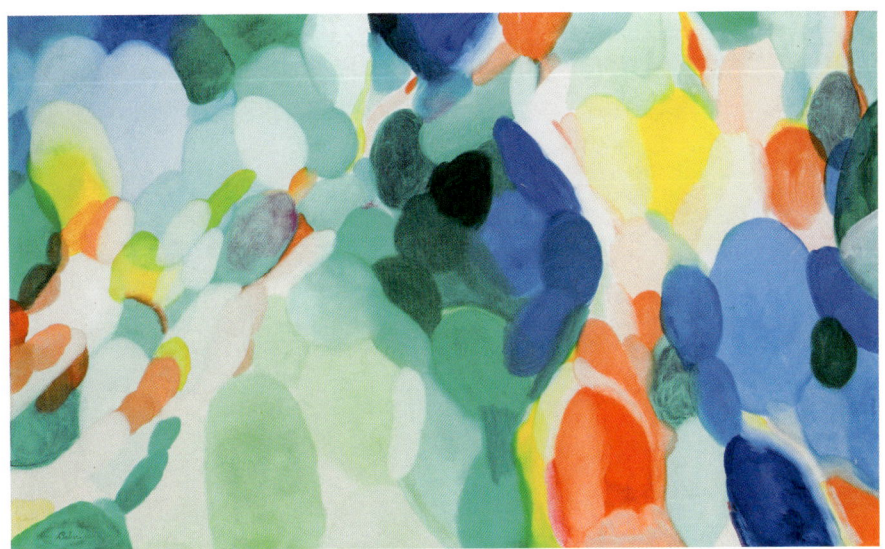

Alice Baber, *The Ringing and the Ringing*, 1967, oil on canvas, 40 x 50 inches, inscribed "For Charles Craig, 1969," private collection, courtesy Shannon's Fine Art Auction.

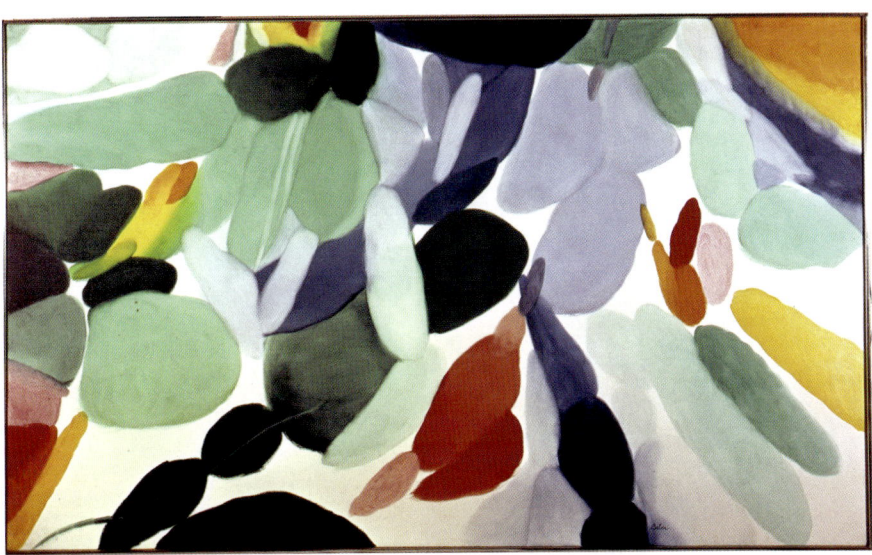

Alice Baber, *Seven Green Leagues*, 1967, acrylic on canvas, 38 x 64 inches, San Francisco Museum of Modern Art, CA, gift of David Kluger.

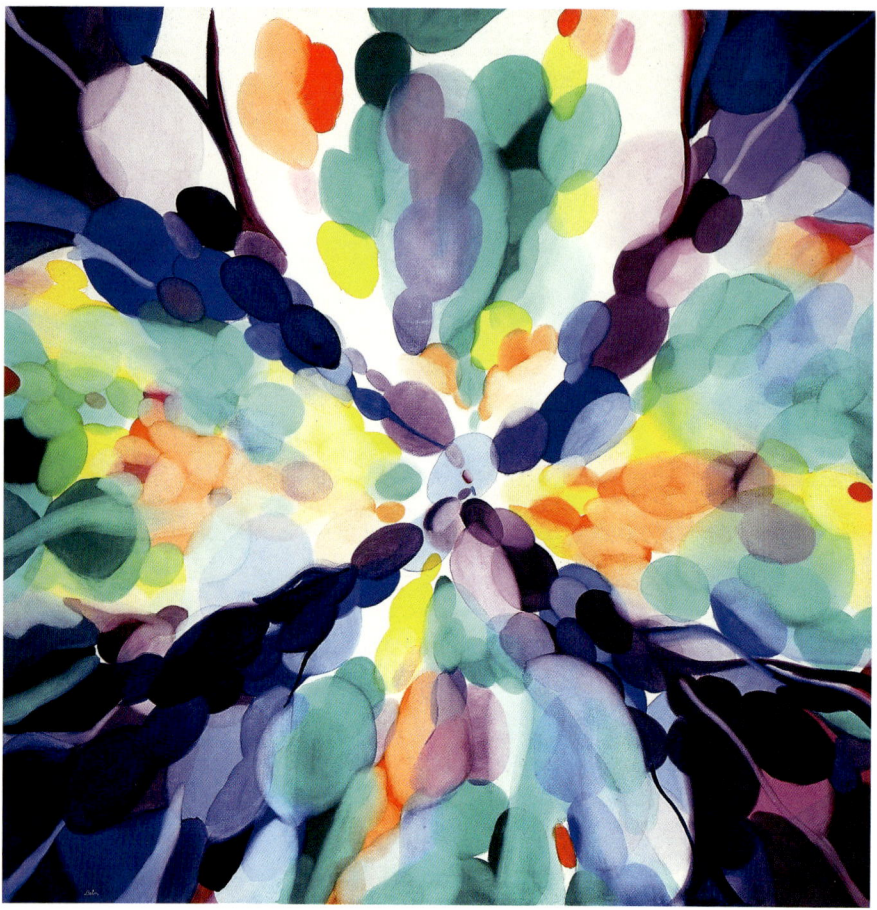

Alice Baber, *Lavender High*, 1968, oil on canvas, 75 ½ x 75 ½ inches,
Blanton Museum of Art, The University of Texas, Austin, TX,
Michener Acquisitions Fund, P1969.6.1.

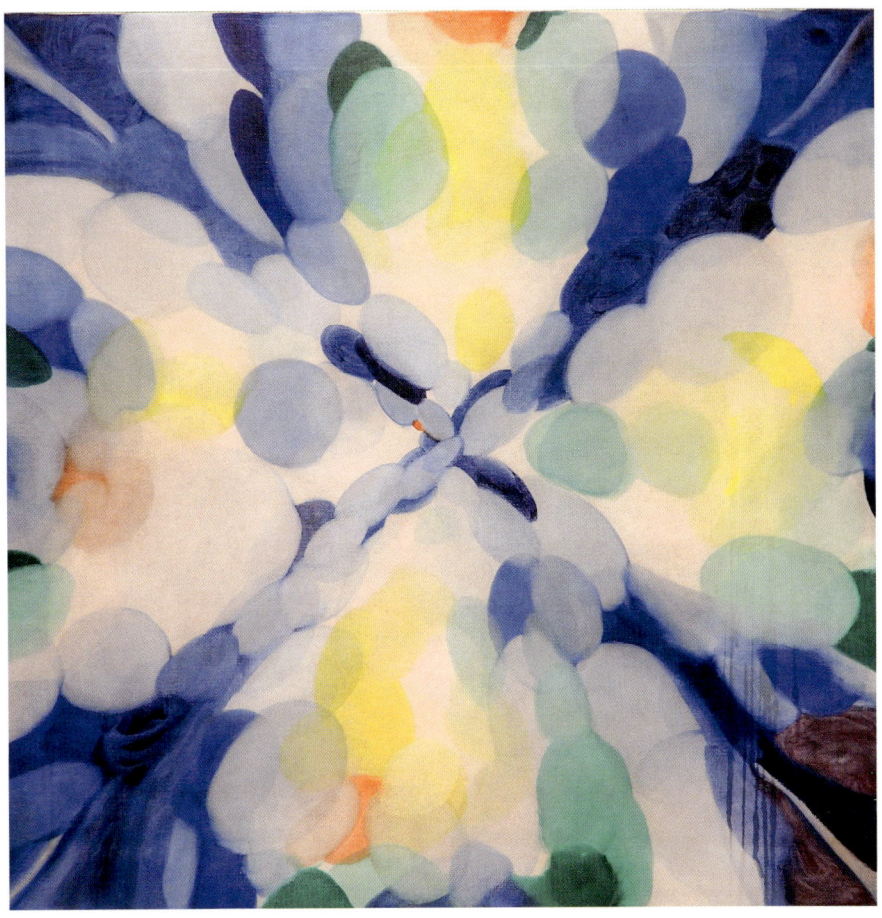

Alice Baber, *Lavender Ways to the Seasons*, 1968, oil on canvas, 33 x 34 inches,
Robert and Christina Tonti, Dallas, Texas.

"I then did a series of 'X' paintings for about five years,
and I still do them sometimes. Paintings in which I use
the 'X' form, but I use the circle moving into the 'X.'"
—Alice Baber, responding to a critic who asked in 1975
why she used the 'X' configuration: "Because I do like it."

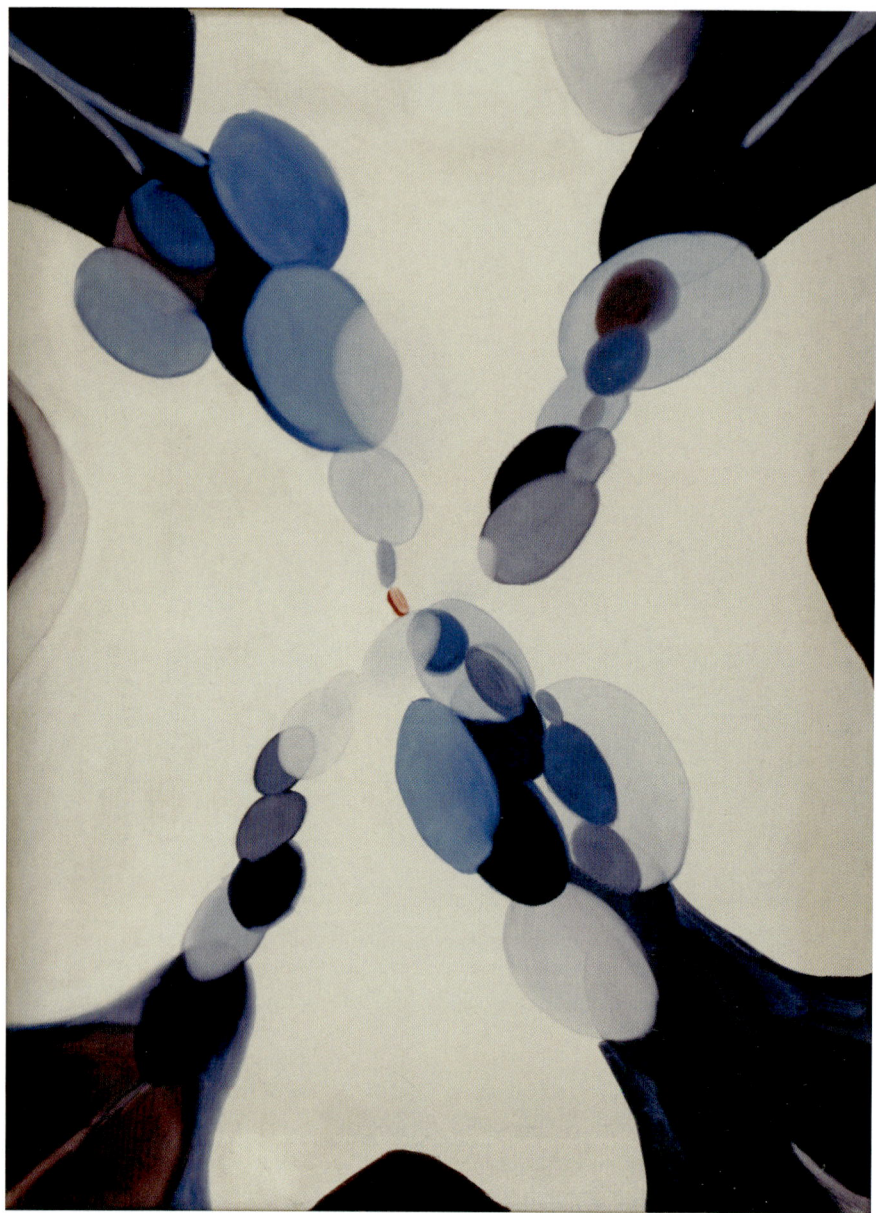

Alice Baber, *The Turning Door*, 1969, oil on canvas, 40 1/8 x 30 inches,
gift of Silvia Pizitz, 1981, Museum of Modern Art, NY, 416.1981.

CHAPTER 6

Further Education in Art
(1946–1951)

B aber attended Lindenwood College for Women from 1946 to 1949, located in St. Charles, Missouri, a suburb of St. Louis. Her high school graduation coincided with the end of World War II, when the large universities were mobbed with returning veterans attending on the GI Bill, which provided for their college education, unemployment insurance, and housing. At the college, Baber majored in art, but she kept up her interest in writing.

In her freshman year, Baber submitted her original poem to the annual contest of the college's Poetry Society, whose purpose was to stimulate "interest in poetry and bring together socially people of similar literary tastes."[1] She won Honorary Membership as well as special notice in the yearbook. Her prize poem was titled "Give Me the Purple-Shadowed Moon," suggesting the focus on color and light that she would continue to pursue in her painting.[2]

Baber's early engagement with poetry, like her love of music, emphasizes her connection to sound—in this case the sound of words, rhythms of speech, and rhymes. In her unpublished notes, she contrasted prose and poetry, noting the "musical beauty" of language as "sound."[3] Whether in poetry or painting, Baber used sensory imagery to create more evocative experiences for her audience. Baber recorded undated notes about poetry, which may be left over from a college class. She made a list headed by Emily Dickinson, followed by Robert Frost, Wallace Stevens, Marianne Moore, John Crowe Ranson, E. E. Cummings, and Richard Eberhart. Her second list headed "Mod. [modern] Verse" begins with her own name, "Baber," followed by Gerard Manley Hopkins, George Orwell, Edith Sitwell, and Dylan Thomas, whose poetry she admired long before she met her future husband, who shared her enthusiasm for the Welsh poet.[4]

Baber's memories of her time in college also include how much she liked Elizabeth Watts, her art teacher there: "She had come straight from Iowa, and she was full of the kind of information that I needed very much. And she taught us to understand and appreciate modern art. . . . Her painting style was probably a moderation of early Guston."[5] Indeed, Watts had studied for her master's degree with Philip Guston, when he taught at University of Iowa and was influenced by American regionalists and Mexican mural painters. This was before Guston, the great figurative painter, dropped social realism for a period of abstract expressionism.[6]

Baber arrived at college knowing what she wanted to study, and it was not Christian religion, even though Lindenwood College was affiliated with the Presbyterian Church and firmly rooted in Judeo-Christian values. Although her paternal grandfather had been baptized, her parents had not been avid churchgoers.[7] Her father told Alice and her sister, "Associate with christian [small c] people. And so live in peace," probably meaning that they should live their lives in accordance with humanist principles rather than following a particular Christian religious sect.[8] Alice recalled: "I remember, at Lindenwood, when they asked me to take the religion course and I didn't want to take the time out to do it, I said, Well, I'll say that I am a Buddhist. And I remember they were very upset about that."[9]

Lindenwood College was close to St. Louis, where Baber recalled going to the art museum.[10] Her annotated copy of the catalogue *40 Masterpieces: A Loan Exhibition of Paintings from American Museums* survives to give us clues as to what she focused on in some of her visits to the museum. This catalogue's illustrations are in black-and-white, so it's easy to see that Baber was recording her thoughts while standing in front of the paintings.

Looking at Paul Cézanne's *Still Life with Apples*, loaned by the Museum of Modern Art, Baber remarked that the "canvas is bare in places."[11] In contrast, she observed that John Constable's 1821 landscape, *Hampstead Heath*, had "rough brushstrokes. No design, Hard to use blue in sky." She considered Lucas Cranach the Elder's *Cardinal Albrecht of Brandenburg as St. Jerome* (1526) to have "lots of color" and called it a "cute picture." The Cranach was on loan from the John and Mable Ringling Museum of Art in Sarasota, Florida, which Baber had visited as a child.

In contrast to the Constable, Baber viewed Honoré Daumier's *The Uprising* (1860), which was on loan from the Phillips Memorial Gallery (today the Phillips Museum) in Washington, DC, as "very dark (why?), good design." She exclaimed over the "rich color" in El Greco's *The Agony in the Garden* (1590), loaned by the Toledo Museum of Art, and the "huge canvas," *The Elphinstone Children*, by the Scottish painter Henry Raeburn. The 1814 portrait, on loan from the Cincinnati Art Museum, measures 78 ½ x 60 ½ inches. About Pierre-Auguste Renoir's *Young Shepherd with Birds* (1911), on loan from the Rhode Island School of Design, she noted: "Lots of color. Figure molded in paint—no outline—blurred edges Dreamlike."

Baber followed up by seeing Rembrandt's *Lucretia* (1666), a canvas on loan from the Minneapolis Institute of Art. She was motivated to look up the story of this Roman woman in Geoffrey Chaucer's *Legend of Good Women*, which she slipped into this catalogue. Lucretia was one of the nine legends Chaucer presented, focusing on the betrayal of women by men, a recurring theme in the poem, and as it turns out, one that would recur in Baber's life.

At the time Baber began attending college, the St. Louis Art Museum had just purchased *Young Men by the Sea* by Max Beckmann (1943), painted during the war years, which the German expressionist artist spent living in self-imposed exile in Amsterdam, after the Nazis declared him to be a "degenerate" artist and included his art in their notorious exhibition, *Entartete Kunst*, which the Nazi Party organized in Munich in 1937.

Baber's time at Lindenwood coincided with the residence of the newly arrived Beckmann, who came to the United States for the first time in 1947 and took the train from New York to St. Louis, arriving on September 18, to teach as a professor of painting for two years in at the School of Fine Arts at Washington University, after which he moved to New York City.

Several of Baber's surviving oil paintings of figures, painted with heavy black lines, suggests her study of Beckmann's work, which she would have absorbed through the impact of his arrival on the local art scene, his influence on her teachers, and her direct observation of his art on view at the St. Louis Art Museum. One faint study Baber made of four male figures in grayish-brown monochrome appears to be a study for her surviving untitled painting of four figures in an interior, which has the somber mood and thick paint associated with the German painter.

Beckmann was known for his many self-portraits and figure paintings, including dramatic triptychs, a format that Baber adopted for several of her later abstractions. Baber would have seen Beckmann's 1943–44 painting, *Les artistes mit Gemüse* (Artists with Vegetable) (CP #4), an oil on canvas (58 7/8 x 45 ¼), interpreted as an allegorical depiction of Beckmann and three friends who fled the Nazis, going into exile in Amsterdam (featured in the exhibition catalogue of Beckmann's 1948 show at the St. Louis Art Museum). In her own untitled painting (CP #4), Baber even repeated Beckmann's composition of four men around a table, three of whom have frontal faces with just one on the right shown in profile. The attentive student, she also imitated Beckmann's focus on the men's hands.

Baber probably read Beckmann's writings excerpted in the 1948 St. Louis Art Museum catalogue. Yet, whether or not she found an early hint to record her own future thoughts and dreams, we find in Beckmann's concepts some parallel interests that will later appear in Baber's own unpublished writings: "And then I awoke and yet continued to dream—painting constantly appeared to me as the one and only possible achievement. . . . I saw William Blake, noble emanation of English genius. He waved friendly greetings to me like a super-terrestrial patriarch. 'Have confidence in objects,' he said, 'do not let yourself be intimidated by the horror of the world.'"[12] Beckmann could have been speaking to Baber when he wrote, "Everything is ordered and correct and must fulfil its destiny in order to attain perfection. Seek this path and you will attain from your own Ego ever deeper perception of the eternal beauty of creation; you will attain increasing release from all that which now seems to you sad or terrible."[13]

One wonders too how Baber would have responded to some catalogue statements made by the German refugee art historian Hanns Swarzenski, then a research fellow at the Institute for Advanced Study in Princeton, New Jersey. "Max Beckmann's high original style has the very disturbing quality of not fitting into a system. He is too independent to associate himself with any established movement, as the Cubists did, the German Expressionists of Die Brücke or the Surrealists. He never joined the cult of the Archaic or the Primitive. He always paints as he does, because he feels compelled to paint that way."[14] Baber later seems to have adopted a similar attitude toward whether she belonged to established movements like the abstract expressionists or the color field painters.

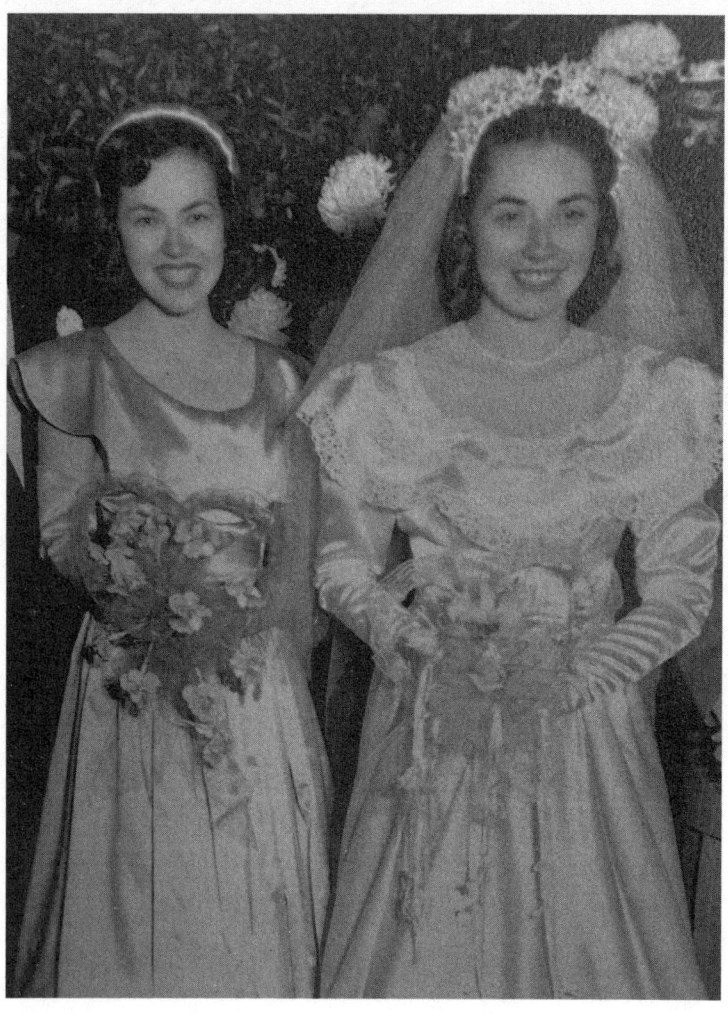

Alice was deep into becoming an artist while her older sister Nancy was busy getting married. On October 17, 1948, Alice served as her sister's maid-of-honor at a formal wedding held at the Presbyterian Church in Kansas, Illinois. Nancy chose the traditional role for women at the time and went on to have three sons. Alice quietly made other choices that ruled out such conventional roles for women.

Meanwhile, at Lindenwood College, Baber took a modern art history course in which, she later told one interviewer, she developed her early interest in Cézanne.[15] She was quick to adopt the French artist's "nervous line," which she viewed as endowing his figures with a sense of movement. But it was also at Lindenwood that Baber recalled taking the advice of Professor Elizabeth Watts: "You have to get out of here and to a big university to study art because we couldn't even have models in the nude or anything." "She was a good teacher because she was a free person," Baber concluded.[16] From her study of Guston-influenced figuration, Baber, encouraged by Watts, moved on, seeking the more liberal instruction believed to be available at a large university.

Baber said that she attended Indiana University in Bloomington to study art with Alton Pickens, because "I had seen his work reproduced in art magazines and I liked it very much."[17] Pickens, born in Seattle, had studied at Reed College and the Portland Art Museum School in Oregon. He lived in New York City from 1939 to 1946, where he was active politically on the Left; his work was published in the *New Masses* during the 1940s.[18] Among his supporters was Lincoln Kirstein—a wealthy collector, author, and curator—who was influential at the Museum of Modern Art and preferred figurative art.[19] Pickens became known for his satirical genre, portrait, and figure paintings that evoke surrealism.

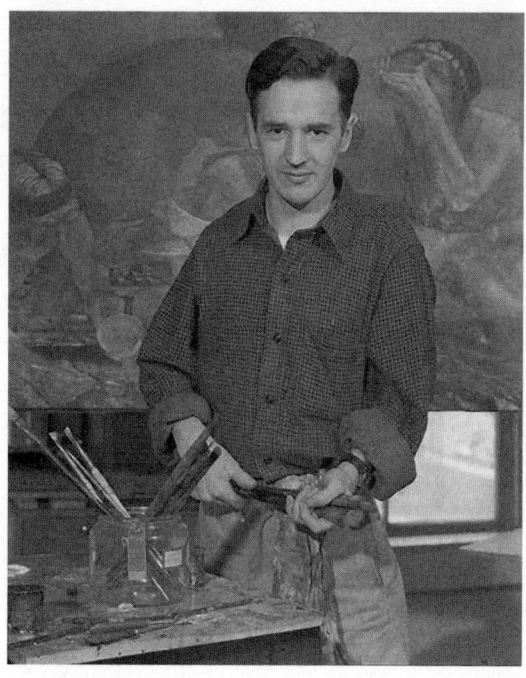

Pickens, who moved to Indiana University in 1946, won attention on campus and in the student newspaper. *The Indiana Daily Student* reported when Pickens won a Blue Ribbon in a competition.[20] Then Pickens was featured as one of nineteen young American artists said to represent "the best in our country" in the March 20, 1950, issue of *Life* magazine, which appeared during Baber's last semester as an undergraduate. In addition to Alton Pickens, the other young artists, chosen from a pool of 450 nominations, included a few—Hedda Sterne and Theodoros Stamos—who would become famous as abstract expressionists, as well as others who today range from less-known to unknown.[21]

The *Life* article inspired *The Indiana Daily Student* to run a feature story about the article headlined ALTON PICKENS GAINS HONORS AS ONE OF BEST YOUNG ARTISTS.[22] Baber and her classmates must have been proud to have their art teacher singled out by *Life*, since the highly influential general-interest magazine, known for the excellence of its photography, was then said to reach a quarter of the nation's population.[23] Baber might also have noticed, however, that only three of the nineteen featured artists—Aleta Cornelius, Honoré Sharrer, and Hedda Sterne—were women.[24]

What Pickens taught at Indiana can be surmised by his notes from 1950 on his studio course that was to serve as an "introduction to art." Of particular interest for Baber is his focus on "transparency, opaqueness, and the illusion of space" as well as the "exploration of the behavior of various paints, e.g. wet, dry, dry brush, effect of various surfaces, transparent and opaque applications, spater [*sic*] on wet and dry surfaces, scraping and wiping off."[25] He also taught "elementary color theory."

Long after her college days, Baber remained loyal to Pickens, praising his instruction, and even insisting in 1974, as one of New York Professional Women Artists, a group of feminists being interviewed by Mimi Poser for her program "Round About the Guggenheim," that Pickens, unlike so many other men of his generation, had not discriminated against women artists.[26] Her opinion was shared by the prestigious women's college, Vassar College, which hired Pickens as a professor in its art department and gave him a show of his work at its gallery in the fall of 1956.[27]

From her study with Pickens, Baber recalled making "abstract paintings, semi-abstract paintings, figures, figures in environment, figures in flattened space."[28] One engaging extant figurative work depicts two black figures, one of which has many bright red lines superimposed upon it. The top of this painting's background is divided between red and bright pink, but the red figure stands on a red rectangle, like a carpet, which is placed upon a yellow ground (CP #5).[29]

What is most striking about this colorful painting is how much it resembles Baber's color pencil drawing *The King and the Old Rug Weaver* (CP #5), which she made in 1939, when she was just ten or eleven years old, to accompany a story that she wrote and illustrated about a character going from India to "Bagdad." The figure on the right in Baber's painting wears a headdress reminiscent of the turbans in her childhood drawing. The scribbled lines within the outline of each of the figures is remarkably similar in concept in both her painting and the childhood drawing. The idea of a rug is also evident in both compositions.

The continuity between Baber's childhood eye and hand and her eye and hand as an adult recalls a quotation of self-analysis by Edward Hopper, some of whose childhood and early commercial work also survives: "In every artist's development the germ of the later work is always found in the earlier. The nucleus around which the artist's intellect builds his work is himself; the central ego, personality, or whatever it may be called, and this changes little from birth to death. What he was once, he always is, with slight modification. Changing fashions in methods or subject matter alter him little or not at all."[30] Although Hopper generalized from his own perspective, we can see that his concept also applies to the development of Baber's visual concepts and memory, whether conscious or not on her part.

What Baber remembered painting at Indiana University were abstractions of the trees on campus, which she flattened and rendered in vivid colors (CP #9). She emphasized about her time in Bloomington that it was her first experience of getting "off the plain," experiencing landscape that was not flat—the hills so evident at Indiana University.[31] Baber later explained to an interviewer, "My move into color was related to trees."[32] At least three surviving untitled canvases of trees with bright palettes appear to be examples from Baber's work in Bloomington.

Baber stated, "I was involved with color and poetry at the time, and I did abstract painting along with realist painting like the other students were doing."[33] She recalled that it was in 1950 that she first saw a painting by the abstract expressionist Clyfford Still, the recollection of which, years later, in 1957, she credited with encouraging her to abandon the horizon line in her own paintings.[34]

Among the other striking stimuli available to Baber in Bloomington was a show in the fall of 1949 of woodblock prints by the nineteenth-century Japanese artist Utagawa Hiroshige, whose stylized landscapes would have appealed to her poetic sensibility.[35] Seeing this show might have prompted her to enroll in the class on Asian art taught by Professor Theodore R. Bowie, a respected author, who was born in Japan to a Russian mother and American father and grew up in both Nice, France, and San Francisco.

The idea of migrating as had Bowie clearly piqued Baber's imagination. She told how Pickens had motivated her to go east: "He said, 'You must go to New York City,' with some sort of poetic remark like, 'where the great ships go out to sea,' which I thought was splendid and which keeps you going in New York. And then he said, 'Go there, and work until you have a group of paintings that are all one group, and this will be your start as a painter.'"[36]

Though painting remained her passion, while at Indiana, Baber also studied graphic design and jewelry with Alma Eikerman—an accomplished American metalsmith, silversmith, and jewelry designer—whose work is now in the collection of the Smithsonian American Art Museum. In addition, Baber studied both art history and journalism. She received a BA from Indiana University in 1950 and then spent another year there doing graduate work before she moved to New York.[37] If the pencil note written on the stretcher reading "fall 1950," is correct, then Baber did not paint her version of Beckmann's *Les artistes mit Gemüse* (Artists with Vegetable) (CP #4) until she began her graduate study at Indiana University. Her memory of seeing Beckmann's work at the St. Louis Art Museum remained vivid. During her last year in Bloomington, she only studied "Oriental art" and painted.[38]

Also attracting attention on campus was Dr. Alfred Kinsey, who, after many years at the university, became in 1947 the founding director of the new Institute for Research in Sex, Gender, and Reproduction, which published *Sexual Behavior in the Human Male* in 1948. Kinsey's celebrity, on campus and then across the United States, must have come to Baber's attention. Kinsey's research was very influential and not only affected the public perception of sexuality internationally but also challenged accepted codes of behavior.[39] Thus, hearing about Kinsey's research and its popularity might also have affected Baber's own perceptions and life decisions.

While at Indiana University, Baber continued writing poetry, which had a relatively high profile on campus. The popular professor who then taught poetry writing was Samuel Yellen, who was also a supporter of Baber's painting teacher Alton Pickens.[40] Yellen at the time was frequently publishing poems and fiction in *The New Yorker* and other prominent journals.[41] Baber would have appreciated the visuality of Yellen's poems, some of which even focused on specific paintings, like Leonardo da Vinci's *Last Supper* and Edward Hopper's *Nighthawks*.[42]

Baber's herself dated to this period (1948–50) a poem she called "Twilight Meeting":[43]

> I go into the blue fields
> Trowelled earth that smells of night mist
> Day's turbined dust returned to collars
> I find my way through the tree lined harvests
> Day has kept the guests in waiting

A summer moon delayed the stage
The wind sings on a comb of locust
And finds me in the orange hedge.

Baber's jingly childhood style has evolved to deliberate four-beat rhythms, plotting an encounter never realized though evoked by way of rural features that approach the surreal ("turbined dust . . . collars," and "tree lined harvests" or "comb of locusts" or "delayed stage"), framed by colors, blue and orange, concluded by wind finding her hedged in.

The rural features, evocative colors, and sounds in nature, although imagined in a new frame, recall Baber's own history on the family farm and the enthusiasms of her doting father. Adin Baber was at one time the owner and custodian not only of farmland but also of what is now known as Baber Woods, located in Edgar County, Illinois, which represents the remnant of a "much larger forest that once occupied most of the Shelbyville Moraine."[44] Adin inherited these fifty-one acres of land from his family, which used the woods as a source of fence rails, lumber, and firewood, while refraining from clearing the land of trees except for a three-acre lot to build two cabins. Adin was proud that since 1898, no trees had been cut, and that the woods had been protected from cattle grazing.[45] Since 1974, Baber Woods, located just a few miles south of Charleston, is owned by the Nature Conservancy, having been donated by Adin Baber.[46]

Adin Baber intended to convey his values to his daughter Alice. From her early childhood, he guided her, encouraging her reverence for nature, and her interest in literature and history. For the summer immediately after she completed her studies in Bloomington, he supported her first travel to Europe to continue her graduate work there. Not surprisingly, Alice chose to go to France, where Adin had worked during World War I. Her passport shows her at age twenty-two en route to Europe by ship, where she arrived in Le Havre, France, on June 21, 1951, and returned home from Southampton, England, on September 8, 1951.

Alice's main destination was just over an hour's journey outside of Paris, where she attended the École des Beaux-Arts (School of Fine Arts) at Fontainebleau for graduate work, studying painting, design, and lithography. Founded in 1923, the school adopted the same mission as its music conservatory, which was begun earlier. By Baber's time, there were classes in painting, printmaking, sculpture, and architecture. Baber recalled that the school was then run by Nadia Boulanger, the revered teacher of many famous composers, including Americans, from Leonard Bernstein and Aaron Copland to Elliott Carter.[47] While in Europe, Baber also managed to tour around France by bus and to visit Switzerland, Rome and Florence, and England, where she went to see Stonehenge and to London.

Baber later wrote notes about the bus trips she took that summer around France: "I loved most of all a château called Vaux-le-Vicomte. This was built by the minister of finance of Louis the 14th & inadvertently caused the downfall of France because the king became so jealous that he built Versailles."[48] Another trip was to Bar-le-Duc, a town in northeastern France, which has the remains of a sixteenth-century château and two churches, one constructed during the fourteenth and fifteenth centuries, and another one with fourteenth-century frescoes. In fact, the architecture in France so fascinated Baber that she later named a painting in her first show after Bar-le-Duc.

Baber's experience studying art in France and getting a taste of Europe added to her aesthetics, her world view, and left her more sophisticated than before. Confident that she could survive in New

York, she chose not to return to Indiana University to finish the credits she needed to earn a master's degree, which might have helped her obtain a permanent position as an art instructor. Instead, she returned ready to make her place in the art scene in New York. When the opportunity to return to France became a possibility, she was more than prepared to take that chance.

CHAPTER 7

Return to France
(1959–1962)

Alice Baber had thoroughly enjoyed studying art in France during the summer of 1951, just before she moved to New York City. Thus, when her relationship with Paul Jenkins evolved, she was more than happy to begin living half the year with him in Paris. Once there, Baber was quick to pursue her own career. Arriving in Paris in 1959, she was still young enough to show at the American Cultural Center, in the center's Premiere Biennale de Paris, also known as the first Jeune Biennale, for artists under thirty-five. The show's organizer, Darthea Speyer, the American cultural attaché, welcomed Baber, just over thirty years old, with an invitation to show in 1959 and then again in 1961, in the Deuxième Biennale de Paris.

Among the other artists included was Baber's acquaintance and contemporary Helen Frankenthaler, who was not living in Paris, although she spent three months in 1958 living in a rented villa in Saint-Jean-de-Luz, France, a small fishing village on the Atlantic coast with her new husband, the artist Robert Motherwell, painting on their honeymoon. In the first of the two Biennale de Paris shows, Frankenthaler won first prize.[1] Like Baber, Frankenthaler created paintings that were known for their beauty and their lyricism, but her technique of "stain painting" on unprimed canvas, which was followed by American color field painters like Morris Louis and Kenneth Noland, attracted neither Baber nor Jenkins.

"Living in a foreign country makes a demand," complained Paul Jenkins in 1966. "An American is a walking representative. The European invariably wants to know where he stands in or for his country . . . no matter what sublime indifference the European may appear to have. You can't be an expatriate unless you have a real avenue of escape. There is no place today an American can go to escape."[2]

Jenkins's career, however, was by now well established, much more than Baber's. Arriving in Paris in 1953, he had come up with a plan guaranteed to ingratiate himself with Michel Tapié, a leading French critic and theorist on postwar art. Jenkins, together with his first wife, Esther Ebenhoe Jenkins, had introduced and edited the book, *Observations of . . . Michel Tapié* in 1956.[3] Paul and Esther, in their introduction, wrote: "One cannot help but feel the uniqueness of the American position. . . . Indigenous artistic expression that expands beyond its engendering boundaries."[4] The book, which was clearly intended to promote Jenkins, was also a tribute to Tapié, reproducing portraits of him by American and French artists: Jenkins, Claire Falkenstein, Georges Mathieu, Henri Michaux, and Mark Tobey.

Tapié was well-known for having organized in late 1952 *Un art autre* for Studio Paul Facchetti, an adventurous gallery located at 17 Rue de Lille on the Left Bank that showed the work of Jackson Pollock, Sam Francis, Jean-Paul Riopelle, Jean Dubuffet, Appel, Henri Michaux, and other vanguard artists. Through the wealthy artist and collector Alfonso Ossorio, Facchetti, a photographer, became in March 1952 the first in Europe to present a show of Jackson

Pollock.[5] The next year, Facchetti gave Jenkins his first solo show in Paris, launching his career.

From Jenkins's studio in Paris in 1959, the dealer and collector Peggy Guggenheim had purchased *Osage*, a work on canvas, and would continue to purchase more of his paintings. He had regular solo shows in New York with the Martha Jackson Gallery beginning in 1956, as well as with the Esther Robles Gallery in Los Angeles and Galerie Stadler and Galerie Karl Flinker in Paris. Jenkins was hot; he could afford to give Baber a boost, but even holding back from that, he had no reason to feel threatened by her energy and ambition, though it may have matched his own.

Artist couples, whether Baber and Jenkins or Frankenthaler and Motherwell, faced the challenge of dealing with competing levels of ambition. When the man was older, dominant, and had a bigger reputation, the relationship was more likely to endure. While Baber moved to Paris to live with Jenkins, they were not yet married. Yet Baber's status at once changed. Having adapted to living alone in New York when it was considered daring, she now had to adjust to living in Paris and to being a woman artist in Paris, which was a bit of a shock, as she recalled: "I didn't like it when I first went there, and then I liked it very much at the end. But I think for me Paris is a city that it's slow to get to know. I was never enamored of it as many people are. . . . It got so it felt like home, or a perfectly natural kind of place to be."[6]

At the time, during Baber's first year living in Paris, she wrote to her father, telling him that a dealer had taken some of her watercolors to sell: "Several critics have been very enthusiastic. The structure is looser in France. One can deal with several dealers. . . . Paris is a hard town, but I came back at the right time."[7] By 1959, Baber's paintings, such as *Persimmon*, an oil on canvas, or her watercolor, *I Saw It Once*, had already become fully abstract (CP #18).

At the time, post–World War II Paris figured in the American popular imagination. Vincente Minnelli's 1951 musical film, *An American in Paris*, inspired by the 1928 jazz-influenced music of George Gershwin, romanticizes the lives of expatriate American artists struggling to make it in the French capital. Some of the songs, like "Love Is Here to Stay," made the adventure seem idyllic, but the struggle to make it as an artist there presented challenging hurdles. Since Paul had arrived in Paris in the spring of 1953, and was already well established and connected to a network of other artists, dealers, critics, writers, and other intellectuals, what remained to be seen was how much he would extend himself to help Alice.

In 1959, just as Baber was beginning to live and work there, several shows in Paris promoted contemporary American abstract art to the French public—almost all of it created by men. The Musée National d'Art Moderne hosted *La nouvelle peinture américaine* (The New American Painting), an exhibition organized by Dorothy C. Miller of New York's Museum of Modern Art. This touring show featured seventeen abstract expressionist artists: William Baziotes, James Brooks, Sam Francis, Willem de Kooning, Adolph Gottlieb, Arshile Gorky, Philip Guston, Grace Hartigan, Franz Kline, Robert Motherwell, Barnett Newman, Jackson Pollock, Mark Rothko, Theodore Stamos, Clyfford Still, Bradley Walker Tomlin, and Jack Tworkov.[8]

Grace Hartigan, who was the only woman included in MoMA's show, was six years older than Alice Baber. However, Sam Francis, who was the youngest of the seventeen Americans and the only one not based in New York, was an exact contemporary of Paul Jenkins, who was not included, even though they both showed in New York with the Martha Jackson Gallery. Being omitted must have rankled Jenkins.

At the same time, a separate show, *Jackson Pollock: 1912–1956*, organized by Porter McCray for MoMA's international program, was also on view at Musée National d'Art Moderne. Jenkins, aware of Pollock's prominence, had worked to forge a link between himself and Pollock shortly before the latter's fatal car crash, even inviting Pollock and Krasner to visit him and his wife Esther in Paris.

Now Jenkins and Baber, the glamorous new couple in Paris, already had friends there, whom at least Paul knew from New York.[9] One person was the painter Joan Mitchell, with whom Paul had earlier exchanged studios. Baber appears to refer to Mitchell and her exotic travel when she writes to her own father in May 1959 about meeting a woman artist who needs adventure and once "found a lost Inca temple in Mex.," referring to Mitchell's 1950 trip to Yucatán in Mexico.[10]

A photograph (mislabeled on the verso as taken in Paris) survives of Baber with the artist Gregory Masurovsky, which appears to have been taken along the canals in Amsterdam, where tourists are often photographed.[11] This photograph was likely taken in 1964, when Baber's work was included in an exhibition *Art in Industry (The Peter Stuyvesant Collection)*, which toured the Netherlands. The collection, with an international perspective, focused on abstract art.

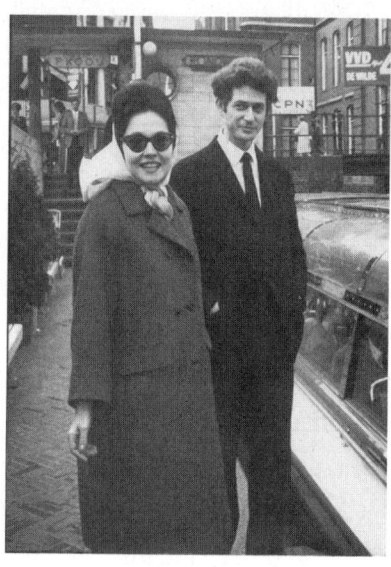

Always interested in seeing new places, Baber would have been thrilled to visit the Netherlands, for, as noted earlier, she told in an interview about her early interest in the seventeenth-century Dutch baroque artist Judith Leyster. Thus, she had a special motivation to want to visit Amsterdam's Rijksmuseum, which not only houses Rembrandt's *The Night Watch*, but many other Dutch baroque master-pieces. Even today, the Rijksmuseum boasts, "When Judith Leyster (1609–1660) joined the Guild of St Luke in 1633, she became one of the first female 'master painters' in art history."[12] Leyster's was just the kind of career that would have appealed to Baber's own ambition.

The existence of this photograph suggests that Jenkins and Baber knew the artist couple Gregory Masurovsky and his wife, the gestural abstract expressionist painter Shirley Goldfarb, who moved from New York to Paris in 1954. Masurovsky was known for his black-and-white drawings and etchings. He and his wife were also part of the circle that included other expatriates such as Sam Francis, Joan Mitchell, and the Canadian Jean Paul Riopelle, all of whom Baber and Jenkins knew well.[13] Although Masurovsky and Goldfarb lived in a modest studio not too far away, they were preoccupied with raising their young son.[14]

Just as Baber and Jenkins arrived in Paris in 1959, James and Gloria Jones also settled there that year, where their home became an important social center for the literary and visual arts scene. Alice wrote to her father about her new friend, the famous American author, noting, "James Jones is related to Daniel Boone. His last book is very serious. The Aunts wouldn't like the first ones—full of profanity like Army men talk. He has a good ear from repeating Army talk & Middle Westernisms."[15] She knew that her father already had an interest in Boone, the archetypal frontier hero of American folklore.

A November 25, 1959, letter from James Jones in Paris to Paul Jenkins in New York confirms their close friendship. It was addressed to Jenkins at 73 Bedford Street, so we know that Jenkins and Baber were living together in her apartment. Jones and his wife, who had entertained Jenkins and Baber just before their departure for New York, reported, "We have not heard anything from Joan Mitchell or any of the other 'reverberations,' of your going-away party. So don't worry your head about that."[16]

Jones also confides: "I had a letter from Ruth Franken [Ruth Francken], quoting or misquoting what you had said to her about the big black painting. She was just leaving for England, I think it was for a show, and she wanted me to 'split the difference or something like that, and pay her $200. . . . This hassling over price like that is all too normal amongst humans, I guess, but it can become unnerving. I don't think I really like the picture that much. So I'm not going to buy it at all."[17] Francken, born in Prague, had studied at Oxford University, lived in New York, and then settled down in Paris.

Jones mentions, "We have not seen Henri since you left. I've been meaning to call him all this time about getting hold of Alice's painting but have not done it."[18] At least one of Baber's watercolors from this moment, *I Saw It Once* (CP #18), is signed, titled, and dated 1959 on the reverse of the paper and signed on the front, on the bottom right. Its warm red, pink, and yellow palette convey an upbeat mood, with several deep purple circles, perhaps implying passion. Baber's abstract composition with circular forms in a vertical format relates visually to at least two of her canvases from this same year: *Persimmon* (CP #18) and *Bon Voyage*, the latter published in black-and-white reproduction in *It Is: A Magazine for Abstract Art*, edited by her friend Philip Pavia.[19]

Jenkins kept *I Saw It Once* all his life and many other examples of Baber's work remained in his estate, although it is not known if these were gifts to him from Baber or, more likely, just a shipment from a show that was returned to him instead of to her, arriving at his place in Paris after they split up. She did inscribe some of her paintings, but none to Paul that has come to light.

At the end of 1959, the first year of Baber's life with Jenkins in Paris, he responded to James Jones, writing to him and Gloria, "Since I've come back I've sworn not to become impatient. Each day I train myself not to jump out of my skin but to be methodical—buy my paint, get set up, and then move in on the white underbelly of the canvas."[20] One gets a hint here of the complex personality that Baber was dealing with. Jenkins did express his gratitude for the couple's help in making Paris seem to have more "reality," writing to thank them for the beautiful farewell party that they held for him and Baber and allowing that he hoped the repercussions from some of the invited and uninvited guests had been minimal. He admitted that he was still shocked by the jealousy of others, but told how moved he and Baber were by their generosity and friendship.[21]

Jenkins confided, "Well I've got one thing in sight since I've been back. I've got a bottle of Old Grand-Dad [bourbon whiskey] in front of me when I write a letter instead of Ricard. The 86 proof has more flavor than the 100 so I guess I'm not a total victim of it."[22] While Jenkins justifies choosing 86-proof whiskey, which is 43 percent alcohol by volume, over 100-proof whiskey, which is 50 percent alcohol by volume, the Ricard he says he has replaced is an anise- and licorice-flavored French aperitif that is 45 percent alcohol by volume, but is often consumed diluted with water.

By his 1968 interview with Colette Roberts, who was asking him about the then-trendy drug LSD, Jenkins spoke about miserable "boredom" during his adolescence and told how he swore that he would forever avoid that: "And from that day forward I've never been bored. I think that boredom is comparable to a sickness as dangerous as alcoholism."[23] Ironically, he made this comment during the period when he was so dependent upon alcohol that those closest to him have commented that he never went out without his flask.[24]

Years later, in a memoir, Kaylie Jones, the daughter of James and Gloria Jones, who would be born the year following this exchange, described her parents and their friends, focusing in on the problem of the day: "Only one word was whispered in the house as if it was the worst insult you could call someone," she explains, "*alcoholic* was a word my parents reserved for the most appalling and shameful cases—drunks who made public scenes or tried to kill themselves or ended up in the street or in an institution. If you could hold your liquor and go to work, you were definitely not an alcoholic."[25]

As a couple, Jenkins and Baber were close to James and Gloria Jones. Their daughter, Kaylie, recently recalled the physical evidence of her parents' friendship with the artist couple: "Two of Alice Baber's gigantic paintings graced my childhood home in Paris, France. One took up an entire wall of our living room, a giant canvas of bright, colorful ovals on a snow-white background. Across the room on another wall was a Paul Jenkins—her husband at the time. His canvas was almost as large, but much darker, a black and charcoal gray form on a white background, that looked a bit like the head of a shark."[26]

While the couple's paintings hung compatibly together in the same salon of the Jones's Paris apartment, after Baber returned for a visit to New York, Jenkins went alone from Paris to London in March 1960, and stayed for two weeks at Dukes Hotel, where Baber wrote him a letter. He was there for his first one-man show in London. It took place March 15–April 2, 1960, at Arthur Tooth & Sons Gallery, located at 31 Bruton Street, which had been around since Victorian times, showing contemporary art, mainly by British and Continental painters.

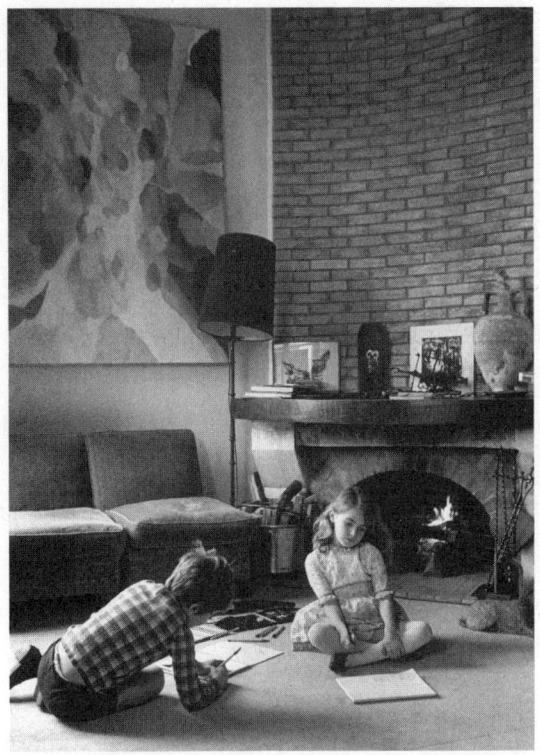

Baber wrote to Jenkins, "It is true that *Zuleika Dobson* by Beerbohm has improved my sense of humor."[27] She had just read the 1911 book, *Zuleika Dobson: Or, an Oxford Love Story*, the English essayist Max Beerbohm's sole novel, in which he satirized undergraduate life. Baber, whom many viewed as a very attractive woman, might have related to Beerbohm's character, Zuleika, described as a femme fatale who has to struggle with gender bias in the all-male domain of Oxford University. The more attractive a woman was perceived to be, the more she was subject to being viewed as a sex object and not taken seriously.

"No new gossip," Baber continues in the letter to Jenkins in London, "except film on D. K. [de Kooning] very professional includes Faulkner and Bucky Fuller. Walter didn't mention so I was discrete."[28] Walter was the Brooklyn-born photographer Walter Silver, who took photographs of both Jenkins and Willem de Kooning in 1959, and a few years earlier had been the companion of Grace Hartigan.[29]

Baber's mentioning in the same context the novelist William Faulkner; the architect, designer, and inventor Buckminster Fuller; and the de Koonings (Willem and Elaine) suggests film footage from the summer of 1948 at Black Mountain, the avant-garde school in North Carolina. It was in 1946 that Willem de Kooning painted his abstract black-and-white canvas *Light in August*, which was a tribute to Faulkner's novel of the same name, which engages with themes of race, gender, and religion in 1920s Mississippi.[30]

Elaine de Kooning, Alice's friend since her early days in New York, had participated in Fuller's attempt to construct his first large-scale geodesic dome. Elaine had also played a role that summer in producing Erik Satie's comic play, *The Ruse of the Medusa*, along with Fuller and others, including John Cage on the piano, the dancer Merce Cunningham, the director Arthur Penn, and the artist Robert Rauschenberg.

Baber concludes her letter by announcing that she is going to Ray Parker's opening and by assuring Jenkins that she loves him.[31] While Baber's letter survived in Jenkins's papers, she appears to have destroyed any letters from Jenkins that she had in her possession, perhaps a measure of how hurt she felt after they broke up.

That spring, Baber wrote to Gloria Jones, telling her that they expected to sail for Europe on June 2 and so would see her soon. She reported: "Paul had a terrific show in England—is now recovered & preparing show here. I have almost worked him up to the idea of a vacation—sea, sky & all that only to get involved myself with the idea of the Venice Bienale [*sic*], where all true artists will congregate as well as dealers, etc."[32]

Baber wrote to Gloria, who had retired from her acting career, that she has heard that she is "in maternity clothes and I'm delighted. I'm no good as a baby sitter (no practice) but I sometimes read aloud to the parents."[33] Her attempt at humor underscores her lack of interest in a detour into motherhood for herself. She mentioned a good evening with the Silvers, which refers to the photographer Walter Silver and his then-wife Libby Durgin, quipping, "I am no longer shy & retiring but scream with the rest."[34] A photograph by Silver from around this time records Baber and Durgin in Jenkins's studio, where there must have been an informal showing of Jenkins's work.[35]

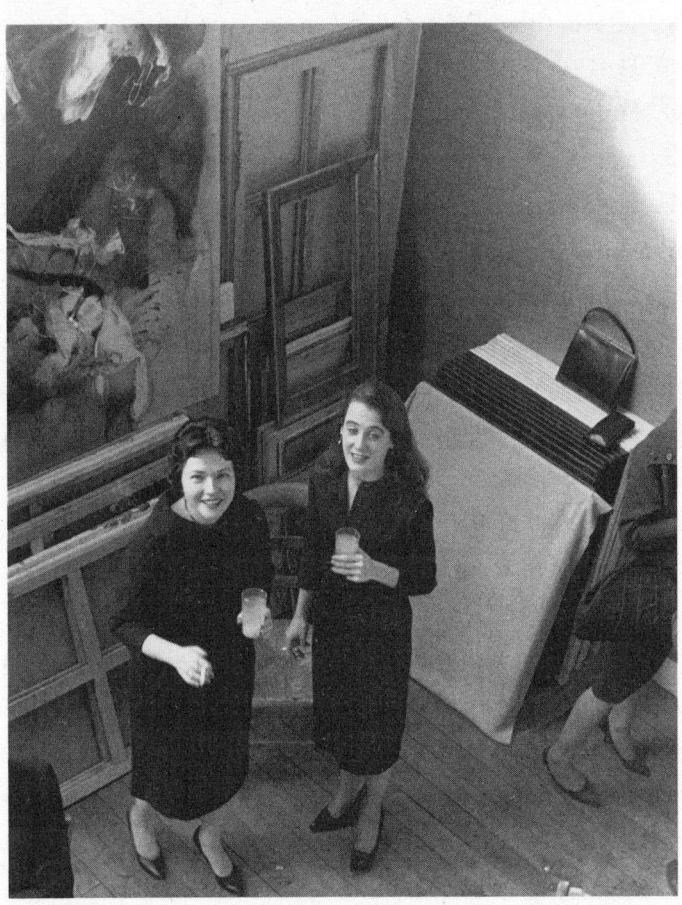

For Baber, the initial period of living in Europe with Jenkins was the most innocent, the most optimistic. She got her wish—the couple vacationed in Spain on the *Costa Brava* from where Jenkins wrote a postcard to the Lassaws, telling them how they were happy to hear from them and that they missed them both. He added, "Hph! Hick! Alice and I are having some native wine and I'm as drunk as a hoot owl." He told of asking for the Greek drink (possibly Ouzo, the dry anise-flavored aperitif that is widely consumed in Greece), which Ibram had once offered them, only to find it unavailable before the fall."[36]

Alice memorialized this idyllic moment in an abstract watercolor that she signed, titled *Porto de la Selva*, and dated 1960 on the picture's verso (CP #19). She recorded her perception of the bright colors and intense sunlight she experienced in Catalonia, vacationing with Paul on the Costa Brava, where the cozy fishing port and the beach attracted international tourists. *Porto de la Selva* portrays the coast of the Cap de Creus, where the sunlight reflects off the water, dazzling the eye of someone who finds local light and local color intoxicating.

In her unpublished manuscript for a book on Jenkins, Baber wrote, "During a trip to Spain Jenkins painted watercolor on white paper. This led him more deeply into problems of translucency and color and presaged his later change from oil to acrylic paint. In acrylic he was able to control the flow of the pigments in much the same way that he did in watercolor."[37] Baber's comments let us imagine the couple, lounging together on the beach, each painting watercolors.

Yet, in his large monograph on Paul Jenkins, the art historian Albert Elsen wrote when "During a trip to Spain in 1959, Jenkins worked extensively in Porta della Selva [*sic*] with watercolor. . . . He recalls becoming more intensively involved with color, perhaps aided by the brilliance of the light experienced working out of doors, and painting on the whiteness of rag papers." Evidently Elsen, who also got the date wrong in his narrative, intentionally omitted mentioning the presence and the likely influence of Alice Baber on Paul Jenkins since he was clearly aiming to please Jenkins.[38] Elsen wrote in the context of this time in Spain, "He was increasingly drawn to sustained transparency of color," which in fact was for Alice Baber a major preoccupation.[39] Several powerful male art historians and critics from Albert Elsen to Irving Sandler were complicit in omitting Alice Baber from the story of Paul Jenkins, essentially excluding Alice Baber from her rightful place in the history of art. Instead, Alice Baber was in the sorority of artist wives who were obscured by the looming shadow of their artist husbands—from Jo Hopper (Mrs. Edward Hopper) to Lee Krasner (Mrs. Jackson Pollock) to Mimi Gross (Mrs. Red Grooms).

There can be no question that Jenkins's letter to the Lassaws, telling them, "I'm as drunk as a hoot owl," documents that this couples' painting vacation in Spain in 1960 (not 1959) was a joint endeavor. Jenkins's drinking might have been a red flag if Baber had wanted to see it. Rather than take note of the level of Jenkins's dependence on alcohol, which was so common during this era, she was probably too deeply in love to pay attention. After all, she had witnessed such behavior since it was endemic at the Cedar Bar, where most of the artists hung out and she too had tried socializing, although she found the place distressing. Despite Jenkins's serious alcohol addiction, he usually managed to be charming in public and continued to produce a reputable body of paintings.

Substance abuse in a partner had already affected Baber's earlier involvement with David Hare. As for herself, she once told an interviewer who asked about the Cedar Bar: "I was highly allergic to tobacco smoke and I was not a heavy drinker because one drink and I usually got sleepy so I didn't go there very much."[40]

A passage in a September 16, 1961, letter from Ernestine Lassaw to Alice suggests how Jenkins's dependence on alcohol was simply accepted by his friends. During 1961–62, while Ibram Lassaw was Artist in Residence at Duke University in Durham, North Carolina, Ernestine was writing to Alice in Paris, reporting on Ibram's beautiful studio, how much their daughter Denise liked her school, and local customs. She notes: "Tell Paul there is not a Bar or Licquor [*sic*] store in town—only Grills. You can buy wine in the grocery store just like Paris, but nothing stronger anywhere! There seems to be licquor [*sic*] at parties so they get it somewhere but we haven't discovered the source yet."[41]

Despite Jenkins's excesses, Baber's life with him was exciting and promising. By early 1961, she wrote a letter to the art writers Irv and Lucy Sandler checking on when they would "stop thru Paris on their way back [from a trip to Germany] or do I have to hold out until September?" She requests: "Do tell the Lassaws all kinds of good things about coming too because I don't want Ernestine to forget her French."[42] The reference was to the French lessons that Alice and Ernestine had taken together. Baber noted, "Paul's show is going very nicely (he is snoring at the moment in a state of blissful repose).[43] We had a press opening for the book and all the usual jazz. Wish you could have attended." She refers to the publication of *The Paintings of Paul Jenkins*, a book by James Fitzsimmons, Kenneth B. Sawyer, and Pierre Restany, just published in Paris by Editions Two Cities.[44]

In this new book, Pierre Restany wrote of "a break in the linear continuity leading from Cézanne through Cubism to geometry—pure or impure, as the case may be. All this had been felt by us and we grew ready to accept this new evidence. But this awareness was spreading among a generation of young artists, weak and naturally divided, torn between the champions of objective painting and the pioneers of *lyrical abstraction*."[45] We take particular note of the use of the term *lyrical abstraction*, since it will later be used to describe Baber's work. Jenkins's show was held at Galerie Karl Flinker at 34 Rue du Bac on Paris's hip Left Bank.

On February 9, 1961, Jenkins wrote to James and Gloria, while he and Alice were staying at the Jones's place in Paris in their friends' absence, telling them how he had just run into Fitzsimmons at the *vernissage* of the magnificent Kandinsky show that he had helped to install.[46] He referred to a show of Wassily Kandinsky's watercolors and drawings that was held at Galerie Karl Flinker and to James A. Fitzsimmons, an American artist and art critic, who in 1956 founded *Art International*, a magazine devoted to the European visual arts scene, published in Switzerland.[47] Now Fitzsimmons had just written about Jenkins in the new book; he would later feature Baber's work in his magazine.

In her 1961 letter to Irv and Lucy Sandler in New York, Baber joked, "No one has informed me as to the Club activities or Cedar Bar fights. How can I keep up at this rate? I'm working hard, have studio set up, and all. Saw Joan Mitchell yesterday—they're all set for the racing boat summer with a house rented from Russian nobility. Riopelle is as usual looking at Châteaux. I as usual promised to help cut the grass."[48]

Baber referred to the artist couple—the American Joan Mitchell, who also showed in New York at the Martha Jackson Gallery, and the Canadian painter Jean-Paul Riopelle—who were independently wealthy and kept separate homes and studios near Giverny. Present at the going-away party for Jenkins and Baber given by James and Gloria Jones, Mitchell and Riopelle were famous painters notorious for their excessive alcohol consumption. That would not have bothered the Jones couple. Their daughter Kaylie later wrote that her father could consume astounding amounts of alcohol "yet still retain his composure. He appeared to judge people he just met by their capacity to imbibe.

The more they were able to drink without falling over or making a fool of themselves, the better he liked them."[49] While Paul Jenkins earned Jones's respect as a drinker, Alice did not indulge at that level.

Alice, referring to Irving Sandler's promised text promoting Paul's art, inquired for her husband, who was clearly eager to have this writing about his art: "As for your critique, Paul awaits it eagerly, but my God you've been busy. He can speak for himself but I know he has some shows in the near future so if you ever have a moment . . . more of this later. Just explain please are you flying directly back to NYC after Germany."[50]

Jenkins had just heard from their mutual friend Ernestine Lassaw: "Irving Sandler is going to Germany to-day for a one week stay to see a big French show. I don't think he will get to Paris.[51] In fact, it was during that same summer of 1961 that Irving Sandler later recalled that he first got to know Jenkins well in Paris. Sandler remembered that he had admired Jenkins's work for years and then had the opportunity to write about it for an upcoming show in Switzerland.[52]

Sandler also recalled spending an evening with Jenkins at the Paris home of James and Gloria Jones on the Île Saint-Louis. Sandler mentions that his wife Lucy was present; however, he makes no mention of Baber, who was surely also there. By the time Sandler wrote his reminiscence signed October 25, 2012, however, Baber was long dead; Jenkins had just died at the age of eighty-eight the previous June 9. It was no time for his widow to hear a recollection that included one of her husband's first two wives, whose mention she did not tolerate.

Ernestine Lassaw, in her 1961 letter to Jenkins, after telling Paul that despite needing to find someone to rent their house for the summer, "it looks like we will chuck it all and come [to France] regardless." Ernestine added a postscript: "Did I tell Alice Dore Ashton is having a baby?"[53] It was surely gossip about the art critic that would interest

Alice, who was then nearly thirty-three years old. There is no evidence, though, that she ever wanted to have a child, as her comments to the pregnant Gloria Jones make clear. As for Jenkins, he did not present himself as a devoted father; in fact, he was quite the opposite. Baber knew this from the time she met Jenkins, but she had already made different choices for her own life.

Baber privileged making and showing art over all else. She was surely pleased to be included in *Modern American Painting*, a show that took place at the Laing Art Gallery in Newcastle-upon-Tyne as part of Newcastle's first arts festival. Organized with sources in England, this show was supported by the USIS (United States Information Service) gallery at the US embassy in London, which by then was part of USIA (United States Information Agency), a government agency aimed at promoting American interests, which operated from 1953 to 1999.

Baber was now showing with much more established American artists, including not only her husband but, among others, the abstractionists Joseph Albers, William Baziotes, Norman Bluhm, Richard Diebenkorn, Helen Frankenthaler, Philip Guston, Al Held, Lee Krasner, Ellsworth Kelly, Morris Louis, Joan Mitchell, Robert Motherwell, Alfonso Ossorio, Theodoros Stamos, Mark Tobey, and Esteban Vicente. With the inclusion of Jim Dine, there was only a hint of the new pop art vogue to come.

During that summer of 1961, Alice and Paul are well documented, making an excursion together with the Lassaws—Ernestine, Ibram, and their daughter, Denise, then fifteen—to revisit Alice's favorite place in France, discovered ten years earlier, when she first visited Europe to study in Fontainebleau. Baber wanted to share her enthusiasm with her good friends. She wrote, "Vaux-le-Vicomte is really an Italian Idea built in France. . . . The great heavy building with a dome is rather sublime, but what I liked were the fountains. . . . abstract rocks."[54] "As you walk towards them," she instructed, "the rocks become enormous heads out of which the water comes from the mouths & then finally on getting closer, these grotesques become grottos again. I was looking for abstraction and I found it. It's hard to find abstraction in France. Nature has been tamed & the people search for the rational."[55]

Snapshots of Baber and friends survive to document their fun on July 2, 1961: Alice and Ernestine, posed wading before the rocks in the garden at Vaux-le-Vicomte, while Ibram photographed them. Ibram also photographed Paul, regally posing alone before the rocks, in a niche in the garden. The Lassaws just missed seeing Alice's work on view in the Deuxième Biennale de Paris, which didn't open until September 29.

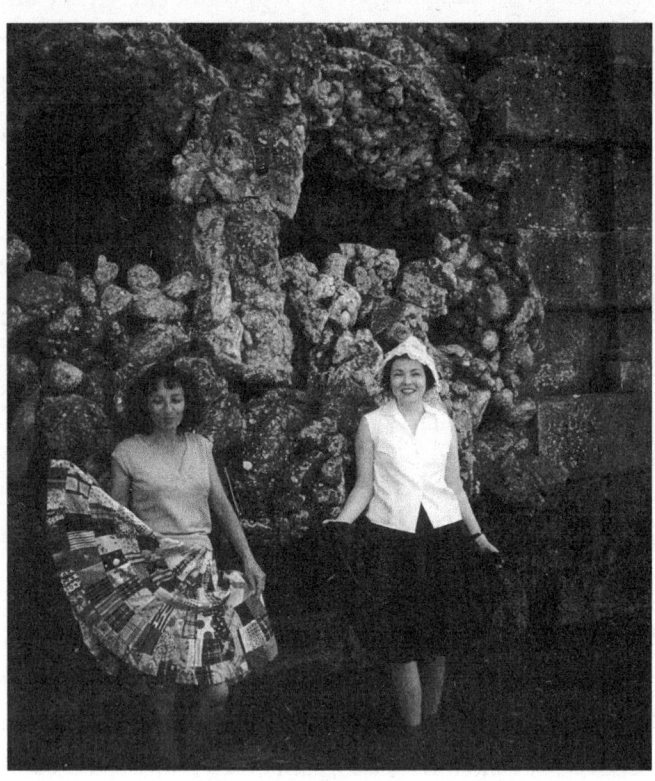

Having spent time for years with Alice and Paul at home in New York, Denise Lassaw was comfortable enough with the couple that in March 1962 she wrote and implored them to let her stay with them in Paris the coming summer, adding, "My mother worries about my (nonexistent) virginity and most likely wouldn't approve of my staying [with another friend] . . . I will be helpful to Alice in any way under my command. I wouldn't bring strange algerian [*sic*] rebels and/or anyone else up to visit, I promise not to get arrested and to try hard to stay out of all trouble, I will get home at a reasonable-ish hour every morning and/or evening . . . well what more could I promise you."[56]

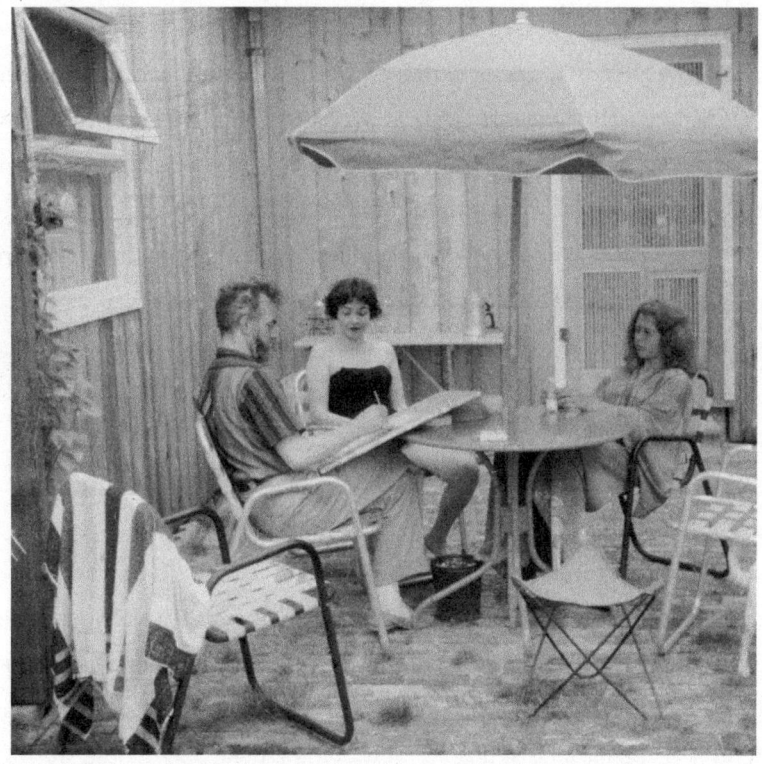

Alice with Paul sketching Denise Lassaw, East Hampton, 1958

Despite their fondness for the Lassaws, Baber and Jenkins were probably not up to taking responsibility for their friends' teenage daughter let loose on her own in Paris. Both were very focused on their own artwork. In July 1962, they had returned from seeing the 31st Venice Biennale, where the American Pavilion featured paintings by Loren MacIver and Jan Müller and sculptures by Louise Nevelson and Dimitri Hadzi.[57] Baber's luminous canvas *Just Arrived* might refer to just such a moment: their triumphal return to "Paris," which, with the year 1962, is inscribed on the overlap of this canvas (CP #21). Her luscious, fluid shapes seem magically lit from behind in this opulent vertical painting, where the colors and dissolving forms enable the viewer's imagination to soar.

Baber was then focused on organizing a show for herself in London at the New Vision Centre Gallery (at 4 Seymour Place in London) to coincide with the moment that Jenkins would be showing again at Arthur Tooth: "As soon as we get unpacked, mentally too, from Venice and do some work I do hope we will come to England. In the meantime I want you to know how much it means to me that you are thinking of giving me an exhibition in your gallery. At this very time I have a body of work which I would like to show you as I feel it offers the range important to a show."[58] Baber also mentioned their in-progress plan to visit Wales. She reported: "The working space problem in Paris is working out well now and I am overjoyed that I can paint toward a show with you."[59]

The gallery director of the New Vision Centre Gallery, Denis Bowen, first wrote to Baber and Jenkins in Paris in 1962. Bowen—a South African artist, gallerist, and promoter of abstract and avant-garde art in Britain—thanked the American couple for "coming to our opening at the gallery in despite of it being a delay to you and in spite of you not being too well."[60] Bowen wrote, "I am noting that Paul's show is March 4 and that you would like yours to 'start the beginning of the next week after that.'"[61]

Baber was trying her best to keep up with Paul, to show where he showed. Her mature work was still developing. It was in Paris in the 1960s that Baber developed her unique method of painting abstractions. She started with a gesso-covered ground on which she applied oil paint in ovoid shapes by using with a rag wrapped around her hand or finger, if she sought an edge. She rubbed thinned paint into the surface of her canvas, allowing the white surface to show through; she could further lighten her shapes through her process of "'lifting' the paint with turpentine."[62] Baber learned to manipulate, overlap, and illuminate her often colorful ovoid shapes into various patterns and to create the illusion of movement, light, and sound.

Baber later explained to a French interviewer how for her "the erasing of color is very important": "Sometimes the most exciting colors I find by lifting, which, when you say superimposing, is the same thing. But when I lift the colors, I find that sometimes the coolness of the color is left (and I never use the term 'hot' or 'cold' in color except in this case) that the residue of a color will have a kind of wonderful cool glow that you don't get, you know, if you haven't lifted because part of the color will lift and part will remain."[63]

As Baber spent more time living abroad, she developed her unique style of painting. She had also begun to absorb more and more European culture, especially from travel to Britain, Spain, Germany, and Italy. Aspects of French culture also affected her work—not only the people she met or the art that she saw on view in museums and galleries, but also what she was reading.

CHAPTER 8

Literary Links
(1963)

Living in France and traveling with Paul Jenkins not only encouraged Alice Baber to experiment with her method of painting but also motivated her to read French literature. Baber became especially attracted to fiction by George Sand and her thoughts about Sand appear in several of her surviving notes.[1] Sand, born Amantine Lucile Aurore Dupin, was an important nineteenth-century writer of fiction and, like Baber herself, a feminist. Sand published under a male pen name and was known to wear men's clothing, at a time when to do so was still controversial in France.[2] "Of all French writers preoccupied with music as expression, George Sand had the technical qualifications to . . . . make music," wrote the scholar Albert Sonnenfeld, noting that Sand played the piano, harp, and guitar.[3]

Sand's 1853 novel, *Les maîtres sonneurs* (translated both as *The Bagpipers* or *The Master Pipers*), tells a story of love set in the contrasting landscapes of the Berry and Bourbonnais regions in central France. This classic novel appears to be the source for Baber's use of the word *Piper*, which she used for many of her titles for paintings, beginning in about 1962, when she was spending half of the year in France, living with Jenkins: *Piper's Message* (1962) (CP #20), *Piper's Near* (1965), *Piper's Mandala* (1968), *The Piper and the Wind* (1972), *Sound of the Piper's Ladder* (1975), *The Colors of the Leader of the Piper* (1975), *The Bridge of the Piper for Virgo* (1975), *White Morning of the Piper's Ladder* (1975), *The Piper of the Blue Ladder* (1976), *Sand of the River Piper* (1976), *The Piper Sees the Ladder of the Jaguar* (1978), and *The Mountain Wing Dances to the Piper's Tune* (1979). Sand wrote in her dedication: "I send you this book, a distant echo of our bagpipes, to remind you that the trees are budding, the nightingales have come, and the great spring-tide festival of nature is beginning in the fields."[4] Not only the beauty of Sand's descriptions of nature but also her synesthetic overlapping of the senses would have appealed to Baber.

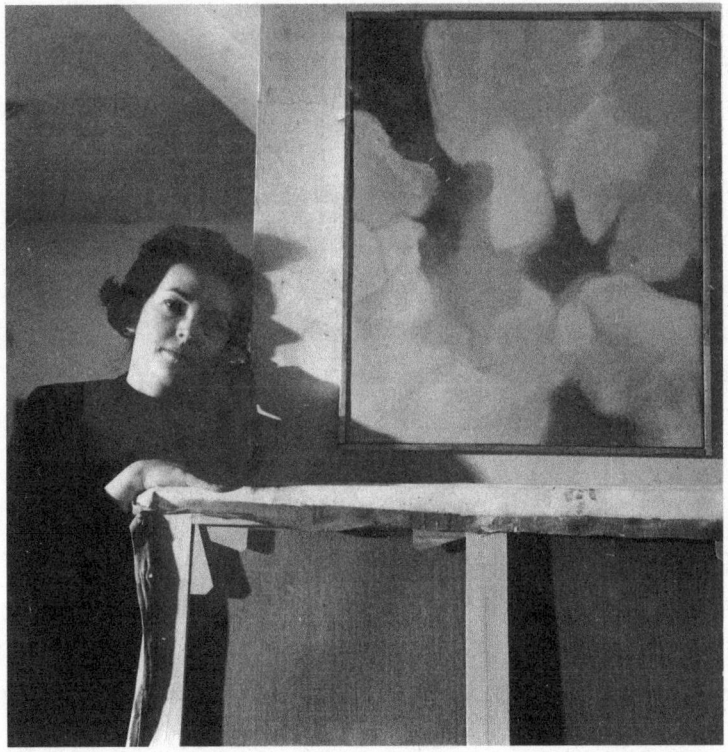

Alice Baber in her Paris studio, 1963, photograph by Marianne Adelmann.

The character in Sand's novel, who seems to resonate with Baber's synesthetic abilities, was a maladjusted young man who, since he desired to play bagpipes, which he could not afford to buy, learned to make music playing a blade of grass as a flute. This appears to be the reference Baber made in her 1966 painting *The Green Reed* (CP #28), for a reed instrument is a wind instrument that uses a vibrating reed to produce sound. The reed is a thin blade of metal or cane as in varieties of grass. In pastoral literature from Theocritus to Virgil, the herdsmen singers make music by playing a panpipe, often made of reeds.[5]

Sand's dialogue tells about a character imagining making music: "When you used to practise on the cornstalks like the herd-boys, you made such a jumble of the tunes that nobody recognized them. In the matter of music, we all thought you more simple than children, who fancy they can play the bagpipes with reeds."[6] Sand's themes would seem to speak with special intensity to Baber and others who experienced synesthesia: "I believe in what you have in your head, but I can't feel certain that you will ever get it out. To will and to do are not the same thing; to dream music and play the flute differ widely . . . all I heard was the wind talking in the trees, or the brook murmuring along the pebbles; but you, you heard something else, and you were so certain of it that I was, too, for sympathy."[7]

The advice the boy received in Sand's novel about following a profession in his art might also have struck a note with Baber: "I know what you have in your ears, in your brain, in your heart,—the music of the good God. . . . keep the music that is so sweet and dear in your secret heart, but don't try to make yourself a piper by profession; for if you do . . . you will become such a fine and delicate musician that all the petty pipers in the countryside will pick a quarrel with you and prevent you from getting custom. They will wish you ill and do you harm, for that's their way to prevent others from sharing their profits."[8] How could Baber, with her synesthesia, not respond to the character Sand has exclaim, "I know now that I am not crazy, and that there is a truth in what we hear within us, as there is in what we see."[9]

Sand's language makes visible the sounds of the wind and the brook just as Baber sought to make visible sounds she named in her titles—from drums to flute to songs—through her early poetry and then through the abstract shapes, colors, and patterns in her paintings, such as *The Ringing and the Ringing* (1964) (CP #29), *Swirl of Sounds: The Ghost in the Banyan Tree* (1976) (CP #43), and *Night Drum* (1977) (CP #45). We can see in Baber's poem from childhood that she referred to her own long black hair as "blown from the pipes of Pan." During the summer of 1940, when she turned twelve, Alice, still remarkably creative and sensitive, wrote this rather sophisticated poem:

> The wind blew all about me,
> As I sat on the hilltop there
> It ruffled the skirt of my long white gown,
> It tugged at my long black hair.
> In the distant hills was a little stream
> As turquoise blue as the sky.
> And the willow trees along it's bank,[10]
> With the wind seemed to wave and sigh
> Beyond the hills came the sunrise
> Shining with golden light,
> And the emerald grass beneath my feet,
> Was wet with dew of the night
> The glorious scene before my eyes,
> Was made by a marvelous hand
> And the wind as it tugged at my long black hair
> Was blown from the pipes of Pan.[11]

Here Baber evokes dawning light, skillfully weaving trimeter with tetrameter and telling rhymes that culminate with the god of pastoral poets, Pan. She makes a leitmotif of her own long black hair. Her early intrigue with the figure of Pan, who could make sounds or music from pipes, resonated in the many titles for paintings that she later created using the term "Piper." Baber had likely read *The Wind in the Willows*, Kenneth Grahame's 1908 novel for children, where Pan appears in chapter 7, "The Piper at the Gates of Dawn." The characters encounter haunting pipe music, from Pan, the Greek god of the wild, shepherds, and rustic music. Alternatively, it is possible that Baber could have discovered Pan in books on classical mythology for children.[12]

Sand's metaphors in *Les maîtres sonneurs* were ideas with which Baber could identify: travel represents a significant part of personal and artistic (musical in the novel) growth; travel symbolizes a search for identity, not just for artistic maturity. As in Sand's novel, travel leads to personal confidence, while it fails to cement personal intimate relationships. Sand's character suffers sickness resulting from the overzealousness of his travel, not unlike the result that eventually cost Baber a life tragically cut short.[13]

Yet, Baber relished that sense of otherness and escape that comes with foreign travel as well as running away from the disappointing defects of her domestic life, first with Jenkins, and then after their relationship floundered. In *Les maîtres sonneurs*, Sand looked at her male hero's arrogance that destroyed his attempt at reaching his artistic ideal.[14] Baber, too, would experience and eventually be compelled to reject Jenkins's arrogance and excesses. For her, Sand's writing became a kind of guidebook filled with feminist insights.

Baber shared her interest in the writings of George Sand with many women artists of her day. Grace Hartigan, aware of bias against women artists, exhibited in New York at the Tibor de Nagy Gallery from

1951 through 1954 under the pseudonym "George Hartigan," which she later said was in honor of the women novelists George Eliot and George Sand.[15]

Baber's love of poetry and fiction encouraged her to show her paintings for the first time in a solo show in Paris, held at Le Mistral bookshop, located at 37 Rue de la Bûcherie, in the 5th arrondissement, which she described as "a bookstore for the writers" that originally opened in 1951.[16] George Whitman, the owner, changed the shop's name to Shakespeare and Company in 1964, honoring both Sylvia Beach's original store and the 400th anniversary of the birth of William Shakespeare.

Next, Baber had a solo show in Paris from January 18 to February 14, 1963 at La Galerie de la Librairie Anglaise (The Gallery of the English Bookshop) at 42 Rue de Seine.[17] Baber recalled: "It wasn't a big show, but as always I put in as many paintings as I could and I had a brochure."[18] The bilingual brochure included statements by Keith Sutton, an English artist who had recently become friends with Baber and Jenkins in Paris, and the American poet and critic John Ashbery.

Sutton wrote: "Such visual modesty and honesty has made a personal art without involving the viewer in a private history. . . . It is as if the artist painted them as a 'singing voice' to create lyrical setting of states of mind, moving, fluid states that pass on or are repeated in variations of rhythm and pace of cloud shadows moving across a landscape."[19] One notices the suggestion that revealing "a private history" was undesirable. Perhaps this taboo reflects political self-censorship during the Cold War, while abstract content could offend no one.

Ashbery noted, "The poetic possibilities of the colors are allowed to grow up normally without interference from the painter, the result being a curiously sharp climate that takes possession of you gradually, and educates you to find perfectly natural all kinds of intervals which would have seemed precarious a moment ago."[20]

Baber's show received a review from "J. M." in *Le Monde*, which, to her satisfaction, described her use of color: "A weightless palette, vapor that flies away like a cloud, bursts on the surface of the painting in blue, violette, orange, green bubbles. . . . Alice Baber walks on clouds with disconcerting ease . . . a total naïve joy in color."[21]

A few days later, Baber received a positive mention from John Ashbery, for "the first show of the American Alice Baber," published in Paris in the *New York Herald-Tribune*: "She uses a richly varied palette of cold colors in abstract paintings whose volumes suggest fruit, rolling landscapes, or clouds. She is one of the most gifted and ingratiating abstract painters to show up in Paris this season."[22] If anyone objected that this capsule "review" was written by the author of the artist's catalogue text, it went unrecorded. Baber also had her Paris show listed in *The Village Voice* in New York, which described her as an "expatriate and member of the New York School."[23] Highly motivated, Baber later explained her personal approach to surviving in the art world: "I did all the things that one has to do. I've never felt that one should wait for the 'big things' before making a move."[24]

Before her solo show in Paris, Baber had participated in a four-person show at Karl Flinker's Paris gallery in 1962, which also included Jenkins, Robert Motherwell, and the late Wassily Kandinsky. Flinker was an interesting figure in the Parisian art world. Arriving from Vienna in 1938, with his father, Martin, who was a Jewish librarian, author, publisher, and literary critic, Karl had fled the Nazi annexation of Austria when he was just fourteen, only to have to flee the Nazi occupation of Paris a few years later. After the war, both father and son, who lost the rest of their family, settled in Paris, and became active in intellectual circles of writers, philosophers, and artists. Karl opened his gallery in 1960 and showed important modernists including, among others, František Kupka, Paul Klee, Wassily Kandinsky, and Jean Hélion.

Flinker, after being introduced to Jenkins by the American painter Norman Bluhm, gave Jenkins a solo show at his Galerie Karl Flinker in 1961, accompanied by a catalogue text by James Jones.[25] In 1963 this same gallery presented a second solo show, *Paul Jenkins: Peintures recentes* [Recent Paintings]. It is not known how Jenkins then felt about having Baber showing at his own gallery, but with her own long-standing engagement with literature and her abstract art, she fit right in.

When Tom Hess, the editor of *Artnews*, corresponded with Jenkins on January 23, 1963, he took the trouble to write, "Tell Alice I've lit several candles for her exhibition—I've always remembered a big beautiful still life she showed in the first March Gallery exhibition."[26]

The couple's linked identity was emphasized on February 28, 1963, when the USIS in London issued a press release that announced AMERICAN ARTISTS TO ATTEND ONE-MAN SHOWS IN LONDON. Baber and Jenkins were described as "two American artists who live in Paris for much of the year will be in London for exhibitions of their work opening here early in March. Alice Baber will hold her first one-man show in London at the New Vision Centre Gallery, 4, Seymour Place, Marble Arch, W. 1. From March 7 and paintings by Paul Jenkins will be on view at Arthur Tooth & Sons. . . . This will be his second one-man show in London."[27]

Keith Sutton's statement from Baber's Paris show at *La Galerie de la Librairie Anglaise* was reprinted for the London catalogue. The statement praised "The simplicity and directness of Baber's paintings" and proclaimed "conviction without being naïve."[28] Beyond Sutton's evocation of Baber's emphasis on linking color to sound and movement, the catalogue also included a formal analysis by the painter and critic Natalie Edgar, who was also Baber's close friend: "Like Genii escaping their concrete confinement, spots of color come leaping out from a solid ground of luminous white in Alice Baber's paintings. . . . The only totality is the state of feeling of the whole painting . . . the experience of the paintings is one of release and expansion of the spirit . . . but well grounded in reality."[29]

Conroy Maddox, reviewing the London show for *The Arts Review*, wrote of Baber, praising her "deceptively poetic sensibility": "She is an artist who has narrowed her form, but not the depth of her feelings, and feeling is everything in her work."[30] The next issue of this publication reproduced an example of Baber's work from the London show, an abstract canvas called *Kingdom of Daylight* (1962–63).[31] The New Vision Centre Gallery was sufficiently pleased that it also included Baber in a group show it sent to Galerie Wirth Berlin in August 1964.[32]

Following their London shows, both Baber and Jenkins were included in a 1963 show called *Modern American Painting* held at the Aberystwyth Arts Festival in Wales. They showed with other well-known abstract artists, including Norman Bluhm, Richard Diebenkorn, Sam Francis, Helen Frankenthaler, Michael Goldberg, Al Held, Shirley Jaffe, Lee Krasner, Joan Mitchell, and Mark Tobey. This show, however, was divided between adherents of abstract art and the new representational style, pop art, represented by Jim Dine, Roy Lichtenstein, Claes Oldenburg, and Andy Warhol. Baber showed three canvases: *Yellow Sentence Suspended Paris* (1961), *Not Quite* (1962), and *Way Over There* (1962). Jenkins also showed three works, while some artists showed only one or two works.[33]

Baber's recent success in the art world did not yet register as financial success. She was still dependent on her father's support, even though his promise of support if she quit her regular day job forced him to live very modestly and to neglect his other daughter and her family. In 1963 Adin continued to give his daughter funds to pay for rent for her studios in two cities and other art-related expenses.[34]

Baber's canvas *Where They Meet* (CP #22) is inscribed on the overlap "Summer Paris 1963." Its bright yet soft palette is closely related to that of *Just Arrived* (CP #21) from the previous year. Her adaptable title could easily refer to the congregation of American artists who gathered at the Aberystwyth Arts Festival. The artists who attended not only met physically, but the divergent trends in contemporary art from abstraction to pop art were also shown together.

Despite the couple's many successes, Baber felt distanced from the European artistic cohort: "We were always the étranger [foreigner], there's no doubt about it. And the international art world there is very amusing, but you know that you're never part of, the sort of the French scene [because] the French scene is itself basically the bourgeois family life . . . So one always feels in many ways a kind of marvelous sense that you're outside of the society."[35] "I think that this has always been the advantage of being in the so-called international world in Paris. And when I went," she recalled, "I suppose there was probably an advantage in the fact that American art had achieved some recognition because possibly we were reported to respect that you know, that at least we'd come of age in America, or something like that."[36] Baber referred to the ongoing international attention paid to abstract expressionism.

Baber and Jenkins planned their annual stay in New York to begin in late autumn 1963. On September 30, 1963, Paul wrote to Ernestine Lassaw to ask if she could help them arrange to get access to Elaine de Kooning's New York studio, which they hoped to rent for the three months that she planned to be away. He explained that he and Alice expected to arrive in the middle of November after Elaine had left, so wondered if she could leave the key along with any necessary instructions with Ernestine. In typical Jenkins fashion, he not only thanks Ernestine, but he reminds her that he will soon be taking her out for lunch.[37]

Baber returned to the United States triumphant. Her hometown was extremely proud of her accomplishments, which prompted the Paris, Illinois, *Beacon-News* to proclaim on November 20, 1963: PAINTINGS BY ALICE BABER WIN ACCLAIM AT ONE WOMAN SHOW IN NEW YORK. The subtitle made another Illinois connection: ARTICLE WRITTEN BY JAMES JONES PAYS TRIBUTE TO TALENT SHOWN ON CANVAS. The article, written by Baber's childhood friend, Mary Ann Morris Tucker, began: "Two impressive experiences within the past month have accorded increased dimensions to the international reputation of a young artist from Kansas in Edgar County." Readers learned that Alice Baber was the daughter of Adin Baber of Kansas, that she had just concluded a successful "one woman" show in New York at the A. M. Sachs Gallery, that the Smithsonian Institution had just acquired her painting, and that she was the subject of an article by James Jones (who came from Robinson, Illinois) in the current issue of *Studio International* published in London. We learn that the painter and the writer, who both came from small towns in southeastern Illinois, met in Paris.[38]

Baber and Jenkins returned to New York from Paris on November 27, 1963, where they had arranged to rent Elaine de Kooning's studio at 827 Broadway while she was away. The couple celebrated all their good news on Thanksgiving Day in 1963 while staying with the Lassaws at their East Hampton home. Ernestine's datebook records her preparation for the holiday, baking pies, yams, and making the dressing for the turkey.[39] The next day, Thursday November 28, the Lassaws met the train, picking up Alice and Paul and Irving and Lucy Sandler. They all had drinks at Bill de Kooning's home then the dinner took place at the home of the artist Wilfrid Zogbaum and his wife Marta. Ernestine recorded that Saul Steinberg and Bill de Kooning were drunk.[40] But by November 30, de Kooning was sober enough to entertain a studio visit for their guests, which they followed with drinks at the home of

Jim and Charlotte Brooks and a party at the Lassaws', who drove their guests to catch the bus back to the city the next day.

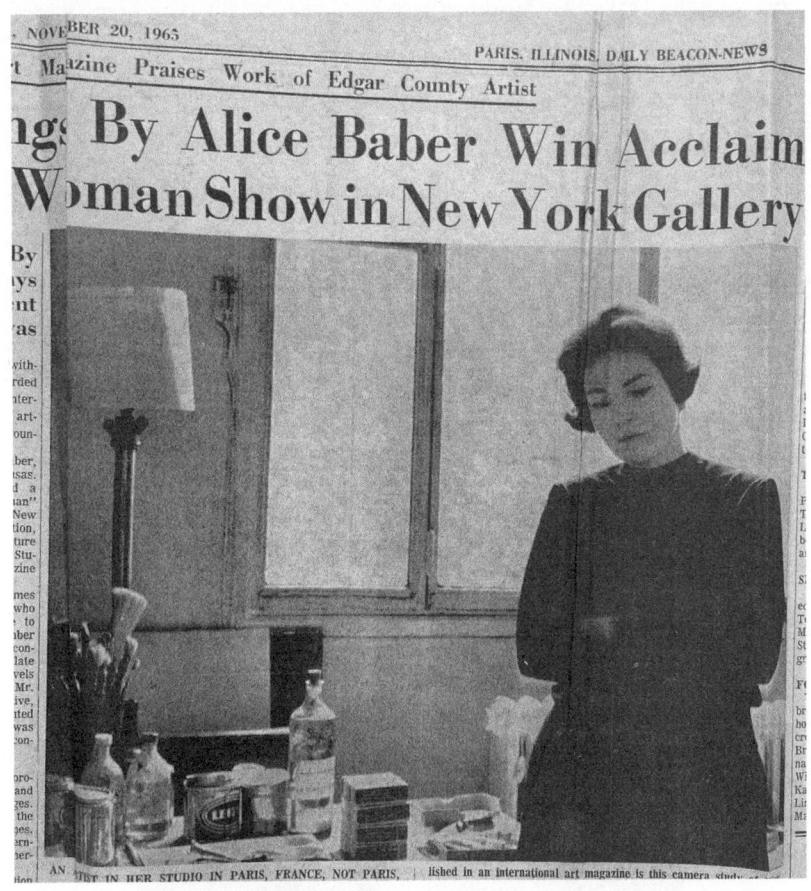

NOVEMBER 20, 1965

PARIS. ILLINOIS, DAILY BEACON-NEWS

Magazine Praises Work of Edgar County Artist

ngs By Alice Baber Win Acclaim
Woman Show in New York Gallery

AN ARTIST IN HER STUDIO IN PARIS, FRANCE, NOT PARIS, lished in an international art magazine is this camera study

Photograph by Marianne Adelmann.

The Lassaws were like family to Baber and Jenkins. Alice's relationship to Paul was so well established that he had met and now corresponded with her father, Adin Baber, who was still living in the family farmhouse outside of Kansas, Illinois. For Christmas Day 1963, Adin traveled to New York to see Alice, who was evidently there without Paul, who was perhaps spending the day with his first wife and their daughter.

Adin, who appointed himself the Hanks family's genealogist, discovered in reading his Christmas mail that his cousin Bryan Hanks, of
Fort Worth, Texas, was also in New York visiting his daughter, Nancy
Hanks. After telephoning and meeting for breakfast, Bryan pressed
them to accept an invitation for Christmas dinner at Nancy's apartment.
Later, recounting the event, Adin spoke of meeting Nancy, as if for the
first time, at least as an adult: "As I looked at these two young women,
I noticed the similarity of them, the Hanks types, the high forehead,
the black eyebrows—Lincoln eyebrows, they have been called—and the
cheekbones and the faces—two beautiful young women."[41] Although this
appears to have been the first meeting of Nancy Hanks and Alice Baber as
adults, the two cousins bonded over their shared passion for the arts and
their fierce independence. At the time Hanks was working closely with
Nelson Rockefeller as the executive secretary of the Rockefeller Brothers
Fund's Special Studies Project.

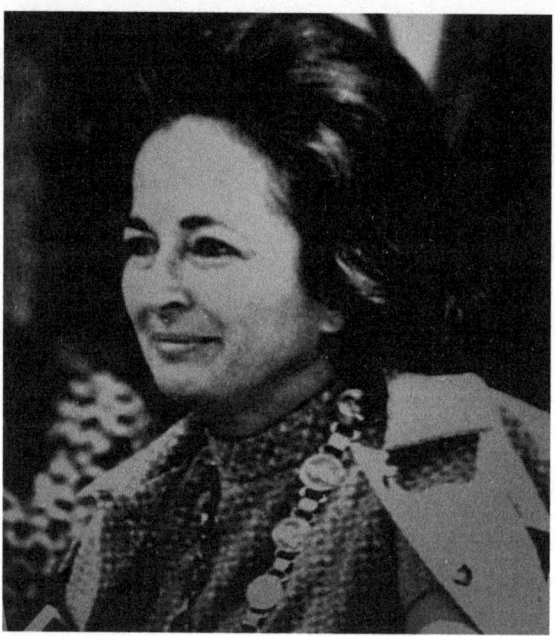

Getting to know Nancy Hanks, Adin always had in mind the earlier Nancy Hanks, their illustrious ancestor, Abraham Lincoln's mother. He also discussed this subject as he continued his correspondence with Paul Jenkins. On January 27, 1964, Paul wrote to tell Adin how pleased he was to meet him and hear about his ideas concerning Lincoln and his mother.[42] He also thanked Adin Baber for sending him an inscribed copy of his book. He praised Alice's painting, pointing out its strengths of color, atmosphere, and space. He added that he was amazed to see such an understanding of painting traditions, as well as her courage to venture into new areas: "It's perfectly understandable why you are so proud of her."[43] Adin responded to Paul: "The nicest thing that I read in your letter is that you say Alice has done a beautiful painting. This favorable criticism from a fine artist is very gratifying to her old 'pappy.'"[44]

Baber remained in New York, while Jenkins went ahead of her to Paris. What Baber wrote to Jenkins in Paris conveys the state of their relationship: "I was so happy to get your telegram today (Thurs. afternoon late). . . . I have missed you so much that I have slept away part of the time rather than getting much done."[45]

Baber reported going to see Paul's paintings on view at the Museum of Modern Art—*Phenomena Junction Red* (1963) and *Phenomena Yellow Strike* (1963–64)—which had both been acquired for the museum's permanent collection. Paul's paintings were featured that fall as two of seven acquisitions of abstract works "painted within the last five years."[46] The other artists featured were Morris Louis, Jules Olitski, Larry Poons, and Jack Tworkov. There was no question that Jenkins had attracted the right kind of influential patrons to serve as his paintings' donors, Mr. and Mrs. David Kluger, and thus received the recognition for which the younger Baber was still searching. Baber's response was completely supportive: "I think your painting looks beautiful."[47]

Baber also reported that her trip to the Museum of Modern Art was in the company of her friend Ann Alpert; Alice wrote to Paul that she and Ann had seen "not one soul we knew, but at least I saw most of it."[48] Baber did tell Jenkins that she had dinner in Chinatown with her old friends Philip Pavia and his wife, Natalie Edgar. Natalie remained a close friend who could be counted upon to serve as reference for her teaching applications. She also reviewed Baber's work in *Artnews* in 1969. Baber had known Philip from her early days at the Club, which he founded, and had recently tried writing about his sculpture. The group ran into Peter Grippe, the artist who first assured Baber that she could attend the panels at the Club. Peter, she tells Paul, "knew Dylan Thomas best," but "Philip said that he heard your speech was very fine."[49]

Baber referred to Jenkins's interest in the poet Dylan Thomas, who died at the Chelsea Hotel, which, coincidentally, had been Alice's first home in New York. For Jenkins, Thomas symbolized his pride in their shared Welsh ancestry. Earlier in 1964, Jenkins had donated to the National Museum of Wales a bust of Dylan Thomas, announced as crafted by the American sculptor David Slivka, who had been a good friend of the poet. According to Denise Lassaw, however, Slivka had telephoned her father to meet him at the mortuary to make the death mask of Dylan Thomas since, as Slivka knew, Ibram Lassaw had studied classical sculpture techniques and was experienced, having produced other death masks.[50] Some years later, Ibram told his daughter that Slivka had taken the plaster death mask that Lassaw had produced, opened the eyes, and added a bit of detailing. Then, with Paul Jenkins's help, he had this cast into bronze, attributed to him alone, and the donation was arranged.[51]

Jenkins's dedication of the bronze cast of Dylan Thomas happened with the help of the Welsh actor Richard Burton in a ceremony in Manhattan, which was later repeated in Cardiff for the presentation of Jenkins's donation to the National Museum of Wales.[52] The Manhattan ceremony, called "For Dylan Thomas," was held in New York at the Poetry Center of the YM-YWHA at 92nd Street, where the bust was accepted by Richard Burton and his father, Phillip, on behalf of the museum in Wales. Thomas's poetry was an enthusiasm that Baber had shared with Jenkins before they met.

Baber's interest in Thomas goes back to her days at college when she placed herself on a short list of admired poets that included Thomas, Gerard Manley Hopkins, George Orwell, and Edith Sitwell.[53] She must have appreciated Thomas for his inventive, rhythmic, and innovative use of words and imagery. Thomas's famous lines at his father's death, "Do not go gentle into that good night /Rage, rage against the dying of the light," must have resonated for Baber with her fixation on light.[54] In 1962 Baber created an abstract watercolor that she called *For Burton in Case*. Since she gave it to Jenkins, it appears to refer to his contact with Richard Burton to enlist him at the presentation of Jenkins's donation of the Dylan Thomas sculpture to the National Museum of Wales.

In the same letter in which she discussed the response to Jenkins at the Thomas program, Baber told him of her plans to spend the weekend in East Hampton with Irv and Lucy Sandler. Irving continued to support Jenkins's work, writing about it on several occasions, although he managed to ignore Baber's art. In fact, the Sandlers met Baber at Penn Station and they all left for a weekend at the Lassaws' in East Hampton.[55] Irving Sandler had also written about Ibram Lassaw's sculpture.

When Baber wrote to Jenkins that she would not be spending the weekend "alone, alone," she also mentioned a party given by the artist Buffie Johnson, so her social life was not exactly at a standstill. Just that day, a Thursday, she told of going to cocktail party given by the artist Ethel Fisher, where she said that she found another guest, the abstract expressionist Theodoros Stamos, "a bore."[56] From there she went on to another gathering of "lively" art collectors.

Baber then shifted to a discussion of Paul's dealer, Martha Jackson, who wanted her to invite her friends, the Slivkas, perceived as "rich collectors," to a gathering in June. Baber demurred, telling his dealer that Jackson already had a great list, and adds of the Slivkas: "They are our friends but not rich or collectors. So she said never mind."[57] Clearly Martha Jackson had confused hardworking poet and editor Rose Slivka and her sculptor husband David Slivka, who never had funds to spare, with another couple.

Before Baber closed her letter, she let Jenkins know that she had sent a check to pay for his daughter Hilarie's summer camp. According to Hilarie, she did not even meet Alice until she was around nine years old, long into the couple's relationship. She recalls Alice fondly, exclaiming, "She was a gem," and telling how Alice found her the perfect tutor when she was struggling with math.[58] She remembers that Alice visited her mother and herself, did puzzles with them, and how she brought them nice presents at Christmas.[59]

Baber ended her letter to Jenkins with a heartfelt message: "Now I want to tell you that I love you so much & all the rest is just to show you that I miss you and don't you go enjoying your freedom too much my darling. I'm glad you stayed with Jim & Gloria [Jones]. I hope nothing is too sad. Tell Karl [their shared dealer Karl Flinker] how much he means to me and then hurry back because I want to eat you up and tell you the story of the three bears. I have a new version. And then you could tell me your version of the 3 bears."[60] The intimacy of her letter alluding to the couple's pillow-talk fantasies suggests her enthusiasm. Yet, her warning to her lover that he not enjoy his "freedom too much" suggests her insecurity about his fidelity and her uncertainly about the durability of their relationship.

Then, just over two months before Baber's thirty-sixth birthday, on June 11, 1964, in New York, she received a Western Union telegram sent by Jenkins at 9:20 from Paris-Le Bourget Airport instructing her, "Pack a small bag STOP We are going to get married STOP Decide where STOP Love you STOP Leap before you look STOP Call you when arrive STOP Our secret STOP Paul."[61] It's clear that they had discussed marriage during the years that they had been living together since he did not need to wait for her reply.

Baber married Paul Jenkins in a civil ceremony performed by a justice of the peace on June 16, 1964, in New Haven, Connecticut. Divorced with one daughter, Jenkins married for the second time, but it was Baber's first and only marriage.[62] Alice's father, Adin, sent out a formal engraved wedding announcement. Among the recipients was Alice's friend, the artist Ethel Fisher.[63] Alice's father sent a handwritten note to her new husband on June 23, just a week after their marriage: "Paul: You have married a very sensitive person; be kind to her. I expect you and she to help one another; the Brownings did so in their poetry. Your wish that Alice should write to me before you do gives me confidence that you have discernment above the ordinary—that was the right thing to do. I am Sincerely Adin."[64] By calling Alice "a very sensitive person," Baber's father perhaps referred to the anxiety that his youngest daughter sometimes suffered, which scientists now know is often related to synesthesia.

About Jenkins, Baber commented, "What I've enjoyed most is being able to talk about art with Paul. Because he's extremely good about thinking about it and so forth. So, I think in those terms of revelations about art that it's extremely helpful to be around people who have an affinity with your own work."[65] At the time of their marriage, both artists were already accomplished; however, Jenkins had had his solo show in 1956 with Martha Jackson at her leading New York gallery, just three years after its founding in a brownstone on East 66th Street in Manhattan. Jackson's gallery then featured an international roster of artists, including Henry Moore, Antoni Tàpies, Alan Davie, Philip Pavia, Louise Nevelson, and Sam Francis. In contrast, Baber's 1958 show had taken place at the much more modest March Gallery, the artist-run co-op she helped to found.

The Martha Jackson Gallery representation added to Jenkins's confidence. He continued to correspond with Baber's father. On August 11, 1964, he wrote to Adin, reporting to him on the recent progress that Alice had made in her career. He told how her paintings had been accepted for the art collections at New York University and the Worcester Art Museum in Massachusetts. He took credit for having helped Alice, even as he credited her father for having helped his daughter.[66] He went on to pay tribute to Adin Baber, pointing out how artists have always needed help, from Van Gogh, who had his art-dealer brother, to Cézanne's father to Robert Browning's family, adding "if anyone has fostered a strong sense of art in his daughter it has been you."[67]

Jenkins's letter documents how Alice felt about literature and discovering that her parents had saved her juvenile poems, suggesting the value of her father's having fostered her imagination, her love of books, and her pride in him. He made clear how happy Alice was to hear the news that he had saved her early poems.[68]

Jenkins then revealed how he viewed his wife's lack of self-confidence as a writer and himself as promoting her, opining that Alice was too self-critical. He admitted to being impressed by the first article that Alice had written for publication, which was about Philip Pavia, the sculptor and her friend since her days at the Artists' Club. He reflected that he was not sure which journal she should publish in, but promised to help find the best venue. It does not, however, look as if the article was ever published.[69]

Jenkins concluded this letter to his new father-in-law with a confident flattery, telling him how proud he was that Alice had him for a father and how much pride he felt to be part of the Baber family by marriage.[70] Although we cannot know how sincere the sentiments that Jenkins expressed were, his effort would seem to indicate his desire for success in his second marriage.

Around this time, Baber sent her father an undated letter, letting him know that she planned "to keep my name professionally." She then discussed her financial situation, telling her father how she was "grateful" for the money that he had been giving her to support her professional expenses. She wrote that "Paul has a small income and has had some luck this last year or two but he uses much of it on being sure that things are done even in a good gallery they usually don't give brochures to artists."[71] She assures her father that Paul, now her husband, can provide her with "food, clothing and shelter," but to keep her two studios (in New York and in Paris) would still require her father's help. While she told her father that she hoped for sales of her art, she explained that at the early stage of her career, she needed to keep her prices low.

Some years later, a 1972 letter from Adin Baber to Alice's sister Nancy addresses the inequity of what he had given to his two children. He promises Nancy to make up the difference to her, which he estimated at approximated $5,000 a year. In 2024 prices, Alice was getting about $50,000 annually.[72] Adin Baber managed to afford to offer Alice this subsidy in a good year by living frugally on just his social security, which allowed him to share the income from tenant farmers who worked his land. His income, however, was not stable and all but disappeared in a "dry" year.

Meanwhile, we know that Baber and Jenkins cut quite a glamorous figure when going out socializing together. Jenkins was very concerned with his appearance; he traded his art in Paris with the designer Pierre Cardin, receiving elegant clothes for himself in exchange.[73]

The Lassaws' daybook reports the two couples dropped by a party at Clement Greenberg's home on February 18, 1964, but since the Lassaws had not been invited, Greenberg sent them away and the four went out for Chinese dinner instead of mixing with Greenberg's other guests.[74]

This encounter took place not long after Greenberg had alienated many artists with his 1962 article "After Abstract Expressionism." Many considered him an elitist dictator for his rejection of postmodern movements such as pop art.[75] Greenberg had rejected the Leftist politics of earlier American artists to favor and promote pure aestheticism or art for art's sake instead. His formalist view was compatible enough for abstract artists like Paul Jenkins and Alice Baber, who focused on issues like light and color.

Years later, when Jenkins's obituary was published in the UK newspaper *The Guardian*, it offered an evaluation of Greenberg's actions toward the painter he once befriended: "Greenberg himself never damned Jenkins, commenting that he and Frankenthaler were special cases, but never again in the four volumes of Greenberg's collected writings did he mention Jenkins, though he wrote fully about Frankenthaler."[76]

Once married, Jenkins and Baber remained a high-profile and attractive couple. But their preferred time together was visiting with their old friends. They spent the Fourth of July weekend with the Lassaws.[77] We know from Ernestine's daybook that they spent time with the Lassaws again on September 2, 1964. When in Paris, however, Baber and Jenkins missed close friends like the Lassaws, although they saw a lot of James and Gloria Jones.

In their shared enjoyment of social interaction and their passion for learning about the art of other cultures, Baber and Jenkins were well suited. Now married and confident as a couple, they would plan a major collaboration and a journey halfway around the world.

CHAPTER 9

First Adventures in Asia
(1964–1965)

Alice Baber and Paul Jenkins shared so many enthusiasms and pursuits that it is easy to imagine their compatibility. Although Baber and Jenkins each loved Japanese art, as someone with an adventurous spirit for travel, Baber had few equals. After their first trip to Asia in 1964, Baber wrote, "Three years ago we went around the world, and I am packed and ready to go at any time again."[1] The impetus for their travel to Asia came from Japan. It was at the Martha Jackson Gallery, Jenkins's own New York gallery, where the group of Japanese contemporary artists known as Gutai had shown in 1958.

Gutai was an avant-garde movement founded by young artists in 1954, which became internationally known for their experimental forms that combined abstract painting with performance and installation. They sought radical new means of expression. Jenkins had first heard from his friend, Michel Tapié, about the critic's travel to Japan to arrange the Gutai's first show at the Martha Jackson Gallery.[2] All this took place in Paris in 1957, before Jenkins's solo show at Galerie Stadler held that spring.[3]

At the time of the Gutai's 1958 show at the Martha Jackson Gallery, Jiro Yoshihara, the movement's cofounder, invited Jenkins to work with Gutai in Osaka, but Jenkins postponed accepting the invitation, perhaps responding to the negative press that the first Gutai show received in New York from critics who yearned for something more traditionally Japanese.[4] Then in the autumn of 1964, Jenkins, surely encouraged by Baber's enthusiasm for foreign travel, arranged to participate with her in a two-person show of small-sized works, as artists in residence at the Pinacotheca, the Gutai's newly established museum space in Osaka. Jenkins recalled in an interview with Colette Roberts that he and Baber were given two small rooms for their shows and that the Gutai group showed miniature paintings at the same time.[5] Since this interview took place on January 11, 1968, before his marriage to Alice Baber fell apart, he was still willing to acknowledge her presence and collaboration. Eventually, her name would be omitted from his version of the story.

The Japanese American artist Matsumi Kanemitsu who, with Baber, was a founding member of the March Gallery in New York, recalled, "In 1964, Paul Jenkins and Paul Jenkins's wife, Alice Baber, my wife Carol and I all went to Japan together."[6] Kanemitsu told an interviewer that when they were both in New York, "I see Paul practically every day, and he go back and forth to Paris and New York. And every time he come back to New York, we get together, almost every day. And we have very close friendship, so naturally, I know more about Paul Jenkins than what Paul Jenkins know himself, you know. And probably vice versa. He know me a lot. And I really respect Paul, his energy. This man really had energy."[7]

Although Kanemitsu was in awe of Jenkins, he barely mentioned Baber, perhaps because he did not take women seriously as artists. He would not be the first man with such a bias, even if it were an unconscious one. Another possibility is that by the time of the 1976 interview, Jenkins had divorced, and his ex-wife, Baber, was not to be mentioned.

Jenkins spent time working with Gutai members, visiting their studios. A work by Sadamasa Motonaga in Jenkins's collection is inscribed, "Nice meeting with Mr. Paul Jenkins at my studio on the 13th Nov. '64."[8] Motonaga was a visual artist and book illustrator, and a first-generation member of Gutai.

In his narrative about the trip to Japan that he took with Jenkins, Kanemitsu mentioned that the California art critic Jules Langsner was often part of their group since he was then in Tokyo on a Ford Foundation grant. Kanemitsu recalled serving as a kind of interpreter for his American friends. Langsner, he recalled, liked to tell the story about his youth when he was in high school in Los Angeles with Philip Guston, Reuben Kadish, and Jackson Pollock, the three future abstract expressionist artists.[9] This would have been of interest to Jenkins and Baber, both of whom had met Pollock. Baber's first art teacher in college had also studied with Guston.

Kanemitsu's admiration of Jenkins would not have escaped the Gutai artists. He insisted that Paul really understood "society, you know, jet-setters, and all these people. It was very important to him. I guess for every artist, it's very important to get to know these people, high-society people. But somehow Paul have [that] kind of personality that high-society people accept him immediately. And same kind of personality Andy Warhol had."[10]

Kanemitsu did make some insightful observations about Jenkins: "Well, Paul, I never see him in a church, but, you see, I think his grandfather [actually his great-uncle] was a preacher. So he have that kind of religious background. Then, also, before he become a painter, he want to be an actor, so he have acting training." He explained how he loved to listen to Jenkins talk and found him fascinating: "And I say, gee, I wish I can talk like Paul," concluding, "Paul is interesting person, that he always talk [about] other people very good—even he dislike the person, he always say nice thing about him, or nice thing about her. And I guess that some people, that's why they were suspicious about him."[11] Jenkins's training from his "preacher" great-uncle, combined with his acting lessons, might have seemed to some competitors like a dangerous combination.

Just before their visit to Osaka, Jenkins had a solo show of his work open at the Tokyo Gallery in the Japanese capital. He and Baber stayed at the International House of Japan, a cultural center cofounded by John D. Rockefeller III and Shigeharu Matsumoto, a noted internationalist, intended to lead "to building a free, open, and sustainable future through intellectual dialogue, policy research, and cultural exchange with a diverse world."[12] Jenkins recalled that the dancer Merce Cunningham was also then in Japan and that they saw a lot of him because they all stayed at the International House and then Cunningham performed in Osaka, where they had their show.[13]

While in Tokyo in 1964, Baber is known to have produced at least two small collages. Both are watercolors on paperboard with collaged elements, each measuring only 10 ½ x 9 ½ inches. When Jenkins and Baber spent some of their time making art instead of sightseeing, Baber turned to collage, which although not her usual medium, allowed her to employ such materials she had at hand.

She called one extant collage *Across the Wide, Tokyo* (CP #23). Its prominent circle might refer to the globe, since it appears to relate to her first time traversing the Pacific Ocean to visit Asia. Baber recalled, "We were very much at home in Japan because we both had looked at, studied & loved Japanese art for many years."[14] The second work produced at the same time as *Across the Wide, Tokyo*, also a collage and watercolor, is known as *Shakespeare Used It*, an unusual reference by Baber to the Bard (CP #23).

What Baber intended by "Shakespeare Used It" is open to interpretation; however, there are well-known expressions that Shakespeare, used such as "sea change," "green-eyed monster," and "love is blind." While Chaucer used the phrase "love is blind" in his *Merchant's Tale* in 1405—before Shakespeare—the dramatist used it in several of his plays, including *Two Gentlemen of Verona*, *Henry V*, and *The Merchant of Venice*; it's still a popular expression in use today.

People are thought to fall in love unwisely with inappropriate partners, whose faults they ignore. If this particular famous phrase dawned on Baber in Japan, it could be because she was experiencing stress from being marginalized both from the vantage of gender bias in a society that was late to recognize women's achievements and as a result of collaborating closely with her new husband, whom she had to recognize was driven by an enormous male ego and his singular focus on his own fame. Or she could have been responding to his alcoholism, which might have been exaggerated in Japan. Following their trip, in July 1965, the Gutai artist Toshio Yoshida wrote to them from Osaka, "I sometimes drink bourbon wisky [*sic*] to recall you to my mind."[15] A year earlier, Jenkins had written to his friend and editor Tom Hess, telling him that he had managed to endure the sixty miles by car riding through the rough Indian landscape to see the Ajanta Caves: "I kept my trusty bottle of Old Grandad by my side most of the way and all the time we were in India we were almost too healthy. That Grand bourbon will kill anything."[16] As late as 1973, Jenkins was featured in a Japanese commercial for Kirin Seagram's Whiskey.[17]

While Baber did not show with Jenkins in Tokyo, the couple showed together in Osaka. As for their reception, Jenkins was the star attraction, while Baber was barely mentioned. A caption for a photograph of Jenkins alone read: "Paul Jenkins at work: Avant-garde artist Paul Jenkins from New York City, accompanied by his artist wife Alice Baber, stays at his old friend Jiro Yoshihara's home in Osaka, where he immediately went to work putting off Kyoto-Nara tours."[18] Jenkins remembered, however, that Mr. Yoshihara took them to Nara and, "thanks to Alice," saw to it that they visited the Ise Jingu, which are two of the most important Shinto shrines in Japan.[19] Dedicated to the Japanese sun goddess Amaterasu and surrounded by ancient forests, every twenty years these shrines are rebuilt in the traditional architectural style to convey spiritual renewal. Baber and Jenkins also visited the great bronze Buddha at Kamakura, which Jenkins recalled for its monumentality and natural setting.

In a group photograph of Baber with Jenkins and others in Japan, she looks unusually unhappy, even glum. Taken on November 29, 1964, this photograph shows Baber and Jenkins at the exhibition in Osaka, together with the Gutai artist Jiro Yoshihara and William S. Lieberman, then a curator at the Museum of Modern Art in New York, said to be attending for "research."[20] While Jenkins was already represented in the permanent collection at MoMA, Baber was not yet in the museum's collection. Now she certainly had come to Lieberman's attention by exhibiting with the Gutai in Japan.

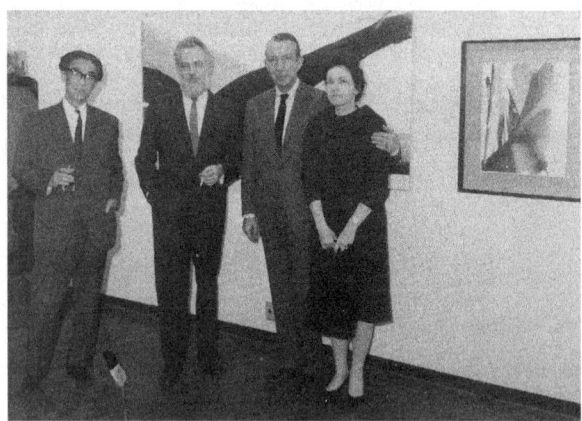

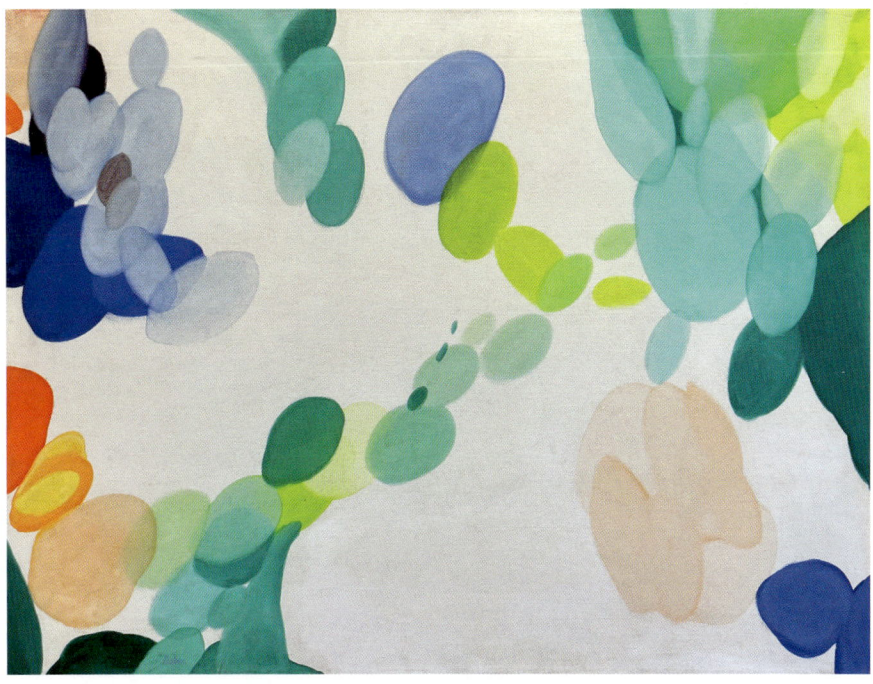

Alice Baber, *Wayward Swing*, 1969,
oil on canvas, 30 x 40 inches,
courtesy Judy Ferrara Fine Art,
Three Oaks, MI.

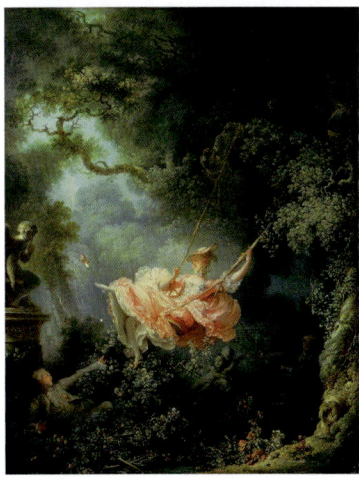

Jean-Honoré Fragonard, *The Swing*, 1767,
oil on canvas, Wallace Collection, London,
reproduced in Rockwell Kent's *World Famous
Paintings*, 1939, owned by Alice Baber.

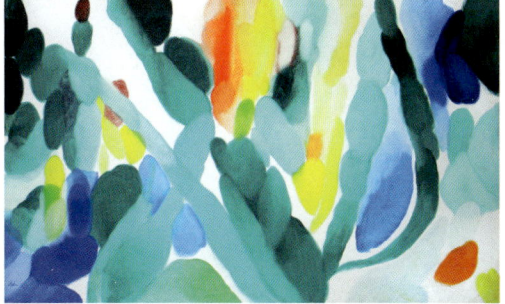

Alice Baber, *Green Swing*, 1966,
oil on canvas, 39 ½ x 65 ½ inches,
Art in Embassies Collection,
Washington, DC.

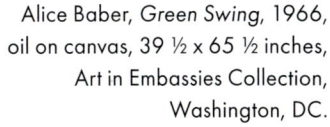

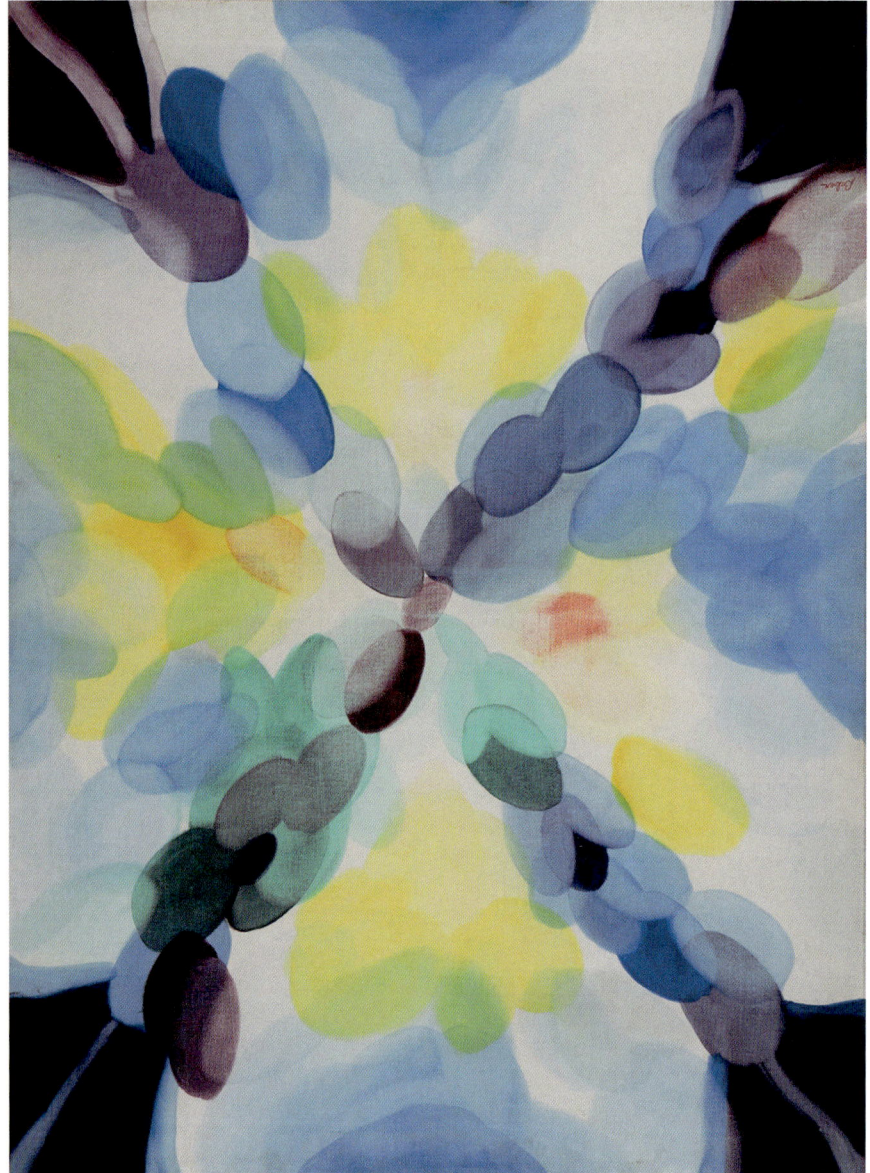

Alice Baber, *Floating Crossing*, 1970, oil on canvas, 40 x 30 inches,
Guild Hall Museum, East Hampton, NY, gift of the Estate of Alice Baber.

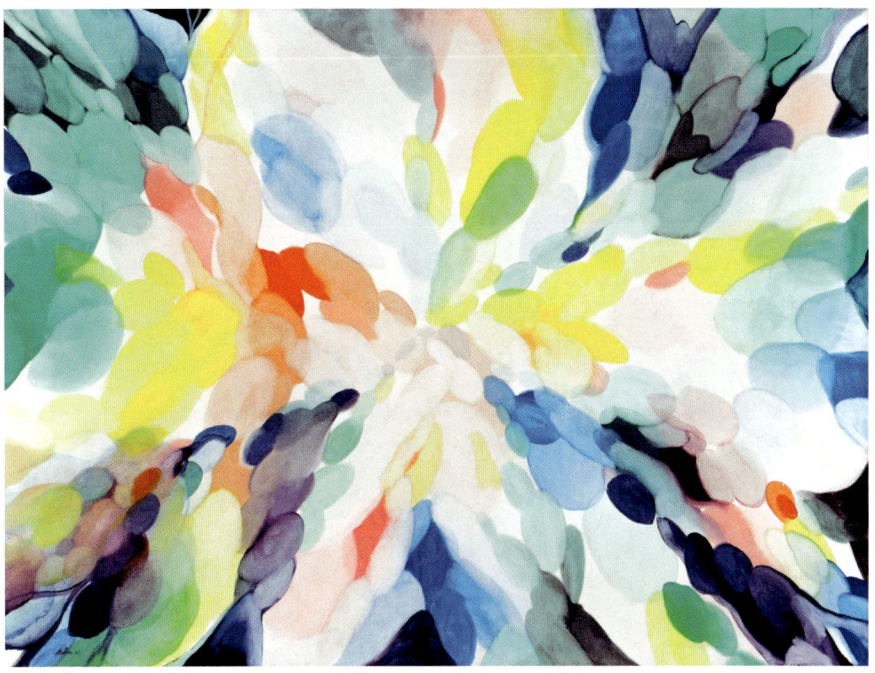

Alice Baber, *Wheel of Day*, 1971, oil on canvas, 58 ¾ x 79 ½ inches,
Santa Barbara Museum of Art, CA, gift of the Artist to the Ala Story Collection.

"Ambiguity is important to me. Recently I discussed
ambiguity with a painter friend. We discussed the circle,
a form that we both use. The circle is a wheel, a wheel
is a clock, is an apple, is an eye, is a sun, is a moon, etc."
—Alice Baber, 1976

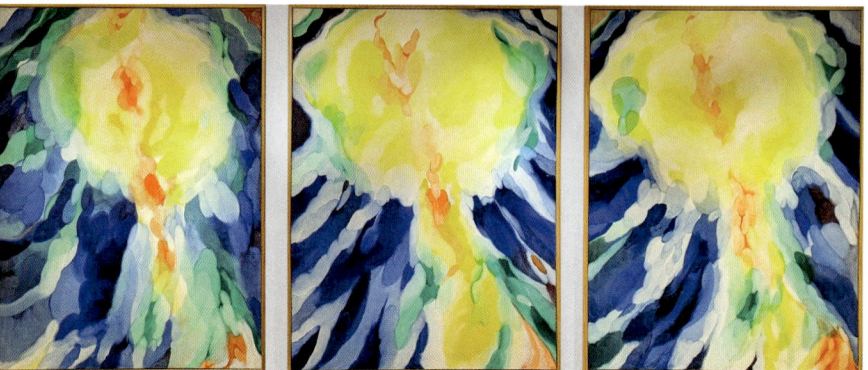

Alice Baber, *Expulsion of the Mythical Kings*, triptych, 1972, oil on canvas, 3 panels, each 77 x 58 inches, overall 77 x 174 inches, Greater Lafayette Museum of Art, IN.

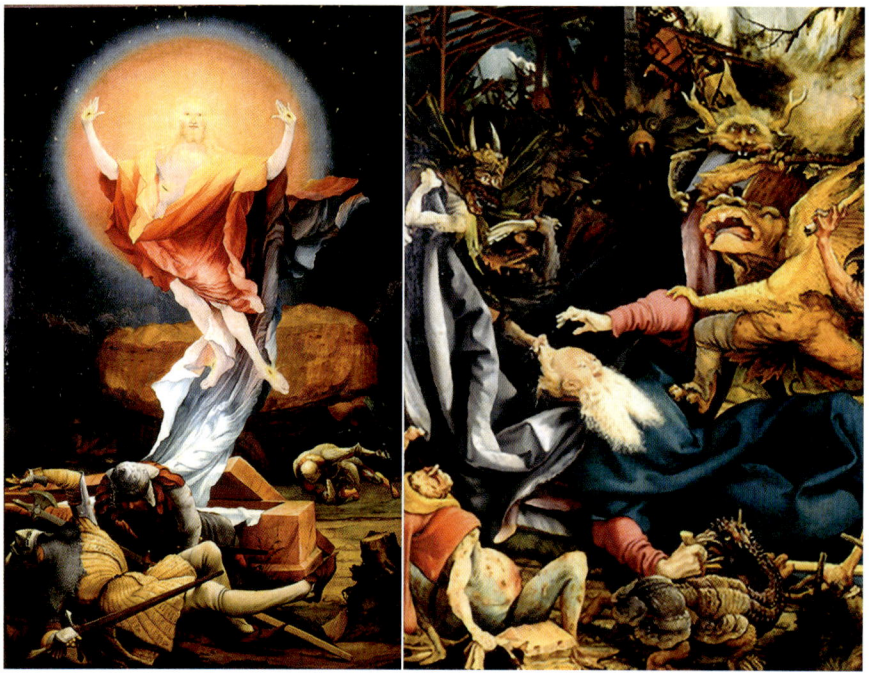

Matthias Grünewald, two details from the *Isenheim Altarpiece*, 1516:
Christ's Resurrection and *St. Anthony with skin affliction*, Colmar, France.

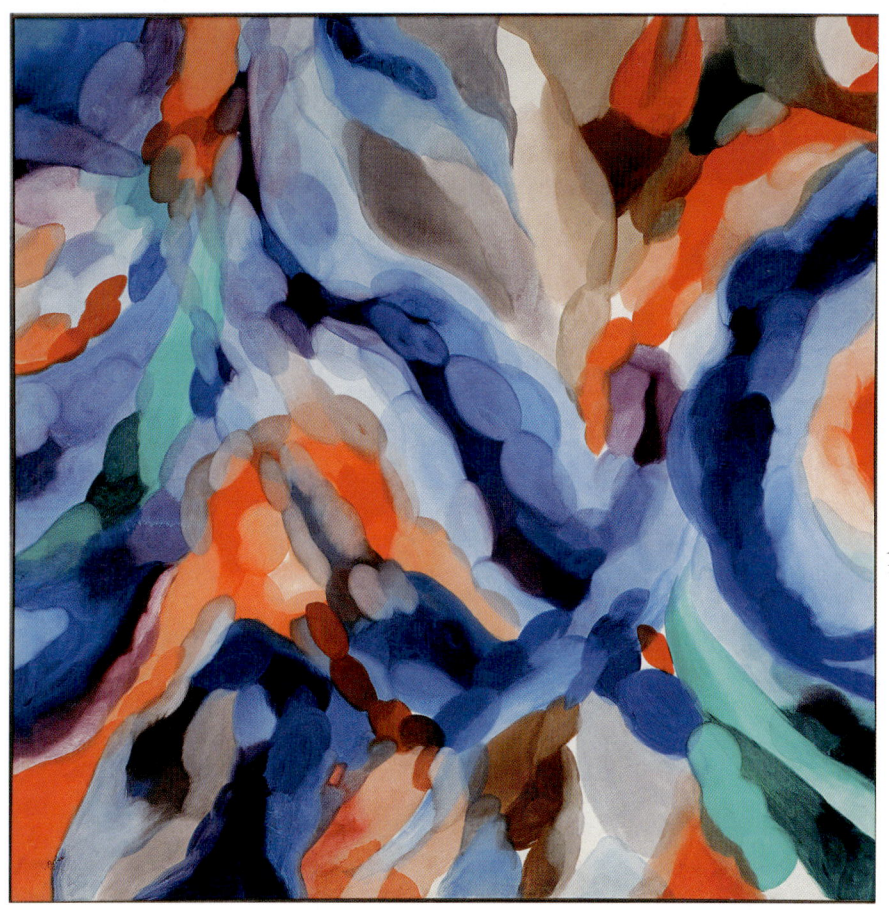

Alice Baber, *Wind Divided Mist the Darker*, 1972, oil on canvas, 80 x 80 inches, private collection.

COLOR PLATE 38

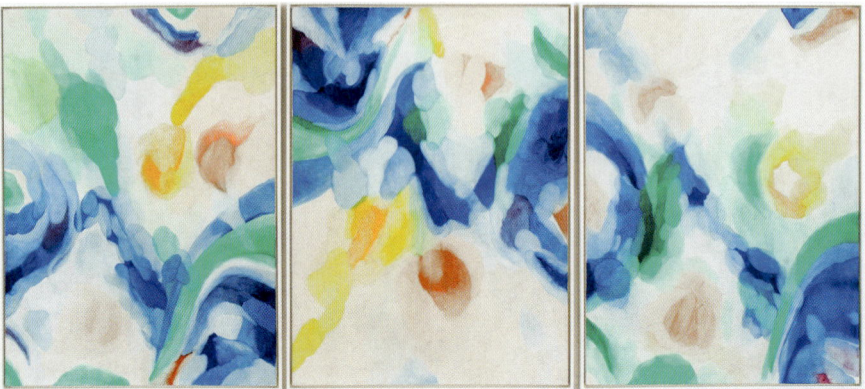

Alice Baber, *Dervishes Before the Palace*, triptych, 1972, oil on canvas, 77 x 174 inches, courtesy Berry Campbell Gallery, NY.

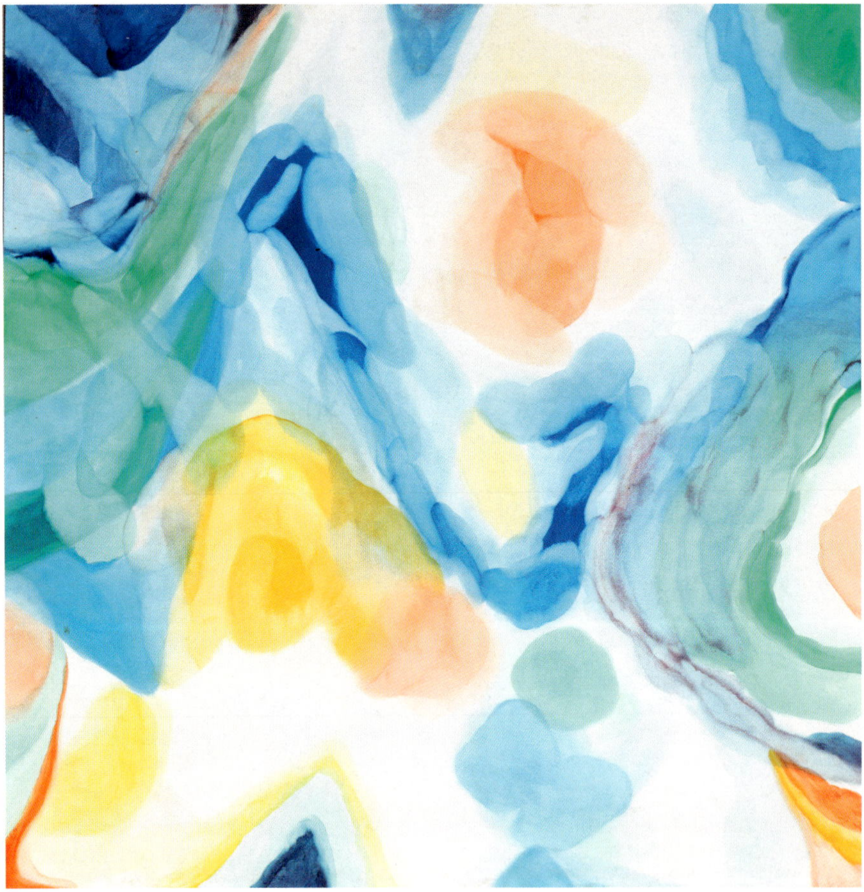

Alice Baber, *Lavender Ladder Turning-Akbar's Hunt*, 1972, oil on canvas, 80 x 80 inches, Whitney Museum of American Art, NY, gift of Richard Galef.

Alice Baber,
Path to the Ladder, 1972,
oil on canvas, 24 x18 inches,
private collection.

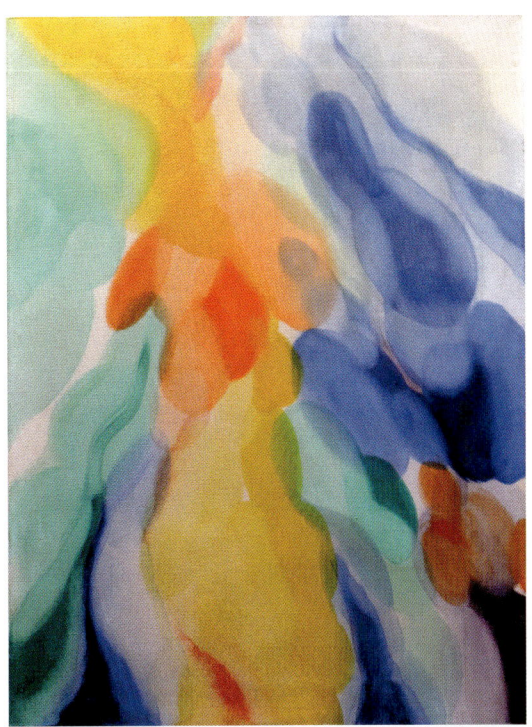

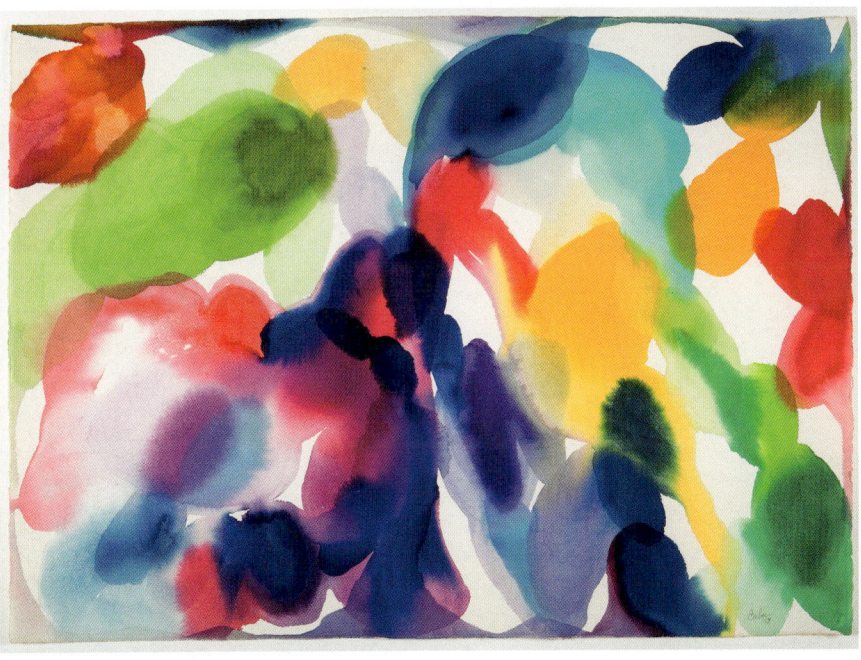

Alice Baber, *Green Dervish Turns to Blue*, 1973, watercolor on white wove paper,
29 1/8 x 41 ½ inches, Worcester Art Museum, Worcester, MA.

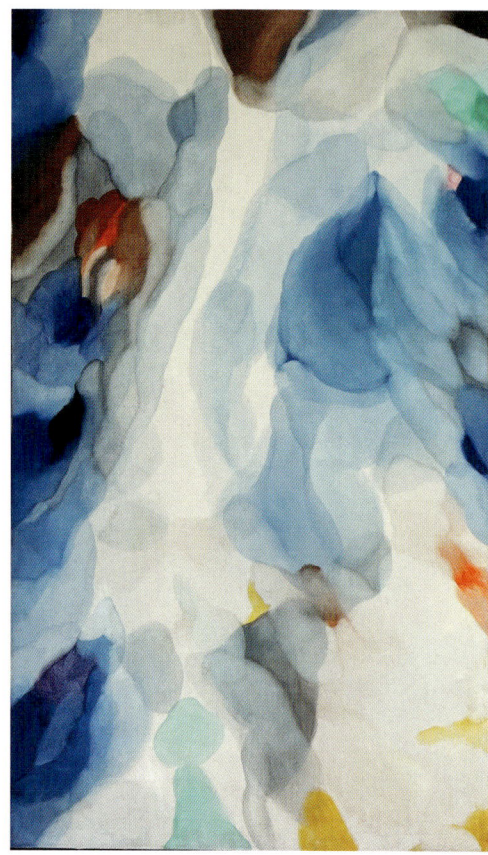

Alice Baber, *Dance of the Wind Cave*,
1973, acrylic on canvas,
63 ½ x 38 inches,
collection of Robert and Ana Greene.

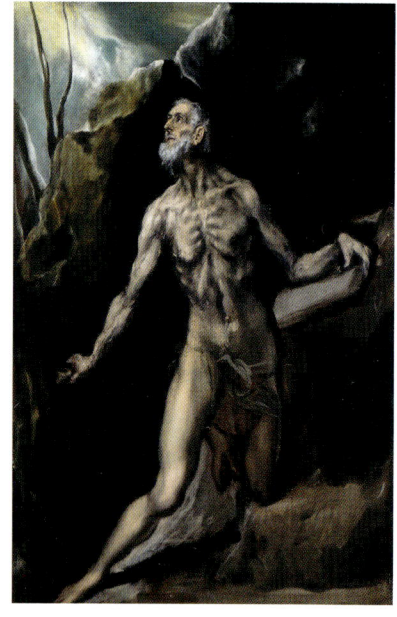

El Greco, *St. Jerome Penitent*, 1610,
oil on panel, 66 x 42 ½ inches,
National Gallery of Art, Washington, D.C.

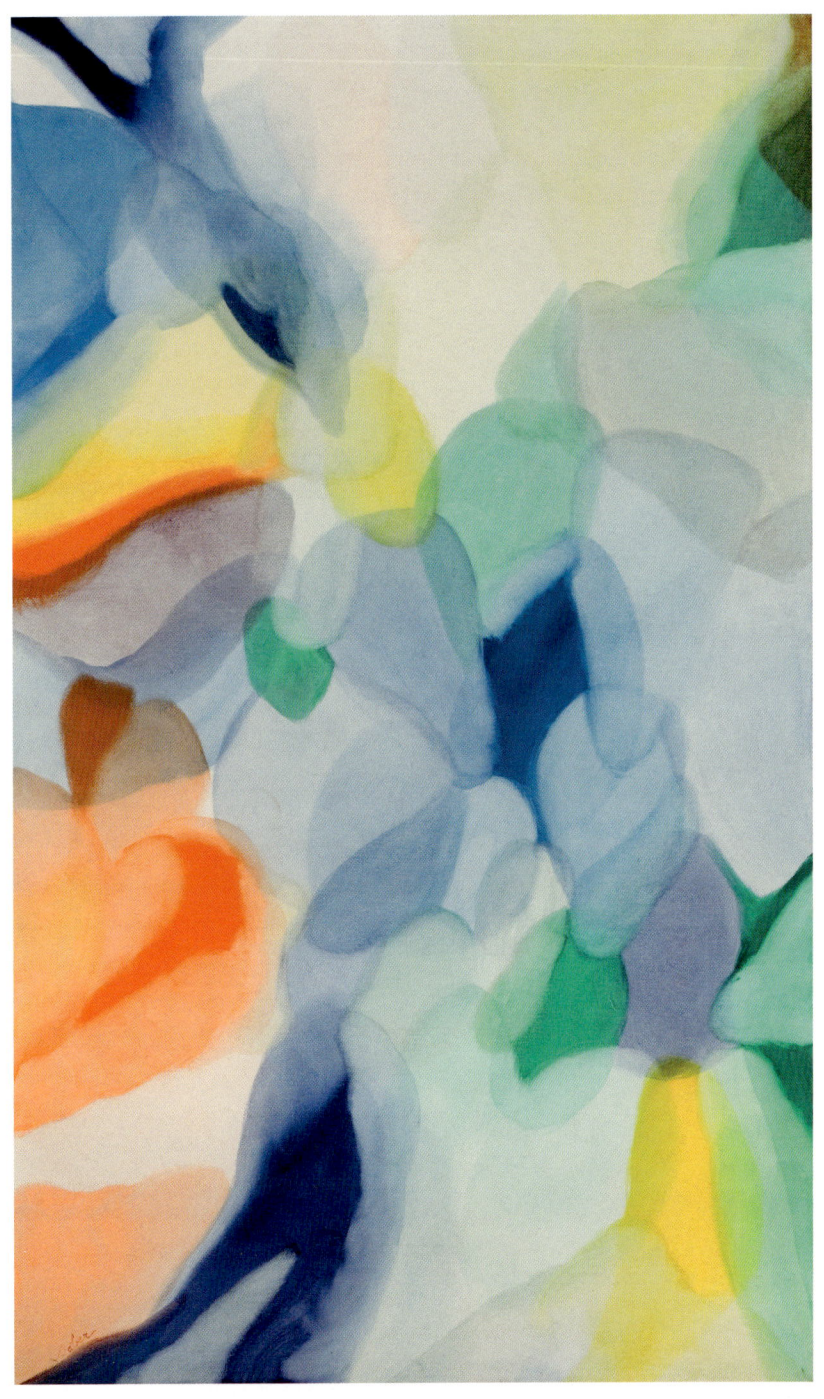

Alice Baber, *The Light in the Depths*, 1975, oil on canvas, 50 x 30 inches, New Britain Museum of American Art, New Britain, CT.

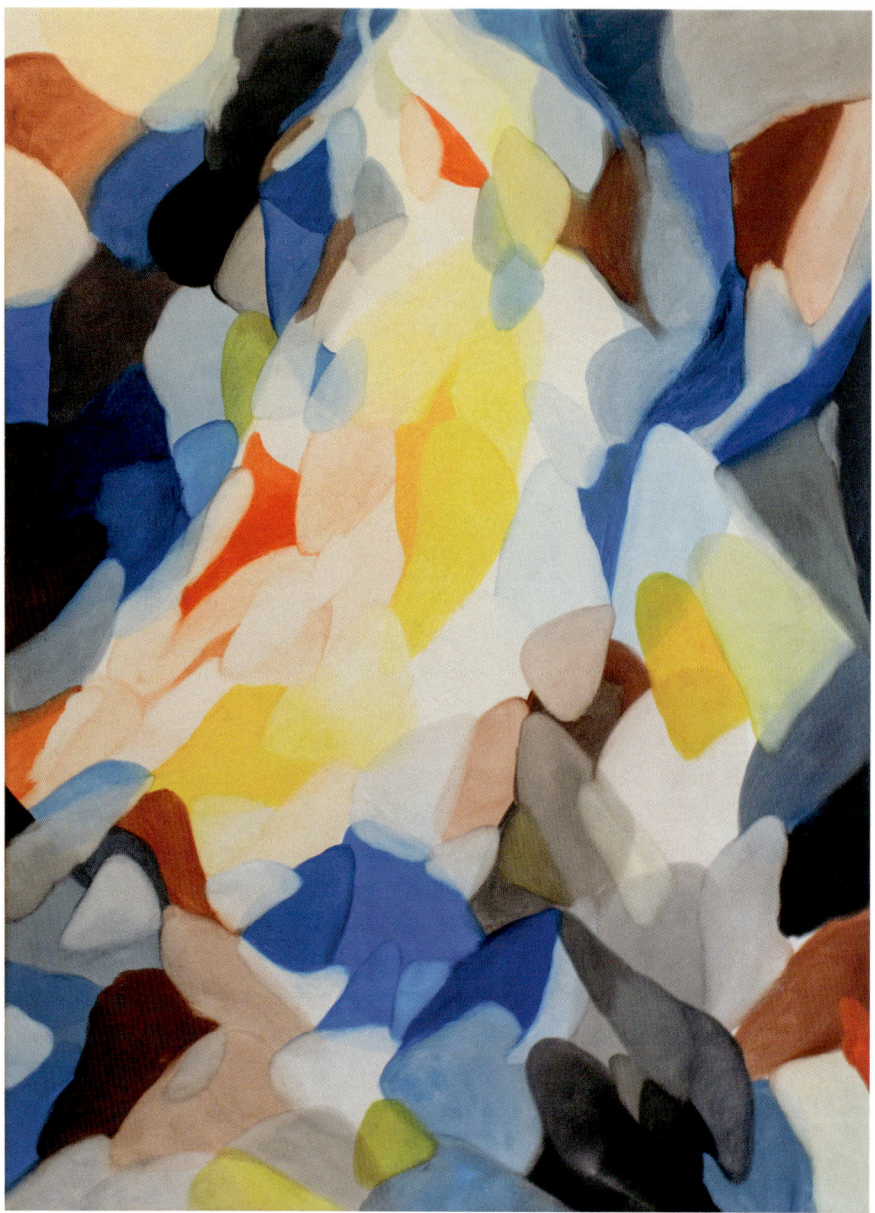

Alice Baber, *Hermit in the Cave of Light*, 1976, oil on canvas, 77 x 58 inches, collection of Jim Carrey.

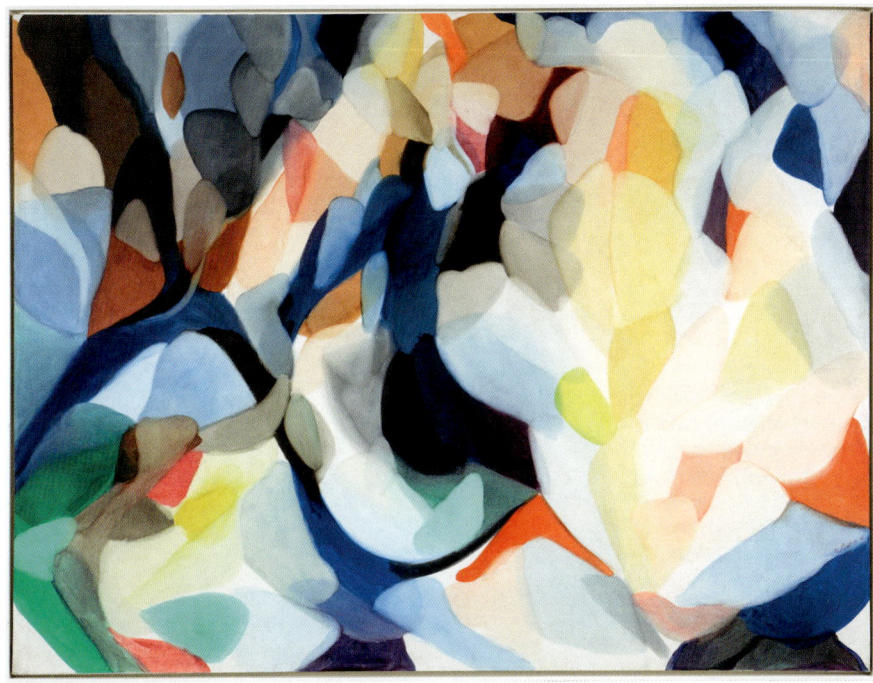

Alice Baber, *Swirl of Sounds: The Ghost in the Banyan Tree*, 1976, oil on canvas, 72 x 95 ½ inches, courtesy Berry Campbell Gallery, NY.

"One of the things that I am interested in is the idea of the painting. . . . I feel that an abstract painting is outer space, and I am in front of it, suspended in outer space, so that there isn't any horizon line. However, there is probably a sense of up and down, and side to side. There is a sense of infinity, which I like very much. And I like the idea of infinity coming way forward, so that you have reverse infinity."
—Alice Baber, 1973

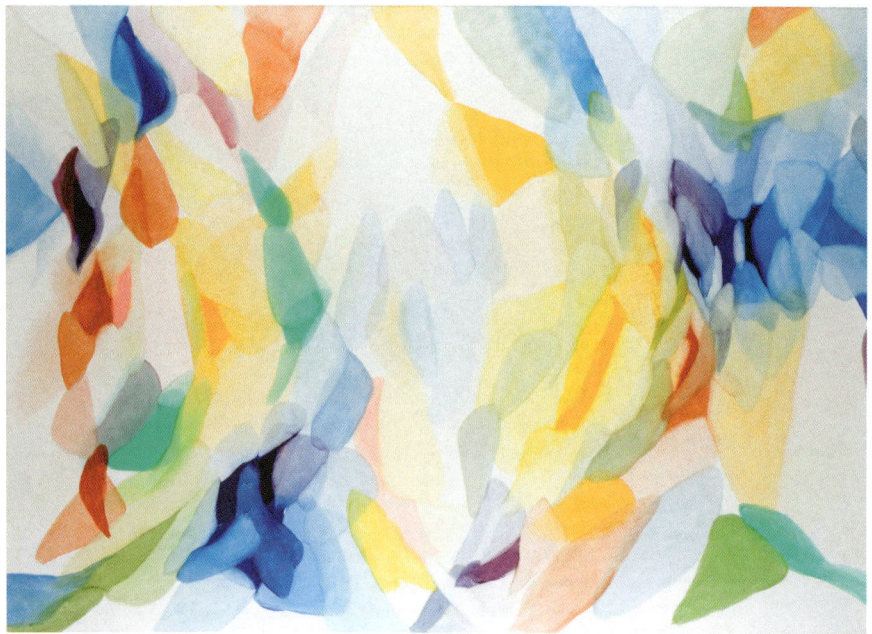

Alice Baber, *Lavender Ladder to the Sun*, 1976, oil on canvas, 72 x 102 ¾ inches,
San Francisco Museum of Modern Art, CA, gift of Dr. William C. Sawyer.

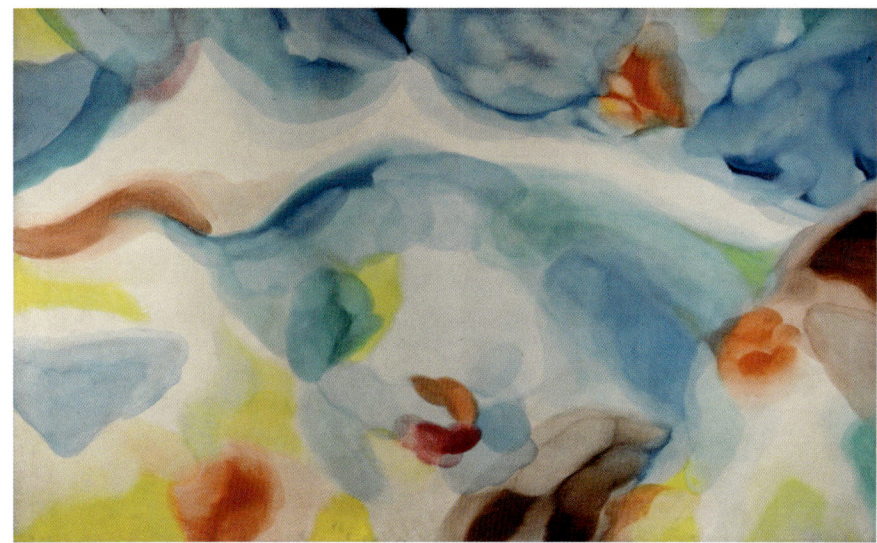

Alice Baber, *Blue Dervish*, 1974, oil on canvas, 37 ³/₁₀ x 63 ¹/₅ inches, National Gallery of Modern Art, New Delhi, India, Acc. no. 2763.

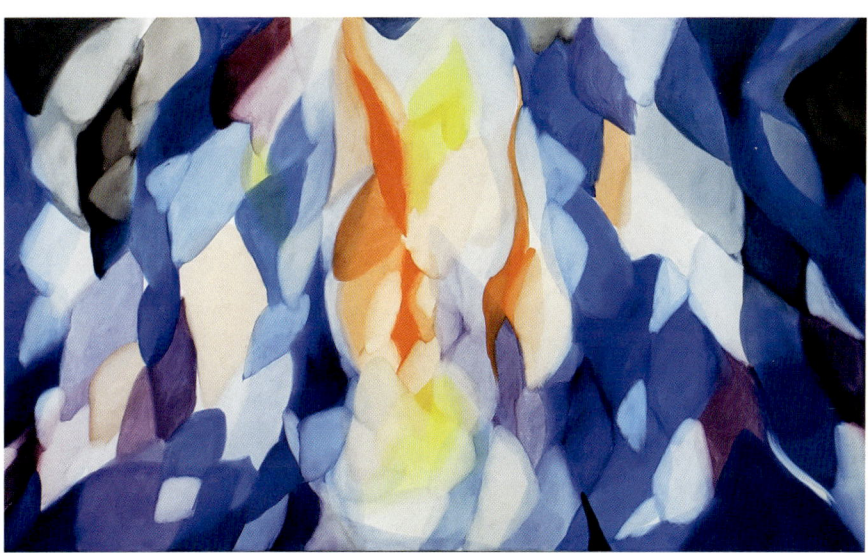

Alice Baber, *Night Drum*, 1977, oil on canvas, 39¼ x 65¼ inches, Castellani Art Museum, Niagara University, Niagara, NY, gift of Dr. & Mrs. Armand J. Castellani, 1989.

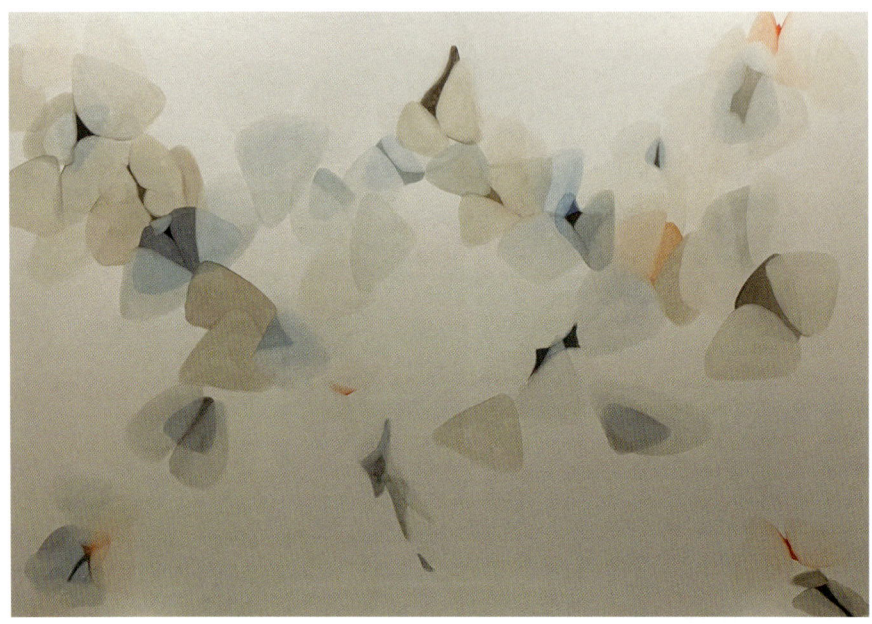

Alice Baber, *The Path of the Grey Falcon of the Dawn*,
1979, oil on canvas, 72 inches x 8 feet,
Metropolitan Museum of Art, NY,
gift of Mrs. Bertram Smith, (1980.314).

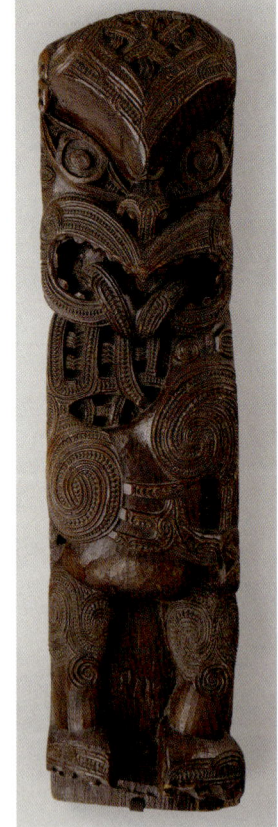

Māori people, *House Post Amo*, ca 1800, wood,
H. 43 x W, 11 x D. 5 inches, Metropolitan Museum of Art, NY,
The Michael C. Rockefeller Memorial Collection,
Bequest of Nelson A. Rockefeller, 1979. (1979.206.1508)

Miriam Schapiro, *Big Ox*, 1967, acrylic on canvas, 90 x 108 inches, Estate of Miriam Schapiro/ Artists Rights Society (ARS), NY, courtesy Eric Firestone Gallery, NY. Baber adapted the form of four diagonal limbs intersecting a central oval open space, a configuration which Miriam Schapiro said that she used in 1967 to express the female body.

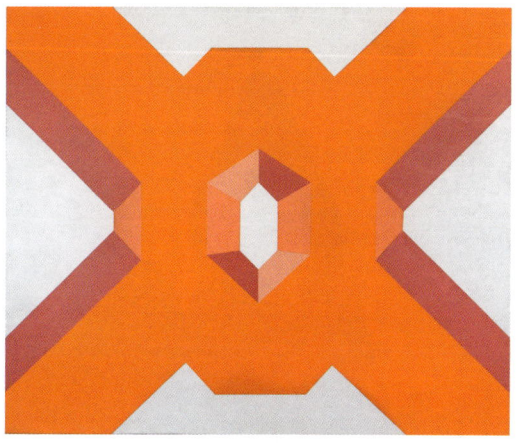

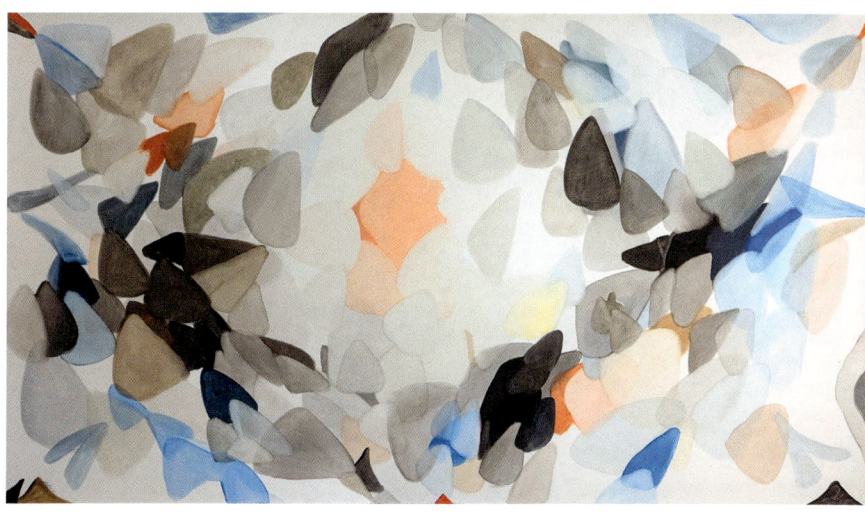

Alice Baber, *The Banner of the Jaguar from the Wind*, 1980, oil on canvas, 30 x 50 inches, Art Museum of Greater Lafayette, IN.

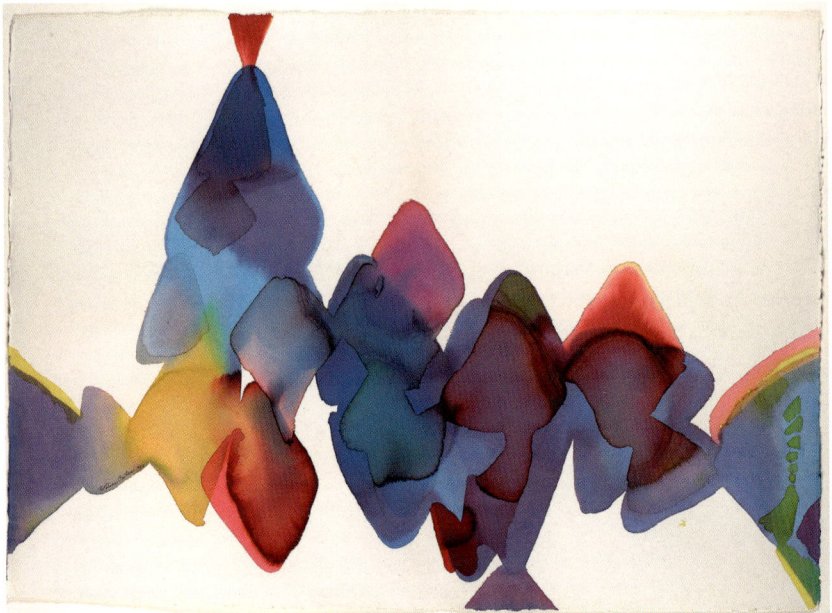

Alice Baber, *The Jaguar Crosses the Rainbow Desert: Sacred Space Series*, 1980, dye-based colored inks on paper, oil on canvas, 30 x 42 inches, Princeton University Art Museum, NJ, gift of the Alice Baber Estate through Norbert N. Nelson, Executor, Class of 1950.

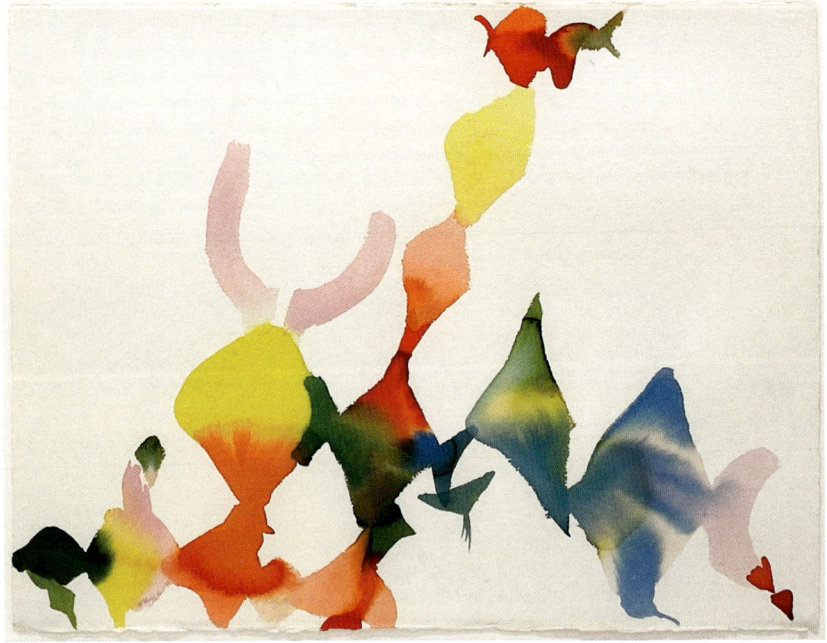

Alice Baber, *Pink Flute of the Jaguar: Sacred Space Series*, 1982, watercolor on paper, 23 x 30 inches, courtesy Taylor Graham, NY.

This two-person show in Osaka is as close to collaborating as Jenkins and Baber ever came. In later years, Jenkins failed to name who the other person in this show was when he presented his chronologies. For these newlyweds, this joint exhibition project remained the most competitive arena to which they would ever subject themselves. The traditional inequities in power and status for women in Japan at this time must have magnified for Baber the perception of having her creativity and her accomplishments minimized. There is no evidence that Jenkins showed any sensitivity to what she was experiencing at the time of their joint show.

Perhaps one should not be surprised that, in 2009, Baber's work was not included and she was barely mentioned in the catalogue of a show called *Gutai and New York*, organized by art historian Ming Tiampo for the Pollock-Krasner House and Study Center in East Hampton, New York, which is located quite close to Baber's last residence in Sag Harbor and also just up the road from the Lassaws. This Gutai show took place in the same art community where Baber had been very active. It is clear now that Baber's omission can be attributed to the fact that most of the art for this show came from Paul Jenkins and his third wife, Suzanne. We now know that Jenkins still owned a large number of early abstractions by Baber, his second wife, whose unfortunate fate was to be erased by Jenkins and his next and final wife.[21]

Less documented than Baber and Jenkins's 1964 trip to Japan is their whirlwind tour of India that followed. Since Baber had written about India in one of her childhood stories, we know that India had entered in her imagination. She recalled, "When we left we decided to go on to India to make a pilgrimage to the Ajanta cave paintings."[22] Besides traveling to see the art in the caves in Aurangabad, the couple also visited Bombay, Agra, and New Delhi.[23] Baber recalled, "We left from Bombay by small plane to go to Aurangabad, the nearest city. . . . We took a slightly broken down taxi for seventy miles over the great Deccan plain. The plain is a plate, high and flat, which has air that creates a euphoric feeling, perhaps because the air, which is a little dusty blows across the Arabian desert. Far in the distance are mountains standing singly shaped like Mayan temples with stairstep sides and flat tops. Finally we came to a beautiful valley."[24]

Baber demonstrated her sensitive perception of topography in her description of the valley, which she recalled "had at the edge a great natural stadium or Greek theater into which we descended, and the caves are carved into the side of this stadium. Some of the caves have sculpture, some have paintings which are visited so much I'm afraid they won't last long. The caves are dark and the guides have photo lights which they move about the intricately covered walls."[25]

The ancient figurative Ajanta murals, dating from before the fifth century, are masterpieces of Buddhist art, which convey emotions through gesture and pose. Baber recorded that the paintings at Ajanta "are very old & very finely drawn & very complicated." She later wrote that she liked "the linear dark and light lines in the Ajanta Caves, the discipline and evocativeness of Persian Gardens, the direct and mysterious quality of Tantric Art."[26]

By Tantric art, Baber referred to spiritual and tranquil abstract forms and mystical diagrams as well as iconographic images conveying the spiritualizing of sexuality.[27] Perhaps having encountered Alfred Kinsey's interest in sexuality as an intellectual field of study at Indiana University later encouraged Baber to collect Tantric art in India. She must have heard about Kinsey's first book, published while she was a student, and perhaps she paid attention to his complementary work, *Sexual Behavior in the Human Female*, published in 1953, just as she was dealing with a succession of demanding men, while trying to make her way as an independent woman and an artist in New York City.

Tantric art is linked to Tantrism, the esoteric ancient Indian traditions of both Hinduism and Buddhism, based on Sanskrit texts, which connect both to the practice of yoga and Shaktism, one of the several major Hindu denominations, where the godhead is considered metaphorically to be a woman.[28]

In Tantra, for example, a yantra is a geometric, pictorial expression of an abstract metaphysical idea. The Kali yantra, which connects to the Goddess Kali, for example, is composed of only downward-pointing triangles, an ancient symbol for the divine power of the female, representing the genitalia of a goddess. Baber told an interviewer, "I've looked at a lot of Tantric art and where it's geometric there—I, you know, I've been interested in the triangles, say from Tantric art."[29] Baber's early interest in the Tantric symbolism of the triangle anticipated the later work of 1970s feminists, most notably Judy Chicago, who made it the shape of the large table in *The Dinner Party*, her monumental sculptural installation of 1979, now on permanent view in the Brooklyn Museum.

Something of Baber's enthusiastic response to India comes from the draft of an undated letter she wrote to Ernestine Lassaw from Paris in January 1965, telling her, "Thought of you at Christmas we were at the Taj Mahal. I loved India. The colors were so beautiful and the atmosphere very intriguing. . . . The Taj is not at all corny as it looks in pictures, but absolutely beautiful because the white rises up from the ground and seems to float," she noted of the tomb monument commissioned in 1631 by the Mughal emperor Shah Jahan to house the tomb of his beloved wife.[30] Alice also informed Ernestine that they were sending her a peacock fan.[31] In India, she explained, "The peacock is thought to be a sacred bird, so that they are allowed to roam free," exclaiming, "We had marvelous adventures in India."[32]

The couple marked their tour of India by posing in a photographic studio aimed at tourists. They were set up to look like a maharaja and his royal spouse enthroned, posed to suggest power, sitting behind a tiger-skin rug, which symbolizes conquest. One cannot miss how stiffly each of them sits, apart from one another, with no sense that they are a loving couple together enjoying a harmonious vacation in an exotic land. This photograph makes it impossible to imagine Paul Jenkins manifesting for Alice Baber anything resembling the love of Shah Jahan for his deceased wife.

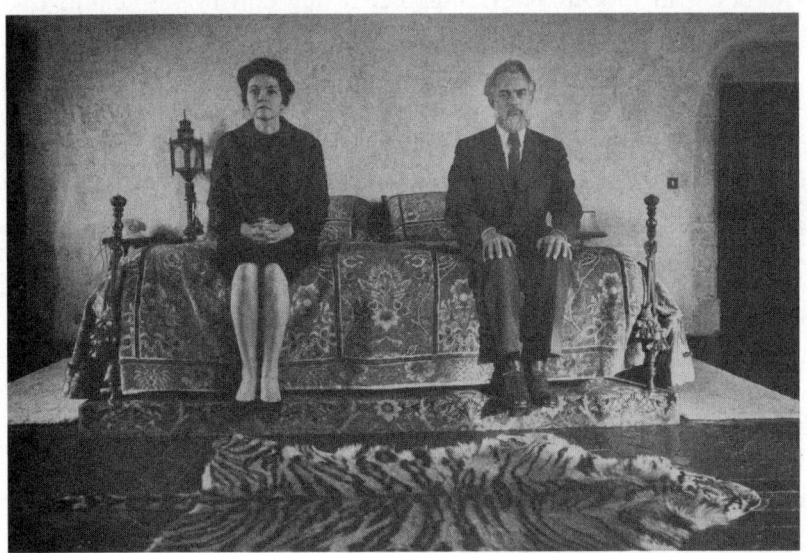

Baber's love of India focused on the colorful "great Bazaar, which has rush hour at sundown."[33] Baber remarked, "When I'm in India I feel as if I have really come home because I am surrounded by the color that seems to me to be the way life really is."[34] She explained, "Color is everywhere: what the people wear, I mean the whole country, there's just no limit to the color. It's hard to imagine in our bleak society how colorful it is."[35]

She elaborated: "Paul and I have seen in our travel some incredible color. In India, long streamers of pink sari cloth being dried near the

Red Fort in New Delhi, a lavender umbrella and orange *Kimono* in a mist on a hillside in Japan, red sweaters in the grey streets in Paris, and that particular golden orange of Notre Dame at sundown, the hard red, yellow, and blue trucks and store fronts in New York, the illusive stones seen by moonlight at Wat Po Temple in Bangkok."[36]

Their visit to Thailand was just a brief stopover on their 1964 world tour. Jenkins wrote to Yoshihara in Japan from Paris, telling him about the eventful night that he and Baber had spent in Bangkok. He told how they attended a dance performance aimed at tourists and then walked over to the walled royal palace, walking around the closed grounds, only to have the palace guard invite them to enter. Jenkins was struck by the contrast with what they saw the next day: "Compared to Nara [in Japan], it looked like Coney Island . . . by day, however by night it was a beautiful fantasy I shall never forget."[37]

In another manuscript, Baber, working on the unfinished narrative that she was writing about Paul Jenkins, stated, "By 1964, after a trip to India, Jenkins was deeply involved in color again."[38] Baber recalled, "I think I've always been interested in the Orient, and the esoteric quality. . . . Of course, we had all the books at home of travels through the Gobi Desert, and that sort of thing, and I decided at an early age I would do that. And India always represented to me a country that would be extraordinarily beautiful, which it is. I haven't been disappointed at all. I think I decided that I would always travel and that I would go to places that appeal to me."[39]

Jenkins wrote to Yoshihara, telling him how much "Alice Baber, that American Woman Painter I am married to" and he appreciated the Gutai's invitation and warmth. As "you can tell from my tone, Osaka was a dream made true."[40] He emphasized just how special the show was for both Alice and himself and thanked his host for the exhibition, while asking him to send the photographs recalling the event.

This artist couple's mutual passion for Asia and its art, which they enjoyed collecting in Japan and India, created another arena for competition between them.[41] At least one book from India survived in the Baber family: *Miniatures and Sculptures from the Collection of the Late Sir Cowasji Jehangir* by Moti and Karl Khandavala Chandra.[42]

Similar statements about what Baber and Jenkins felt while traveling together made it unclear who felt what. Baber's handwritten undated note states, "It has been said that traveling is either an experience we shall always remember or one we shall never forget. And my chief concern in travel is to observe & remember color."[43] Another time, Baber explained, "I'm involved with a kind of color memory, which is a combination of memory and fantasy. I paint out of that bank. It's important for my brain to travel because I don't understand anything until I do travel, and once I've traveled, there are even more mysteries."[44]

Following their travels in Asia, on Wednesday October 27, 1965, the New York furrier–art collector Jacques Kaplan hosted "a party in the honor of Alice Baber (Mrs. Paul Jenkins).[45] The dress was black tie. The French-born Kaplan was famous for giving "lavish parties at his Upper East Side apartment for his Bohemian friends, disappearing as the evening wore on and checking into the Westbury Hotel to enjoy a good night's rest."[46] "I turned into a sort of East Village beatnik on Fifth Avenue," he later recalled.[47] He was known to have hired artists such as Frank Stella and Richard Anuszkiewicz as designers and for trading furs with artists for their art. Besides Baber, among the other women artists in Kaplan's circle were Joan Mitchell and Lee Krasner (both of whom had shown at the Martha Jackson Gallery), each of whom had for a time been known as part of an artist couple.

Baber was "like a peacock," recalled the artist Ce Roser, who showed along with her in many feminist shows; she remembers Baber as "very active, very beautiful," exclaiming that she wore a glamorous fur coat, and that men were drawn to her.[48] Roser recalls that Paul Jenkins was "always on, possibly quite dominating" and felt that Baber was quiet, not talking much.[49]

Now that they were married, Alice and Paul were celebrated in the art world as a celebrity artist couple. ACCLAIMED COLORISTS VISIT LAND OF COLOR: "MR. AND MRS. PAUL JENKINS ARRIVE FOR HIS SHOW" read the caption for a newspaper photograph of Alice and Paul together in Arizona on November 19, 1965.[50] The exhibition of Jenkins's work was at the Gallery of Modern Art in Scottsdale. The local paper described the couple as an "internationally acclaimed contemporary painter and married to another highly talented and respected painter—Alice Baber." Paul was described as a "silver-bearded clear-eyed painter" and a "soft-spoken artist," who said about his art, "It's like a compulsion to become involved with a color," continuing, "It has a hidden meaning. I can only find out about it in painting, not in my own thoughts."[51]

Switching to a description of Alice, the article continues, "Alice Jenkins [*sic*] also is concerned with the luminosity of color, its play, and interplay, but from circles of color, she has moved to less sharply defined forms and darker, more somber overlappings of pigments." The reporter added that "James Jones, the author of 'From Here to Eternity,'" had described Alice as "dealing with 'the tragedy of light.'"[52]

Baber's father wrote to Alice that he was "delighted to learn from, a 1000 miles away, about the outstanding brochure of Paul's show in Arizona. She said, 'My, he's something!' I thinks so too."[53] This was the opinion of his younger cousin, Nancy Hanks, who mattered to Adin Baber because Hanks was such a successful administrator and connoisseur of the arts.

From 1969 to 1977, Hanks, appointed by President Richard M. Nixon, was the second chairman ever of the National Endowment for the Arts, an independent federal agency intended to act as funder of the arts and arts education, established by Congress in 1965. Hanks's genuine interest in and support for Baber's art must have helped Baber negotiate her successful relationship with US Department of State programs that eventually enabled her to travel, lecture, and show around the world.[54]

Baber and Jenkins seem to have respected each other's work. They surely shared ideas and opinions about art, but one wonders about the evolving levels of competition between them. In a 2002 study, *Intimate Creativity: Partners in Love and Art*, the authors, a married couple, Irving and Suzanne Sarnoff, weigh in on equality between couples where both are creative: "In heterosexual pairings, sexism is a prevalent form of injustice. Even without consciously malicious intent, men may attempt to exploit or belittle their female partners. And those women, while suffering from such treatment, may submit to it because of their own internalization of self-abasing stereotypes."[55]

Baber may have given Jenkins one of her large abstract watercolors as late as 1968—*Flourish with Beaming*, which is signed and dated that year. If it had not been intended as a gift, it seems likely that Baber would have wanted it back. It projects a boldness and a clarity that is not always so emphatic in her work. It turns out that this is also one of many works by Baber that Jenkins held onto and kept hidden until the end of his life.

Sometime around the time that their marriage took place, Baber began writing the manuscript she called "Paul Jenkins: The Painter." Heavily corrected handwritten pages and the unpublished typescripts remain in her papers, suggesting that the writing of this narrative was rather complicated, even burdensome. She began her introduction with a statement that could apply to her own work: "The world of Paul Jenkins is one of elemental light, moving color, and changing form."[56]

Since Baber was still working on this major book project as late as 1968, one wonders if it was her attempt to save the faltering marriage. It's difficult to imagine the egocentric Jenkins, who also published his own writing, working on a book about Baber or any other artist. She wrote: "The palette of Jenkins has a rich overflowing translucence, the nuances of brilliant hues, the flashing of winded things, the unearthing of buried treasures displaced unfurled into open spaces. Jenkins is an intense colorist."[57]

Baber explained about her own work, "My intention from the very beginning was to try to find a way that didn't remind me of a thousand other people that I had seen. And I think that that's one of the problems that we have today . . . I think that . . . I think I am easily bored by something I have already seen. So my ideal is to do something that's off the beaten track . . . something really unusual."[58] It is interesting that Baber—who had studied, appreciated, and collected Asian art—had internalized the Western goal of innovation rather than the Eastern respect for copying earlier traditions and revering old masters.

About the influence of Asian art on her work, she commented, "Oriental art. I don't use it consciously, but I think that it does have not so much an influence as the way I do a kind of critical analysis on my own work or on it there's some kind of tie. For example, in the *tanka* at the end of the room, in the center part of the mandala there is a square, and that particular *tanka* is rather recent it's only fifty years old, I suppose, give or take a few years and it's rather bright in color, compared to most *tankas*."[59] Tankas, also written as *thangkas*, are hanging scrolls or fabric temple banners that present painted picture panels often representing Buddhas, mandalas, or great practitioners, which are sewn into or bordered by a textile mountings.

Baber explained that her friend, the artist Robert Slutzky, had looked at her tanka and "commented immediately on the positioning of the white diagonal, and the green and then the orange, you see, because he immediately read into the kind of thing that he loves in a painting. And I hadn't seen that before, and now when I see it I'm delighted with what Bob has seen in it. But I usually see something in it that's in my own work. I mean, whatever your eye starts picking up, you pick up wherever you're looking."[60]

Even with their time spent traveling in Asia, living in Paris, and exhibiting abroad, Baber and Jenkins managed to spend regular annual periods in New York, where the art market still mattered for their careers. To be with Jenkins, Baber had departed for Paris before her career was fully developed. What she needed now was a New York dealer to promote her career.

CHAPTER 10

Finding a New York Dealer
(1965–1966)

B aber's passion for Asian art and culture must have strengthened the bond with her dealer Abe Sachs. Beginning in October 1965 and lasting through 1978, Baber had at least eight solo shows in New York with Abe Sachs at his A. M. Sachs Gallery, which was initially located at 822 Madison Avenue at 69th Street, but in 1968 moved to 29 West 57th Street and, for a time, would concurrently have a second location downtown in Soho.[1]

Sachs was until 1960 a dealer of Chinese antiques (porcelains, scrolls, early bronzes, and pottery). Political turmoil leading up to the Cultural Revolution (1966–1976) curtailed his collecting trips to China, so when he exhausted his inventory, he opened a gallery for contemporary art in 1964.[2] Baber, whom Sachs viewed as a "colorfield painter," was among the first artists he represented. Among the many other artists that Sachs eventually showed were Warren Brandt, Power Booth, Jackie Ferrara, Susan Rothenberg, Peter Hutchinson, and John Ferren.[3]

Baber wrote to Abe Sachs on July 24, 1965, from Biarritz in the South of France, while she and Jenkins were on their way back from another vacation in Spain, where they visited Madrid and El Escorial, a large royal complex built in the late sixteenth century during the Renaissance. In Biarritz, an elegant seaside resort, they had arranged to meet their friends James and Gloria Jones.

Baber thanked her new dealer for setting the date, October 19, 1965, for her first solo show with him in New York and reassured him that she would return to Paris in two days and would send him her biography at once.[4] She explained that they expected to be back in New York during the second week of August and added, "We enjoyed Madrid very much and spent a lot of time at the Prado. The American Embassy was very nice to us, and, as a result of the trip will be hanging my work and Paul's work in the theatre part of the Embassy residence. The Dukes have a good modern collections already started on loan from the Woodward Foundation," she wrote, referring to the US ambassador to Spain, Angier Biddle Duke, and his wife.[5]

That August 10, just before departing Paris for New York, Baber wrote to Jack Mayer, an art dealer in Paris, telling him, "I am leaving for you 11 watercolors. Four of these you have selected, seven of these come from work this summer and we have chosen them for you to see and to add to the others, should they interest you. I have been thinking about the price. It means a great deal to me that you are showing them, framing them, and I would like to offer as much incentive as possible. I know your strong tendency to place work well and not just sell it."[6] Thus, Baber said that she only asked 150 New Francs each, noting, "I am delighted to have watercolors in your hands."[7] She ebulliently reminds him of the impending opening on October 19 of her show at the A. M. Sachs Gallery in New York and informs him of James Jones's article coming out in *Studio International* that September. She tells him that she will be in Copenhagen on Friday and that they leave for New York from there.[8]

By 1965, when Baber first showed with A. M. Sachs, her work had already been abstract for several years. She impressed a reviewer in *Artnews*, who saw in her paintings "soft, light-puffed forms edging close to one another," but then quipped that her darker colors "make an effective bang—like cannons firing together."[9]

Baber must have been pleased, for we know that she explained her intention with reference to another of her abstract canvases, *Just Arrived* (CP #21), from 1962, which has a mysterious floating light. "Nobody's supposed to read anything into it," she insisted. "When you're working on movement in color and form or something of what I call the whole idea of colored wind moving across the canvas then when you have a number of ideas; a lot of things happen that may create their own kind of ambiguity within the structure, that may or may not lead to a reading of it in the sense of subject matter, traditional subject matter."[10] Following Baber's suggestion, one could perhaps read a green human figure with a red head on the right side of her canvas *Where They Meet* (1963) (CP #22), but perhaps it's just random biomorphic shapes she observed when she painted it in Paris that summer.

Baber's title for the canvas, *Seven Wonders* (1966) (CP #26), with its bold yellow curve of light, could be a reference to the seventh wonder of the ancient world—the Lighthouse of Alexandria, built by the Ptolemaic Kingdom of ancient Egypt during the third century B.C.E.—but maybe not. "In the final stages of the painting, I usually add glowing lights," wrote Baber, "I create the center of the vortex. It is as if I am deciding where Atlantis is. I breathe yellow onto the painting, the only real light for me."[11] She referred to the fictional island that Plato described as part of an allegory on the hubris of nations; said to have been lost beneath the sea, Atlantis remains a place of the imagination.[12]

Such abstract work seemed too challenging to Alice's father. Although Adin Baber believed in his daughter, he was not confident that others would understand her abstract work. He wanted to continue to help her financially, so he wrote to her near the end of 1965, arranging to buy many of her paintings, which he hung about the farmhouse and eventually planned to donate to museums, telling her, "I wish to rename some of them, so people begin to get a glimmer [out] of Abstraction. One that I call 'A Fiery Mist and a Planet' to an observer, he promptly replies, Oh yes, 'Creation.' The two Everglades is good, but I add, 'Edge of the Everglades where the tangled trees grow from water.' Oh yes, I see the water now!"[13] (CP #16)

But for critics and art dealers, Baber's enigmatic and poetic titles were already evocative enough. Baber's 1966 show (November 15–December 3) at the A. M. Sachs Gallery earned another *Artnews* review from Baber's friend, the painter Natalie Edgar, who picked up on Baber's concern with creating the illusion of movement through color, observing how her forms pulsated.[14]

Baber also received a *New York Times* review from Grace Glueck, who observed, "Disks and puffs of pure bright color drift lyrically over a white field toward a gentle vortex, bumping one another like colored balloons at a children's party."[15] She felt that Baber's greatest success was in her large-scale paintings like *"Axe in the Groove,* where the white canvas is almost completely suppressed."[16]

The 1966 painting in question is inscribed by Baber on the stretcher *"Axe in the Grove,"* not the spelling error, "Groove," that was published in the *New York Times* review. Baber's original title and her interest in figurative speech call to mind the dual definitions of Grove as "a small wood or forested area, usually with no undergrowth" or "a small orchard or stand of fruit-bearing trees, especially citrus trees: a grove of lemon trees." Given Baber's visual memories of her girlhood in Florida, her interest in painting trees in college, and *The Everglades* (CP #16), her memory painting of walking into a hammock of bald cypress trees, the latter definition might well apply, especially given the flowing green shapes in the center of this canvas.

Axe in the Grove could also refer to Baber Woods, the family acreage that Adin Baber protected and proudly kept from the ravages of cattle farming and commercial ventures to harvest wood by clear-cutting the virgin land (CP #27). Adin Baber's reverence for nature, his determined proscription against clear-cutting forests that are sacred, makes one think of the Lakota and various other Indigenous tribes who regard particular forests or other natural landmarks as sacred places.

Baber's consideration of protecting the woods also recalls the story of the "Sacred Grove" visited by the youthful Joseph Smith, the founder of Mormonism and the Latter-Day Saints movement. Members of his family are said to have "become seekers themselves in the Presbyterian church at Palmyra township, New York."[17] The Smiths' farm was located on native forests—land—purchased for their farm. A second account is said to have taken place in 1907, when a visitor from Utah to the "Sacred Grove" met the church's caretaker, who claimed that his late father "had never used an *axe in the grove* except to remove dead timber" and he urged his son to respect the wooded area in similar fashion since he believed "that this was the very forest in which Joseph Smith had prayed and experienced the grand theophany which was the origin of the Mormon religion."[18]

By theophany, the caretaker referred to an appearance of God to human beings. Alice Baber could have heard this story while attending Lindenwood College, which was affiliated with the Presbyterian Church.[19] Baber's titles sometimes have spiritual references, about which she commented, "I usually title things, like if they were religious. I didn't really give them full religious significance. Like the Jacob's Ladders, I didn't call Jacob's Ladders, I just called [them] 'Ladder.'"[20]

Another 1966 work that relates to the content, palette, and form of *Axe in the Grove* is *Ladder Forest* (CP #26).

Thus, Baber's frequent use of the word *ladder* refers to the biblical patriarch Jacob's ladder.[21] The ladder featured in Jacob's dream during his flight from his brother Esau as told in the Book of Genesis: "And he dreamed, and behold a ladder set up on the earth, and the top of it reached to heaven; and behold the angels of God ascending and descending on it."[22] Thus, Jacob's ladder became the colloquial name for a bridge between the earth and heaven. Baber told an interviewer, "Most of the forms in my paintings move upwards, kind of a Jacob's ladder."[23] Christian theology speaks of "climbing up the heavens towards the light of God."[24]

Such a reference to divine light is not surprising for Baber, who was familiar with Judeo-Christian teachings from her Presbyterian college. Some of Baber's contemporaries also referred to the story of Jacob; for example, *Jacob's Ladder*, a 1957 abstract painting by Helen Frankenthaler, whom Baber knew, has been in the collection of the Museum of Modern Art since 1960. Baber said that a title was "a sort of poetic expression of what's in the painting, but it's not real poetry, it's after all a title."[25]

Baber titled many of her canvases with *ladder*—for example, *Wind Ladder* (1960–1961), *Floating Ladder* (1962–1963), *Dark Ladder* (1965), *Sun Ladder* (1965), *Ladder Rising* (1965), *Ladder Forest* (1966) (CP #26), *Light Ladder* (1966), *Path to the Ladder* (1972) (CP #39), *Lavender Ladder Turning-Akbar's Hunt* (1972) (CP #38), *Ladder Fire on the Mountain* (1973), *Purple and Blue Ladder Turning North* (1976); and *Lavender Ladder to the Sun* (1976) (CP #44). About *Lavender Ladder to the Sun*, she wrote, "The color lavender is chosen as the starting point and as the finishing point. The ladder is a kind of Jacob's ladder which takes the painting into outer space."[26]

Baber titled several of her paintings with the name of Akbar the Great, the Mughal emperor, who reigned from 1556 to 1605, descended from Turks, Mongols, and Iranians, who was known for his policy of religious tolerance and as a patron of the arts at his courts in Delhi, Agra, and Fatehpur Sikri, which Baber visited on her 1964 trip to India.[27] On her trip to Iran in 1974, she might have thought about Akbar's efforts to unite distant lands of his realm through loyalty, expressed through an Indo-Persian culture, and to himself as an emperor with near-divine status. In addition to *Lavender Ladder Turning-Akbar's Hunt* (1972) (CP #38), Baber named paintings *Akbar's Dream* (1973) and *Akbar's Shadow* (1974).

Baber's own attitude toward religion remained one of searching, not of piety. On June 27, 1968, she noted, "Finding God is one thing. Expressing Him is another. Art is *expressing* him."[28] That fall she signed up for "History of Buddhism" at Columbia University, taught by Professor Robert F. Olson.[29] The catalogue describes the course content as "change and continuity in the development of Buddhist thought and institutions during the expansion of Buddhism from India to Tibet, China, and Japan."[30]

Five years later, in 1973, Baber claimed, "I'm almost a Buddhist," recalling her initial curiosity at Lindenwood College, where she rejected taking a course on Protestant Christianity "so I wouldn't sort of play with the idea, but I remember thinking that this would be my way out, and so maybe in some strange way, you see, I thought this was the escape from our world into something else better, more interesting and fuller."[31]

Baber not only attended lectures on Buddhism, she also received the monthly announcement from the Ramakrishna-Vivekananda Center at 17 East 94th Street in New York.[32] This organization maintains a temple in Manhattan and a summer cottage at Thousand Island Park,

New York, where Swami Vivekananda lived and taught in 1895, combining Hindu religion and philosophy. Once Vivekananda's teachings attracted American artists, like the early modernist painter Marsden Hartley; now, decades later, Alice Baber.[33] One of Baber's undated notes reads, "I object to the metaphors of religion like sound, rain coming, etc."[34]

Yet, the more that Baber traveled, the more open she was to spiritual beliefs from other cultures. When writing to friends in Germany about her participation in an upcoming show in Cologne, Germany, at the Kölnischer Kunstverein in 1966, she enthused, "We had a marvelous summer visiting Russia. Moscow, Leningrad [Saint Petersburg], and Kiev. We were there for eleven days and were impressed by the beautiful icons, the Pushkin Museum and the Kremlin."[35] They visited a monastery outside of Moscow in Sergiyev Posad, which at the time had been renamed Zagorsk in 1930 by the Soviets. Baber and Jenkins first saw and were impressed there by the icons of the medieval Russian painter Andrei Rublev. From a photograph of the interior of the couple's home, it's clear that they managed to acquire at least one Russian icon, a portrait of a male saint.[36]

Yet, for the most part, Baber's audiences did not perceive her spiritual explorations.

As for the Kölnischer Kunstverein in Cologne, Baber did have a solo show there from September 13 to October 9, 1966.[37] She was trying to figure out how she could be in New York for the opening of Paul's one-man show on November 1 and then for her own solo show on November 15, but also get to the opening in Germany, to which she would have to fly for just a few days—"If there is an opening in the sky," she wrote the organizers, Lore and Andreas Becker, "I am looking forward to your opening." But she warns that if she cannot get there, "Dear Karl [Flinker, her Paris dealer] has promised that he will come on my behalf."[38]

The illustrated Cologne catalogue included paintings like *Seven Wonders* (1966) (CP #26) and *Ladder Rising* (1965); it featured a translation of the 1965 article by James Jones, "Alice Baber and the Tragedy of Light." But another publication was uppermost on Baber's mind. She informed the Beckers that "Paul's play arrives from the publisher September 5 and he looks forward to sending a copy to you and Dr. Feldenkirchen. He will be very happy for you to see it and is very proud of the way it looks."[39]

Paul's play, *Strike the Puma*, was published in France in English in 1966 by the Paris publisher Éditions Gonthier. The cover noted: "Paul Jenkins is known by his astrologer as a true sign of Cancer. His passport would reveal that he was born in Kansas City, Missouri, on July 12, 1923. As a painter he is known in New York, London, and Paris as an *Abstract Phenomenist*. In this play he investigates phenomena in another form." In fact the dedication of the play was to "G. J. & J. J. & A. B. & G," which would be to Gloria Jones and James Jones, and Alice Baber and G., who is identified as a principal character, "with obvious references to G. I. G."[40] By G., Jenkins referred to the philosopher, mystic, and spiritual teacher George Ivanovitch Gurdjieff, who taught the wisdom of self-awareness, urging people to become conscious of themselves and not to live out their lives in a state of hypnotic "waking sleep." Gurdjieff believed in the potential to awaken to a higher state of consciousness and serve our purpose as human beings.[41] This was a philosophy that Jenkins referenced more than once.

The task of promoting Jenkins's work before Baber did whatever she could to promote her own art seemed to be a role to which she, as his wife, was assigned. Somehow, as here, she managed to juggle both roles. At the time of her solo show at the A. M. Sachs Gallery in the autumn of 1966, Baber's 1964–1965 canvas, *Noble Numbers* (CP #24), was on loan by the Smithsonian Institution to President Lyndon Johnson's

White House as part of its program of loans of American art.[42] Yet, despite such indicators of career success, Baber never received the same level of early recognition achieved by her exact contemporary, Helen Frankenthaler, who, early in her career, had the clear advantage of being introduced to movers and shakers in the art world as the girlfriend of the influential art critic Clement Greenberg.

CHAPTER II

Questions of Identity
(1966–1968)

A lice Baber's career seemed to be about to take off when the Paris art dealer Karl Flinker, whom Baber shared with Paul Jenkins, told her in 1966 that Michel Seuphor, the art critic who founded the abstract artists' group Cercle et Carré, which included Wassily Kandinsky and Le Corbusier, would include two of her paintings in his book on American art.[1] Seuphor had already included Jenkins in his 1957 book, *Dictionary of Abstract Painting*, writing that he was "a painter of charm and mystery. The half-colours and the flickering light of nighttime."[2] Flinker wrote to her as "Mrs. Alice Baber-Jenkins" at the Paris home she shared with Paul Jenkins at 15 Rue Decrès, imposing an involuntary name change that suggested that she risked losing her separate identity from her artist husband.

Jenkins, who occasionally published articles in *Artnews*, wrote to his friend and the magazine's editor, Tom Hess, on April 6, 1966, to remark upon Alice's intensity in creating new work: "Alice is working up a storm and has done some paintings that are downright disturbing to my tentative sense of inner security." He said that Hess might view the new work when he came to Paris. At the same time, Jenkins noted that his exhibition would be open at Arthur Tooth & Sons, his gallery in London, May 17–June 5.

The gradual blurring of Baber's professional and personal identities came with repeated references to Baber as "Alice Baber Jenkins," the artist's wife. This change of name seems to have been imposed particularly in England. Baber was photographed with Jenkins on May 28, 1966, at his opening at the Arthur Tooth & Sons Gallery. That July 2, 1966, "Alice Baber Jenkins the Lyrical Abstract Artist" appeared in *Tatler* in a feature headlined THE AMERICANS AMONG US.[3]

When Baber was not present solely for the purpose of supporting Jenkins, however, she was written up as "Alice Baber" in *Tatler* on September 3, 1966, as showing her work at the Women's International Art Club in Whitechapel Gallery along with other invited artists: Elisabeth Frink (the English sculptor and printmaker), Françoise Gilot, and Sonia Delaunay, the latter two artists whom she probably already knew from Paris.[4]

Baber and Jenkins were in England from the middle of May 1966, staying at the Eyrie Mansion at 22 Jermyn Street, London, SW1, as Alice wrote to Paul's aunt Louise (Jenkins), an accomplished soprano, who lived in England, but had been ill.[5] Recalling the duties of earlier generations of male artists' wives, Baber seems to have become Jenkins's secretary, for she also wrote from Paris for Jenkins earlier that month to Diane and Irvin Shapiro, New York friends who lived in the posh Hotel des Artistes at 1 West 67th Street in Manhattan, thanking them for writing to their friend, Mr. Harold Myers at *Variety*, about the film festivals, which could feature the new film about Jenkins. Baber offered that she and Jenkins planned to take the couple to a "marvelous restaurant near Notre Dame," and added "Paul hasn't forgotten his promise to Diane about the small painting that she waited for so patiently."[6]

Just before leaving Paris, on September 22, 1966, Jenkins wrote to Baber's father, thanking him for the copy of Alice's poems and telling him how joyous the poems made him feel, even moving him to tears. "There is something so poignant about Alice's thoughts in words, and I am ever grateful to you for protecting them."[7] Jenkins really seems to have connected with Adin Baber, telling him how he was anticipating meeting Nancy Hanks, whom Alice would phone when they were back in New York to tell about their exhibition and arrange a studio visit.[8] He was pleased to report that his Broadway studio building had just installed an elevator to make such visits easier.

On Christmas Day 1966, Alice Baber was featured in an article by Grace Glueck in *The New York Times* as leading a revival of the Club, which her friend the sculptor Philip Pavia had founded at 39 West 8th Street in 1949, a few years before Baber had arrived in New York in the fall of 1951. The informal gatherings of abstract expressionist artists and others, such as the mythographer Joseph Campbell or the composer John Cage, had stimulated Baber in her first years in the city. The idea of the revival was to reinstate the panel discussions on Friday nights. Baber had teamed up with artists Pavia, Lester Johnson, Fay Lansner, Raymond Hendler, and Sideo Fromboluti to reconstitute the Club. Unfortunately, Pavia told Glueck that they did not welcome "anti-art people, who think you don't have to know about things like composition and drawing to be an artist."[9] When Glueck asked, he admitted that the exclusion included Andy Warhol, which doomed the revival to be perceived as conservative, no longer vanguard.

Baber's statement was much more constructive and politic. "'So far, the response has been great,' says the artist Alice Baber, one of the new Club's prime movers. 'Of course the new Club won't be just like the old one—nothing ever is. The old Club had so much *energy*. It gave a lot of vitality to the New York scene. Artists need a place to go and see what's doing, after spending so much time in isolation in their studios.'"[10]

Jenkins wrote to Baber's father in February 1967 to tell him what a marvelous moderator Alice had been at the Artists Club the previous week. "It was her idea to say that Tenth Street was a state of mind and not just a place or time," he said praising not only her delivery, but the content of her performance.[11] He took credit for helping edit Alice's speech and claimed that she had been anxious before the program started. He added "Even if Alice did yell at me from time to time, I felt that I contributed to this drama about to take place."[12] Evidently, Jenkins did not take Alice's efforts at performing in public as seriously as she did.

Jenkins was still much better known than Baber and male artists were in much greater demand. After informing his father-in-law that he was about to receive the Corcoran Biennial's silver medal and quipping, "Why, before you know it, your son-in-law is almost going to become 'respectable,'" he added how he had received an invitation for February to speak at the Albright Art Gallery in Buffalo, but had only been willing to accept if they also invited Alice to speak, which they did. As a result, the couple also participated on two radio shows with Sandy Liesberg at WOR. Jenkins boasted that he was creating new requests for them to speak together.[13]

Jenkins also told his father-in-law how Alice had sought out a voice instructor to take lessons in microphone techniques. He observed that she always had that speaking ability when she took the trouble to practice in advance. He opined that many people in the art world were now admiring Alice.[14] He closed this line of thinking with a loaded comment: "She is quite innocently becoming someone who represents other people and their feelings in the struggling art world, something I knew would happen."[15] What Jenkins doesn't reveal to his father-in-law is how his wife's growing influence makes him feel.

Adin Baber responded to this news of his daughter by confiding in his son-in-law, "I am very proud to hear how Alice did a magnificent job of moderating at the artist's club. Tenth street is verily a state of mind. Her first painting of the green Everglades (really a hammock) and a flaming funeral pyre (CP #16) are what created in my mind the thought that she must leave McCall's and give full time to Art."[16]

The charming couple now shared their family connections and social networks in both New York and Paris. Clues to Baber's social networks in the French capital are evident in a 1968 letter from her friend, the American artist Zenaida Gourievna Booyakovitch, known as Zuka, who lived and worked in Paris. Zuka painted and exhibited portraits of Alice Baber (1962), Joan Mitchell, and others, which the critic Pierre Schneider wrote about when she first showed them in 1965 at the Galerie Lambert.[17] Zuka's frontal portrait bust of Baber projects the coquettishness of a Barbie doll. Writing to Alice three years later, Zuka reported having had dinner with their mutual friend, the American art dealer Darthea Speyer, who, while cultural attaché in Paris for the US embassy, had put Baber's work in two Jeune Biennales.[18] With similar familiarity, Zuka also mentioned the American abstract painter Shirley Jaffe, with whom she had just gone to some gallery openings in Paris.

Their Parisian network of friends fragmented when Alice and Paul separated in 1968 and divorced in 1970. Few clues as to what caused the couple's breakup emerged. Although some who knew her then recall Alice as strong and stoic, refusing to discuss what happened, Ann McCoy, who first met Baber through the collector Charles Craig in Santa Barbara, well after the marriage ended, opines that "Paul was a huge narcissist."[19] Of course, artists need to some degree to focus on themselves, on their own creativity.[20] But such a focus might easily mean that one spouse in an artist couple might be envious of their partner's success or level of ambition.

Baber's papers contain some notes that she scribbled hinting at what she thought went wrong with the marriage: "What was his relationship to Esther? His ex-wife?," she asked after it was too late for the answer to make a difference.[21] "The first partner is haunted by being used against loneliness. Infidelity is because one or the other cannot be alone, they never admit they cannot be alone." "I don't have the luck of Geo. [George] Sand said the woman, my lovers don't die. They go away to marry young beautiful . . . with money." "He was fearful of the devil the insanity in himself." "Being with Paul is like being a criple [*sic*] with fiction."[22] She also wrote: "The nice quiet evenings are the ones that are fatal because that's when I like him again."[23] A separate page, undated and handwritten, states, "He projects evil on me." "Paul said don't try to be so original (he equates this with devil's advocate) when he brings in cliché even in an offbeat way. I react with trying to take it toward the original."[24] It seems as if Baber felt that Jenkins made her choose between him and her own artwork, to which she was more devoted.

Another cryptic page read at the top: "Going to beat me till the blood runs down my legs."[25] In the middle, she has the word, *healthy* with an arrow drawn, pointing to "nobody most of all my father . . . no son of a—" At the bottom of the same page, we read, "Do it and get it over with so I can get on with my life." This appears to refer to leaving Paul.

One wonders if while splitting up, the couple squabbled over possession of their Asian art collection. Baber's notes state, "My husband & I are painters but we both have a passion for collecting, especially ivories. Our ivory collection includes a number of netsukes [miniature sculptures, originating in seventeenth century] which come from Japan . . . small animals carved in many subjects such as animals or plants."[26] It appears as if Jenkins held on to that collection.

Baber might have made these notes when she and Jenkins were interviewed for a feature in the November 1967 issue of *Art in America* by Joanna Eagle on "Artists as Collectors." The article compares the couple with another pair of abstract painters, Helen Frankenthaler and Robert Motherwell, noting, "In both cases, each artist collected before his or her marriage. The Motherwells' interests range over many periods and varieties of art; the Jenkinses concentrate almost exclusively on Oriental."[27] We learn of Jenkins's long fascination with ivory objects, which he began collecting in Paris in 1957. "He still has the piece he bought then, a flat ivory hook from Brittany used to unravel fish nets. On one side is a sailor holding a bottle; on the other the wife is all dressed up, as Jenkins puts it, for 'Sunday-go to meetin.' Jenkins likes the tactile attraction of ivories and now has over thirty pieces."[28]

Baber had catered to Jenkins's special interest in ivories, when she gave him the first of his many ivory knives. A photograph of Baber and Jenkins accompanied this article.

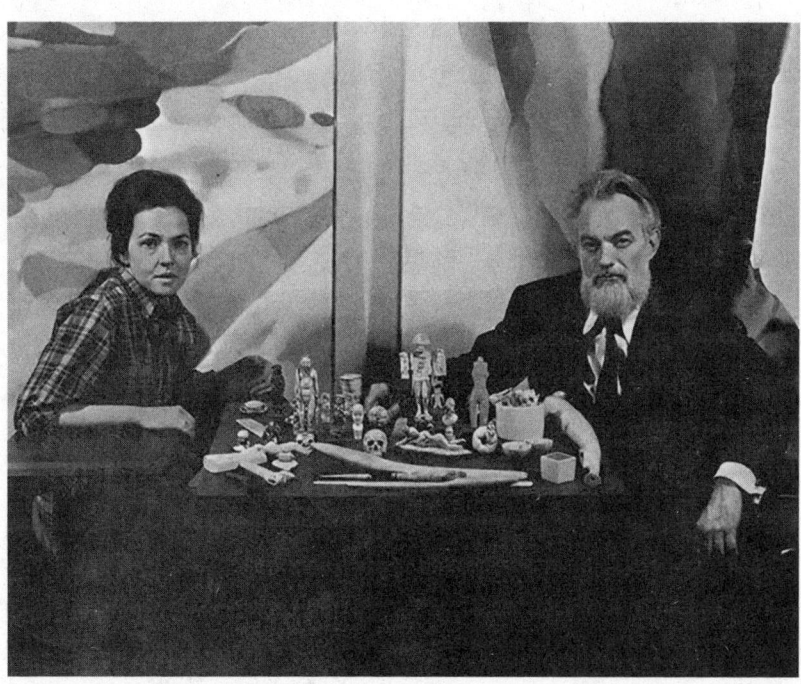

The photographer, John D. Schiff, caught the stoic couple looking a bit glum, sitting at a table covered with ivories from their collection. The caption identifies two canvases visible in the background as Baber's 1967 oil painting, *All of The Seasons*, and Jenkins's 1967 canvas, painted in acrylic, *Phenomena Samothrace*. The two artists appear as equals, though fail to show any human connection beyond possessing together the collection that they show off here. What a striking contrast to how they posed together with such affection in 1958 for the photographer Fred McDarrah at the Sam Francis opening. Within five years of this feature on collecting, both collecting couples—the Motherwells and the Jenkinses—would divorce.

The tension between Baber and Jenkins also seems apparent in a portrait painted in 1967 by Ethel Fisher, which she called *Alice Baber and Paul Jenkins*. She makes an emphatic point by depicting a serene Alice alone, seated in an interior with a portrait of the absent Paul hanging on the wall behind her. Alice, who holds both a pair of gloves and a large umbrella across her lap, appears to be about to depart. The portrait on the wall is unmistakably Paul, emphasizing his large trademark beard, even as he holds a book open with his right hand. Paul's portrait is done in dark shades of gray, almost in grisaille, and is hung against a contrasting bright yellow wall. Baber's head overlaps the lower left corner of the portrait, almost as if she is trapped by his virtual presence, unable to leave him.

Fisher showed *Alice Baber and Paul Jenkins* in two versions: the first smaller version on paper (18 x 20 inches) was on view in New York City in a show of artists portraying themselves and others, which was called *Artists by Artists*. This show took place at the Capricorn Gallery, on 11 West 56th Street, May 16–June 3, 1967. The larger version of this portrait on canvas (51 x 40 inches) was shown in the 18th Annual Silvermine Guild of Artists' New England Exhibition from June 3 to July 4, 1967 in New Canaan, Connecticut.

In exhibiting this portrait in two versions, Fisher made public her view of her friend Alice's unhappy predicament, leaving only the reason for her distress unstated: Alice, who had been betrayed, was now married to a man who was having an affair with a younger woman. To make matters worse, Jenkins was involved with a young woman who worked in the art world. The show's participating artists showed with many galleries, including Paul's gallery, Martha Jackson, where the young woman was employed. This portrait had to have stimulated gossip.

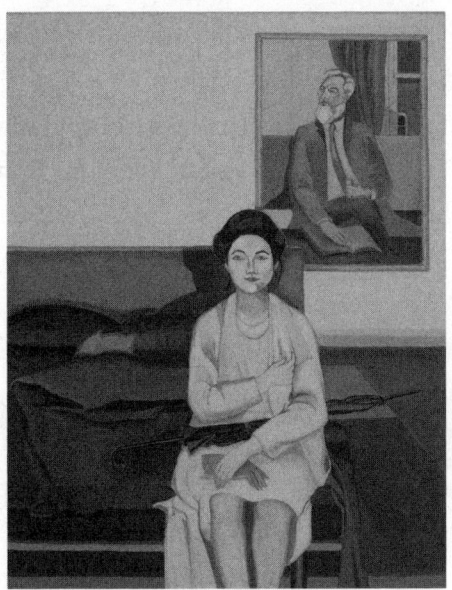

Baber had known Ethel Fisher for many years. Fisher recalled that she met Baber in New York during the late 1950s. "I was instrumental in getting her work represented by A. M. Sachs Gallery in New York," Fisher asserted.[29] One of Fisher's small collages, dated 1965, includes Baber's name in its design. It also includes a fragment of Fisher's New York address on East 89th Street. Although Fisher could have observed the tension in her friend's marriage, she might also have heard about it directly from Baber. In a picture that speaks volumes, Fisher's extraordinarily perceptive portrait records her friend's anguish and disappointment in love.

Another of Baber's friends, the California sculptor Betty Gold, who met Baber in 1970, when she was in a show in Santa Barbara, recalls that, for Alice, "Paul Jenkins was not an easy person," and that "Alice just couldn't take it anymore. He didn't allow her any room. He wouldn't share his contacts. He never helped her. Typical male artist: he wanted everything for himself."[30]

It turns out that Jenkins actively pursued other women in his studio, while he was married to Baber, who still lived on Bedford Street. Jenkins did not have to look very far. At the Martha Jackson Gallery, he found attractive her new young assistant, Katherine Komaroff, a recent graduate in art history from the University of California at Berkeley, who arrived in New York in 1964, the year Jenkins and Baber married. Jenkins, then just forty-one years old, was two decades older than Komaroff and twice married. At the distance of sixty years, Komaroff recalls that Paul was "very elegant" and "one of a kind with lots of interests." She does say that Jenkins had a "serious drinking problem" and "walked around with a flask," which his daughter confirms.[31]

By July 19, 1967, Jenkins wrote to Mr. and Mrs. Frederick Wiseman, thanking them for a visit to their magnificent home to see their art collection that he had made together with his dealer, Martha Jackson and "Mrs. Komaroff."[32] On August 1, 1967, Jenkins sent a letter to one of his collectors, telling them that he was then living in his studio at 831 Broadway in New York.[33]

It's not clear exactly when Jenkins's affair with Komaroff began, but by the time that Martha Jackson died on July 4, 1969, Komaroff left New York with Jenkins to live with him in Paris, initially accompanied by his daughter. It was the first and only time that Hilarie Jenkins, then fifteen, visited her father in Paris. Komaroff, at just twenty-six years old, was thrust into the role of a part-time stepmother to a teenager; she also began to work for Paul as his archivist and she managed sales of his art. A friendly letter of July 24, 1969, to Paul from Esther, his first wife and Hilarie's mother, tells him that their daughter is "home again" and that she had "a wonderful time."[34]

Before they left for Paris, Komaroff recalls that while Baber came to Paul's openings at the Martha Jackson Gallery, she did not think that the couple lived together. She recalls that she thought that they maintained separate studios and that Baber lived alone in her apartment on Bedford Street. She says that she saw no evidence of Baber's clothes at Jenkins's studio.[35] It appears that for a time, Jenkins led a double life, one with his wife in Baber's Bedford Street apartment and another with his mistress in his studio on Broadway. Komaroff recalls Baber as someone "very reserved" with "a rather cool exterior" and as "a very elegant woman who was very devoted to her own art."[36] Baber's devotion to her own work must have been challenging to Jenkins, who expected his wife to focus on him.

Baber's friend Natalie Edgar recalls hearing gossip about Paul's involvement with the young assistant at the Martha Jackson Gallery. She asked Alice about this rumor, and Alice declined to say anything. "She was tough," Natalie remembers about her friend.[37] Only when the dissolution of her marriage finally seemed inevitable in the spring of 1968 did Baber abandon Paris. Although she retreated to New York, she later told one interviewer that she left Paris when its peaceful qualities gave way to the student revolution and unrest in the spring of 1968.

Although civil unrest did disturb France for seven weeks in 1968, especially during May, when daily life was disrupted by mass demonstrations, national strikes, and the occupation of universities, Baber had other reasons to depart Paris. Civil discord in her own home let her to return to living in Greenwich Village, settling alone into her old place on Bedford Street. Like Jenkins, Baber had also held onto her own studio, at 597 Broadway, where she painted.

Baber expressed her aesthetic rationale for returning to New York when she exclaimed, "New York is a very good place to come back to because the light is tough and clear. The color is vivid. I realize in visiting the Midwest that in winter at least, the color is absolutely eaten by the atmosphere."[38] A few years later, Baber reflected soberly, "I left for Paris, so I lost a couple of years. But I gained a European experience and a lot of showing in Europe and around the world."[39] But while her mind could justify returning to New York, her heart was still stuck in Paris.

How some other women artists viewed Baber when she returned from living in France part of every year can be inferred from the way Ce Roser, Baber's fellow feminist artist, recalled her from this time: "Alice was so dressed up and glamorous after coming back from Europe. The rest of us were trying to be Beatniks. We wore corduroys or blue jeans."[40]

One poignant page of Baber's random uncatalogued notes can be dated after its New York postmark of May 3, 1968. It is a mailing from the Howard Wise Gallery in New York addressed to Mr. & Mrs. Paul Jenkins and is covered with her random notes scrawled in different directions. She wrote: "You don't like doing the wrong thing. Can you explain why I want to come see you. To see you makes me nervous—it's punishment. I have so much anxiety. I want you on my side. I am horribly depressed not to go to Paris—I am cut off from part of my existence. Perhaps he could let me come for a few days."[41]

Baber's other notes are clearly dreams, for she wrote, "I dream that I have a key to work in a big studio near my place (On 7th Ave) to paint the wall white for some reason. The people in it—a couple are friendly. Bill de Kooning also has a key. He came in without knocking & the younger man starts to yell 'You can't come here so often.' I am afraid de Kooning will get angry so I rush over & tell him that I am there. We go to Jack Delaney's."[42] Jack Delaney was the proprietor of an eponymous restaurant at 72 Grove Street in the West Village, who died of a heart attack in January 1966, although the dream appears to have taken place later.[43] Jenkins liked to boast that his studio on Broadway had been Willem de Kooning's before he took it over in 1963.[44] When she woke up, Baber realized how much simpler her life was with just one studio because she used to have several (between New York and Paris) and would forget to pay the rent from time to time.

Another time she recorded this dream: "We are working at Mourlot. My mother & sister & Paul are there on Xmas day I am not dressed when Mrs. Mourlot comes to the office. I am wearing a 2 piece dress & my underwear shows. I am very embarrassed." Since her mother died during World War II, when Alice was just fifteen, she could not have been present with Paul, whom Alice did not meet until the late 1950s.[45] The setting for the dream was at Fernand Mourlot, a famous commercial print shop located in Paris, where Jenkins produced lithographs in 1965 and Alice imagined them each working there at the same time.

One of Baber's dreams seems to sum up what went wrong in the marriage: "When I say to Paul 'the sky is falling' it is a natural event—he says (the play, (his drama) the human drama must go on) I say we must go to the press to tell the world about the natural catastrophe." It was as if they were operating on different planets or with different responses to the world around them.

By 1969, Jenkins had produced at least two works that he named after Katherine Komaroff, his young lover: a print in an edition of three hundred that he called *Phenomena Katherine Wheel*, and, in 1971 a large canvas he called *Ore Lode Vein (Phenomena Katherine Wheel Horoscope).*[46] Instead of a partner who competed, Jenkins found, for a time, someone who was less demanding than Baber, who would have felt hurt if she saw these autobiographical titles that he gave to his latest artworks. In 1967, Jenkins, the sycophant son-in-law, painted *Phenomena near Baber Woods* but by 1969, the unfaithful husband produced *Phenomena Katherine Wheel.*

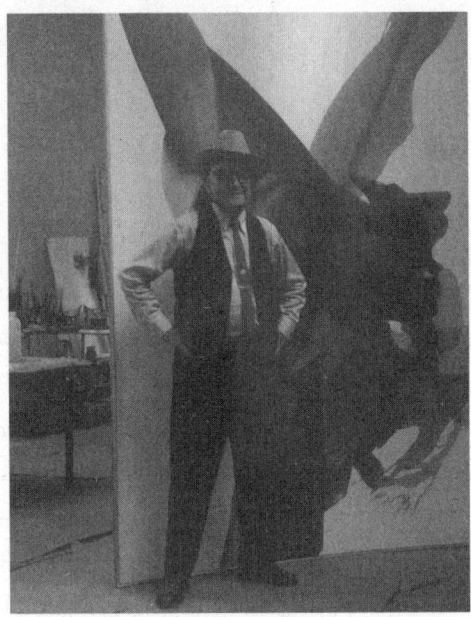

Adin Baber in Paul Jenkins's New York Studio posing

by *Phenomena Astral Signal,* ca 1965

News of the couple's separation reached the art historian and Stanford University professor Al Elsen, who wrote to Jenkins on April 12, 1969, confiding, "The news about you and Alice was depressing as I am very fond of Alice and her recent paintings are the best she has done. I hope that both of you are able to continue working without serious setbacks."[47] Jenkins wrote on May 26, 1969, to Elsen, who had already begun work on a huge monograph on his painting, telling him that he would be pleased to learn that Alice's show, then in its second week, was such a success and that he had spoken to her dealer, Abe Sachs, who said that sales had been good and that he was planning to extend the show another week. He also reported that he had spoken with Baber and told her that people were talking about how well her paintings were received.[48]

Jenkins appears to have felt some concern over the appearance of his behavior. He had written to their close friends Jim and Gloria Jones on April 19, 1969, telling them that Alice was soon to have a show of her work and that she had a new studio of two thousand square feet, located at Broadway and Houston Street in Soho, a short walk from her home, and that there were some good folks in the building.[49] He added his observation that Alice had been enjoying "a full social life and a very quiet, discreet private life." He boasted that she had received an important commission for a 4 x 20 foot painting and speculated "I think I can safely confirm that Alice will go on painting until the day she dies and will probably have a reputation as important and meaningful as Georgia O'Keefe [sic]," adding "We continue to see each other, but not nearly so much, of course, as we did last year."[50] He then asserted that he helped Alice with advertising, catalogue layout, suggestions about her painting, and "all the things that are imperative to both of us in the jungle of art."[51] Jenkins claimed, "She looks like a million dollars."[52] His perception that their mutual friends were concerned about Alice and thought him a cad is palpable. Since he had a practice of selling his paintings to his dealers rather than consigning them, he concludes by mentioning Kathy, whom he reported continues to despair exasperatedly over my "business acumen," for his young companion now also served as his manager.[53]

Meanwhile, as news that the couple's marriage had ended spread throughout the art world, others wrote to Jenkins to express their regret. Sam Kaner, an art dealer at the Court Gallery in Copenhagen, wrote on May 29, 1969: "We hear you and Alice are separated and this made us all sad, but you two happy?" Not a very tactful remark but hearing such comments as Paul carried on his affair with Komaroff must have been very tough for Baber. By then he had been appearing publicly with Komaroff in Paris.[54]

Yet, despite this public presence of Paul with his young mistress, Alice had not yet told her father that her marriage had ended. On July 15, 1968, Adin Baber wrote a letter to his daughter with a copy to Paul: "I am completely abashed that you neither answer my letter and card nor telephone. Also your answering service is evasive. Do not do this to me. I have had the same trouble reaching Paul. What is this?"[55] Adin reminded his daughter that "last October, you told me that Paul had had a fall down a stairway in France, and being unable to paint, had no income. I agreed to honor your overdrawing checks until your show, and hoped for sales. My June statement from the bank shows that you and I are about to be in a financial crisis."[56] He then informed Alice that he was putting into her account her inheritance from her grandfather and canceling her "overdraft privilege," since he had to "pay fertilizer bills to stay in business."[57]

After the marriage ended, Baber's life became even more nomadic. She now needed to augment her income by teaching art, so she often moved about to be an artist in residence. She managed to teach painting at New York University in 1968 and drawing at Pratt Institute in Brooklyn in 1969. Baber taught both art history and studio courses at Queens College of the City University of New York in 1970. Her November 6, 1968, application form lists as references departmental chairman Louis Finkelstein, as well as faculty members James Brooks and Herbert Aach, her friend the painter Natalie Edgar, and John Ferren.

Ferren was not only a fellow artist represented by the A. M. Sachs Gallery, but someone whom Baber knew from both his important leadership role at the Club in the mid-1950s and from when they had both participated in the same group show in 1958. Ferren's abstractions were influenced by both Wassily Kandinsky and Zen Buddhism, both of which interested Baber. By this time, Baber also shared with Ferren a history of living in Paris, though his time there was much earlier, during the 1920s and 1930s. Ferren met and befriended many important Parisian avant-garde artists from Marcel Duchamp and Joan Miró to Pablo Picasso and Henri Matisse.[58] At the moment when Baber was challenged to recreate her life as an artist without her constant companion of the last decade, Ferren's support of her talent and professionalism mattered.

CHAPTER 12

Feminist Imagery and Activism
(1969–1973)

A s the feminist movement gained attention during the late 1960s, artists and writers began to challenge the dominance of men in the arts, seeking attention and opportunities for women. Some banded together in group protests to attain visibility, while others got busy organizing alternative programs and locales. Alice Baber not only made efforts to show her own art, she worked to establish venues for other women to exhibit their art, to discuss feminist issues on panels, and to search for new ways to create a sense of community.

Baber continued to show her work in New York at the A. M. Sachs Gallery, which held another solo show of her paintings from May 17 to June 5, 1969. The show caught the attention of the critic Peter Schjeldahl, who reviewed it for *Art International*: "Alice Baber deploys numberless blips of gorgeous color on her canvases, creating vertiginous images full of light. The greatest density is often maintained in the corners, as blips of all sizes and degrees of transparence build and swirl in and about the relatively empty center. . . . these paintings are pleasurably enough read on the level of simple kaleidoscopic spectacle, somewhat reminiscent of the dazzling free-form 'light shows' that accompany rock and roll concerts."[1] Schjeldahl, however, expressed his discomfort at the possibility that Baber's "reliance on the *O* motif" had "some symbolic significance," which must have referred to his abhorrence of the then trendy ideas about "central core imagery" and feminist art.[2]

Prominent American feminist artists—such as Judy Chicago, Miriam Schapiro, or Hannah Wilke, for example—tried to empower women by referring to women's central core, their shared body part that they saw as making them the victim of patriarchal abuse leading to the marginalization of women.[3] Baber's large painting, *Lavender High* (1968) (CP #30), measuring 80 x 80 inches, of which a black-and-white reproduction of an image from the show that accompanied this *Art International* review, does in fact demonstrate a central vortex of oval lavender shapes convulsing at the pale blue center.

The configuration of an X-shape in *Lavender High* brings to mind Miriam Schapiro's 1967 canvas, *Big Ox* (CP #47), which has diagonal limbs intersecting a central open space and which Schapiro intended to express the female body. Schapiro later described this image as her "explicit cunt painting (that) was a real cry in the darkness . . . for something besides the symbol of the phallus."[4]

Such an *x* configuration became a favorite motif for Baber, who repeated it in various paintings over several years, including in *Lavender Ways to the Seasons* (1968) (CP #31), *Departure for Lavender (Lavender at the Turn)* (1968), *Floating Crossing* (1970) (CP #34), and *Day of Sounds* (1971). She commented in 1975 that after doing a kind of pattern of circles, "I then did a series of 'X' paintings for about five years, and I still do them sometimes. Paintings in which I use the 'X' form, but I use the circle moving into the 'X.'"[5] When asked why she used the *x* configuration, Baber responded to the critic, whose disapproval she perceived: "Because I do like it."[6]

Baber's coyness about the metaphorical meaning of such forms could be explained by her desire to function as an artist in both New York and Paris without inflaming European critics, who were usually even more sexist. The next year, the critic Lucy Lippard warned of the perils women artists faced in Europe in a 1976 article, "The Pains and Pleasures of Rebirth: European and American Women's Body Art": "One does not call oneself a feminist in polite art society in Europe unless one wants to be ridiculed or ignored. All of this must be partially due to the lack of an organized feminist art movement in Europe and of any alternative galleries or magazines for women artists. In the resultant void, middle-class, generally apolitical women have become the purveyors of what, in another context and with a higher level of political awareness, might be seen as radical political imagery."[7]

Lippard exclaimed, "It is no wonder that women artists so often deal with sexual imagery, consciously or unconsciously, in abstract . . . styles," lamenting how often women feel compelled to please the male audience and even engage in self-exploitation, which Baber clearly refused to do.[8] Yet, whether or not Baber's abstract x imagery intentionally contained any unacknowledged female symbolism, it raised no barrier for the Blanton Museum of Art at the University of Texas at Austin, which purchased *Lavender High* in 1968 with its James Michener Acquisitions Fund.[9]

At this particular moment in time, Baber's repeated choice of the color lavender calls to mind the phrase *Lavender Menace*, which Betty Friedan, president of the National Organization for Women (NOW) first used in 1969 to describe what she perceived as the threat of lesbians to NOW and the entire women's movement, fearing that feminists would be dismissed as "man-haters."[10] Although Baber had already used the word *lavender* in several titles a year earlier, in 1968 the color had already been associated with gay men, because of its link to early twentieth-century women's fashion. While Baber might have used *lavender* in her titles in 1968 without thinking about its metaphoric meaning, as a feminist and a fan of metaphors, she must have realized its significance after the public controversy over Friedan's figure of speech in 1969.

A group of women, including the authors Rita Mae Brown and Karla Jay, disrupted the Second Congress to Unite Women in May 1970, showing up wearing T-shirts emblazoned with LAVENDER MENACE and distributing copies of a manifesto titled "The Woman Identified Woman," which put lesbians at the center of feminist politics for their political, cultural, and erotic resistance to patriarchy.

Baber appears to have quietly joined with many heterosexual feminists, who declared themselves "political lesbians" to affirm their solidarity with lesbians and their important commitment to other women. Thus, Baber continued to use lavender for a number of her titles, such as *Lavender Evening* (1970), *Lavender Ladder Turning-Akbar's Hunt* (1972) (CP #38), *Green Light Crossing Lavender Ladder* (1972), *The Lavender Bridge to the Ladder* (1974–1975), and *Lavender Ladder to the Sun* (1976) (CP #44). Baber's discretion was such that her personal expression of empathy for lesbian women and solidarity with their cause could appear in her carefully chosen titles for her abstract art without making her politics obvious to everyone.

Baber's friend, the painter and critic Natalie Edgar, by then married to Philip Pavia, was the "N. E." who reviewed for *Artnews* Baber's solo show in 1969 at her gallery, A. M. Sachs.[11] This review was much more matter of fact, descriptive without the gender anxiety of Peter Schjeldahl's response, when Edgar enthuses over "colored disks speeding along like tumbleweed. Bright viridians, cavernous purples, spinning yellows, steely magentas fall one over the other. Suddenly their paths converge toward the viewer and the disks zoom in, falling towards *him* like rain. Just as suddenly, they ascend like colored sky-rockets, curving toward pinpoints in the sky."[12] It is interesting that although the reviewer speaks of Baber's "complex and liberating compositions," she (or her editor) has chosen to refer to the viewer as "him," designating male viewers.[13] But then, we must recall that this was the era when women artists still had what were called "one-man" shows.

Baber's status in the art world was reinforced by the publication of a color reproduction of her painting on the cover of *New York Quarterly* in the winter of 1970. At the time, Thomas Victor, who was the journal's senior editor, had a Baber painting hanging on the wall of his studio. He later recalled in response to a query from her sister Nancy, "Alice was a friend of mine. We took a Shakespeare reading course together and worked on a brochure of her work. I did the photos. I also arranged for her to have the cover image of the first issue of *The New York Quarterly*."[14] "Alice was a delightful friend to me," he added. "We all miss her."[15] The "brochure of her work" refers to Baber's monograph published by the Women's Interart Center, where she helped to organize their International Women's Art Festival in 1975.

This same issue of *New York Quarterly* also included the poet and art critic John Ashbery, who had written about Baber's work in 1963: "There is nothing acid in the pure dissonance of the faint but strong oppositions of forces marshalled and observed in her work. The poetic possibilities of the colors are allowed to grow up normally without interference from the painter, the result being a curiously sharp climate that takes possession of you gradually, and educates you to find perfectly natural all kinds of intervals which would have seemed precarious a moment ago."[16]

By the late 1960s, both Ashbery and Baber had returned from Paris to live in New York. Despite this relocation, Baber managed to have another solo show in Paris, this time at the Galerie Lambert on Rue

Saint-Louis en L'Île, which earned a review in *Le Monde* on July 2, 1970: "The American Alice Baber has gradually oriented her painting towards a search for ever more precise structured colored shapes. The disordered blurred spots have given way to transparent ovoidal shapes organized according to a very particular scheme, emerging from the periphery of the canvas. The light foggy clusters are as if irresistibly attracted towards the center of the aerial pictorial space."[17] The gallery's announcement featured a photograph of an adorable Alice Baber, crouching before an abstract canvas in her studio, captioned by a quotation taken from James Jones's early essay, appearing first in English and then in French translation: "In her continued study of light and the tragedy of light, Alice Baber has brought to us now a kind of 'celestial painting.'"[18]

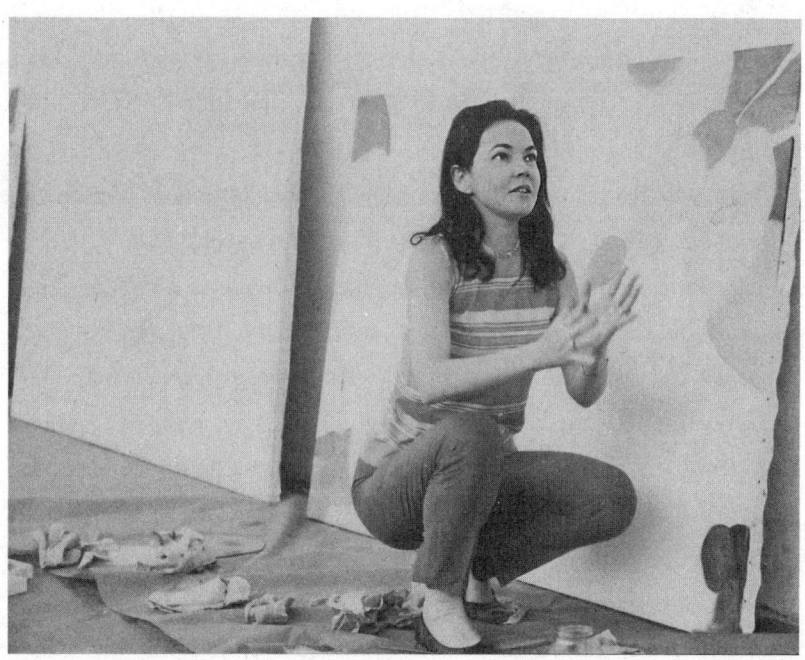

Back in New York, Baber still could not bring herself to tell her father that her marriage to Paul was over. On April 23, 1970, Adin Baber wrote to Nancy's husband, Chuck McNeill, of "a delicate situation," explaining, "The past year, when talking to Alice I would ask about Paul. Her laconic answers always were Oh, he is all right. Now I have always been super-sensitive so felt that something was awry. Upon arrival in New York, I was placed in Paul's part of the apartment and soon discovered no man's clothing but asked no questions of Alice until the last hour before we started to the train station. I then asked: 'Are you and Paul estranged?'"[19]

Adin had felt close to Paul, but this trip he had not called at his son-in-law's New York studio. To her father's probing question, Alice responded limply, "I do not know—I do not care to discuss it." Adin interjected, "I must ask one more question, are you legally married?" He reported to Chuck that Alice responded "yes." He then asked, "What are your plans?" and reported, "Alice answered at length that she is being well recognized as a future artist; that she would like to paint a few more years and move back to the farm. She added, 'No one has a home in New York City.'"[20]

Adin, who never lost his faith in Alice's talent, continued: "Personally, I expect her to become such a famous artist that she won't leave New York City for long. On the other hand, my friend, the famous [writer] Mari Sandoz would leave New York for a few months to return to her loved Sandhills, Nebraska. No one can predict what a person of genius may do."[21]

The painter Archie Rand, who got to know Alice when she showed at a New York gallery next to his own (on the same floor), observed Alice's "devotion to 'painting' that some of us understood when not in the thrall of Clem's dictums. In fact, I once talked about Alice's work to Cora Cohen, who with me, was shoved onto the circumference of Clem's domain." He recalls some of his "friends, dumping on Alice's work for no reason as it seemed to me to be perfectly in concert with the aesthetic territory in which we were all working. At that time A. M. Sachs became referred to as not as 'good' as the small satellite Emmerich-flavored galleries like Elkon and Goldowsky on which Clem had sprinkled holy water . . . there was no incentive for Alice's work to be discounted by anyone other than for the interference of some outside prodding. There was nothing inherently heretical in her work that couldn't fit into the larger tent."[22]

By December 1970, but perhaps as early as April, Alice was seeing Richard Galef, an accomplished industrial and landscape designer, who, like Jenkins, was five years older than she. Baber could have met Galef during the time she spent soon after moving to New York, working for the designer George Nelson. Born in New York City, Galef attended New York University, then served in the US Army during World War II, going overseas, where he worked as the editor of the army newspaper *Stars and Stripes*. Later, to manufacture his designs, he opened his own factory in Williamsburg, Brooklyn. He read widely. Baber shared Galef's love of literature, poetry, and nature.

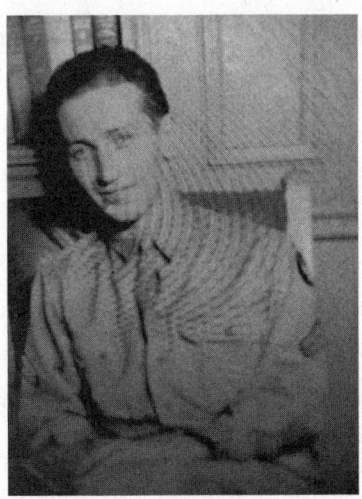

"Richard" [Galef] appears with Alice in the Lassaws' discreet day-books with no other identification.[23] By December 17, 1970, Ernestine Lassaw notes that they got picked up by Alice and Richard to go to a party given by the painter Buffie Johnson, whose guests included many of the New York School artists, including their close friend Elaine de Kooning, who had shown with Baber at the March Gallery.

Richard Galef entered Baber's life in New York, filling the void left by Paul. She continued with the A. M. Sachs Gallery, having a solo show on view March 27–April 20, 1971. James R. Mellow, the same critic who had reviewed Baber's first solo show at the March Gallery in 1958, reviewed this latest one for *The New York Times*. Mellow tried to categorize Baber and another contemporary abstract woman artist, Jo Baer, who was showing elsewhere, as two "serialists." The article's sexist content was thinly veiled, and even the headline—TODAY'S SERIES LINE-UP: BABER AND BAER—makes a near pun on Baber's name as "Babe," combined with an evocation of the macho sports world, which today would be considered politically incorrect.[24] "Strictly speaking," Mellow tried to explain, Baber's "current show is the latest of several in which she has displayed a consistent, abstract imagery—translucent oval or ameboid forms that are marvelous for the radiance and delicacy of their colors—is not a serialist in the orthodox sense in which the term gained currency in the sixties. She does not rely upon the same, shape or size format for all her pictures; nor are her paintings necessarily intended to be seen as an ensemble."[25]

Mellow remarked upon Baber's "subtle inflections of color and brushwork that indicate the signature of the artist, so to speak, rather than the impeccable surfaces, the machine-finished look that many hard-core serialists favor. If Miss Baber's paintings are to be categorized as serialist, it is with the qualification that they are *soft-core serialism*."[26] Mellow undermined what he called "the effectiveness of her work" by his unfortunate but intentional choice of the sexist metaphor then popularly known for its association with softcore or hardcore pornography in film, where the director either chooses to make body parts visible or not.

"The recent paintings are rich, quite beautiful and deft in their handling of forms and colors—overlapping reds, yellows, greens, purples—and can be enjoyed as individual works," Mellow acknowledged. "Seeing them en masse, one can appreciate the cleverness with which the painter has developed a potentially monotonous idea."[27] Mellow admitted, "The pleasures here—in paintings like 'Gale to the Light,' 'Wheel of Day' (CP #35) and 'Wheel of Sound,' with their striking modulations of color and light—are considerable. If the term is not totally pejorative nowadays, Miss Baber adds a distinctly *feminine* grace and suavity to the ranks of contemporary abstraction—and with a style and imagery that is uniquely her own."[28] At this moment of burgeoning feminist protest, most women artists felt that being stereotyped as making feminine art was "pejorative," as Mellow himself knowingly suggested.[29]

A review of the same show in *Arts Magazine* pronounced her paintings "very much of the moment" and reproduced three of her canvases, *Grove of the Piper* (1968), *Day of Sounds* (1970), and *Lavender Turning to North* (1970). "The resulting abstractions are direct and sensuous of inner feelings, feelings of buoyancy, lyricism, and an inner spirituality. Depth and space are attained by careful overlapping of veils and color, generally in the shape of ellipses," wrote the anonymous reviewer.[30] This less polemical reviewer observed Baber's "movements in this group of paintings emanate from the interaction of an implied X-shape crossing at various points in the picture plane. A balance of these elements is achieved through a controlled composition gaining the utmost advantage of light, color, and harmony."[31] There was no effort to impose political meaning where Baber had painted abstract forms.

Such attention in the press as Baber received from her shows in New York was very important in helping her obtain a continuous stream of teaching jobs, especially since she never finished her master's degree, which she had begun at Indiana University during the year following her undergraduate studies. Thus, it was significant when Baber was associated with such internationally prominent artists as the Dutchman Karel Appel, the Hungarian-French Victor Vasarely, and the Spanish Antonio Saura in a feature story in *Newsweek*, on April 12, 1971.

Baber's large and colorful canvas *Before Sounds* had been acquired by the Turmac Tobacco Company in the Netherlands. *Newsweek* told the story of the company's managing director, Alexander Orlow, a Dutch industrialist, who had theorized that color in the visual environment in the form of abstract art, displayed high on the walls above the machinery in the factory's work hall, would create a better environment and help keep the workers on the job.[32] His collection had already grown to more than five hundred artists, including Baber.[33]

Baber's work was clearly known internationally by this time. In 1966 a London newspaper had referred to "Alice Baber Jenkins the Lyrical Abstract Artist."[34] Thus, it was odd when on May 25, 1971, *The New York Times* reviewed a show opening at the Whitney Museum of American Art presenting a donation of a collection of contemporary abstract artists put together by the dress manufacturer Larry Aldrich, and claimed that Aldrich had coined the term *lyrical abstraction*. Yet the phrase had been in earlier use in English in London in 1966: "Alice Baber Jenkins the Lyrical Abstract Artist," so clearly Aldrich did not coin this term.[35] Baber's work was not included in Aldrich's collection, but the show's relevance is that the term would be used years later to describe her work by *The New York Times* in her obituary.[36] Eventually, in 1975 the Aldrich Contemporary Art Museum did invite Baber to participate in its panels and lectures on women artists.[37]

At the time of the Whitney show, the reviewer David L. Shirey explained: "Like baroque or abstract expressionism or almost any general art tag, lyrical abstraction is one of those vague terms that can at once embrace sweeping similarities as well as differences in styles and personalities. Nothing could sustain this observation more than the current lyrical abstraction exhibition at the Whitney Museum. . . . 33 young American artists, and they run a gamut of artistic persuasions."

Claiming that Aldrich had identified a trend in American painting, the museum explained that in coining "'lyrical abstraction,' Mr. Aldrich used the expression to describe an art that is, in his words, 'lyrical,' 'sensuous' and 'romantic' in colors that are 'softer' and 'more vibrant,' a visually 'beautiful' art."[38] Shirey noted that "color-field painting belongs primarily to the sixties, and lyrical abstraction hardly reacted against it. As a matter of fact, it freely used the colors and techniques of color-field painting to soften what it borrowed from abstract expressionism. If lyrical abstraction leans most heavily on abstract expressionism, it is by no means a return to it. It lacks the force, impact and sense of fundamental creativity of abstract expressionism."[39] Finally, Shirey gets to the point of lyrical abstraction: "It is not interested in fundamentals and forces. It takes them as a means to an end. That end is beauty. Beauty is not always achieved. But when it is, lyrical abstraction has fulfilled its purpose."[40] To the extent that Baber's works can be considered lyrical abstraction, she often achieves that sought-after beauty.

As for the history of the term *lyrical abstraction*, we must consider that the use of the term in the United States followed its use in Paris, where as early as 1947 the French art critic Jean José Marchand has been credited with coining its name.[41] *Lyrical abstraction* is also said to have been a component of Tachisme, when the name of this movement was coined in 1951 by Pierre Guéguen and Charles Estienne, the author of *L'Art à Paris 1945–1966*.[42] All of this, of course, took place long before the beginning of *lyrical abstraction*, the term described in the United States as "coined" in 1971 by Larry Aldrich.

At least one online source dates "Lyrical Abstraction ca 1945–1960" and defines it as "the least strident sub-variant of the wider *Art Informel* style—itself one of the most important European modern art movements of the post–World War II period—Lyrical Abstraction (or 'Abstraction Lyrique') was a French style of 20th century painting in the manner of American Abstract Expressionism. Compositions were sensuous, romantic and painted in a loose gestural style."[43] This same source defines the meaning of lyrical abstraction by explaining that it "was not a specific school or movement, rather a tendency within *Art Informel*. See it as a balanced, elegant, (sometimes animated, sometimes soothing) style of abstract art which is nearly always charged with content taken from the natural world. Often marked by sumptuous colour, its harmonious, painterly beauty may be contrasted with the harsh, angst-ridden and dissonant imagery produced by other *Art Informel* groups like COBRA, or recent Neo-Expressionists."[44] This definition could well apply to Baber's work. With her abstractions, we can find many references to the natural world either in her titles or in her comments—from her 1975 canvases like *Sound of the Wind* or *Sound of the Cloud* to the pale triptych that she said she produced after witnessing mists enveloping Machu Picchu in Peru.

Baber's connections to European aesthetic developments included her solo show from June 16 to July 12, 1971, at the Galerie für Zeitgenössische Kunst (Gallery for Contemporary Art) at Bornstraße 10/11 in Hamburg, Germany. Even given Baber's success at getting shows and positive critical reception, times were still very difficult for women artists, most of whom still had much less opportunity than men to sell their work or to obtain permanent teaching jobs.

Thus, Baber continued to scramble to augment her livelihood by teaching, surviving a rather nomadic, fragmented existence. In 1970–1971 she was a visiting professor at the University of Minnesota in Minneapolis. Baber later admitted to having felt unsettled: "The only place that I had any trouble painting at all was in Minnesota," where she was both teaching and had a show at the university's gallery. "The snow was so white there was no color," she admitted, adding, "I ended up painting dark paintings with sort of flames, red flames, as if they were fireplaces, you know. Or all-white paintings, with just a few colors."[45]

One of Baber's untitled poems seems to relate to her experience in Minnesota, where she traveled to earn money, the "nomad's gold":

Glass buds, form upside-down in hollows, and flail
Enormous bones, hair, flesh and nomad's gold,
Frozen three times as moving icy snails
Have crept and fallen in the changing fold.
Hot breathing ice has worn its rivering way
Down eyes and nose and mouth to belly and toes.
Travelling continuously night and day.
In sheets of colors, speckled with salt snow.
As purple heaps the space of rocky-go.
Breathing the teeth of horns in aggregate.
Dark lanterns move and shift light blow by blow.
The marble gaps its mass of silty weight.
Cross over, one-step, at this open hour,
Green moss, step-two: brown earthy, brine wind, re-flower.[46]

Reaching beyond the childish jingles and almost surreal tetrameter and trimeter, she attempts pentameters in their sonnet form, yet still her imaginative take on objects, textures, plants and animals, stepwise struggle, elemental lights and darks recalls another of her notes, "What saved me that winter was a trip to Santa Barbara where I went in advance for the next year. As soon as I saw all the tropical things I was alive again. And then I went back and I painted like crazy."[47] But when she did spend the following semester at the University of California, Santa Barbara, she reacted to the Pacific Ocean, claiming, "The light is too bright. You almost can't see what you're doing. It's like an experience rather than an environment to work in."[48]

Baber visited Southern California as a participant in the show *Trends in 20th Century Art*, a loan show drawn from the permanent collection of the San Francisco Museum of Modern Art, which took place from January 6–February 1, 1970 at the Santa Barbara Museum of Art, organized by Ala Story. Baber was written up in the "Women's News" section of the Santa Barbara paper: "This internationally known artist was a bit of a disappointment. She didn't look at all the way I had imagined her, you know, sort of O'Keefe [*sic*, for Georgia O'Keeffe] or Nettleson [*sic*, Louise Nevelson intended]. She looks like a New York fashion model and has the enthusiasm and warmth of a deb."[49] Because she was so attractive, Baber had to deal with stereotyping and being dismissed as a model or a debutante, "deb," for short, suggesting that she behaved like a young woman of marriageable age from an upper-class milieu rather than a courageous woman who had chosen the role of artist and was a kind of bohemian rebel in disguise. At the time, she was already forty-one years old.

This journalist, despite her ridiculous stereotype of how women artists should look exotic, as in O'Keeffe's intentionally austere appearance or Nevelson's dramatic costumes and emphatically huge false eyelashes, did pronounce Baber's three oils in the show "very exciting," although only Baber's *Seven Green Leagues* (1967) is listed in the catalogue.[50]

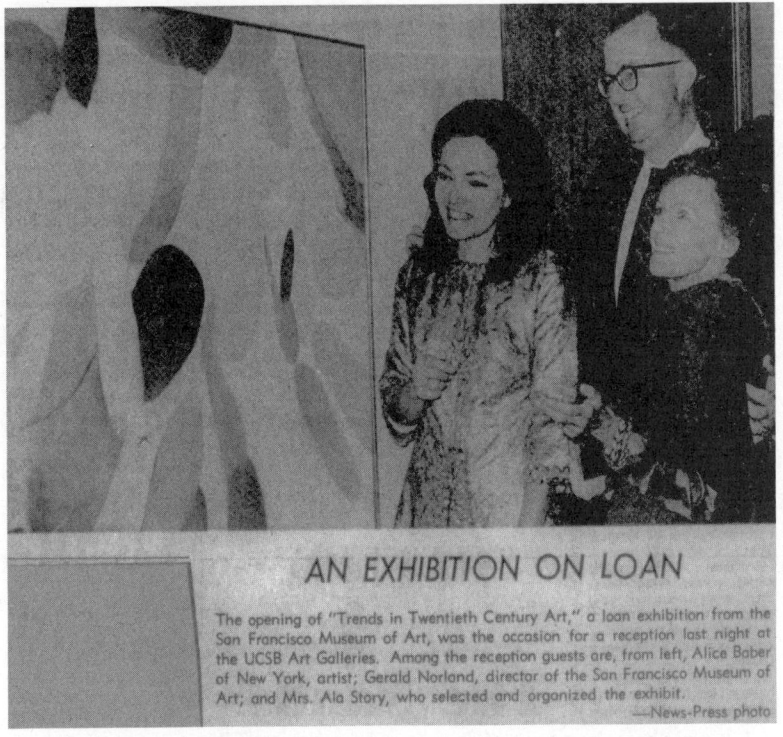

AN EXHIBITION ON LOAN

The opening of "Trends in Twentieth Century Art," a loan exhibition from the San Francisco Museum of Art, was the occasion for a reception last night at the UCSB Art Galleries. Among the reception guests are, from left, Alice Baber of New York, artist; Gerald Norland, director of the San Francisco Museum of Art; and Mrs. Ala Story, who selected and organized the exhibit.
—News-Press photo

Baber posing in front of *Seven Green Leagues* (1967)

Baber wrote that she painted *Seven Green Leagues* (CP #29) in France and that "the title comes from a folk story about a giant's movement. The painting is involved with upward leaps and the metaphor of awkward growth."[51] The folk story to which Baber referred is known in French as *Le Petit Poucet*, where seven brothers from a poor family are saved from starvation and a hungry ogre when the youngest and tiniest of the brothers manages to steal the sleeping ogre's magic "seven-league boots," which enable the wearer to go from one mountain to another in a single step and to jump over rivers.[52]

From fairy tales to poetry, Baber's creative imagination helped her relate to her nephews when, while showing in *Trends in 20th Century Art* in Santa Barbara, she took the opportunity to visit her sister Nancy and her family, who at the time lived nearby. Always enthusiastic, she arrived with paint and canvas to give her nephews painting lessons. Nancy's younger son, Geoff, who was then about fourteen years old, was struggling with a homework assignment to analyze "Mother to Son," a poem by Langston Hughes. Aunt Alice, he recalls, volunteered to help him. Totally comfortable with poetry, she easily explained the meaning of the assigned poem, with its line "Life for me ain't been no crystal stair," which Geoff recalls understanding as "Life is not a bowl of cherries."[53]

While still on the West Coast in 1970, Baber first met the sculptor Betty Gold, who lived and worked in Venice, California. The two became friends. "I don't know why—I was like a little sister," Gold recalled, "Alice was eager to go places and do things. I loved her art."[54] Gold's sculpture emphasized color, but the two women made very different kinds of art, not causing Baber to worry, as Gold remembered she did when she found other friends copying her work.

Although Baber valued her family, women friends, and feminist activities, she did not limit herself socially or professionally to such circles. In Santa Barbara, Baber was friends with the collector and banker Charles Craig, whose tastes and acquisition included contemporary artists like Baber, Stanley Boxer, and Norman Bluhm; early modernists, including David Burliuk, Max Weber, and Suzanne Duchamp; and ancient sculptures from Asia, Africa, the Mediterranean, and South America.[55] Craig owned Baber's 1967 canvas, *The Ringing and the Ringing* (CP #29), which she inscribed on the verso "For Charles Craig April 1969." This inscription documents that Baber had earlier been in Southern California, where Ann McCoy recalls that she was one of many house guests at Craig's Santa Barbara home. *The Ringing and the Ringing* is another example of Baber's linking colors to sounds and movement, which was a direct response to her synesthesia.

An invitation reproducing Baber's *Yellow Swing*, "To meet Alice Baber" for cocktails at 21 West Arrellaga Street, Charles Craig's Santa Barbara home, on January 4, 1970, documents the friendship of Baber and this most important California patron—who, however, was gay, and not a suitor to replace Paul.[56] In a lecture Baber gave in Santa Barbara in 1976, she recalled her visits there in 1970 and 1971 and the creative community that she found despite the drama of the moment: "I painted for two months in the garage of Charles Craig. I painted the terrible fire in the mountains and the earthquake. I have painted Margaret Mallory's grape arbor and Robin and Ernest Jones's rose garden, Irma Kellogg's quiet pool and many other memories from Santa Barbara."[57] Baber referred to the San Fernando earthquake on February 9, 1971; while its epicenter was to the south of Santa Barbara, the shock was felt for three hundred miles along the Southern California coastal region.[58] Her friend Margaret Mallory was a documentary filmmaker, who with former Santa Barbara Museum of Art director Ala Story founded Falcon Films in 1947 to produce films on art and artists.

Returning to her life in New York, Baber continued to see Richard Galef. The two spent the weekend of July 30, 1971, visiting the Lassaws in East Hampton. For August 1, Ernestine recorded the hot summer weather in her daybook, noting that they had lunch on the beach, went to the opening of a collage show, had cocktails at the Ernsts' (referring to the artist Jimmy Ernst and his wife Dallas), and went to dinner at Stephen Talkhouse, a popular live music venue and bar in nearby Amagansett. Baber, however, no longer prioritized being with a companion. The demands of her career came first.

Although Baber was still seeing Galef on February 22, 1972, when they had dinner in New York City with the Lassaws at Lüchow's before attending an opening at the MoMA, she was focused on promoting a group that she had formed of like-minded artists. Together with

Herbert Aach, Baber organized a group of five artists, who, though working in different styles, emphasized color in their work, which they called Color Forum, since they got together and talked about color at the 23rd Street Workshop Club, a successor to the Club.[59] Baber served as guest curator for a related show held in 1972 at the Blanton Museum of Art at the University of Texas at Austin. She wrote an essay for the catalogue, as did three other members of the forum: Herbert Aach, Gabriele Rosenberg, and Robert Slutzky.[60]

At the time of the group, Gabriele Rosenberg and Robert Slutzky were married.[61] Since they subsequently divorced and Rosenberg changed her name to Gabriele Roos (with whom I was later acquainted) I did not immediately realize that Rosenberg and Roos were one and the same person.[62] According to the biography in the catalogue of Baber's show *Color Forum*, Rosenberg was born in Hamburg, Germany, in 1932, just before Adolf Hitler came into power in 1933.[63] The family of four emigrated in 1938; however, years later, Rosenberg decided to change her name and buried her previous identity, even her prior achievements.

In *Color Forum*, Rosenberg's essay, "On Color," states, "Visual narration in film seems to have begun at just about the time when painting began to free itself from narration's hold and to search for other aesthetic and expressive means. . . . Voice becomes an integral part of the gestalt of a human being—without it the sense of that person becomes quite flat, unfinished."[64] In a sense, Rosenberg turned her own history from part of a famous narrative to an abstract creation.

In addition to these artists who contributed catalogue essays, the other artists Baber included in this show were considered to have color as their "obsession," including Pat Adams, Josef Albers, Sam Francis, Sam Gilliam, Joyce Kozloff, Robert Natkin, Ray Parker, Ad Reinhardt, Mark Rothko, and Clyfford Still.[65]

In her "Curator's Notes" for the catalogue *Color Forum*, Baber stated, "My own point of view leaned heavily to the pre-eminence of color—what I call 'color hunger'—that has motivated my own work and my selections. I have also looked for magic, poetry, eccentricity, saturation, overemphasis, and so forth."[66] On a more personal level, Baber wrote what can be called her most basic philosophy: "Pure color and hue for their own sake, on one level, and as metaphor on another, are what interest me."[67] She explained that in selecting the show's artists, she began with a list compiled by Herbert Aach and then, working with the rest of the group and the gallery's director, Donald B. Goodall, decided on the final participants.

Baber's synesthesia—her tendency to link color with sound—is apparent in her curator's notes in the *Color Forum* catalogue: "There is some emphasis in this show on low-keyed statements about high-keyed spectrum colors; that spectrum colors are 'sweet' and that they are carried into unusual juxtapositions, set the teeth on edge like the high sweet quality of Mozart; that 'hot' and 'cold' concepts must have new definitions for flat color passages as opposed to modeled color."[68]

Commenting on her own essays in *Color Forum*, Baber stated, "I wrote an article about color, in which I described colored memory of my own that I thought would relate in a way to my work, going through each color. And later on I read something or other that Kandinsky wrote, which is not the same as mine, but I thought it was such a good way of showing it when I was doing it."[69]

For example, Baber wrote in her essay on color: "Purple: it can be black or grey or green or blue or lush or puritanical. I use it for rivers or mountains, and pilgrimages, all trips to far places, for wild winds and for the shadows on the ground of eagles carrying snakes, and the evocation of the effervescent lonely but happy souls thinking of pink and yellow and green in vast gardens."[70]

In contrast, she considered: "Orange is not so difficult; the actual pigment can be made transparent easily but it can turn into brown light or become sick with green mixed badly, or can make a splendid opaque grey. Orange is primitive; it makes Easter eggs or Peruvian mats and kimonos in the rain, and blonds with feather boas, beach towels and umbrellas, magazine covers, and principalities beyond the seas."[71]

Baber left notes about her talk at a panel related to the *Color Forum* show. She chose to explore color as metaphor in four categories. From Baber's earliest career to the end of her life, metaphor remained central to her interests. For the panel discussion on color, she wrote, "When color is freefloating, it is already a metaphor of the artist's view, color seen from all sides, from over, above, under, around and from afar. This floating world intrigues me; the everyday mimetic world is too specific. Freefloating color deals with the transformation and suspension of things."[72] Baber referred to "multiple imagery—abstract imaging—images created by color lost, found, flooded with light or grazed by shadow comes close to expressing elements of nature both seen or imagined, in the garden, the city, lost kingdoms or whatever. The use of the color can be both universal and specific."[73]

Baber wanted to explore "the meaning of the choices of the colors by the artist which results for myself from color hunger. No two artists attribute the same feelings or ideas or moods to the same colors and it becomes very personal."[74] Baber discussed a third kind of metaphor that she called "'the metaphors of process.' As you are working, colors and forms change under your hands, new ideas emerge. These may have disappeared when the painting is finished but traces will remain as gentle ghosts."[75] Baber pointed out a fourth "kind of metaphor that might occur, is in the final reading of the surface of the painting that the artist and viewers see together and which can easily become symbol or allegory."[76]

Here Baber makes it evident that she was aware of symbolism that could be read into her own abstract art by diverse sets of viewers. That would include the *x* configurations that feminists or anti-feminists read into her art as gender markers in the late 1960s and early 1970s. She was, of course, long aware that an *x* could just be a mark for someone, often illiterate, intended to take the place of a signature, or just used to mark a choice in voting.[77]

Baber also wrote that another kind of metaphor related images to titles and even to the color in a painting. As examples, she cited "whether de Kooning read Faulkner, who titled Jackson Pollock's work," referring specifically to whether Barnett Newman titled Pollock's 1952 painting known as *Blue Poles*.[78] She added, "Robert Delaunay has described the effect of color as a blow to the forehead. For me it is a healing process of clearing the mind, the Rorschach Test thinks of the effect of color as color-shock."[79] She referred to the psychological test in which people's perceptions of inkblots are recorded and then interpreted to measure personality characteristics or emotional functioning.[80]

Baber had given the matter of abstraction a lot of thought: "One of the things that I am interested in is the idea of the painting. . . . I feel that an abstract painting is outer space, and I am in front of it, suspended in outer space, so that there isn't any horizon line. However, there is probably a sense of up and down, and side to side. There is a sense of infinity, which I like very much. And I like the idea of infinity coming way forward, so that you have reverse infinity."[81]

Baber related this concept of reverse infinity to "a Sonia Delaunay tapestry," noting in 1973 that she was "writing an article on her. I know her and I admire her work very much. And she just had a show, and so I'm trying to write about it."[82] Baber had met the Ukrainian Jewish immigrant Sonia Delaunay in Paris through their mutual friend, the American painter Buffie Johnson.[83] "I found Sonia Delaunay absolutely extraordinary to know as a friend and she was very brilliant," Baber later commented. "She was knowledgeable. She was a very intense kind of person. . . . I think that it has been one of the greatest pleasures of my life, knowing Sonia Delaunay."[84] Baber admired how Sonia Delaunay helped young artists, but very secretly: "She very quietly and generously helped artists and was just someone that when I would be going back to Paris I would go to see her and we would look at Paris from her eyes, her eyes as a painter. I found that very exciting."[85]

Like many feminists, Baber had an interest in finding role models among earlier generations of women artists. From April 20 to 22, 1972, Baber took time to attend the conference of Women in the Visual Arts held at the Corcoran Gallery of Art in Washington, DC, from which she kept her annotated program. She appears to have attended workshops by artists like June Wayne, who offered "Survival Techniques of Women Artists" or the curator Marcia Tucker's "Problems of Curatorial and Directorial Positions in Museums." Baber marked on her program the critic Cindy Nemser's "Analysis: Critics and Women's Art," and the photographer Lisette Model on "Women in Photography."[86]

Although Baber's ongoing concern with color and abstract art does not relate directly to her activism in the women's movement, she took time away from her own painting and teaching to write about other artists' work as well as women's themes. In the spring of 1973, Baber showed at Fordham University's Lincoln Center's campus in a show called *IX Painters*, in which nine women each showed one work. The critic Joseph Mascheck reviewed the show for the April issue of *Artforum:* "An accompanying catalogue, in tabloid form, announces 'IX PAINTERS—9 Styles' (styles come cheap?) and quips coyly, 'Coincidentally, all the painters are women.' The two most professional efforts were Alice Baber's *Wind Divided Mist the Darker* (1972) (CP #37)—something like a color-field work seen through a kaleidoscope."[87]

Mascheck mentioned that he preferred the much larger women's show at the New York Cultural Center, which took place that same year. Despite the trouble most women then had to show their work, Baber's painting, which won early attention in this show of just nine artists, *Wind Divided Mist the Darker*, resold at Sotheby's on September 28, 2023, for $698,500, reflecting the surge of interest in Alice Baber and in women artists in general.

That larger group show at the New York Cultural Center was called *Women Choose Women*; it was initiated by the group Women in the Arts.[88] Baber was chosen in 1973 as one of 111 women artists in this show notable for its selection committee, which included the feminist art historian Linda Nochlin and artists Pat Passlof, Ce Roser, and Sylvia Sleigh, the latter three in the show. Among the other artists were some whom Baber knew or would soon know well, including Dorothy Gillespie, Buffie Johnson, Gabriele Roos, and Joan Mitchell. Reproduced in the catalogue was Baber's large canvas *Green Light Crossing Lavender Ladder* (1972), measuring 77 x 58 inches.

The feminist art critic Lucy Lippard remarked in her introductory catalogue essay for *Women Choose Women* that "New York museums have been particularly discriminatory, usually under the guise of being discriminating."[89] Lippard's comment was quoted in *The New York Times* review of the show, written by none other than James R. Mellow, who had reviewed Baber's shows in 1958 and 1971. Now, although he stated, "The strongest showing is made by the realist painters," he noted, "But there are some fine abstractions, too: Alice Baber's delicate veils of color . . ." naming her first in that category before claiming, "Women, too, appear to have a natural instinct for color. Or is that another male myth learned at a mother's knee?"[90]

The New York Times, probably responding to charges of sexism for Mellow's review, decided to run a feature story written by the visual artist and writer Roslyn Drexler, who singled out just four of the artists, who were already "known to the public": "Joan Mitchell, Alice Baber, Nell Blaine, Mary Frank."[91] In a review of *Women Choose Women* for *Artforum*, April Kingsley referred to an idea she attributed to Judy Chicago and others that women's bodies, including her "centrally located uterus—condition her work as an artist." Kingsley dismissed the theory that these factors tend to produce "centrally focused paintings or sculpture and a preponderance of circular, ovoid, or box shapes in overlapping flowerlike concentric structures," arguing, "I am afraid, however, that despite the logical neatness of this theory, precious little work can be found, in this show at least, that conforms to it. Alice Baber's centrifugally massed, ovoid fingers that overlap like petals of a single giant flower provide the only perfect example of such an image in the entire show."[92]

Baber must have chosen to show this particular work, perhaps because she wanted it to fit in or even to be provocative, for her commitment to feminism was sincere. At this time, she also expended energy in writing about other women artists. In December 1973, her article on Sonia Delaunay was featured in *Craft Horizons*. Baber, having had her marriage to Jenkins fail, must have been curious how Sonia and Robert Delaunay functioned as an artist couple, especially a pair like the Delaunays, who, like Baber and Jenkins, both explored color and light, and sometimes exhibited together. Baber was already on record that she found too much cubism in Hans Hofmann's teaching, so the cubism in Delaunay is not what attracted her. In her article Baber self-reflexively quoted Delaunay, "Colors are notes of a poetic language which expresses states of soul."[93]

Just months earlier, Richard Galef had photographed Baber in her New York studio. The photograph, dated 1972, is artfully posed, capturing Baber in profile before several of her canvases and looking at her watercolors, seen on the floor and in a storage box. The next year, Galef donated Baber's oil painting *Lavender Ladder Turning-Akbar's Hunt* (1972) to the Whitney Museum of American Art (CP #38). Measuring eighty inches square, the canvas was a substantial gift. Since Galef was not known as a photographer, it appears that he made this one as personal work for a good friend, whose painting he then donated to the Whitney. Even before I discovered that the name "Richard" appeared with Alice in the Lassaws' daybooks, Galef's sensitive photograph of Alice and his donation of a major painting to a museum suggested that Baber and Galef had more than a professional relationship. Only later did I find confirmation in the Lassaws' discreet daybook notations.

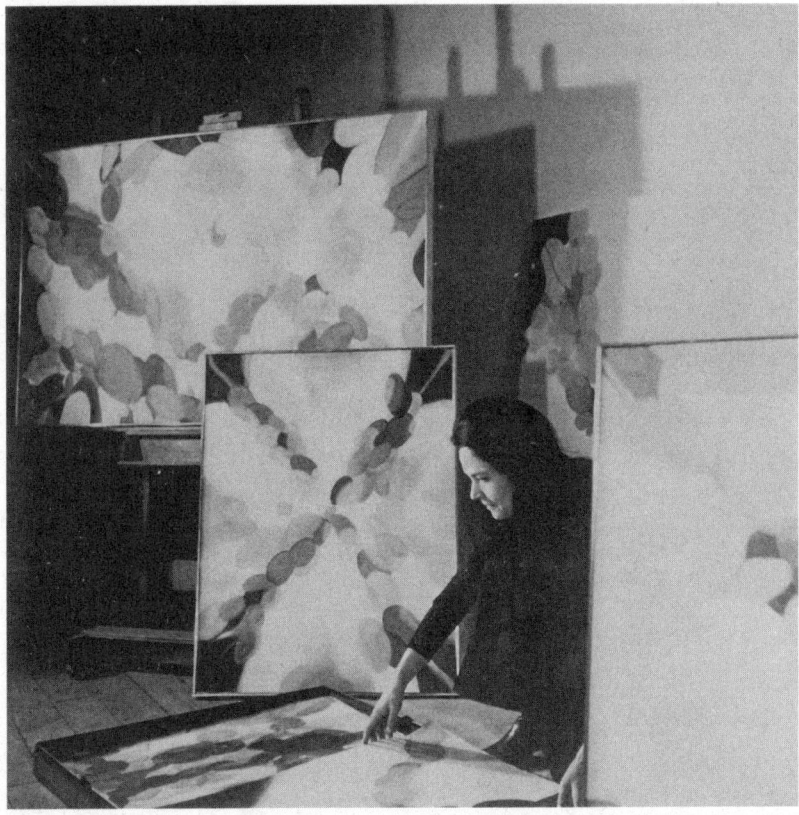

CHAPTER 13

Nomadic Challenges
(1973–1975)

When not globe-trotting to promote her work, Alice Baber relied upon teaching to sustain herself. From 1972 to 1973 she taught studio art at the State University of New York at Purchase. That year, we know that she assigned as textbooks Rudolf Arnheim's *Art and Visual Perception* (1971) and Bates Lowry's *The Visual Experience* (1967).[1] In the book by Bates Lowry, who was the director of the Museum of Modern Art from 1968 to 1969, Baber must have liked the chapter on color, which states, "The perception of color is the single most strongly emotional part of the visual process. Our reactions to color are often strong and immediate, and we associate the most diverse experiences and emotions with certain colors."[2] Baber would have appreciated Arnheim's discussions of light as well as color. He wrote that "light is more than just the physical cause of what we see. Even psychologically it remains one of the most fundamental and powerful of human experiences."[3]

While Baber was clearly engaged by teaching and feminist activism, she was fortunate to have forged a supportive and ongoing relationship with her dealer, Abe Sachs, who was so enthused about Baber's work that in January 1973 he showed her paintings in A. M. Sachs Gallery's two locations. Uptown, at 29 West 57th Street, her recent paintings were on view, while downtown, its Soho branch, at 141 Prince Street, presented her earlier paintings from the 1960s and 1970s.[4] The printed notice for these shows reproduced Baber's canvas *The Piper Sees the Ladder* (1972).

Roberta Smith reviewed both these shows for *Artforum*, describing some thirteen years of Baber's work, including several triptychs: "Several paintings from 1959–62 consist of round edgeless spheres which spread into each other. The use of a narrow range of bright color, which varies mostly in terms of value, encourages this spread. . . . The paintings are soft and static, like hazy clouds."[5] Smith concluded that Baber's "titles further the naturalism inherent in this kind of imagery. The paintings sometimes represent specific, often turbulent occurrences: *Dervishes Before the Palace* (CP #38), *The Piper and the Wind*, *Hunt in the Mountain*, *Expulsion of the Mythical Kings* (CP #36)."[6]

The recurring turbulence Smith observed, from Baber's allusion to aggression in her titles with words like *expulsion* or *hunt*, could be seen as a metaphor for the dissolution of Baber's marriage. At the same time, however, Baber's interest in movement links directly to her synesthesia. With regard to the movement inherent in each of these titles, Baber wrote, "I also use color to make movement (not gesture) to cause the forms to move all over the canvas—around and about, across, up and down, sometimes in one direction and at different speeds—some fast, some slow."[7] She later claimed to "like movement and suspended movement."[8] Baber's ongoing focus on conveying movement in painting relates her work to the psychologist Heinrich Klüver's observations about synesthesia.[9]

Baber explained, "Color makes light. Some light moves over the surface as if this wind were moving it, that was the kind of color light that first interested me, but now I am more interested in light within each color so that the separate colors move across the canvas as if each were a separate colored light cast from different places in space."[10]

Baber's love of light eventually led to her finding a home of her own with "lovely light and I am bathed in it, painting away," as she described her own place in Sag Harbor on the east end of Long Island.[11] Visiting her close friends, the Lassaws, and occasionally housesitting for them, encouraged Baber, by the summer of 1973, to rent her own place, and eventually to purchase a home where so many New York artists spent their summers. She told friends that the light on the open fields reminded her of the Midwest.[12]

Baber also recalled meeting fellow artists on Long Island, including, for example, the painter Conrad Marca-Relli, a founder of the Club, when he came over to the Lassaws' home while she was visiting and commented on the images in a book of Paolo Uccello's Renaissance drawings that she was studying, telling her, "See, we're not interested in the sky behind the battle."[13]

Another abstract expressionist whom Baber met, probably also through the Lassaws, was Adolph Gottlieb, whom she recalled seeing at the home of Balcomb Greene in Montauk at the tip of Long Island. She recalled looking out at the water and the rocks and asking Gottlieb: "'What is that something in a painting that you want to get?' And he said, 'Well, I always call that the meat and potatoes.' Isn't that wonderful? I said 'Oh, my God.' I certainly wouldn't have thought of anything as simple as that or as basic an answer. I am not sure to this day that I have an answer."[14]

Spending more time on Long Island, Baber began to show her work at the Elaine Benson Gallery in Bridgehampton, nearby her Sag Harbor home. Just a few months earlier, from February 3 to March 1973, Baber's small canvas *Blue Float* (1967) was included at the Montclair

Art Museum in a show of the collection of Harold and May Rosenberg, longtime residents of East Hampton and close friends of the Lassaws.

While Harold Rosenberg does not appear to have written anything substantial about Baber, his wife, May Natalie Tabak, wrote a few lines about her friend, whose critical reputation was growing.[15] In January 1975 Tabak wrote, "Alice Baber's by now familiar forms and glorious colors evade all ritualistic observation of scientific laws of color phenomena. At a glance we immediately recognize her gamboling gametes despite their ceaseless amoeboid metamorphosis . . . whatever we chance to discover in our encounters with Ms. Baber's works, we welcome, we welcome as joyous relief from the tedium of predictable art."[16]

The development of Baber's art responded to the last three trips that she made to India, from 1972 to 1976. The announcement for her two January 1973 shows at the A. M. Sachs Gallery stated, "She recently returned from her second trip to India where she added to her *own* collection of Tantric art."[17] Some of these art works—including a Russian icon and "Tantric Buddhist miniatures from Tibet" had been photographed in an installation in Baber and Jenkins's home to accompany *Art in America*'s 1967 article on artists who collected.[18] Now she announced that she was collecting by herself, not with or for him. For Baber, however, India was not just an opportunity to shop. She favored India as a destination that satisfied her love of color, often making her recall having reveled in "long streamers of pink sari cloth being dried near the red fort in New Delhi."[19]

Another time Baber said, "I think India's probably the most fabulous place I've ever been. The color is incredible there."[20] It was not just the color of India, she insisted, but the culture that appealed. At some point, Baber was studying Buddhism, a topic for some of the lectures she attended in New York, at the 92nd Street Y, by such speakers as the Argentine author and poet Jorge Luis Borges, who wrote a book on Buddhism, or Alan Watts, the British writer and speaker, known for interpreting and popularizing Buddhist, Taoist, and Hindu philosophy for a Western audience.[21] Watts became famous among the counterculture for his book *The Way of Zen* (1957); he argued in *Psychotherapy East and West* (1961) that Buddhism could be thought of as a form of psychotherapy, which would have appealed to Baber, who was constantly recording her dreams, which often reveal the anxiety she suffered.[22]

Baber's study of Buddhism can be seen as preparation for her third trip to India, in January 1974, when she had a one-person exhibition in New Delhi at the Chanakya Gallery, run by Shami Mendiratta.[23] A review of the show noted how one responded to the vitality and energy that caused the "surging streaming magnificence of light and colour. Nothing else matters."[24] Another reviewer stated that "Alice Baber's inspiration comes from colours, orange saris being dried outside the Red Fort in Rajasthani women in bright 'edhinis' [pure silk saris] at work. She remembers all these details and puts them on her canvas in oil colours which carry the freedom of water paints."[25] At the time of her show, the National Gallery of Modern Art in New Delhi purchased Baber's painting, *Blue Dervish*, for it's permanent collection (CP #45).

Back in New York, Baber joined with other feminist activist art-ists during the summer of 1974, when she, together with Dorothy Gillespie and the other twelve members of New York Professional Women Artists (Seena Donnerson, Joyce Blum, Joyce Weinstein, Mary Abbott, Sari Dienes, Ann Gillen, Buffie Johnson, Fay Lansner, Ce Roser, Theresa Schwartz, Margot Stewart, and Susan Weil), staged a portable walk-thru outdoor exhibition in Battery Park in lower Manhattan, which then briefly moved to Central Park at 60th Street and Fifth Avenue for several weekends in September. The journalist

Anna Quindlen reported that "Alice Baber painted large circular transparent shapes to form what she calls 'a tree of life.'"[26] The poignant purpose of the show was to call attention to the work of the group of women in New York Professional Women Artists, which institutional gender bias made necessary.

That fall of 1974, Baber was one of the fourteen New York Professional Women Artists who participated as a group in teaching at the New School for Social Research in New York a course called "Women Artists Past to Present." The other participants included Mary Abbott, Therese Schwartz, Margot Stewart, Buffie Johnson, Fay Lansner, Sari Dienes, Susan Weil, Ann Gillen, Seena Donnerson, June Blum, Joyce Weinstein, Ce Roser, and Dorothy Gillespie. Baber's lecture was announced on the course flyer as "Sexual Characteristics of Color."[27]

The course had just begun on September 19, when Baber's supportive father died at the age of eighty-two on October 7, 1974. Shortly after the funeral, Alice invited John Kern, her eldest nephew, who was returning from a stay in Europe, to come and live for several months in her studio on Broadway in New York, which was not otherwise being utilized much due to her travels. Kern recalls that his aunt had a record player in the studio and an amazing record of Portuguese music. He recalls that they spoke about the arts and how much they influence each other, reflecting their own era, but also how they can reveal new directions. He also remembers that she considered Johann Sebastian Bach the greatest artist ever.[28] The love of music that she shared with her nephew reflects its centrality for her painting.

Baber was also drawn to music from foreign cultures, including the music known as *sema*, which comes from a Muslim religious order, a mystical sect known as Sufi, which originated in Islamic Persia in the thirteenth century. Their melodies, which are aimed at creating spiritual transcendence, employ a reed flute and the rhythms of a double-headed drum. This music is associated with dervishes, who whirl or dance as a devotional exercise.

Dervishes Before the Palace is the title Baber gave to her 1972 triptych (CP #38). Her abstract canvases feature forms that appear to leap across the three panels to evoke whirling dervishes, men who choose lives of material poverty, embracing love and service to reach God. The sect was founded by the son of Rumi, the widely read lyrical poet and Sufi mystic. Baber painted in 1973 an expressive watercolor she called *Green Dervish Turns to Blue*, the forms and colors of which also evoke movement (CP #39); and in 1974, *Blue Dervish* (CP #45).

Baber, who clearly had interest in traditional Persian culture, had committed to go to Iran in December 1974, for a show of her work that opened on December 5 at Gallery Ala of the Iran America Society in Tehran. The timing was difficult, since she had barely time to adjust to losing her father before she had to leave for Iran. For the bilingual brochure for this show, Baber chose to feature an excerpt from James Jones's essay discussing "the tragedy of light."[29]

In Tehran, Baber met with Ms. Mahnez Afghami, the minister of women's affairs, and visited a women's center. In connection to her show, Baber presented a talk on "What's New in American Art." Her show took place during the time of the secular and authoritarian rule of Mohammad Reza Shah Pahlavi, commonly referred to as "the Shah." The works Baber showed included canvases called *Cradle of Lapis Hermit* and *The Flag on the Mountain*, which were for sale. She conducted some art workshops in Tehran.[30] Baber's trip also involved traveling in the provinces for the first ten days.

It turns out that Baber was accompanied in Iran by her friend Richard Galef with whom she had been having a significant romance, which for a time withstood her peripatetic lifestyle.[31] How close

Baber's friendship was with Galef remained unknown to me until I ran into Margaret Poser in the audience of a panel about Alice Baber that I participated in at the Berry Campbell Gallery in New York.[32] I had not seen Margaret for years but remembered her well. I met her through her mother, Mimi Poser, who, for her WNYC radio program, interviewed Alice Baber in 1974, and then me, on an unrelated topic, a few years later.

Margaret was eager to share with me her memories of meeting Alice Baber at a dinner held at her parents' Manhattan apartment. Alice, she recalls, was accompanied by Richard Galef, and they were showing slides of their trip together to Iran in December 1974 on Joe Poser's projector. Margaret remembers seeing their slides of Isfahan, the Iranian city with outstanding seventeenth-century architecture, which especially interested her because at the time she was at Harvard, taking a course on Islamic art with the noted art historian Oleg Grabar.[33] Thus, the couple's relationship, which had begun by 1970, well before Galef photographed Baber in 1972, was still on in early 1975, when this dinner took place.[34]

Baber introduced Galef to her friends James and Gloria Jones, who in 1975, after sixteen years in Paris, moved to East Hampton, long a gathering place for artists and writers. James Jones claimed that eastern Long Island was a "beautiful" place to live and work: "I'm getting older. I've still got a lot to do. And I got the feeling that the only real cultural excitement is happening in the U.S."[35]

Their daughter, Kaylie Jones, recalled: "Alice was a close friend of my parents, and remained so even after her divorce from Paul. Shortly after we moved to Sagaponack, Long Island in 1975, Alice bought a house just down the road in Sag Harbor, and spent many evenings sitting around our dining table in the kitchen of our old farmhouse."[36] Kaylie remembers Richard as "quiet, sweet."[37] She characterizes Alice as "a good sport, willing to try anything. Gloria really loved her," and says that Alice "was beautiful, like a Victorian countess."[38]

As happy as Baber was to have her old and dear friends as neighbors on Long Island, she was not content to stay close to home. She was driven instead to travel to exotic locations like India and Iran, expecting to find inspiration for her paintings. A few months following Baber's show in Iran, *The New York Times* published an article captioned SOTHEBY'S HAS STRUCK OIL SELLING ART TO IRANIANS, a clipping of which Baber kept in her papers.[39] Internationally acclaimed works of contemporary art, such as Jackson Pollock's *Mural on Indian Red Ground* (1950) and abstractions by Mark Rothko, were purchased during Iran's 1970s oil boom under the supervision of Queen Farah Pahlavi.[40] As for Baber, beyond a potential new audience for her work, travel to such foreign places continued to fuel her imagination, providing new contexts in which she could experience color.

Another of Baber's longtime friends from France, the American expatriate painter Joan Mitchell, wrote to her around this time, telling her, "We're sitting here with plenty to drink—Talking old times and thinking of you in the most appreciative terms—believe that! Alice—French mail strike so I couldn't write you about your father—I'm so sorry—was in N.Y. for 4 days & am out here at Sally's drinking with Charles & we are thinking about you . . . You're having a show in Iran?—marvelous—do come to Vétheuil for more than lunch please Charles is moving in on me next week."[41]

Baber and Joan Mitchell were not just women painters who shared the experience of dealing with gender bias, even while showing in New York and in Paris—they shared something much more significant. Both were synesthetic artists whose senses were attuned to linking colors with sounds, letters, or other senses like taste. They shared their perceptual sensitivities with many other visual artists from Vincent van

Gogh to Wassily Kandinsky. Anxiety associated with synesthesia might have contributed to both Mitchell's excessive drinking and to Baber's stress, but this cause for anxiety was not known during Baber's lifetime. Contemporary neurologists had not yet focused on synesthesia.[42] Yet mutual sensitivities from synesthesia could also have added to Baber and Mitchell's enduring friendship.[43]

Baber's linking color to sound is behind her pale canvas, *Sound of the Wind* (1975). Such work in Baber's solo show at the A. M. Sachs Gallery from February 1 to 20, 1975, got reviewed in *Art in America*, where the critic Al Brunelle commented, "Alice Baber's new 'white' paintings demonstrate her unique and substantial contribution to color painting more forcefully than does her earlier work, wherein the dazzling deployment of vibrant color tended, happily enough, to intoxicate rather than inform."[44]

At this point, Baber had a record of showing regularly since 1965 with Abe Sachs, about whom she said in an interview: "Yes, he's done well for me and I think he has done well as a dealer and for all his artists. I mean, I think he has a very good eye. He has a good eye for color when he looks at paintings. And I think his choice of stable has by and large been quite interesting all this time."[45] Sachs also helped her get shows around the country, often at university galleries or small museums, but women artists still had a much more challenging terrain to navigate. This was especially helpful since Baber was seen by Robert Littman, who worked at the A. M. Sachs Gallery, as "timid."[46] Others viewed her as "genteel" or as having "mid-Western reserve."[47]

In March 1975, students in the Feminist Art program directed by Miriam Schapiro at CalArts in California sent requests to many women artists, imploring them to "write about your own work. We believe that your art deserves to be perceived as you intended. We hope that the publication of this book will provide a means for the beginning of a new critical language. Responsibility for the place of women in history rests with women."[48] The project requested photographs of the artists and their artwork with a deadline of just a month away. Baber was pleased to be included with this group of seventy-eight women, some of whom were older and much more established than she. Some of the others included—besides Schapiro—Eleanor Antin, Judith Bernstein, Audrey Flack, Grace Hartigan, Lee Krasner, Alice Neel, Betye Saar, Joan Semmel, and June Wayne.

Baber submitted her 1974 canvas, *The Bridge of Sounds*; the photograph of herself in her studio taken in 1972 by Richard Galef; and a statement about her process and preferences: "I start a painting from color or color memory. I wake up in the morning and feel the need of color and I begin to work. I use circles as forms: open, closed, crossing over each other and crossing the whole space. The shapes originally evolved from still life materials, circles which gave me open and closed form. I am interested in color movement and color leaps, and in color vibrations, that occur from colors that can be picked up from different parts of the canvas."[49]

The Lassaws' daybook records that Alice and Richard left their East Hampton home on September 1, 1975, the end of Labor Day weekend. From around this time, Kaylie Jones recalls that, as a teenager, she was very impressed when Richard Galef showed up with lots of high-quality medical marijuana for Alice to smoke, which was intended to help her deal with the nausea she experienced from chemotherapy treatments to treat melanoma.[50] Yet, Baber's long relationship with Richard Galef was about to end. In July 1975, he met the woman to whom he would propose marriage three months later.[51] He might have perceived that Baber was more devoted to her art than she could be to any man, or, perhaps, either Galef or Baber feared that she would not survive her battle with melanoma.

Baber, energized by feminist activism, once again turned her attention to showing in 1975 with New York Professional Women, in an exhibition held at the New School for Social Research. Along with Baber, the members showing art were June Blum, Sari Dienes, Seena Donnerson, Dorothy Gillespie, Buffie Johnson, Fay Lansner, Ce Roser, Therese Schwartz, Margot Stewart, Joyce Weinstein, and Susan Weil.[52]

In between her travels, feminist activism, and illness, Baber still managed to paint. One such example from this hectic period is her 1975 oil on canvas, *The Light in the Depths* (CP #41). Compared to works from a decade earlier, like *Pink Change* or *Bright Safe* (both 1965) (CP #25), Baber has simplified her forms and rendered them much more distinct. Many of the forms swirl toward the center of the later composition with a focus around a dark blue vortex, which recalls the earlier concept that Baber discussed as "the idea of infinity coming way forward, so that you have reverse infinity," as in her interpretation of Sonia Delaunay's work.

Such formal analysis, however, was not the focus of Baber's teaching from 1975 to 1978, in New York at the New School for Social Research. Instead, with her friend—the artist, curator, and administrator Dorothy Gillespie—she taught a popular course called "Functioning in the Art World: New Roles for Artists, Curators, Collectors, Administrators, Students, and Community Leaders," which was aimed not at teaching "how to make it," but instead about how to make "community" to develop mutual goals for success.[53] The New School catalogue promoted this course as: "For the person who wants to become an essential part of the art world, this course explains the way to enter any or all of the different aspects—who is important in each aspect and how they overlap to form the whole *Art Scene*."[54]

The fall term was concerned with "the curator; the collector . . . the artists; the teacher; hanging a show and moving a show; art and grants;

and public relations." The second or spring term stressed "styles in art; styles in life; galleries and alternatives; journalism and art; museum trustees; structure and non-structure in art organizations; how to give an art world party; the problems of fund raising; and can we make a better art world?"[55] At the time, almost no art history department taught such topics, which would have been invaluable for beginning curators, especially young women, who were transgressing gender barriers. This course was revolutionary.[56]

This collaboration, and the enduring and mutually supportive friendship between Gillespie and Baber, functioned despite the different paths each had chosen in life. Gillespie was not only an active artist, but she had married and raised three children.[57] Such "community," stretching across different lifestyle choices, Baber had achieved through her energetic engagement with feminist activism.

Baber was active with the Women's Interart Center, located at 549 West 52nd Street in the Hell's Kitchen neighborhood on Manhattan's West Side, which became known, from 1971, as the first women's alternative space in the city, a trailblazing New York exhibition space sponsored by the artists' collectives Women Artists in Revolution (WAR) and Feminists in the Arts. Baber served as a trustee of the Women's Interart Center, working together with high-profile art stars such as writer, activist, and sculptor Kate Millett; painter Alice Neel; and sculptor Louise Nevelson. Baber, who served for a time as the head of the steering committee for the Fine Arts Museum of the Women's Interart Center, managed to be a feminist activist without seeming radical, just as she had managed to convince her high school classmates that she was artistic without being bohemian. Baber was simply skilled at being subtle.

Baber's activities with the Fine Arts Museum of the Women's Interart Center included organizing a series of special events to salute "1975: Women and Art" with a panel on May 7 (which was recorded), moderated by Alice Baber. The panel was called "The 1975 Art World/The Women in It." Panel participants were Howardena Pindell, an American artist, curator (then at MoMA), and educator; Judith Van Baron, teacher, curator, and administrator; Isabel Bishop, painter and graphic artist; and Mary Garrard, the art historian, who was then heading up the Women's Caucus for Art, which was trying to encourage women's studies in art and art history.

As the panel's moderator, Baber had to deal with Isabel Bishop's opening statement, which was in the form of a provocative question that she insisted on repeating: "Do you find that there is such a thing as women's art? I wonder." Baber interjected diplomatically, "This is one of the most interesting problems that we have to discuss in the women's movement in a sense. There are many, many shades of opinion on that." Bishop repeated: "I just don't see that it's ever been established that there's a women's art. Or that women are discriminated against in exhibitions."[58]

Bishop tried to provoke a debate, asking her co-panelist, Judith Van Baron, then serving as the director of the Bronx Museum, why anyone would want to have a show with art by women only. Van Baron noted that she was one of the few women to direct a museum. In fact, Bishop had often been privileged to be chosen as the token woman in exhibitions and also chosen as the only woman to serve on the editorial board of *Reality*, a short-lived artists' journal from the early 1950s produced by men, including Edward Hopper, Raphael Soyer, Alexander Dobkin, Joseph Solman, and Sol Wilson.[59] Bishop, who enjoyed being the "token woman," had little empathy for other women artists.

Bias against women in the art world made Baber's nomadic existence necessary. She had to keep on the move to support herself as an artist, whether teaching or showing her work. She expanded her audience by traveling to Palm Beach, Florida, for her first solo show at the Palm Beach Gallery in March 1975. Her canvas *Bridge of Sounds* (1974) was featured in the show's publicity. In June 1975, Baber spent time visiting with her sister Nancy at their family's home, near Kansas, Illinois, not far from Paris, Illinois, where the local newspaper identified her as "an artist of international renown."[60] Mary Ann Tucker, the journalist who wrote this feature, was a childhood friend of Alice Baber, who also attended the same schools, in the class after Alice.[61]

That August 1975, Baber was included in the notable show *Women Here and Now*, organized by artists Joyce Kozloff and Joan Semmel, shown at Ashawagh Hall, a community center frequented by artists in East Hampton. Along with the work by the two organizers and Baber, the show included many other leading women artists, among them Elaine de Kooning, Audrey Flack, Jane Freilicher, Buffie Johnson, Fay Lansner, Betty Parsons, Miriam Schapiro, and Hedda Sterne.[62] At this show's opening, Carolee Schneemann, known for multimedia works engaging her own body, presented the first performance of *Interior Scroll*, one of her most notorious works, in which she appeared to report sexism while reading from a scroll that she slowly pulled out of her vagina.[63]

Consistently more decorous than overtly radical, in 1975 Baber organized a large international show of women artists called *Color, Light, and Image* for the Women's Interart Center to mark International Women's Year, designated by the United Nations. The show, open from November 13, 1975 through January 30, 1976, featured 115 women, including such familiar names as Louise Bourgeois, Sonia Delaunay, Audrey Flack, Shirley Jaffe, Pat Passlof, Sylvia Sleigh, May Stevens, and Jane Wilson.

This women's show Baber organized was much larger in scope than most previous ones, including art not only from the United States and

Europe but also from Asia and Africa. The review in *Art International* by Phyllis Derfner pronounced the show "impressive apart from Feminist concerns, while it advanced the cause of women in art with an admirable openness and evenhandedness. In participating in this show, women served their own best interests and equally those of art. This was an event where the gap between unrelated, strictly esthetic and narrowly Feminist issues was effectively bridged."[64]

At the time of this large international show of women artists, the Women's Interart Center published a monograph, *Alice Baber*, which reproduced an inscribed photograph of Baber by Arnold Newman and included Baber's own essay on "Color," as well as excerpts of previously published writing by John Ashbery, Al Brunelle, Natalie Edgar, James Jones, Keith Sutton, May Natalie Tabak, and Rose Slivka.[65]

The contribution by Slivka, Baber's editor at *Craft Horizons*, for her article on Sonia Delaunay, was a poem, "Song to the Color in the Paintings of Alice Baber," dated January 7, 1975.[66] Slivka took up the connection of Baber's love of travel to her absorption of the colors she responded to in the interesting places she kept visiting, citing Isfahan, the historic city in Iran, known for its spectacular Persian architecture, its mosque with blue tiles. When Slivka began, "In Isfahan, the yellow lions of light outrun the river," she referred to Baber's recent canvas, *Isfahan Remembered* (1975).[67] The poem's images are abstract like Baber's art, but the final line reads "the last color of dreams," which seems very appropriate given Baber's focus on color and her demonstrated interest in recording her dreams. Yet for Baber, reference to the memory of Isfahan could also signify the loss of her traveling companion.

Baber must have invited Slivka to write something to accompany her work in the exhibition and catalogue *Women Painters and Poets*, organized for the Visual Artists Coalition Inc. for a show at New York

University's Loeb Student Center dedicated to the United Nations declaration of International Women's Year.[68] Slivka's poem appeared in the show's catalogue next to a reproduction of Baber's canvas *Ladder Tree of the Hermit*, and across from a painting by Baber's good friend Dorothy Gillespie, accompanied by a poem by Helen Adam.

The monograph on Baber also included a longer essay by the poet Richard Howard, who was also a close friend of the older abstract expressionist Lee Krasner, and liked abstract painting.[69] Howard wrote of Baber's art: "The several paintings, so similar, so discrepant, are renditions of the ecstatic apocalypse (if as I think an apocalypse means the casting out of intermediary images, those determinations which stand between identity and process), demystifying the 'ominous' colors of the expressionists, as Ashbery has already noted about this artist . . . we have agreed, in the convention of our speechlessness about such things, to call them beautiful."[70]

Later that year, Baber left New York to visit Paris, Illinois. The occasion for this visit was a show of her watercolors in Edgar County, Illinois, at the new Bicentennial Art Center and Museum on East Washington Street (known today as the Link Art Gallery). Her return to the family home around the time her father died probably inspired this show, which was called *The Tragedy of Color*, once again echoing the interpretation of the writer James Jones.[71] Alice and her sister Nancy attended the show's opening reception given by the Paris Art League.[72]

Baber, once her relationship with Richard Galef ended, began to focus even more on her painting. She tried her hand at curating, but while interesting and diverting, the minimal fees paid for such part-time work would not enable her to sustain her painting career. She once again turned to foreign travel, not only for inspiration, but also to support herself and to continue showing her art. She managed to finance this venture by being completely available, adaptable, and agreeable.

CHAPTER 14

Color Hunger: Appetite for Latin America (1975–1977)

nterviewed in 1975, Alice Baber was asked if she chose her colors when she started a painting or if she worked in layers, deciding as the painting progressed. She responded with her usual explanation: "My choice of color comes from something I call 'color hunger.' I wake up in the morning and have a tremendous desire for a color. When I start a painting, I find that I can't help but use that color, and then I find that that color will dictate some of the other colors. Sometimes I repress myself because I know that technically I have to build up to that color I have in my mind."[1]

Baber also recounted that she kept "a certain number of paints handy; I know which brands will produce certain things, so I always have great stacks of tubes of those around. So finally, you do have a palette, and that palette is always available, and from that point on, it is up to your mood and your emotions."[2]

Baber was so immersed in color she could project her own emotions onto the palettes of other painters. She published an insightful article, "Gorky's Color," in the catalogue for a show that opened in October 1975 called *Arshile Gorky: Drawings to Paintings*, organized for the Blanton Museum of Art at the University of Texas at Austin, for which Baber served as assistant curator, working with Isobel Grossman. This was Baber's second project for this museum under the direction of Donald Goodall, for whom she had organized the successful *Color Forum* show in 1972.

Baber's observations about Gorky are revealing for what they tell us about her own perceptions. "The ambiguity of possibility, the recurrence of the suspended line, occurs for a thousand reasons," she wrote, adding, "Gorky emphasized what most painters later in the fifties were admonished to avoid, the finding of multiple images wanted or unwanted in a work, the implication of subject matter. From the fifties to the seventies, the mystique of flat space and nongeometric, nonorganic, nonsubject matter continued to be a dictum around town."[3] Baber seems especially self-reflexive when she wrote: "The artist finds shapes, chooses, moves the hand; the mind finds ambiguity. It isn't always the same story. Artists play with form as executioners play with death. When painters talk together, we talk about materials and ambiguity of space and form and color."[4]

"The implication of subject matter" runs through Baber's abstract work, sometimes drawing meaning from the idiosyncratic titles, which often repeat favorite themes like Piper, Path, Ladder, or Swing, or concepts like sound, light, or color. Baber focused not only on her own interest in color, light, and shadow but also on Gorky's use of light and shadow. She mentioned in her catalogue essay that she owned an untitled 1936 drawing by Gorky.[5] Baber clearly viewed Gorky's life and work with empathy and admiration, which she had developed upon first arriving in New York.

Thus, Baber managed to work successfully on a show of a male artist whose work she admired, even while she actively sought to promote herself among women artists who identified with feminism. With other women artists, who lived both in the Hamptons and in New York City, Baber continued to show at the Elaine Benson Gallery in Bridgehampton in 1976, where openings provided a social hub for summer visitors.[6]

By the fall of 1978, Baber was finally able to purchase the house on Hampton Street in Sag Harbor, which she had been renting since 1974.[7] Baber traveled so much, however, that she had little time to enjoy her vacation home on Long Island. Around this time, she also relocated her city home from the West Village to her studio at 597 Broadway, just south of Houston Street in Soho, the former industrial neighborhood, which then attracted many artists with its ample cheap loft space.[8] Ann McCoy remembers that Baber's loft was huge and a fourth-floor walk-up.[9]

From 1973 to 1976, Baber was able to teach in New York at the School of Visual Arts and at the New School for Social Research. Anticipating her exhibitions in California, she became a visiting artist at the University of California, Berkeley, for the spring term in 1976. From June 2 to July 6, 1976, she had a solo show at the Santa Barbara Museum of Art, while concurrently from June 8 to 25, 1976, the William Sawyer Gallery, located on Clay Street in San Francisco, accorded Baber a solo show, *Celebration of Color*.

Thomas Albright reviewed Baber's show for the *San Francisco Chronicle*: "She could extend that title [*Celebration of Color*] to cover the entire show, although she would have to add a few words about space, movement and sensuous paint surfaces, for her finest paintings celebrate all these forces, and with a rare strength and beauty."[10] He described Baber's abstractions as "made up of broad, lobular shapes that resemble rounded beach stones. These become scaffolds for applications of richly harmonized oil colors, some full and intense, others vaporous and transparent, unified by a softness of surface that resembles the sensitive touch of a pianist."[11]

Around this time, Baber began to work frequently for the United States Information Agency (USIA), a government agency devoted to the practice of public diplomacy that operated from 1953 to 1999, most centrally during the Cold War years.[12] She had already participated in the US Department of State's Art in Embassies program, lending for several years her paintings for exhibition abroad in many countries.

The USIA repeatedly sponsored Baber's travels, during which she showed her artworks, lectured, and gave well-received demonstrations about how she created her art. Her abstract style fit the needs of the USIA for American art that could circulate without having politically provocative content. Baber's only political visibility at home was in the sphere of feminist activism, which was mainly positive and of interest to her audiences in the countries where she was sent at the time of her engagement. For example, the USIA would not have chosen to sponsor a feminist in countries that had specific government policies repressing women.

Adaptable and personable, Baber worked well for the USIA's mission statement: "To understand, inform and influence foreign publics in promotion of the national interest, and to broaden the dialogue between Americans and U.S. institutions, and their counterparts abroad."[13] One of the program's stated functions was to "bring the benefits of international engagement to American citizens and institutions by helping them build strong long-term relationships with their counterparts overseas."[14]

For example, Baber explained her art in a slide-illustrated talk in Guadalajara, Mexico, which has a large American expatriate community. A feature in the local paper covered the event and concluded, "Her enthusiasm for expression in color, with her personal charm and personality, made for an enjoyable and enlightening experience."[15] Baber's papers include evidence of the lasting friendships she formed with many of the people she met in her official travels.

When Baber visited Mexico during the summer of 1975, she planned to return for an exhibition of her work there and to give some lectures for the USIS in Mexico City.[16] She did have an exhibition in Mexico City in December 1976.[17] Her show in Guadalajara opened on May 13, 1977. The vivid colors in Mexico, like those in India, appealed to Baber's sensibility.

Back home, Baber's solo show at the A. M. Sachs Gallery, from February 5 to 24, 1977, earned respect from Dennis Masback, who, not yet thirty years old, was probably the youngest artist then showing with Sachs, having just participated in a group show there in 1976, before he gained a solo show the next year. He recalls not only Baber's work with its focus on color and movement, but that "Alice was sweet to me, a gentle nice person," who was "very generous with me."[18] Baber's show was reviewed by Grace Glueck for *The New York Times*: "Miss Baber continues the abstract imagery she has shown over a period of years—translucent amoeboid forms in delicate colors that drift and swirl on fields of white. Of late the palette has become paler, and several of these paintings have a lovely quiet lyricism, particularly the very light canvases in which color is almost a trace element, such as 'The Dream of the Jaguar.'"[19] Glueck found Baber's watercolors less interesting than her canvases.

At the time, watercolor as a medium seemed out of fashion, although the earlier abstract works of Georgia O'Keeffe were still very much admired. In another review of this show, Baber herself was quoted, explaining, "Shapes emerged as I worked . . . lotus, heat, light. Overall intense colour dissolves shape and bathes form with pulsating vibration. This is energy. It controls the subject matter and makes it more mysterious as it changes."[20] In her review, Ann McCoy declared Baber's paintings "both mysterious and masterful. . . . The works are studies in light and colour in the purest sense."[21]

Other specialists of the watercolor medium admired Baber's work. The artist Lawrence Goldsmith featured examples of Baber's work in his 1980 book, *Watercolor Bold and Free*.[22] He reproduced Baber's watercolor *The Floating Tree of the Jaguar*, noting that "boldness of conception led to boldness in design and execution. Nothing was allowed to impair this purity of purpose."[23] Baber's inclusion in such a book would help in her effort to hold academic positions as a visiting artist.

Goldsmith also reproduced Baber's *The Sound of the Wind (Sacred Space Series)* in conjunction with his advice on composition, where he suggested concentrating on a single shape, which would earn her "the utmost freedom in all directions." Goldsmith commented on Baber that she was "somewhat protozoan, this artist has structured an arrangement full of variety and vibration. She has superimposed some shapes and let others overlap, but most are clearly visible. In contrast, she has faded the outlines of just one. Her orchestration of color is mainly in a range of blues. The red and brown-violet shapes therefore offer pleasing shocks. Her plain background allows for a range of value changes, and lets each shape be seen with lucidity."[24] Goldsmith noted that Baber had traveled extensively in South America and that she enjoyed "tropical light, when possible by water," and that in her New York studio Baber remembered what she called "the light of my travels."[25]

In fact, Baber and her paintings traveled widely. Ever adaptable, from 1976 to 1978, also under the auspices of the US Department of State, Baber exhibited and lectured in thirteen Latin American countries.[26] Highly motivated, Baber sometimes solved the problems of the high cost of shipping and unreliable customs between countries by carrying her entire show herself, as she suggested in a February 7, 1977, letter to Helen Hughes, director of the Instituto Cultural Dominico Americano, in Santo Domingo, Dominican Republic: "I bring work with me for a show in a roll under my arm. I can bring enough oils and watercolors in this way for a large space—stretchers could be sent down in advance. It makes more sense than forwarding things from Mexico or Bogotá, because air shipments are so sporadic, and so are customs conditions in various countries. Therefore, I would be happy to exhibit and lecture in July."[27]

In 1976 alone, Baber spent five months traveling and exhibiting her work for the USIA, spending a month and a half each in Brazil and in Mexico, and the rest of that trip in Colombia, Costa Rica, Guatemala, Haiti, Jamaica, Nicaragua, Panama (and the San Blas Islands), Paraguay, Peru, Santo Domingo, and Uruguay.[28] In 1977 she had solo shows in Bogotá, Colombia, and Guadalajara, Mexico. The catalogue for this last show in Mexico reproduced translated excerpts of her essay for the 1972 show she had curated called *Color Forum*.

For some catalogues for her shows in Latin America, several earlier reviews were translated into Spanish, including the longer 1975 essay, "Alice Baber y lo Bello" [Alice Baber and the Beautiful], which the poet and essayist Richard Howard had written originally for the monograph published by the Women's Interart Center.

Baber's success is evident in voluminous and time-consuming correspondence with friends made along the way and in the fact that the USIA kept scheduling and promoting her. For example, from Uruguay, Assistant Cultural Affairs Officer Rose S. Berstein wrote to Baber on January 4, 1977, to say that her photograph was featured in the US embassy's new calendar and her successful appearance in Montevideo was one of "the high points of our 1976 programming."[29]

From Brazil, where she participated in a seminar, Baber was complemented: "Your teaching professionalism was especially noted and recognized and materially contributed to the aforemention [*sic*] success. One could feel throughout the seminar the real interest and enthusiasm generated by you in your classes, by your obvious knowledge of your subject field and the interest you took in discussions with the participants and your fellow colleagues."[30]

"Her lectures were primarily about painting, with an emphasis on color: yet, everywhere she went Cultural Officers were interested in the Feminist Movement in the US, and wanted to know more about the status of women artists here," Joellen Bard reported.[31] "In Latin America," Baber explained that she saw "the beginnings of an international camaraderie among women artists."[32] "More North American art should be seen in Latin America and more Latin American art seen in the United States," Baber stated.[33]

In Brazil, Baber helped to organize and participated in a special session concerning "the new working woman: at home and on the job."[34] Having organized and participated in many feminist exhibitions in the United States, Baber observed that the distinction between contemporary painting and sculpture and women's traditional crafts was rapidly disappearing in the work of feminist artists like Judy Chicago or Miriam Schapiro.

Of her travels in Latin America, Baber commented, "It was also educational for me because I've always been obsessed by color myself and especially fascinated by the way they use color in the folk arts and crafts."[35] What Baber saw at home as the reevaluation of traditional women's crafts like quilts she could apply to crafts in Latin America from *molas*, the colorful reverse-appliqué rectangles from the San Blas Islands (an archipelago in Panama) to native embroidery in Mexico's Yucatán. Baber was reported to have said that contemporary "cottage arts [crafts] . . . not shown in museums is beginning to appear there."[36] Baber collected many examples of *molas* that featured imaginative animals and abstract patterns, originally made as blouses by Native women.

Baber was reported as describing the art that she had seen in Mexico as an "'ambiguity of forms,' especially in embroidery, 'which can be considered an art form and is sometimes even worth having signed.'"[37] Baber regularly purchased brightly colored handwoven Indigenous garments, several of which she brought home as gifts for her dear friend Ernestine Lassaw, at least one of which Ernestine proudly modeled in a photograph.

Ernestine's daughter Denise wrote of Baber: "Each time she returned from an adventure in India, Central America, or Asia she brought armfuls of handmade clothes as gifts. Before I was a teen my 'style' was set—wearing Alice's dresses embroidered with feathers, small mirrors, or hand-woven nubby plant-dyed fabric. These delights were not yet sold in New York City. Perhaps this made me look weird, but I belonged to a rare tribe and I was proud to wear our colors."[38]

Baber reflected upon the aesthetic impact of her travels in Latin America, "The fabulous colors delighted me, but I was also very much moved by the snow on the mountains. I got involved with the idea of things that appear and disappear in snow. I translated that interest into dealing with a very white painting where the light seems to pour around the forms, so the forms themselves seem to get lost."[39] She had solved the problem that she had first confronted in the winter she had spent teaching in Minnesota.

Baber had returned to New York by January 5, 1977, when she wrote to Asta Rose Alcaide in the USIS program division at the US embassy in Brasília, Brazil, to thank her: "At long last I'm back in New York. The last half of my trip ended with a month and a half in Mexico City. . . . I've had a marvelous trip and I am home in New York now for five months but will be heading back to Bogotá for a show at the Centro Colombo

Americano. I have so many adventures to recount that you will have to come to New York to hear them."[40] Baber writes about her forthcoming workshop in Bogotá and proposes that they consider holding one in Brasília. She asks for news of Brazil and offers, "I'll write more later about how it rained in Machu Picchu, how the peso fell in Mexico and the luminous color on the top of the mountains in Haiti."[41]

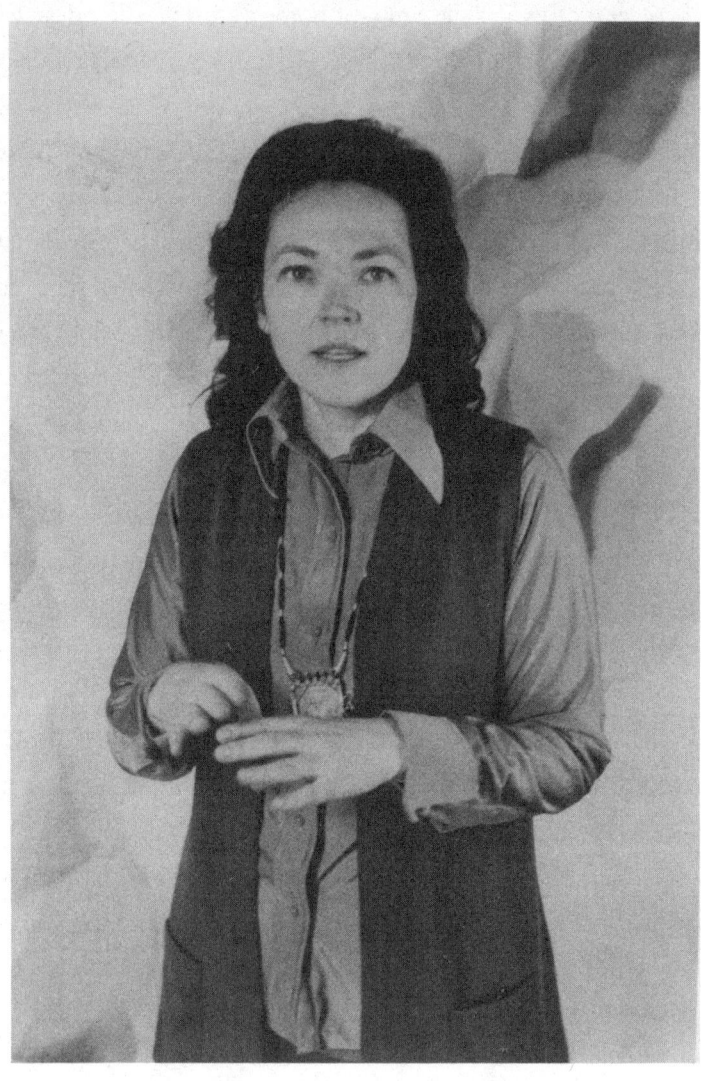

Baber was clearly enjoying her experiences traveling, but she perhaps underestimated the toll it was taking on her health. In a January 7, 1977, letter to Lorene Araujo in Brazil, Baber thanks her for the "absolutely splendid time that I had in Fortaleza. It is one incredible memory.... Thank you for finding doctor Marsillse [*sic*]. I had the father's name and he gave the son's name whom I saw. He told me I was in perfect health and it turns out that he likes modern art and his wife is a private dealer."[42]

In retrospect, it seems clear that Baber was not in perfect health. Yet her extraordinary stamina and love of travel do recall the annual trips her family had made from Illinois to Florida for more than a decade during her childhood. The change of scene and regional cultural diversity in plants, food, and climate seem have instilled in Baber a deep appreciation for difference and for local color, since she was always eager to explore the globe—from Delhi to Tehran to Tegucigalpa or San Salvador or Caracas. "More than anything else," she admitted, "I love to travel. I rationalize that I travel for the sake of my painting, but I know that I would travel anyway."[43] Baber identified Peru and India as two of her favorite places.[44] The title of her 1976 painting, *Purple and Blue Ladder Turning North*, seems to allude to travel.

Baber's extensive travel in Latin America inspired her many titles referring to jaguars, which are found in the countries she visited during her tour of Latin America for the USIA in late 1976. While on tour, Baber gave her usual demonstrations of her personal method of painting, held exhibitions of her artwork, and gave slide-illustrated lectures on color. In Peru, Baber recalled "looking at these jaguars in some early woven fabric; I came back with the idea of the jaguar and the force of the jaguar and so I used that in a lot of titles."[45]

In Mayan mythology, jaguars symbolize strength, ferocity, and courage, which influenced Baber's titles for these and other canvases:

Dream of the Jaguar (1977), *Path of the Jaguar* (1977), *The Ring of the Garden of the Jaguar* (1980), *The Summer Dream of the White Jaguar* (1980), and *The Banner of the Jaguar from the Wind* (1980) (CP #47). From her "Sacred Space" series, Baber also painted a number of late watercolors that reference jaguars such as *The Jaguar Crosses the Rainbow Desert* (1980), *Blue Flag of the Jaguar* (1981), and *Pink Flute of the Jaguar* (1982) (CP #48).

Relating to the title *Blue Flag of the Jaguar*, Baber wrote about blue: "Painting can be read six ways and that the simile and metaphor can be seen as follows: blue as blueness, blue as nonblue, blue as the virgin, blue as the nonvirgin; blue as sky, blue as nonsky."[46] "Everything should be painted blue and one should live in it and on it because it is space and because it is time," she added.[47] The jaguar is also associated with the prediction of things to come, perhaps because these felines have binocular vision, meaning each eye can work by itself, which enables better depth perception.[48]

In the case of Baber's 1978 triptych in the Guggenheim Museum, the three panels are called *The Piper Sees the Ladder of the Jaguar*, *The Lighter Cave of the Hermit and the Jaguar*, and *The Jaguar Finds a Mountain Under the Sea*. Baber said of the "white painting": "The light pouring out from around the forms is a memory of Machu Picchu when a white mist covered the whole mountain."[49] She showed the earliest completed works from these "white" paintings in Bogotá, but explained that this series was "influenced by my Latin American trips, especially the one to Peru."[50] She added that the jaguar "I remember from a weaving in the museum in Cuzco is probably a metaphor for feline energy, the hidden mountain could mean a repository of knowledge and the sea refers to the churning of the sea of milk, the Indian and Cambodian myth of the differentiation of the universe, when a great snake moved."[51]

Although jaguar images recur across Latin American culture, from motifs in folk art to fiction by Jorge Luis Borges, one cannot ignore that Baber's use of jaguar imagery follows Paul Jenkins's full-length play *Strike the Puma*, which was published in Paris in 1966 and produced off-off-Broadway in 1968.[52] According to the Lassaws' daybook for Wednesday May 22, 1968, they traveled to New York to see Paul's play performed, which they pronounced "excellent." The play debuted at The Theatre, located at 78 West 3rd Street in Greenwich Village. *Strike the Puma* had been chosen by Vasek Simek to present in his Equity showcase, intended to explore new plays and to expose "the work of actors, directors, playwrights to small professional audiences in the form of theatrical experiment."[53]

Jenkins said that the meaning of *Strike the Puma* was to end man's "self-hatred." He told an interviewer that this was a universal problem of mankind that had to be vanquished. He discussed his interest in the philosophy of the spiritual teacher George Ivanovitch Gurdjieff, a mystic who taught that people should awaken to a higher state of consciousness to serve our purpose.[54] Jenkins maintained that Gurdjieff inspired him to comprehend the perils of power, saying of his own play: "It's a Faustian theme really."[55] He added that some of the other characters' identities were in jeopardy of being lost. Jenkins often turned to Gurdjieff, whose teachings he probably encountered in Paris, after the philosopher's death there in 1949.[56]

Although one assumes that "A. B." in the play's dedication is Alice Baber, one cannot help but wonder if Baber inspired the character of Maya, described as "she curves. She can be thin or full, but she is cat-like . . . Age 33."[57] Baber was not quite this age when she and the older Jenkins first became involved. In the play's prologue, the character Omen Rangel Thorndyke tells the audience that his name has changed overnight from Owen to Omen, and then proceeds to admit,

"There was some general concern about the title, 'Strike the Puma,'" but he explains, "The Puma is an unusual and mysterious animal. It has the distinction of being the leading predator of the New World. It has uncanny skill as a killer . . . But for all its ruthless and inexorable strength it is puzzled in its contacts with man and notoriously timid."[58]

In contrast to the choice Jenkins made to use the puma in the title of his play, Baber chose to title multiple paintings with the word *jaguar*, which is said to be one of the most aggressive species known to humankind and one of the world's most dangerous predators. Popular lore might hint at what provoked Baber, after her divorce, to title paintings after jaguars—even if she did so on an unconscious level. Despite the puma's ability as a predator, the jaguar is said to have more speed, strength, and a deadly bite force. While a jaguar would be challenged in a fight with a puma, jaguars are reputed to be extremely aggressive and fierce in defending their territory.[59]

While Baber probably never got over the intense betrayal she felt from Jenkins's infidelity, which he insensitively revealed to art world gossips, she had moved on. She was able to enjoy the status that her art had attained as she exhibited internationally and watched multiple museums acquire her artworks.

CHAPTER 15

Recognition, Then Becoming Very Gray
(1977–1982)

Defending her place in the art world, Alice Baber had a show of her work from February 28 to March 18, 1977, at St. Mary's College of Maryland, a public college some ninety-seven miles south of Baltimore. At the time, older, more famous American women artists like Lee Krasner were still dreaming and scheming how to get a retrospective in a major New York museum like MoMA.[1] While the locale at St. Mary's College seems less than central to the art world, the school produced a professional exhibition and an impressive catalogue, edited by Professor Norton T. Dodge, who reprinted excerpts from earlier reviews and articles about and by Baber.

Dodge, a scholar of Soviet economics, did pioneering work on the role of women under Joseph Stalin.[2] He is best known for saving and smuggling to the West nearly ten thousand works by dissident underground artists from the Soviet Union.[3] Dodge was long rumored to have been a CIA agent, but he later said that he paid for his collecting with family money that came from investing early with the future multibillionaire, Warren Buffett.[4] Dodge's Cremona Foundation registered the copyright to Baber's catalogue and was the first listed sponsor of her show.[5]

Just how Dodge, a major Sovietologist, met Baber remains unknown, as does her connection to St. Mary's College and its gallery.[6] It is possible that Baber and Dodge met through Baber's devoted cousin Nancy Hanks, who had worked with Nelson Rockefeller and his brothers Laurance and John, when she "served as executive secretary of a group that included Henry Kissinger and that published 'Prospects for America–The Rockefeller Panel Reports' on foreign policy, defense, education and social and economic affairs."[7]

The St. Mary's College Gallery director and associate professor of art, Jonathan Ingersoll, who was said to have "arranged" the show, wrote a brief essay for Baber's catalogue that emphasized "as in music, where leitmotifs emerge to play significantly against countermotifs, Alice Baber discovers potent images which function in the same way. These images, as she introduces them into her work, appear, disappear and reappear, again and again permitting the spectator to voyage in the worlds she has created."[8]

The catalogue lacks a checklist of the show (which could have been a separate page slipped in); however, it reproduced a number of Baber's paintings, including several from American public collections: *Lavender Ladder Turning-Akbar's Hunt* (1972) (CP #38), *Open Staircase* (1964–1965), *Sun Ladder* (1965), *The Key of Sound and Light* (1976), *Wheel of Day* (1975) (CP #35), *Noble Numbers* (1970) (CP #24), and *Akbar's Dream* (1973).[9] Among the loans to the show that were then privately held was *Mountain Ladder* (1970), loaned by Baber's cousin Nancy Hanks; the watercolor *Red Sand of the Mountain* (1974); and the canvas *Dream of the Jaguar* (1975), both loaned by Norton T. Dodge.[10]

The catalogue excerpted and reprinted a poem on Baber by the Brooklyn poet, playwright, and novelist Norman Rosten, as well as prose on Baber by James Jones, John Ashbery, Keith Sutton, Richard Howard, Natalie Edgar, Al Brunelle, May Natalie Tabak, Grace Glueck, James R. Mellow, Thomas Albright, and Janet Solinger, then a prominent arts administrator at the Smithsonian Institution, who also loaned to the show a 1976 canvas, *The Colors of the Leader of the Piper*.

Baber's own essay, "Color," written for the *Color Forum* catalogue in 1972, and her essay, "My Paintings Are My Diary," from the time of her 1976 solo show in Santa Barbara, were also reprinted in the catalogue.[11] In the latter, Baber wrote, "The paint answers back, so there is always a dialogue. I want the viewer to create part of the meaning. Ambiguity is important to me. Recently I discussed ambiguity with a painter friend. We discussed the circle, a form that we both use. The circle is a wheel, a wheel is a clock, is an apple, is an eye, is a sun, is a moon, etc."[12] Baber's diary entries are poetic, evocative, and make liberal use of metaphor and simile: "The tangled memories of my travels are like embroidery threads of many colors caught up in a patterned wicker basket, intertwined with two hoops and a large lost needle. Or like spinning balls of yarn covered by feathers falling from Montezuma's coat."[13]

Like the storied Aztec emperor Montezuma, Baber had begun to qualify as the subject of an origin story. Baber looked back to her beginnings in the New York art world, when she participated in the show *Tenth Street Days: The Co-ops of the 50s*, organized by the artist, educator, and writer Joellen Bard. Baber showed her 1959 painting, *Bon Voyage*.[14]

Baber was also invited to speak on a panel that took place at the Pleiades Gallery in New York on January 5, 1978, called "More About Tenth Street Days—and Beyond," moderated by Joellen Bard. The other panelists included the artist Joan Gedney, the critic Dore Ashton, Phoenix Gallery director Helen Thomas, and the gallerist and publisher of *Art Speak* Bruno Palmer-Poroner.

Having been well received around the globe, Baber took issue with Bard's argument that New York co-op galleries should be for Americans only, "no foreigners," as reported by the artist Jean Cohen, who recorded that Baber expressed concern for foreigners and came with a "lively and extensive list of suggestions for 'Beyond,' and noted the vacuum that exists for Black artists, particularly in museums. And what of artists coming back from war?" adding, "Alice recalled also that women in the '50s were expected to queue up behind the older (male) artists for recognition."[15] As early as 1978, Baber was both sensitive and courageous to call out the bias that existed in museums against both artists of color and women.

Reached more than four decades later, Bard did not recall moderating this panel, although she remembers that Dore Ashton, with whom she had studied, did not want Alice Baber in the related show and claimed not to like her work. Bard also recalled Baber's link to Nancy Hanks, head of the National Endowment for the Arts (NEA), and ascribed the agency's failure to fund her project to Baber's influence, which, however, seems highly unlikely. Bard also denied that she ever spoke against including "foreigners," commenting that Jean Cohen must have taken this remark "out of context."[16] The sentiment that Cohen reported, however, is echoed by Bard's own published 1977 article, "Alice Baber: Mission to Latin America," which Bard did not recall writing. She wrote, "I can't help thinking that artists in the United States need as much help as those in Latin America."[17]

After I sent her own published article on Baber to Bard, who taught art in New York City public high schools for thirty-four years, she responded that she had forgotten writing it and that although she was "advocating for American artists" at the time, she did not mean to imply that she did not like Latin American artists. Bard, who was then president of the Association of Artist-Run Galleries, said that she considered that she had a duty to promote American artists.[18]

As for Ashton's dismissal of Baber's abstract art, the most likely explanation was that she rejected it as apolitical, "art for art's sake," meant only for aesthetic pleasure, lacking any social-political purpose or messaging. Dore Ashton was definitely not a feminist and known not to support other women—from Baber to Lee Krasner to this author. But even more damning for Ashton was Baber's known relationship to her powerful cousin and friend, Nancy Hanks, who was appointed to head the NEA by President Richard Nixon and had a close relationship with Nelson Rockefeller.[19] In contrast, Ashton has been described as having "unashamedly left-leaning politics and modernist stance [that] garnered both allies and enemies—most notably the senior art critic of the *Times*, John Canaday, who fired her in 1960."[20] As for Baber's personal politics, there is no evidence that she expressed her concerns beyond her strong identification with feminism and her support for equal rights for women, ideas that were not then popular among most Republican women.

Yet Baber was surely encouraged and perhaps advised by Hanks, whose biographer asserts "was never a feminist."[21] Despite their fundamental political difference, Baber won repeated exhibition support from the United States Information Service (USIS), which the NEA, an independent government agency, could not directly influence.

While working for the USIS, Baber was well placed to meet Clara Diament Sujo in June 1977 in Caracas, Venezuela. The two women met over dinner and Baber got to see her "wonderful collection," which Sujo founded there in 1969 as "Estudio Actual."[22] Sujo championed Latin American and women artists, including Hedda Sterne, Louise Nevelson, and Marisol Escobar.

In writing to thank Sujo, Baber noted that she had sent her a copy of the catalogue from her show in Bogotá and wrote, "Mrs. Carter came to Bogotá. My show was the cultural event and so we met," referring to First Lady Rosalynn Carter.[23] Baber reported, too, that she had visited Quito, Ecuador, and purchased "some pre-columbian shell ceramics musical instruments and looked at the churches."[24] They planned to meet again at the end of August. But by the time that Sujo opened her CDS Gallery in New York in 1981, it would be too late to collaborate with Baber as one of the women artists she promoted.

By now, Baber had achieved a name for herself. She kept busy with other solo shows in 1978 at the Kunst-Galerie 63 in Klosters, Switzerland (from February 18 to March 4), then at the Allen House Galleries in Louisville, Kentucky. She told how in Louisville "three men came in from an advertising agency. And one of them said to me, 'Do you ever paint realistically?' And I said, very spontaneously to him, 'But to me my pictures are very realistic because this is the way I see the world.' And he looked at me and laughed. And then I laughed too, because I realized that it truly is. I am painting a kind of celestial outerspace [sic] in many of the works and sort of rearranging the forms, rearranging the universe to my satisfaction."[25] Baber added that she found "all the light and color that I think is kind of the ideal space that I like to be in, or look in or see."[26]

Following Louisville, in May 1978 Baber showed at the Frances Aronson Gallery in Atlanta. Baber attended the opening in Atlanta, recalling, "I used to travel to Atlanta as a child, so I am very impressed to see the city now."[27] She would have stopped by Atlanta on the regular automobile trips from Illinois to Florida that she and her sister made with their mother.

Though Baber loved travel, she had a brief respite during the summer of 1978, when her schedule permitted her to spend a few precious weeks staying at Ernestine and Ibram Lassaw's East Hampton home while they were away traveling. (She was surely renting her own home for the summer to make ends meet.) During this interlude, she had time to see Gloria Jones; however, James Jones had passed away from congestive heart failure at the age of fifty-five on May 9, 1977. Their daughter, Kaylie, recalls: "Alice's eyes carried an expression of constant surprise, as if everything were fascinating to her, and every moment new."[28] The loss of James Jones, her friend and supporter, at such a young age must have made Baber much more aware of her own mortality, especially given her own experience with melanoma. After a brief interlude on Long Island, however, she resumed her frenetic exhibition and travel schedule.

In October 1978, Baber's solo show opened in Highland Park, Illinois, at a gallery called "the art package ltd.," which billed her works as "a joyous celebration of light and image. She creates poems of colour, deftly orchestrating a dance of transcental [sic] energies."[29]

The theme of women artists was central once again when Baber participated in a conference in Paris in 1978 called "Women Changing Society New York/Paris" or "Colloque Sur La Condition Feminine" on November 7 and 9 at the American Cultural Center.[30] The press release described Baber as an "active as a member of many women's organizations."[31] "The women's art movement in France is of special importance to me," she stated, "since I enjoyed the opportunity of doing my graduate work at Fontainebleau and lived and worked in Paris for eight years."[32]

Months earlier, when the conference was being planned, Baber wrote to a friend in Paris about preparations for the program and efforts to have a women's show in Paris, possibly at "the Musée d'Art Moderne (the head being a woman). . . . If not a woman's show how about Ibram Lassaw & I having a 2-person. Something like, the Metaphor of Continuum. I'm determined to use Metaphor for something. Susan Sontag just used it in her last title, so it's safe."[33] In 1978, Baber had been reading Sontag's newly published *Illness as Metaphor*, which compared metaphors used to describe tuberculosis and cancer, pointing out that society's metaphors for disease adversely affected the afflicted.[34] Although Baber's own fatal disease of melanoma had already been diagnosed, at the time, despite her memory of her mother's fragility and early death, she thought that she had beaten the disease.[35]

It was in 1972 that Baber conceived of a major new work as a triptych, which she called *Expulsion of the Mythical Kings* (CP #36). As for painting triptychs, after claiming that she favored a "certain amount of concealment," Baber admitted, "There's Grünewald in there, but sort of by chance; I was painting one day, and there was a golden circle in there, and then I go back and I look at the Grünewald."[36] She spoke of Matthias Grünewald's monumental Isenheim Altarpiece of 1515, located in the Musée Unterlinden in Colmar, France. Her comment about "a golden circle" refers to the inner right panel depicting the resurrection of Christ (CP #36), who is shown set against the night sky surrounded by an orb of bright "divine" light.

In preparing to paint her own abstract triptych, Baber was attracted to the brilliant orb of spiritual light, outlined in a blue ring, that envelopes the head and upper body of Grünewald's resurrected Christ in yellow, orange, and red body halos rising like the colors of flames. Baber evidently discussed the influence of the Isenheim Altarpiece on her *Expulsion of the Mythical Kings* with Virginia Pitts Rembert, who wrote confirming this influence in her essay for the 1982 show that turned out to be Baber's memorial retrospective: "The golden circle at top was inspired by the radiant aureole of Grünewald's 'Risen Christ' in the Isenheim altarpiece."[37]

In retrospect, we can imagine that Baber was drawn to the metaphor of hope in the depiction of the resurrection of Christ placed on the right panel of this spectacular altarpiece (CP #36).

Baber's initial diagnosis of melanoma, a usually fatal skin cancer, occurred around the time that she painted *Expulsion of the Mythical Kings* At first, she believed that she had beaten the disease, which would ultimately take her life, however, it would be difficult to erase all fears of a recurrence. While the precise date of her first diagnosis of melanoma is not known, most melanoma metastases occur within the first few years after diagnosis, although some documented cases recurred ten years or more after the initial diagnosis.

Baber's interest in Grünewald's Isenheim Altarpiece in the context of her own disease is particularly fascinating because of the skin afflictions Grünewald depicted. He painted this, his largest and most memorable work, for the Monastery of St. Anthony in Isenheim, near Colmar in Alsace, a region that has alternated between Germany and France according to the fortunes of war. This monastery was known for its dedication to hospital work. Its monks were celebrated for the care they gave to sufferers of skin diseases such as syphilis, plague, or ergotism, then known as "St. Anthony's Fire," which was caused by eating rye grain infected with fungus, leading to hallucinations and attacking the central nervous system, resulting in death.

While suffering with skin cancer, Baber sought comfort and consolation, searching for her own miracle of recovery. One imagines that she found hope not from the image of Saint Anthony, who is depicted suffering plague-type skin sores and vivid hallucinations, or from the Crucifixion of Christ, depicted in a state of intense suffering with twisted hands and with numerous wounds, thorns, blisters, and running sores, but from the figure of the resurrected Christ, who is shown as having miraculously triumphed over earthly afflictions (CP #36).[38]

Studying Grünewald and reading Sontag, Alice Baber appears to have tried to intellectualize her serious illness, distancing herself from its imminent threat. In this endeavor, she followed her father's example in recovering from his mental illness. Adin Baber owned nine volumes of *The Diary of Samuel Pepys*.[39] Reading Pepys's account of the Great Plague of London (1665–1666), which documented the rising death toll and people's fears, Adin escaped the difficulties of the Great Depression and focused on his own health challenges, making concentrated efforts to maintain his equilibrium. Likewise, Alice, once diagnosed with melanoma, which has a high risk of spreading, soldiered on.

Baber routinely put her illness aside, as when she went to Paris just to speak at the conference on women. From there, she had to rush home, choosing to focus once again on her own art instead of feminist politics or her health, although there was probably little that she could have done to stop the progression of her disease. She had another solo show at the A. M. Sachs Gallery from December 2 to 30, 1978, capping off a very busy year.

This time the *New York Times* reviewer Vivien Raynor characterized the artist as "a prominent colorist since the early 60s, Alice Baber has charted a course somewhere between Abstract Expressionism and Color Field painting."[40] *Artnews* called this same show "Baber's palest show to date—and clouds are the reason . . . Baber's pale canvases *The Jaguar Speaks to the Mountain of Light* (I, II, and III) were inspired by a trip to the extraordinary archaeological site of the Incas in the Peruvian Andes, Machu Picchu. Despite its high altitude, due to its proximity just south of the equator, Machu Picchu rarely has significant snow. Yet, Baber encountered a fierce storm, which cloaked the ancient Inca site in clouds while she was there. She thus enjoyed sensations different from those most tourists experience when visiting Machu Picchu."[41]

Despite the distractions of globe-trotting, Paul Jenkins's name came back into the limelight and to Baber's consciousness through the publicity associated with the release of the 1978 feature film *An Unmarried Woman*, directed by Paul Mazursky and starring Alan Bates and Jill Clayburgh.

The film received even more publicity when it was nominated for three Academy Awards.[42] Ironically, since it was widely publicized that Paul Jenkins produced the abstract paintings used in the film and taught Bates how to perform his pouring technique as a painter, the film's plot came too close to that which caused the demise of Baber's and Jenkins's marriage. Although not quite their story, the movie was nonetheless an account of marital infidelity, with characters that included an art gallery assistant and a male artist, none of which Baber wanted to remember.

Around this time, Baber commented in a letter to her friend Ann McCoy, "You are right about love life. Very difficult!! Accounts for my attempting Devil may care approach. We can write advice to women artists some day. Almost everybody has a fling in Berlin, did Shirley tell you about hers? It may still be on."[43] Baber had come a long way since her initial infatuation with Jenkins and her devotion to him.

Instead of focusing on the past, Baber wrote notes about her experience of color and light as she traveled from eastern Long Island on January 20, 1979: "I took the early train this morning after a cadmium scarlet sunrise across the horizon of Sagaponac [sic]. As I progressed to New York City, snow was in the air and the sky turned from clear blue grey to ochre gray. Then just before the snow fell to pink grey and then purple grey." She explained, "I have been painting grey and white paintings since my last trip to South America. The forms finding and losing themselves like mountains in clouds."[44]

Baber wrote, "For me the process of painting begins in color hunger, light hunger, and dark hunger, the need to find form and space. The experience of looking, turning, moving, changing, then, sorting, shifting, and grinding the thoughts of the hand onto the 'sacred space.'"[45] Baber repeatedly called up the metaphor of sacred space as central to her abstract work, as we have seen in her painting *Axe in the Grove* (1966) (CP #27).

Baber was nonetheless sometimes a puzzle to journalists who were assigned to cover her. In February 1979, Baber traveled to her solo show at the Buscaglia-Castellani Art Gallery of Niagara University, located at the northern limits of the City of Niagara Falls, New York. She wrote to her friend about going to this show in Niagara: "The falls are very nice in winter, very contained, the top is like green jade."[46]

A local reporter, who met Baber at the opening reception in Niagara, declared her to be a paradox: "One minute she was all practicality—recommending artists borrow ideas for filling up corners from Titian, telling why she likes oil better than acrylic: 'I find oil has a certain type of sparkle you can't get with acrylic.' The next minute, raven-haired and radiant, Baber beamed at a local artist she had just met. 'I could tell you are a painter by your spirit,' she said."[47] When Baber explained why she preferred abstract art to realism, the journalist reported her explanation: "Then, a figure appears. I call it 'the little green doggie in the corner. Sometimes the figure is a jaguar. Other times, the Hindu 'Krishna child' or 'the Virgin.' Do you put it in or leave it out," she asked the audience. And the conclusion: "Baber puts it in. Then she transforms the whole scene to an abstract array of amoeboid shapes which barely suggests the original vision, but communicates her initial emotions intact." She concluded, "Baber's work is interesting. It grows on one."[48] The journalist concluded correctly that although Baber's work is abstract, it nonetheless reflects her psyche, her inner or spiritual content.

From April 21 to May 16, 1979, Baber showed in *Women Artists of Eastern Long Island* at the Guild Hall Museum in East Hampton and took part in a panel discussion about the regional show copresented with the American Association of University Women. The others on the panel, which was moderated by the art critic Phyllis Braff, were the artists Perle Fine, Fay Lansner, and Buffie Johnson.[49]

Each artist had just one work in the Guild Hall show, which had to be on paper, a collage, or sculpture. Baber showed *The Secret Mirror of the Jaguar*, a watercolor that she had painted while staying at the Lassaws' home the previous summer.[50] She recalled that she "painted large watercolors, working in great peace to the sounds of birds in a bird bath. The light filtered through a transparent roof [of Ibram's studio], and I worked on the floor with round flowing forms. This is the work that I am showing at Guild Hall."[51]

"Besides the white paintings, and the green-blue watercolors," Baber summed up, "I have also worked this year on a series of dark Nocturnes while reading *The [Master] Pipers* by George Sand. Whenever I read more about her, I realize the energy, and the vast amount of work that she did from midnight to morning reminds me of the power of the colors of the night."[52]

Sand's narrative of the developing relationships of two sets of lovers conveys her belief that women should be treated as equals to their partners in marriage, a sentiment that Baber clearly shared, but had not found possible in her own experience.

In August 1979, Baber, ever itinerant, was artist in residence at the Tamarind Institute, at the University of New Mexico, where she produced lithographs. She called the series she produced at Tamarind "The Four Corners Series," and they included *Ceremony: Rock and Dancing Yellow*; *Preparation of the Fetish: Air, Light, Sun, Rain*; *Ancestor of the Wind*; *Ceremony of the Dancing Jaguar*; and *Road to the Ceremony of the Blue Dance*.[53] Baber named her Four Corners Series for the Four Corners Monument that marks the quadripoint in the Southwest where Arizona, Colorado, New Mexico, and Utah meet. An untitled abstract lithograph on black paper, which survives in a printer's proof, lacks Baber's usual sense of transparency and light.[54]

Following Tamarind, Baber produced her next lithographs in Europe, where she had a commission in September 1979 from Ediciones Polígrafa in Barcelona for a series of five prints in six colors.[55] She called this group her "Catalonian Diary Series" and gave them titles like *The Texture of the Mountain Becomes a Wing*, *The Wing of the Mountain Turns to Light*, *The Space Between the Mountains Is a Dance*, *Ceremony of Dancing Jaguar*, *Ancestor of the Wind*, *The Wing of the Mountain Dances to the Piper*, and *The Shadow of the Mountain Becomes the Light*.[56]

Commenting on these lithographs by Baber, who had previously made prints in 1967 and 1974 and, earlier still, had studied lithography in the summer of 1951 at Fontainebleau, the curator and former art dealer Constance Kane explained that in comparison to Baber's watercolors, "The graphics are one step removed by their inherent properties. As a result the memories are more delicate as if not to disturb the perception of the moment;" she explained that Baber "takes us with her on her colour-laden journeys."[57]

Baber's contribution as an artist was recognized by Eleanor Munro, whose 1979 book, *Originals: American Women Artists*, mentions Baber in the chapter titled "Women of the Third Wave: Sisters of the Crossroads." Munro wrote, "It was also a time when, as in years to come, among all the invention, obfuscation, flamboyance and fakery, there could also be seen artists pursuing with quiet self-knowledge and freedom, ways that may not be epochally new but are still open to the most varied personal interpretation, like various generation Abstract Expressionist painters Alice Baber, Natalie Edgar and Emily Mason."[58] Munro's mentioning "various generation Abstract Expressionist painters" is a reference to the so-called first-generation painters like Lee Krasner, who was a full generation older than Baber, but Munro might also have meant that Baber's work extends beyond the definition of abstract expressionism to color field painting.

Baber's studio, which she opened for charity benefit tours by such groups as Smithsonian Associates and Brandeis University, was described as hosting "a glittering collection of Indian, Japanese, Iranian, and Pre-Columbian art."[59] Extant photographs document Baber's collections and decor, which reflected her life as a world traveler. Her last loft home and studio was featured in one book on lofts and in another on rug collecting.[60] Remarkably, Baber, when just ten years old, had written a story about a rug weaver in Baghdad, so her interest in rugs, the Middle East, and Asia developed very early (CP #5).

Besides learning that Baber had at least two cats and many houseplants, we see from photographs of her loft that she not only collected handmade rugs but also masks from diverse cultures and Buddhist *thangkas*, which typically depicted a Buddhist deity, scene, or a mandala. She had a large and dramatic decorative ceiling hanging, which she identified as an Indian wedding canopy.

Virginia Pitts Rembert, who got to know Baber, reported that she found inspiration from her travels and from "things she has brought back to wear or embellish her studio: embroidered black tunics from Pakistan, Turkoman jewelry, Kalim rugs used by Iranian tribesmen, Indian temple hangings and a wedding canopy. Tibetan Thankas, prints and miniatures of many kinds—Japanese, Persian, and Indian."[61]

Not only attracted to such exotic art that she found in her travels, Baber also collected modern art, including, as previously noted, a drawing by Arshile Gorky. Baber was featured as a curator and collector in an investigative 1977 article about art collectors for *The Feminist Art Journal*. She answered questions posed, stating that she owned approximately fifty paintings and works on paper, which were mainly abstract, and that she had acquired them "privately," as opposed to some collectors, who acquired their collections entirely from galleries or auction houses.

Baber, who surely traded her own artwork with her friends, said that 30–40 percent of works in her collection were by women artists, which was the highest percentage among the collectors surveyed. Brenda Price, the artist who conducted this survey, presented her findings in a chart; in her capsule comments on each of the collectors, she described Baber as "Refined Bohemia; looks to help women artists."[62] This was in sharp contrast to a collector like Richard Brown Baker, whom Price reported as collecting over a thousand works with a very small percentage of women artists, and whom she described, "The collection mirrors the collector: courtly, crammed full of detail, knowledgeable, exhaustive."[63]

Baber recalled when a woman once came to her studio from the magazine *Antiques* to look at her rugs and kilims, and told her, "Oh well, you don't have the ones with natural dyes, although some of them do have natural dyes because some natural dyes are very brilliant."[64] But Baber explained that she loved "the ones with very bright colors. I think the very fact that the artists or the craftspeople went to those dyes when they had a choice shows something. They liked them too."[65]

Despite her love of collecting, Baber kept her focus on creating art. Her illness is reflected in her abandonment—at least on canvas—of the rainbow colors that had so long engaged her. While Baber had experimented with white-and-gray paintings as early as 1971, by 1979, when she painted *The Path of the Grey Falcon of the Dawn*, her canvases no longer featured the lively colors in her earlier work (CP #46).

The enigmatic yet significant title of this canvas, *The Path of the Grey Falcon of the Dawn*, reveals much more about the artist and her times than is immediately apparent. The allusive title ultimately confirms what we already know about Baber's lively intellect, her feminist politics, her curiosity about other cultures, and her love of foreign travel.

Even after dealing with her cancer diagnosis, Baber could have been imagining a trip to New Zealand once she had read about the Māori king's thirty-five-year-old daughter, Princess Piki, who, following six days of mourning, was chosen by the tribal elders to become their first woman leader. The princess, after being chosen as her father's successor to lead the Kīngitanga (the Māori political movement in New Zealand), announced her decision to take her mother's name, Te Atairangikaahu, which translates from Māori as "falcon of the dawn."

The *New York Times* obituary for Princess Piki's father, King Korokī, the long ailing leader of the Kīngitanga political movement, who died on May 18, 1966, explained that the princess had performed his duties during his long illness.[66] The article noted, "No woman has ever held the title, but there have been greatly influential women leaders among the Māori. Princess Piki is therefore considered to be a possible choice."[67]

In fact, the princess would serve as Māori queen for more than forty years, the longest reign of any Māori monarch. Her reign is said to have inspired a Māori cultural renaissance, which supported century-long efforts by the Māori to repair the cultural and economic damage resulting from European settlement. In the mid-nineteenth century the Kīngitanga began to contest growing pressure to sell tribal lands.[68] Some Māori called for unification and an end to intertribal conflict, taking as their model British culture with its single sovereign.

It's not surprising to find that the cosmopolitan Baber, who for most of a decade divided her time between New York and Paris, had been reading about New Zealand's Indigenous Polynesian people, the Māori, who originated as settlers from East Polynesia, arriving in New Zealand in several waves of canoe voyages between roughly 1320 and 1350. While we don't know precisely what Baber read about New Zealand

and the Māori, we do know that she learned about nautical exploration through her father's engagement with such histories. Adin Baber owned at least nine volumes of Richard Hakluyt's multivolume *The Principal Navigations, Voyages, Traffiques and Discoveries of the English Nation*.[69] Alice might also have encountered histories of Captain James Cook, who circumnavigated the North and South Islands and wrote about the intelligence of the Māori and the promise of New Zealand as a site for colonization. Since childhood, Baber's imagination was constantly nourished by foreign places, travel, and history.

Māori art and culture would have caught Baber's attention following the January 26, 1979, death of Nelson Rockefeller, who had been her cousin Nancy Hanks's lover. It was announced in February 1979 that Rockefeller had bequeathed part of his art collection to the Metropolitan Museum of Art: The Michael C. Rockefeller Memorial Collection, which included a number of Māori objects, including, for example, a Māori House Post Figure (Amo) (CP #46).[70] Baber would likely have seen this fascinating wood carving exhibited at the Met in 1969, 1972, and from 1972 to 1974.[71] Yet, it appears to be the unusual story of Princess Piki that captured the imagination of Baber, a devoted feminist activist.

Feminist imagery in her abstractions had been called out earlier, as we have seen, by some reviewers, especially men, who claimed to see references to female genitalia. Whatever Baber might have intended in the way of feminist imagery, she expected to be exempt from having to identify or confirm such imagery to her audience, including such critics. Despite the abstract forms and composition of *The Path of the Grey Falcon of the Dawn*, Baber expressed content subtly through imagined shapes and colors arranged in a meaningful way. She had earlier commented about "the finding of multiple images wanted or unwanted in a work, the implication of subject matter," because she had experienced this herself and was aware that symbolism could be read into her own abstract art by diverse audiences.[72]

Baber's arrangement of forms in *The Path of the Grey Falcon of the Dawn* echoes the *x* motif that she used earlier in her career, which we have seen relates to Miriam Schapiro's notorious 1967 canvas, *Big Ox* (CP #47). Like Schapiro's painting, Baber's has four diagonal limbs intersecting a central oval open space, a configuration with which Schapiro said that she intended to express the female body, a solution, as Schapiro later explained, to express her "real cry in the darkness . . . for something besides the symbol of the phallus."[73]

Baber's own struggle to express her feminism through her abstract forms is also embedded in another part of her title for *The Path of the Grey Falcon of the Dawn*. Baber used the term *path*, meaning "a choice or way of living; a doctrine," a course of action or conduct, something that she believed in or followed. For her, that doctrine would be equal opportunity for women.

Baber not only painted but since childhood had written poetry. Her love of metaphoric meaning encouraged her repetition of favorite words such as *path*, which recur again and again in Baber's titles. Consider, for example, her earlier paintings, all oil on canvas: *Path to the Ladder* (1972) (CP #39); *Path of the Jaguar,* (1977); *The Blue Drum Path to the Open Coast* (1977).[74]

The color gray in *The Path of the Grey Falcon of the Dawn* also has multiple implications. The predominant color for falcons is certainly gray, but the pale palette of this canvas is also suggestive of a particular time in Baber's life. The painting's pale gray palette with its subtle elements of lavender and tan echoes Baber's concerns of the moment. She abandoned—certainly for this canvas—the bright rainbow colors that had so long engaged her.

Baber followed *The Path of the Grey Falcon of the Dawn* with other
pale paintings. She painted *The Summer Dream of the White Jaguar*
(1980) just as she was struggling with illness that would be diagnosed
as terminal cancer. On her use of color, she had earlier commented, "I
think that the change in subject matter comes, with the use of color,
in a tapering off of interest in rendering. Because you no longer have
to gray down the forms or find ways of making a third dimension or
reproducing reality in some fashion. And as your own sense of color
approaches your own sense of poetry and fantasy, I think the priorities
begin to change."[75] Baber had commented about emotions and colors
in 1973, "Anything that's particularly sort of gloomy becomes very
gray."[76] This was an echo of her father's use of gray in his own poetry
at the time of her mother's tragic early death.

Baber's shift to shades of gray is also reminiscent of the abandonment of color by Mark Rothko as he coped with the depression that
eventually led to his suicide.[77] Baber, who recalled meeting Rothko
at Ibram and Ernestine Lassaw's home, was more constructive in
dealing with her fatal diagnosis.[78] Her poem *Night*, written years earlier, during her first years in college, expresses her experience of pain:

Night
Only the ticking of the clock to prove
that time moves,
Eternity! Marked by the hours
it gives.
Only the rattling of a dry tin roof
above me
Proves that the old house still
breathes and lives.
Night is made of sleep for those

who can find it.
But for impatient pain; the other part
There's only the patter of mice
come in the darkness
To nibble at the shell around my heart.[79]

Baber's narrative is now more intelligible, as she expresses her vulnerability. As she faced her own serious illness, Baber, who had put Rothko's work in her *Color Forum* show in 1972, did not, however, completely give up on color in her own work. Instead, she continued to experiment with vivid dye-based color inks on paper as in her of *The Secret Mirror of the Jaguar* (1978) or *The Jaguar Crosses the Rainbow Desert: Sacred Space Series* (1980) (CP #48).

Baber explained her "series of paintings which I call the *Sacred Space Series*. And I got the idea of the kind of sacred space in ancient cities where several blocks would be devoted to; in this case it was the ancient cities of the Middle East and they were devoted to the Goddess. And, I thought the idea of taking a space would be interesting. Whether the thing that I do in that space is sacred, is something else. It's a question about the attitude about the space."[80]

In 1980, the year after Baber painted *The Path of the Grey Falcon of the Dawn*, Mrs. Bertram Smith (aka Louise Reinhardt Smith), a well-known collector of modern art and, since 1965, a trustee of the Museum of Modern Art, gave this large Baber canvas to the Metropolitan Museum of Art. Although Mrs. Smith gave a few other paintings to the Met, she left most of her collection to the MoMA.[81] In fact, Mrs. Smith owned *The Path of the Grey Falcon of the Dawn* for no more than a year. The unstated implication is that Mrs. Smith made her gift to promote Alice Baber, who already anticipated the gift of another painting to the collection of the MoMA but also wanted to be represented with a major work in the Met. Louise Smith was clearly close to Bill Lieberman, the curator who had moved from the MoMA to the Met, and, as it happens, he had met Alice Baber in Osaka, Japan, in 1964, while she was showing with the Gutai. Although how Louise Smith met Baber remains unknown, she would have known Nelson Rockefeller at the MoMA and, perhaps through him, possibly met Baber's cousin Nancy Hanks, who had been closely associated with him.

It seems fitting that it was a woman who collected and gave the Met its first painting by Alice Baber, since the artist painted *The Path of the Grey Falcon of the Dawn* as a covert feminist image, an homage to an accomplished woman in a distant culture, who obtained both high status and lasting respect. Baber's message—her content—was perhaps not intended to be deciphered during the artist's own lifetime, but was instead calculated to speak to posterity, to those interested enough to read the clues she left behind. Baber, however, could not have imagined that the Metropolitan Museum would hide Mrs. Smith's gift of her prized painting by keeping it in storage for the next forty-five years.[82]

Interviewing Baber for *Women's Art Heritage* on WBAI-FM radio on March 21, 1980, Alexandra de Lallier noted that Baber was about to leave on a tour of solo shows of her work, including venues in Los Angeles; Lima, Peru; Frankfurt; and Paris. "I like to travel so much," Baber responded, admitting that she found it "sometimes a little fatiguing."[83]

"When in the early 80s Alice was diagnosed with cancer and underwent a grueling treatment," Kaylie Jones recalls, "she never lost her good humor or her enthusiasm for life. I went to see her in her Sag Harbor home shortly before she died. Alice was sitting up in bed, her head encased in a metal brace that was screwed right into her skull and looked like a Medieval instrument of torture. Yet she was still smiling, still wearing that expression of surprise and good cheer."[84] Kaylie Jones took her mother Gloria to see Alice; the two women's friendship dated from 1959, when they both moved to Paris.

Against all odds, the determined Baber had remained active as a painter, holding three solo shows in 1980: in Los Angeles at the Gallery West in March; in Lima at Gallerie de l'Arte Nueva; and *Alice Baber: Color, Light and Image* the Amerika Haus in Frankfurt in October, coinciding with the Frankfurt Book Fair.

Although Baber was not present at the opening in Frankfurt, the public affairs officer at the American consulate reported to her that among the visitors to her show were the popular writers Erich Segal and Erica Jong, the latter a famous feminist.[85] When Baber traveled to Los Angeles for her show in March, staying with her friend Betty Gold, her Atlanta dealer Frances Aronson sent her a telegram: "Knock 'Em Dead Alice Love Frances."[86]

In February 1981, Baber traveled to Indiana and served as a juror for the annual Wabash Valley Art Show held at the Swope Art Museum in Terre Haute. The works selected for the show came from artists living in Indiana, Illinois, Kentucky, Michigan, Ohio, and Tennessee.

Baber took the opportunity to visit with her old friend, Norma "Ronni" Frazier Templeton, who had been her sorority sister at Indiana University. Both women came from the same corner of Illinois and the two became friends after each transferred to Indiana University.

The next month, just over two years after her last show at the A. M. Sachs Gallery, Baber had a solo show in New York at the Lillian Heidenberg Gallery in March 1981. Baber's serious illness and pre-monitions of death alone might explain why she suddenly switched from her longtime gallery, A. M. Sachs, to showing with the Lillian Heidenberg Gallery. By then, the A. M. Sachs Gallery had moved upstairs to the fourth floor at 29 West 57th Street to a much-reduced space.[87]

Reviewing the Heidenberg show in the *East Hampton Star*, Phyllis Braff described "Baber's rhythmically repeated curving high-keyed colored shapes emphasize lyrical transparencies and musical relationships that recall synchromist ideas pioneered in Paris shortly after the birth of cubism."[88] Braff, however, had met Baber and realized that Baber was searching "for a color quality that will emphasize particular expressive goals."[89] She also realized that Baber had an interest in associating her abstract forms with "spiritual sensations" and noted that the artist had been influenced by the time she had spent in South and Central America.

By June 1981, Baber was just home from the hospital, having been diagnosed with a form of bone cancer (which is how the earlier diagnosed melanoma was spreading) that would prove fatal.[90] Both Baber's nephew and Ann McCoy recall hearing that Baber's cancer began as melanoma.[91]

Perhaps both her spirituality and her passion for painting sustained Baber at this difficult time. In 1981 and 1982, she was still painting watercolors such as *The Purple Jewel of the Jaguar* or *Pink Flute of the Jaguar* from the "Sacred Space" series (CP #48). In early March 1982, Baber visited her cousin Nancy Hanks at her home in Washington, DC. Hanks's assistant, Pat Fisher, recalls that Baber was suffering from bone cancer, but "being an artist, wanted to go to the National Gallery." "Alice is dying of cancer," Hanks told Fisher, "But she doesn't want to be treated as if she were dying. I'd like you to take her to the gallery, but, you are not to help her up the stairs! You just let her walk around with her head held high."[92] Both women, who were not just cousins, but close friends, were dying of cancer at the same time.

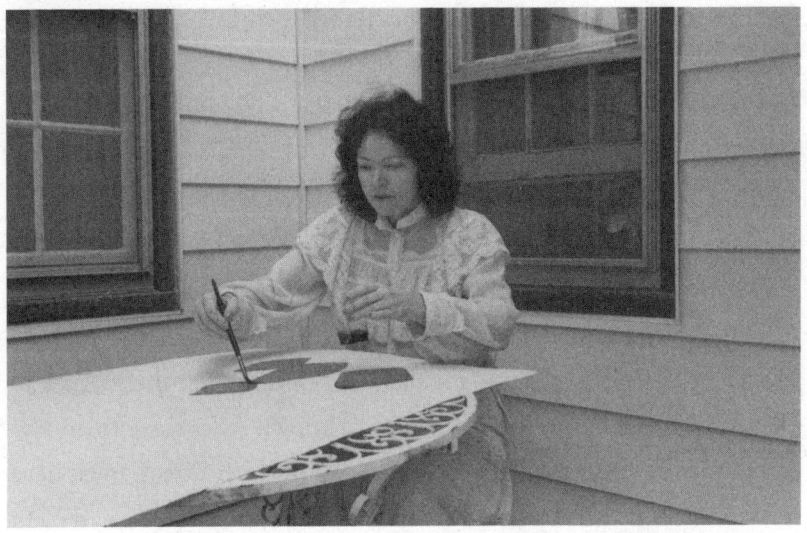

Ann Chwatsky photographed Alice painting, Sag Harbor, NY, 1981.

During the period of Baber's last illness, she grew close to Norbert Nelson, who became the executor of her estate.[93] The artist Ce Roser, who participated in many feminist shows and other activities with Baber, recalls that Nelson was devoted to Baber. He entertained by giving lavish parties at her home in both Sag Harbor and New York City so that she could see friends in the art world.[94] Alice Baber signed her last will and testament on April 8, 1982, while she was a patient at Lenox Hill Hospital in New York.

The spring/summer 1982 issue of the *Woman's Art Journal* published the following comment by Elsa Honig Fine, its founding editor: "When we were preparing the material on Alice Baber for the Spring/Summer 1982 WAJ, we knew were in a race against time. Baber was seriously ill, and we wanted her to be able to share this homage to her life and art. Indeed, the issue gave her great pleasure; it added focus and meaning to her final months."[95] This issue, which suggests the esteem for Baber's art and activism in the women's movement,

featured two important articles on Baber's work: "Alice Baber" by
Sylvia Moore and "The Watercolors of Alice Baber" by Alexandra
de Lallier.[96] The latter article emphasized the importance of Baber's
observation of reflected light.

On August 31, 1982, Ernestine Lassaw recorded in her daybook
that she went to Sag Harbor to see Alice.[97] On September 15,
Ernestine went to the hospital with Alice. Four days later, she was
there to see Alice. On September 20, Ernestine visited Alice and took
Elaine de Kooning, noting "she bought painting" and then "Alice to
New York Ambulance." Elaine, who had known Alice since their days
together at the March Gallery cooperative on 10th Street, must have
wanted to cheer Alice, who might have worried about having sufficient
funds to cover her mounting medical bills. Genuinely fond of Alice,
Elaine painted a posthumous portrait of her from memory. Alice's death
was "a terrible blow" to Gloria Jones, her daughter Kaylie recalled. Her
mother "could barely talk about her old friend" and "Alice's paintings
remained in their place of honor in our home."[98]

On September 7, 1982, Paul Jenkins, Alice's ex-husband, wrote to
her, telling her how much he admired her courage. He referred to the
name of a book that they had read together,

> That name Under The Name of Saturn seems to suit us
> sick or well . . . sober or drunk.
>
> I so often remember you saying how from time to time
> one had to hit bottom to surface again. Now that I am able
> to look back I want you to know how much it meant to me to
> share our mutual predicament. Aspiring to paint beyond
> everything else.
>
> I feel only now that I am beginning to see beyond the
> rim of the stretcher.

Jenkins continued his guilt-ladened typed letter to his dying ex-spouse, when it was far too late to repair the damage he had inflicted on her in their failed marriage. He admitted that he had become more aware and less patient with his knowledge that he had engineered his own downfall, when he claimed that he would have "loved only to serve" others. His salutation for this strange letter is "Much love, Paul."

Since this hand-signed letter is found in the Paul Jenkins Papers at the Archives of American Art and not in the Alice Baber Papers, we cannot be sure that Jenkins even shared a copy of it with her. It's even possible that he wrote this letter just to look good for posterity. His reference to "under the name of Saturn" suggests that the couple had read the 1963 book *Born Under Saturn: The Character and Conduct of Artists* by Margot and Rudolf Wittkower, which investigates the history of the folklore that artistic inspiration is a form of madness, a madness directly expressed in artists' unhappy and eccentric lives.[99] The book surveyed artists in "documented history from antiquity to the French Revolution," while we can also think about the troubled mental health of more recent artists from Vincent van Gogh to Mark Rothko. From this reference to *Born Under Saturn*, it is also possible that Jenkins wanted to acknowledge difficulties that he had caused Baber, which he knew related to his own lack of sobriety and self-control.

Among other friends who thought to visit Baber in the hospital was Richard Galef, with whom she was close in the early 1970s and who accompanied her on her trip to Iran.[100] Also in touch with Baber at this time was Arlene Bujese, then the director of Phoenix II East, a gallery in Washington, DC, that showed Baber's work. Bujese recalled that Nancy Hanks called her to arrange to buy one of Alice's paintings anonymously, asking that Arlene telephone the ailing Alice and tell her that someone with another name (any name; Bujese says that she chose Carmichael) had just made the purchase. Bujese recalls that Baber, who died a few days later, was very pleased to get the news that she had sold a painting to this new collector.[101] Hanks died on January 7, 1983, just a few months after Baber.

On September 22, Ernestine recorded that she picked up Alice's mail, but then for October 2, 1982, Ernestine recorded, "Alice died in the early hours."[102] Paradoxically, Dorothy Seiberling's article mentioning Alice Baber appeared in *The New York Times* on October 3, 1982, a day after Baber's death in Lenox Hill Hospital.

This *New York Times* article was a feature story about the show *The Artist and the Quilt*, which, according to Seiberling, had begun when the artists Charlotte Robinson, Alice Baber, and Dorothy Gillespie met for lunch in January 1975 and wanted to do something special to celebrate International Women's Year. The trio settled on honoring the unsung creative women of the past, who used their artistic vision and sewing skill to make quilts. They proposed a museum show of quilts designed by contemporary artists but executed by traditional quilters.[103] The latter goal became a complicating factor that slowed down the project.

As well as Baber, Gillespie, and Robinson, the project's original participants included Miriam Schapiro and Joyce Kozloff, both prominent members of the Pattern and Decoration movement, and Isabel Bishop, Rosalyn Drexler, Mary Beth Edelson, Elaine de Kooning, Alice Neel, and Betty Parsons, as well as Faith Ringgold, who was already known for her own story quilts.[104]

Baber, who loved working with her colleagues, not only missed celebrating her contributions to *The Artist and the Quilt* but also being present at her own solo show, about to open in at the University of Alabama Gallery, which was featured in the *Tuscaloosa News*, also on October 3, 1982, the day after her death. Baber was identified as a "well-known New York artist," who works in the "color abstractionist mode"; a "colorist" who experiments "with the varied effects that are possible with color as a result of using unorthodox types of paint and methods of application. Miss Baber rubs oil in transparent layers that appear to open much like curtains or veils, revealing cavernous depths or spatial vistas which are highly suggestive to the imagination."[105]

In conjunction with this show, the art collector Silvia Pizitz, who was born in Birmingham, Alabama, and studied at the Grand Central School of Art in New York, where she settled, donated paintings by Baber to the Birmingham Museum of Art and the University of Alabama Gallery, which organized Baber's 1982 show. Pizitz's patronage included her donation of Baber's painting to the Museum of Modern Art in New York in 1981 (CP #32).

Baber's funeral took place at 2:00 P.M. on October 6, 1982, in the front yard of the Baber farmhouse in Illinois, with the service conducted by the Reverend Phillip Snider.[106] The family's funeral books record, "Alice's cherry casket on front porch in dappled sunlight, flowers around it."[107] Two of her nephews, Geoff and Bill Kern, played flutes, and the third and eldest, John M. Kern, "read Psalm XC from big old Baber bible" and Deuteronomy 6:4–8, which begins, "Hear, O Israel: The LORD our God, the LORD is one." The other two speakers were Norbert Nelson, her friend and executor from New York, and her friend, Sharon Theobald, then the director of the Greater Lafayette Museum of Art.

Alice Baber was buried in Fairview Cemetery in Kansas, Illinois, but the USIA kept touring shows of her art that had already been scheduled at the time of her death—in Haiti, a show of watercolors and lithographs took place at the Musée d'Art Haïtien du Collège St. Pierre in October 1982. Fran Switt, who worked with Baber in cultural affairs at the USIA, wrote to Norton Dodge on October 21, 1982, a postcard that was the invitation to Baber's show in Haiti: "It is with great sadness that I write to you, knowing how much we all miss Alice.

She participated in the preparation of this show. I know she would have loved the opening. We all raised a glass of champaign [*sic*] to her memory. This show will tour the Caribbean."[108]

The show, *Alice Baber: Luz y Color*, continued in February 1983 at the Galeria de Arte Moderno in Santo Domingo, Dominican Republic, and from March 20, 1983, Baber's watercolors and lithographs were shown at the National Gallery of Jamaica; the same show, called *Alice Baber: A Journey of Light and Color*, visited Port of Spain, Trinidad and Tobago from April to May 1983.

In 1982 the Greater Lafayette Museum of Art (GLMA) established the Alice Baber Memorial Collection of both her work and of other artists in her circle, many of whom donated work, including Elaine de Kooning, Paul Jenkins, Dorothy Gillespie, Will Barnet, Stanley Boxer, Ann Chwatsky, Audrey Flack, Connie Fox, Helen Gerardia, and several others. Arnold Newman donated two photographs from 1968, one of Alice and one of her and Paul Jenkins.

Baber's close friend Dorothy Gillespie, with whom she shared a love of bright color, donated one of her sculptures to the GLMA. The museum's director at the time, Sharon Theobald, had, as a student in 1960, met Baber through Gillespie, when she and Baber were both teaching at the New School in New York City. When Theobald was interviewed by the local paper, she recalled that "Baber had known for several years that she was dying and she expressed to Theobald her need to share her works with friends."[109] Baber was quoted as having told Theobald, "I can always go home, but I'll never really go home until my paintings go home."[110]

Theobald volunteered to organize a retrospective of Baber's work, which opened in Paris, Illinois, near where Baber was born, in January 1983, and then traveled to the Greater Lafayette Museum of Art in March 1983. This was the same show that had begun at the

University of Alabama. For the catalogue, the essayist was Virginia Pitts Rembert, who was then chair of the Department of Art at the University of Alabama. Rembert, who had gotten to know Baber from interviewing her beginning in 1975, recalled in 1982 that Baber had "a will that is apparent in fostering her own career and in bucking her present traumatic illness. There are also a mental acuity that belongs only to the intelligentsia, and an aristocratic demeanor that belies her mid-western heritage."[111]

Baber knew about the creation of the memorial collection for the GLMA and "even recommended other contemporary artists whose works should be part of it."[112] One of the artists to donate a work was Audrey Flack, who had shown with Baber in many women's exhibitions, and who wrote, "I knew Alice for many years and have decided to participate in the building of the Alice Baber Memorial Collection by giving you a work of mine."[113] Flack, despite her brief early period painting abstract expressionist canvases, donated a later work that was photorealist in style.

Baber also bequeathed one of her own paintings to the GLMA. Ironically, the museum shows a monumental canvas by Paul Jenkins on its website, but there is no mention of Alice Baber, the artist who was the reason for the memorial collection.[114] Theobald recalled that Jenkins asked her, "How big is the largest painting you have by Alice Baber?" Competitive even after Baber's death, Jenkins donated this huge painting, intent on dwarfing his ex-wife's work.[115]

To raise money for the Alice Baber Memorial Fund at Guild Hall in East Hampton, New York, where Baber spent time in the summers, there was a sale "at advantageous prices" of Baber's works held at the Elaine Benson Gallery in nearby Bridgehampton, from September 30 to October 2, 1983.[116] A report in the newspaper announced that more than $8,000 had been raised for the fund. Paul Jenkins, as Baber's ex-husband, was one of the three people who appeared in the accompanying photograph taken at the gallery.[117] Perhaps he regretted his role in destroying his second marriage, but he surely could not resist another opportunity for publicity.

The Swope Art Museum in Terre Haute, Indiana, acquired the 1967 painting Jenkins called *Phenomena near Baber Woods*, which he named after the conservation efforts of his onetime father-in-law with whom he had corresponded.[118] Adin Baber, Alice's father, purchased *Phenomena Near Baber Woods* from the artist and had it shipped directly to the museum in August of 1967. Ironically, the Swope had recently exhibited this monumental work without making any reference to Alice Baber, without whom neither the title nor the association with Indiana would exist. The painting inspired a local composer, Jack Nesser, to create a work in 2024 to raise funds for the Terre Haute Symphony Orchestra.[119]

The chairwoman of the Guild Hall benefit on Long Island was Baber's longtime friend Ernestine Lassaw, whom Annabelle Hebert, then the director of the museum and cultural center, wrote to thank for her help in the fundraising campaign.[120] Ernestine staged a yard sale to raise funds by selling off Alice's clothes. Aware that Alice's clothes reflected her friend's creativity and personality, Ernestine labeled and kept a sheet of paper, penned by the artist Mercedes Matter, on which Ernestine set prices at $5–$20 each, totaling $140 for items such as a "striped Guatemalan skirt," "a lime green and shocking pink Persian coat," a purple cotton Indian blouse, a red cape, and "Japanese evening [*sic*]."[121] Even in death, Alice Baber's wardrobe testified to her love of color.

The Lassaws' daughter, Denise, reflects: "I had many mothers in the art world of the 1950s. Besides my birth mother, Ernestine Lassaw, and my god-mother Elaine de Kooning, there was Alice Baber, a radiant being with very white skin and black hair. She was a person who brought colors to life."[122] "Although Alice looked soft, her mind was a finely sharpened tool, not to be distracted by foolish things. She could hold her own on any subject," Denise insisted.[123] "From Alice and my other mothers I learned to be an independent thinking human. We didn't doubt our naturally clever minds, and did not conform to a society that had lesser expectations of our sex. Alice and my other mothers were creators of beauty. If one creates beauty, what does it matter what sex you are? But I am glad they are being more fully appreciated now, even if they have to wear the label of 'woman' artist."[124]

Baber adored the Lassaws. She left them one of her few personal bequests as her executor Norbert Nelson wrote to them: "She valued the warm and supportive friendship which you both gave her over so many years very much, and wanted to give you some small pleasure which you might otherwise not have had. I know she hoped it would bring you some small joy."[125]

Baber appeared posthumously in the 1982 book *25 Artists by Hans Namuth*. Edited by the art dealer Arlene Bujese, the essay on Baber was a reprint of James Jones's 1965 article, which she must have chosen. Each artist received a full-page color reproduction of one work: Baber's painting was *For a Book of Kings* (1974).[126] But more poignantly, Namuth photographed Baber at work in her studio especially for this book, recording her valiant efforts to produce watercolors in her final days. Namuth stated about his new photographs taken for this book: "Among the six I added this year alone was brave and beautiful Alice Baber, who just died."[127] Thomas M. Messer, then the director of the Guggenheim Museum, described Namuth's interpretation in this haunting photograph of Baber in his foreword: "Alice Baber, as most of us have never seen her and none of us ever will again, her lovely features attenuated but still intact, her head held and contained within a metal halo vest, as she deploys her pure and exquisite artistry against the cancer in last, gallant rear-guard action since overpowered."[128]

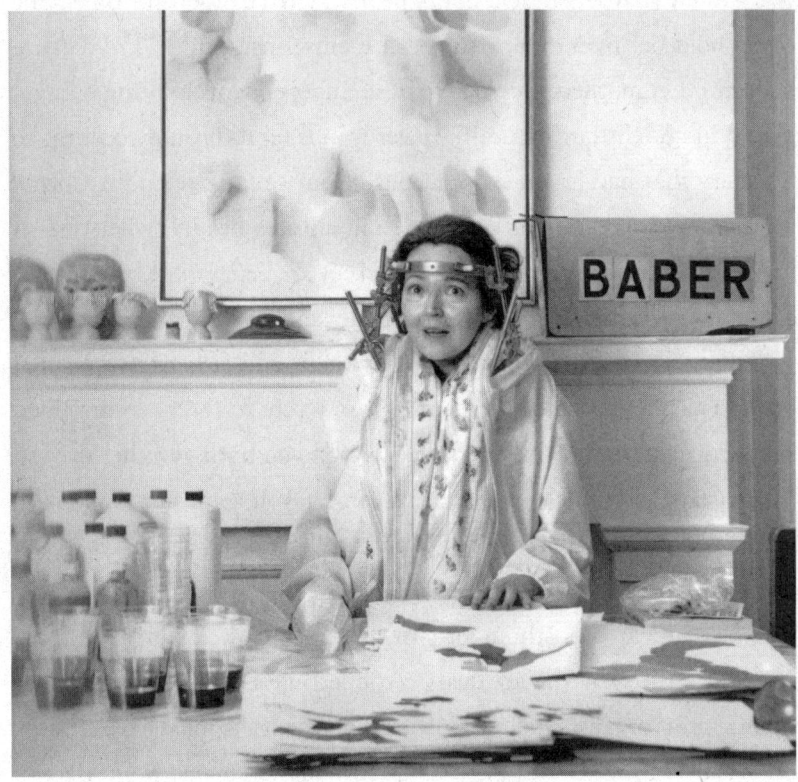

Hans Namuth photographed Alice painting, Sag Harbor, NY, 1982.

In search of Baber's story, I finally tracked down someone who recalled what happened to the Alice Baber Memorial Library at Guild Hall. The art critic and curator Phyllis Braff, who both wrote about Baber for the *East Hampton Star* and who included her in a show she cocurated for Guild Hall, recalled, "Yes, I knew Alice Baber. She was a special person. Sense of classic, refined beauty in every way. Genteel. Dedicated to her project commitments."[129]

Braff stated and surely believed "Guild Hall eventually decided (after installing the Alice Baber Memorial Library) that the public would be better served if the collection was housed at the EH library across the street. There is a commemorative bookplate in each volume."[130] Sadly, however, Alice Baber's books have vanished without a list of them or any trace of how they were discarded.

In New York, Baber's art is in the permanent collections of the Museum of Modern Art, the Guggenheim, the Whitney, and the Metropolitan Museum of Art. Dozens of public institutions, in the United States and abroad, now own Baber's paintings, each of which, though rarely shown, deserves to be on view. In fact, Baber, whose stunning body of work is now being rediscovered, was the subject of three gallery shows in New York and one in London in 2024. Thus, Alice Baber is doing much better than most women artists of the past, who too often remain buried by bias against women artists.[131]

ALICE BABER:
SELECTED PUBLIC COLLECTIONS

Arkansas Art Center, Little Rock, AR
Art in Embassies, U.S. State Department
Art Museum of Greater Lafayette, Lafayette, IN
Berkeley Art Museum and Pacific Film Archive, Berkeley, CA
Birmingham Museum of Art, Birmingham, AL
Blanton Museum of Art, University of Texas at Austin
Castellani Art Museum of Niagara University, Lewiston, NY
David Ownsley Museum of Art, Ball State University, Muncie, IN
Dwight Frederick Boyden Gallery, St. Mary's College of Maryland,
    St. Mary's City, MD
Fine Arts Museums of San Francisco
Fort Lauderdale Museum, Florida
Fralin Museum of Art at the University of Virginia, Charlottesville
Georgia Museum of Art, Athens, GA
Grey Art Museum, New York University
Guild Hall Museum, East Hampton, NY
Herbert F. Johnson Museum of Art, Cornell University, Ithaca, NY
Hood College, Frederick, MD
Israel Museum, Jerusalem, Israel
Katzen Art Center, American University, Washington, DC
Kemper Museum of Contemporary Art, Kansas City, MO
Knoxville Museum of Art, Knoxville, TN
Link Art Gallery, Paris, Illinois
Los Angeles County Museum of Art
Lowe Art Museum, University of Miami, Coral Gables, FL
Marianna Kistler Beach Museum of Art, Kansas State University,
    Manhattan, KS

Metropolitan Museum of Art, New York
Mount Holyoke College Art Museum, Holyoke, MA
MSU Broad Art Museum, Michigan State University, East Lansing, MI
Museum of Modern Art, Bogotá, Colombia
Museum of Modern Art, New York
Nasher Museum of Art at Duke University, Durham, NC
National Gallery of Modern Art, New Delhi, India
National Museum of Women in the Arts, Washington, DC
Neuberger Museum of Art, Purchase, NY
Newark Museum of Art, Newark, NJ
New Britain Museum of American Art, New Britain, CT
Princeton University Art Museum, Princeton, NJ
Raclin Murphy Museum of Art, University of Notre Dame,
    Notre Dame, IN
Rose Art Museum, Brandeis University, Waltham, MA
San Francisco Museum of Modern Art
Santa Barbara Museum of Art, Santa Barbara, CA
Solomon R. Guggenheim Museum, New York
Smithsonian American Art Museum, Washington, DC
Swope Art Museum, Terre Haute, IN
University of Alabama Gallery, Tuscaloosa
Weatherspoon Art Museum, Greensboro, NC
Whitney Museum of American Art, New York
Worcester Art Museum, Worcester, MA
Wright Museum of Art, Beloit College, Beloit, WI

DRAMATIS PERSONAE

Aach, Herbert (1923–1985)
Abbott, Mary (1921–2019)
Abrams, Ruth (1912–1986)
Adam, Helen (1909–1993)
Adams, Pat (1928–)
Albers, Joseph (1888–1976)
Albright, Thomas (1936–1984)
Alcaide, Asta Rose (1920–2016)
Alpert, Ann (1914–1997)
Ames, Elizabeth (1885–1977)
Antin, Eleanor (1935–)
Armento, Rocco (1924–2011)
Arnheim, Rudolf (1904–2007)
Ashbery, John (1927–2017)
Ashton, Dore (1928–2017)
Baber, Adin (1834–1902)
Baber, Adin B. (1892–1974)
Baber, Alice (1928–1982)
Baber, Asa (1832–1915)
Baber, Dexter Dole "Deck"
   (1867–1965)
Baber, Frederick (1876–1940)
Baber, Nancy (1926–2005)
Baber, Lois Mary Shoot
   (1892–1943)
Bacon, Peggy (1895–1987)
Baer, Jo (1929–2025)
Bard, Joellen (1942–)
Barnes, Djuna (1892–1982)

Barr, Jr., Alfred H. (1902–1981)
Bates, Alan (1934–2003)
Baziotes, William (1912–1963)
Blaine, Nell (1922–1996)
Beauchamp, Robert (1923–1995)
Beckmann, Max (1884–1950)
Benson, Elaine (1924–1998)
Bernstein, Judith (1942–)
Biala, Janice (1903–2000)
Bishop, Isabel (1902–1988)
Bissière, Roger (1886–1964)
Blaine, Nell (1922–1996)
Bluhm, Norman (1921–1999)
Booth, Power (1945–)
Booyakovitch, Zenaida Gourievna
   "Zuka" (1924–2016)
Bourgeois, Louise (1911–2010)
Bowen, Denis (1921–2006)
Bowie, Theodore R. (1905–1995)
Boxer, Stanley (1911–2010)
Braff, Phyllis (ca 1930–)
Brandt, Warren (1918–2002)
Breton, André (1896–1966)
Breton, Aube (1935–)
Brooks, Charlotte Park
   (1918–2010)
Brooks, James "Jim" (1906–1922)
Brown Baker, Richard
   (1912–2002)

Bujese, Arlene (1938–)
Burton, Phillip (1904–1995)
Burton, Richard (1925–1984)
Canaday, John (1907–1985)
Chicago, Judy (1939–)
Chwatsky, Ann (1942–)
Clayburgh, Jill (1944–2010)
Cohen, Jean (1927–2013)
Cornelius, Aleta (1923–2002)
Craig, Charles (19??–19??)
Cunningham, Merce (1919–2009)
Davie, Alan (1920–2014)
de Kooning, Elaine Marie
    Catherine Fried (1918–1989)
de Kooning, Willem (1904–1997)
Delaunay, Robert (1885–1941)
Delaunay, Sonia (1885–1979)
Derfner, Phyllis (1947–)
Dienes, Sari (1898–1992)
Dobkin, Alexander (1908–1975)
Dodd, Lois (1927–)
Dodge, Norton T. (1927–2011)
Donnerson, Seena (1924–2020)
Dove, Arthur (1880–1946)
Dreyfus, Shirley (1922–1995)
Drexler, Rosalyn (1926–)
Duchamp, Marcel (1887–1968)
Duchamp, Alexina "Teeny"
    (1906–1995)
Dzubas, Friedel (1915–1994)
Edelson, Mary Beth (1933–2021)
Edgar, Natalie (1932–)
Eikerman, Alma (1908–1995)
Eliot, George (1819–1880) (born
    Mary Ann Evans)
Elsen, Albert (1927–1995)
Engle, Jules (1909–2003)
Ernst, Max (1891–1976)
Ferrara, Jackie (1929–)

Ferren, John (1905–1970)
Fine, Elsa Honig (1930–)
Fine, Perle (1905–1988)
Fisher, Ethel (1923–2017)
Fitzsimmons, James (1919–1985)
Flack, Audrey (1931–2024)
Flinker, Karl (1923–1991)
Flinker, Martin (1895–1986)
Focillon, Henri (1881–1943)
Francis, Sam (1923–1994)
Frank, Mary (1933–)
Francken, Ruth (1924–2006)
Frankenthaler, Helen (1928–2011)
Freilicher, Jane (1924–2014)
Frink, Elisabeth (1930–1993)
Fromm-Reichmann, Frieda
    (1889–1957)
Galef, Richard (1923–2015)
Gambini, William "Bill"
    (1918–2010)
Garrard, Mary (1937–)
Gedney, Joan (1925–2013)
Georges, Paul (1923–2002)
Gerardia, Helen (1903–1988)
Gillen, Ann (1935–)
Gillespie, Dorothy (1920–2012)
Gilliam, Sam (1933–2022)
Gilot, Françoise (1921–2023)
Glueck, Grace (1921–2023)
Goldsmith, Lawrence (1916–2004)
Gold, Betty (1935–)
Gold, Herbert (1924–2023)
Goldfarb, Shirley (1925–1980)
Goldwater, Robert (1907–1993)
Goodall, Donald B. (1912–1997)
Goodman, Sam (1919–1967)
Gorky, Arshile (1904–1948)
Gottlieb, Adolph (1903–1974)
Grabar, Oleg (1929–2011)

Graham, John (Ivan G.
Dombrowsky) (1887–1961)
Greene, Balcomb (1904–1990)
Greenberg, Clement (1909–1994)
Grippe, Peter (1912–2002)
Guggenheim, Peggy (1898–1979)
Gurdjieff, George Ivanovitch
(1866–1949)
Guston, Philip (1913–1980)
Hale, Robert Beverly (1901–1985)
Hanks, Nancy (1927–1983)
Hanks, William (ca 1650–ca 1704)
Hare, David (1917–1992)
Hare, Elizabeth Sage Goodwin
(1878–1948)
Hartigan, Grace (1922–2008)
Hasen, Burt (1921–2007)
Hazelet Drummond, Sally
(1924–2017)
Heidenberg, Lillian (1949–)
Hélion, Jean (1904–1987)
Herrigel, Eugen (1884–1955)
Hess, Thomas B. (1920–1978)
Hofmann, Hans (1880–1966)
Holtzman, Harry (1912–1987)
Hope, Henry (1905–1989)
Hopkins, Budd (1931–2011)
Howard, Richard (1929–2022)
Hutchinson, Peter (1930–)
Iolas, Alexander (1908–1987)
Ireland, Richard W. (1925–)
Jackson, Martha (1907–1969)
Jaffe, Shirley (1923–2016)
Jenkins, Esther Ebenhoe
(1922–2018)
Jenkins, Hillarie Paula (1954–)
Jenkins, Paul (1923–2012)
Johnson, Buffie (1912–2006)
Johnson, Lester (1919–2010)

Johnston, Ben (1926–2019)
Jong, Erica (1942–)
Jones, Gloria (1928–2006)
Jones, James (1921–1977)
Jones, Kaylie (1960–)
Judd, Don (1928–1994)
Kane, Connie (Levene)
(1930–2021)
Kanemitsu, Matsumi "Mike"
(1922–1992)
Katz, Alex (1927–)
Katz, Leslie George (1918–1997)
Kern, John M. (1954–)
Kingsley, April (1941–2023)
Kissinger, Henry A. (1923–2023)
Kline, Franz (1910–1962)
Klonis, Bernard (1906–1957)
Klüver, Heinrich (1897–1979
Kozloff, Joyce (1942–)
Kramer, Hilton (1928–2012)
Krasner, Lee (1908–1984)
Kuniyoshi, Yasuo (1889–1953)
Lamba, Jacqueline Breton Hare
(1910–1993)
Lansner, Fay Gross (1921–2010)
Lassaw, Denise (1945–)
Lassaw, Ernestine (1913–2014)
Lassaw, Ibram (1913–2003)
Leslie, Alfred (1927–2023)
Levene, Sam (1905–1980)
Lewitin, Landès (1892–1966)
Lincoln, Nancy Hanks
(1784–1818)
Lippard, Lucy (1937–)
Littman, Robert R. (1941–)
Lowry, Bates (1923–2004)
Louis, Morris (1912–1962)
Lurie, Boris (1924–2008)
Maddox, Conroy (1912–2005)

Rockefeller, Lawrence S. (1910–2024)
Rockefeller, Michael C. (1938–1961)
Rockefeller, Nelson (1908–1979)
Rosenberg, Gabriele [Roos] (1932–2022)
Rosenberg, Harold (1906–1978)
Roser, Ce (1925–)
Rosten, Norman (1913–1995)
Rothenberg, Susan (1945–2020)
Rothko, Mark (1903–1970)
Rublev, Andrei (ca 1360–ca 1430)
Ryan, Ann (1889–1954)
Saar, Betye (1926–)
Sachs, Abraham M. "Abe"
Sachs, Paul Joseph (1878–1965)
Sage, Kay (1898–1963)
Sand, George (1804–1876) (born Amantine Lucile Aurore Dupin)
Sandler, Irving (1925–2018)
Sandler, Lucy Freeman (1930–)
Sargent, Paul Turner (1880–1946)
Schapiro, Miriam (1916–2015)
Schorer, Mark (1908–1977)
Schuyler, James (1923–1991)
Schwabacher, Ethel Kremer (1903–1984)
Schwartz, Theresa (1928–)
Segal, Erich (1937–2010)
Seiberling, Dorothy (1922–2019)
Seliger, Charles (1926–2009)
Semmel, Joan (1932–)
Seuphor, (Michel 1901–1999)
Sharrer, Honoré (1920–2009)
Shoot, Mary Elizabeth Wilhoit (1851–1933)
Shoot, Tilford Taylor (1848–1905)

Shulman, Alix Kates (1932–)
Sihare, Laxmi (1929–1993)
Silver, Walter (1923–1998)
Simek, Vasek (1928–1994)
Sleigh, Sylvia (1916–2010)
Slivka, David (1914–2010)
Slivka, Rose (1919–2004)
Sloan, John (1871–1951)
Slobodkina, Esphyr (1908–2002)
Slutzky, Robert (1929–2005)
Smith, Joseph (1805–1844)
Smith, Louise Reinhardt (Mrs. Bertram) (1904–1994)
Solinger, Janet (1922–2020)
Solman, Joseph (1909–2008)
Solomon, Hyde (1911–1982)
Sontag, Susan (1933–2004)
Soyer, Raphael (1899–1987)
Speyer, Darthea (1919–2014)
Spillenger, Ray (1924–2013)
Stamos, Theodoros (1922–1997)
Sterne, Hedda (1910–2011)
Still, Clyfford (1904–1980)
Story, Ala (1907–1972)
Sujo, Clara Diament (1921–2020)
Sutton, Keith (1924–1991)
Suzuki, Daisetsu Teitaro (1870–1966)
Switt, Frances F. (1937–2002)
Tabak, May Natalie (Rosenberg) (1810–1993)
Tanguy, Yves (1900–1955)
Tapié, Michel (1909–1987)
Templeton, Norma "Ronni" Frazier (1927-2019)
Theobald, Sharon (ca 1945–)
Thomas, Dylan (1914–1953)
Thomas, Helen (1920–2013)
Thomas, Yvonne (1913–2009)

Tice, Clara (1888–1973)
Tucker, Marcia Silverman
  (1940–2006)
Tworkov, Jack (1900–1982)
Van Baron, Judith (1942–)
Vicente, Esteban (1903–2001)
Victor, Thomas (1938–1989)
Vivekananda, Swami (1863–1902)
Ward, Eleanor (1911–1984)
Watts, Alan (1915–1973)
Wayne, June (1918–2011)
Weil, Susan (1930–)
Weinstein, Joyce (1931–)
Wiese, Otis Lee (1905–1972)

Wilfred, Thomas (1889–1968)
Wilke, Hannah (1940–1993)
Wilson, Sol (1896–1974)
Wilson, Susanna Winslow
  (1916–2003)
Wittkower, Margot (1902–1995)
Wittkower, Rudolf (1901–1971)
Wright, Frank Lloyd (1867–1959)
Yellen, Samuel (1906–1983)
Yoshihara, Jiro (1905–1972)
Yunkers, Adja (1900–1983)
Zogbaum, Marta (1932–1984)
Zogbaum, Wilfrid (1915–1965)
Zubrin, Edith (1926–1977)

APPENDIXES: PUBLISHED ESSAYS

Curator's Notes by Alice Baber

Color by Alice Baber

Gorky's Color by Alice Baber

Sonia Delaunay by Alice Baber

My Paintings are My Diary by Alice Baber

Memoir of Alice Baber by Denise Lassaw

CURATOR'S NOTES
BY ALICE BABER, GUEST CURATOR

The Color Forum[1] was founded a few years ago by a group of five painters. To quote Herbert Aach, the group's organizer, "Our work can be best described as possessing a conceptual override on color. Or, one might say that color in the broadest sense is the most important, perhaps the most significant factor in our work. Since the problems arising from such a concept are of such huge proportions, this banding together is basically intended for the exchange of information and ideas, esthetic and scientific, for problem solving and in the hope of developing an oral syntax, a common articulation, to broaden the base of communication on color, not merely for this group and other artists, but also for all those who are interested in color in all its phases."

As the group met, it became immediately apparent that, from the point of view of style, our works, though dissimilar, shared a common emphasis, color, which I feel is the *raison d'être* in the work. This commonality brought us together and we have met various times for discussions, taping a number of these for the record. The importance of these discussions was to give us all an understanding of the range of problems that we face in our work.

There was extended discussion about the relationship of form to color. We felt that in one sense the two were almost inseparable, but that in another sense color takes preeminence as the prime mover over all the other elements in the painting.

My own point of view leaned heavily to the pre-eminence of color—what I call "color hunger"—that has motivated my own work and my selections. I have also looked for magic, poetry, eccentricity, saturation, overemphasis and so forth. Others of the group were deeply based in architectonic and structural problems, and it was the intermingling and exchange of the differences of opinion that made our sessions lively.

In preparation for the "Color Forum" show, Herbert Aach compiled a list of artists and the group spent long nights adding the names and deciding on the scope of the show. After we established a basic list, I worked toward choosing the show. Dr. Donald B Goodall, the director, was extremely helpful at all times and at all phases of the show, and the exhibition reflects his interest and help.

I would like to thank the galleries and the collectors who so generously have loaned work to the show, and especially the artists who allowed my visits to infringe upon their studio time and who understood at once what I meant by color, both specifically and generally. This is an artists' show and we would like to have had space for others. My hope is that the show will continue in other years.

Our original plans to try to show works from the entire twentieth century became too large to encompass comfortably. We therefore concentrated on recent years and we did not attempt to overcategorize or designate in art-historical terms.

Pure color and hue for their own sake, on one level, and as metaphor on another, are what interest me. On another level, materials affect art. Acrylic, whether actually used or not—and it is rather evenly divided in the show—has affected the last decade in terms of thinness, flatness and matness.

Art comes from the materials used, from art, and from nature, which means that painting can be read six ways and that the simile and metaphor can be seen as follows: blue as blueness, blue as non-blue; blue as the virgin, blue as nonvirgin; blue as sky, blue as nonsky. Assuming that there is a great emphasis now on color as hue and as an expressive subject, I would like to point out in addition that there is some emphasis in this show on low-keyed statements about high-keyed spectrum colors; that spectrum colors are "sweet" and that they, carried into unusual juxtapositions, set the teeth on edge like the high sweet quality of Mozart; that "hot" and "cold" concepts must have new definitions for flat color passages as opposed to modeled color.

In the selection of the show we have tried to present a finely honed point of view about color which has been developed by the Color Forum. The exhibition is not the cutoff point, since the problem of color is constantly changing. I see it as the beginning, leaving the question of color open.

COLOR
BY ALICE BABER

M y early work was still life and from it came the tree of life, the celestial garden, the rivers the mystical ladders, colored wind and rain, plants made of jewels, mythical springs, and the final rim of the universe.

In India I have seen long streamers of pink sari cloth being dried near the red fort in New Delhi, a lavender umbrella and orange kimono in the mist on the hillside in Japan, red sweaters in the grey streets of Paris, the golden orange of Notre Dame at sundown, the hard red, yellow and blue store fronts in New York, and the iridescent mosaic tones illusive in the moonlight at Wat Po temple in Bangkok.

When I first conceive of a painting, I must feel a certain color. I see it everywhere, I feel it, I hear it, I taste it, and I want to eat it. I start from the driving force of the color. I feel one color (color hunger); then comes a second color to provide light, luminous light. It will be the glow to reinforce the first color. I then discover the need of one, two, three, or more color which will indicate and make movement, establish the psychodynamic balance in midair, allow freedom to take place, add weight at the top and bottom of the painting, and create mythical whirlpools between larger forms.

By this time, I can begin to evaluate what I have been painting in a driven way. It is a painful time, for it can be the moment to preserve what I have or to change the painting. Then I think about the color consciously. I must add what is needed. The right darks, the right lights have to be there, and I must know the forms which have been created by the colors' work as forms.

In the final stages of the painting, I usually add glowing lights and change areas of local color if they come out too strongly as local pigment separated from the rest of the painting. It is here and at this moment that I can force the local color through light to take its significant or meaningful place in the painting. If it has not already happened, I create the center of the vortex. It is as if I am deciding where Atlantis is. I breathe yellow onto the painting, the only real light for me; it is like the inter-reflection of beaten gold shapes. (White as a light is also valid, but, irrationally, I contend that it is not light, because for me it is blue, and blue does not reflect, it is solid.)

Color makes light. Some light moves over the surface as if the wind were moving it, and that was the kind of color that first interested me, but now I am more interested in light within each color which causes the separate colors to move across the canvas as if each were a separate-colored light cast from different places in space.

Purple: it can be black or grey or green or blue or lush or puritanical. I use it for rivers or mountains, and pilgrimages, all trips to far places, for wild winds and the shadows on the ground of eagles carrying snakes, and the evocation of effervescent lonely but happy souls thinking of pink and yellow and green in vast gardens.

Red as a pigment is very heavy; it is best treated as fire and light or as transparent plants seen through filtered light, translucent all day suckers, or as red peppers well-polished or raspberries or cherries up to the elbows (red plastic boots are more difficult). Red should never be used as blood, or buckets of red paint, but it can be a Chinese res-taurant, a French hotel, school children in sweaters, trucks, prelates of high orders, and Picasso's little bit of red in each painting.

Orange is not so difficult; the actual pigment can be made trans-parent easily, but it can turn into brown light or become sick with green mixed badly or can make a splendid opaque grey. Orange is primitive; it makes Easter eggs or Peruvian mats and kimonos in the rain, and blonds with feather boas, beach towels and umbrellas, magazine covers, and principalities beyond the seas.

Then there is pink—how difficult to control! A great deal of white must be placed in sticky gobs on the palette, add cadmium red light still dull—add alizarin—still uninspired. Shall one use rose madder guaranteed to fade by Windsor Newton himself? Or throw it out and use a nice pink acrylic—it shall be found! Pink is light, pink is the shadow of sunset. Made very fine with turpentine and no white; it is the color of India, paladins embroidered in gold. Pink is all form and body but I prefer not to use it erotically, because it so naturally belongs there, but rather as the esoteric, the transcendent transition.

Black. I remember only once seeing it as a stripe on a German flag, in the great tulip garden near Amsterdam. Black belongs to Goya, to Velazquez, to Murillo and gangster cars, the insides of old cannon, and the little Princes in The Tower. Perhaps I shall take a long length of it out onto the bills and let it move in the wind and then I shall know it. I see a photographer covered in a black velvet square in a Renoir flower garden and I see strange black creatures with black matting over the eyes and high above them the ravens turning on Malabar Hill.

Green. Veridian green, chrome green. Wonderful. Terre Verte belongs to the great masters of Siena (green-Mondrian casts you out). Green should be used for sky, not problems of Proserpine, and awakening and nighttime and movement across the canvas and gently rainbowed with yellow to make blue parabolas . . . and running through it and floating in it.

Blue. Lapis and Thalo, sea captains and kings. Blue makes painting possible, it mixes with everything, it makes transitional tones, and universes of flat space; it can be transparent or opaque, mysterious or open, innocent or authoritarian, poignant, sad, wild with glee. Everything should be painted blue and one should live in it and on it because it is space and because it is time.

Yellow, the greatest color of all, a thick horrible local pigment. It must be forced onto the canvas into the only light we really know, the light of all the Gods—of all amber and heat, summer shades and parchment, and carved ivory held to the windowsill and hot yellow winds and heavy yellow flowers flailing the spring, and sport cars and yellow doors, the golden fleece, and Cytherea, and yellow mountains, but most of all the persuasive light under the sheets where worlds are spun in the mind of golden cobwebs to the top of the ladder, to the outer continuum.

GORKY'S COLOR
BY ALICE BABER

M y mother told me many stories while I pressed my face into her long apron with my eyes closed. She had a long white apron like the one in the portrait, and another embroidered one. Her stories and the embroidery on her apron got confused in my mind with my eyes closed. All my life her stories and her embroidery keep unraveling pictures in my memory. If I sit before a blank white canvas . . ."[1]

We have Gorky's own words and letters describing his color and his imagery[2] and we have his ideas as he immersed himself in art history, with his intellectual and emotional responses,[3] and we have his direct experience with nature, lying looking at the grass,[4] or teaching students, a matchbox held before his eyes, relating "a fixed point . . ." to "the world in front of him."[5]

Another written source for color, form, fantasy, and space are his descriptions—"blue rock half buried in the black earth with a few patches of moss placed here and there like fallen clouds" written on the *Garden of Sochi* series.[6]

To examine his palette leads to "plums of color," as Gorky called them.[7]

We choose our ancestors and we search for them. The painting, *Still Life*, c. 1924–26, Michener Collection, The University of Texas at Austin, is an example of early color, breathtaking and rich. I think that such color relates to Eastern carpets, gelim type, of Caucasian or Northern Turkoman colors, the soft green, the brown, the purples, the pinks, the rich alizarin orchestration. The spatial leaps of the pink in the back to the middle space, the overlaying of color and line and the color also remind me that Gorky used the best paint available. These colors were purchased with love and used with urgency.

I would like to mention as possible color sources both Armenian and Russian high and folk art as well as Caucasian, Turkoman, and Iranian color and form. Many worlds flow in and around Christian Armenia. Gorky discusses Armenian old masters in a letter to his family[8]—the free-floating spaces of the medieval painter, Toros Roslin, and others. These works are fascinating because of both their color and range.

Russian folk art combines primary color—red, yellow, blue—employs red and blue together, and also combines unusual lavender and offbeat tints.[9] Although the 19th century had already introduced Chevreul, chemical dyes, and discoveries of Far Eastern art, it seems to me that the greatest color input in the 20th century arrived with the Russian immigration to Paris—that, together with clear color from the South of France and Moorish Spain. Somehow, Miró and Kandinsky seem closest to Gorky in color choices.

Gorky's intense color usage followed his earlier Cézannesque washes. He then became involved in still life and cubism, and Ethel Schwabacher says that "at this time a potential colorist, he turned decisively in the direction of form and structure."[10] In fact, Gorky was deeply involved with color at all times.

Both Schwabacher and Stuart Davis have discussed the heavy impasto that Gorky used on some of his early paintings. Davis described Gorky as squeezing out ". . . half a dozen tubes of each color . . . to acquire a viscous consistency. When ready to paint, he transferred this small fortune in pigment to one or more canvases with a palette knife. . . ."[11]

The changes of color involved with cubism might well lead one to think that the change to emphasis on the black line (once and for all put down, as opposed to the earlier line of many changing colors and overlays) and the changing of color in between so that the pigment is built up high, was a discipline involved with the relation of drawing to color in terms of grayscale.

In the impasto paintings of Gorky the spreading on is done with thoroughness, painted and overpainted; one sees the color saved by form, the form then re-enforced by color. In *Composition*, 1938–39, owned by Donald and Isobel Grossman, the whites spread about, gently and elegantly covering and revealing hints of worlds beneath, an overlay approach that brings the white forward to the flat plane, to what later becomes the scumbled scrim of the landscape still lifes.

In thinking about the color choices in these paintings with the cubist emphasis, I decided to examine *Cahiers d'Art* to see what Gorky himself could have seen at the time. The first point is that all the reproductions were in black and white. The second is that Gorky's fine eye chose unerringly the works strong in black line, as well as the autonomous line of Picasso's *Crucifixion*, 1927, an autonomous line completely abstracted in Gorky's *Nighttime, Enigma and Nostalgia*, 1931–32. One becomes excited and gets the feel of the magazines, hot off the press; Picasso, Matisse, Gris, Ernst, Masson, Kandinsky, Miró, and an abundance of primitive art, including Scythian and Catalonian. (Incidentally, Masson's loose line seems weak in reproduction. However, Julien Levy said that much later, when Masson was in America, Gorky was interested in meeting him but could not speak French and Matta was more accessible as a friend.)[12]

In 1935 Gorky worked for the WPA Mural Project in Newark and gives some interesting color ideas.

"To add to the aggressiveness of these shapes, I have used such local colors as are to be seen on the aviation field—red, blue, yellow, black, grey, brown—because these colors were used originally to sharpen the objects so that they could be seen clearly and quickly. . . .

"In the other three panels, I have used arbitrary colors and shapes; the wing is black, the rudder yellow, so as to convey the sense that these modern gigantic implements of man are decorated with the same fanciful yet utilitarian sense of play that children use in coloring their kites. In the same spirit the engine becomes in one place like the wings of a dragon, and in another, the wheels, propeller, and motor take on the demonic speed of a meteor cleaving the atmosphere."[13]

Referring to the first balloon ascension he says, "In the shock of surprise everything changes. The sky becomes green. The sun is black with astonishment . . . the earth is spotted with such elliptical brown forms as had never been seen before." The transference of color from one form to another is a colorist's delight.[14]

More changes in paint application begin to occur at the end of the *Garden in Sochi* series.[15] In *Pirate I*, Gorky used washlike water color, allowing the wet paint not only to run but also to make form through the etched lines of the edge of the washes. There are also larger areas of wash only, the sides left open—*Pirate II* has much scumbling. *Water of the Flowery Mill*, 1944, uses all techniques, scumbling, dripping, wash. *The Plow and the Song*, 1947, owned by Mr. and Mrs. Milton A. Gordon, is involved with scumbling; the Oberlin College painting of the same subject, with wash. The fluid light created by the scumble or washes creates a scrim in space—it intimates color beyond the transparent tent of Gorky's chosen space.

In *Making the Calendar*, 1947, a warm brown which both covers and reveals, and in *Agony*, 1947, the reds and browns remind me of Rothko's color later on. The reds in Gorky's painting, from the very first and throughout his life, are important and are painted with great nuance.

Once, at a meeting of artists, Gorky suggested that everyone do a work using only red, white, and black. There was consternation felt by some of the other artists and one can only assume that Gorky enjoyed the idea of setting the problem.

Gorky's color is a powerful part of his mastery. As I walked into the exhibition of the Peggy Guggenheim Collection in Paris (at the Orangerie, Summer 1964), in a room full of Gorky and his confreres, for me Gorky took the room and the show by his color alone. "Like a blow with a fist"[16] (as Robert Delaunay has described the effect of certain colors).

If the line indeed came first for Gorky, as is repeatedly stated, it is almost secondary in the reading of the works where he immerses himself in color. Line and color are integrated because linear felicity requires the placing of lines, at the last, over color, if color has blanked out the original format of lines. Color becomes a primary wash, middle link, or a last change.

Along with color, one of the excitements of following Gorky's work is the frequent interweaving of shapes which return like old friends throughout his work. The color is related to the subject matter. I feel that the color is most frequently derived from still life and imposed onto and into landscape (the title *Landscape Table*, 1945, emphasizes this idea). As he began to turn from cubist still life to a kind of abstract landscape, he maintained many habits from still life. The upturned table becomes the scrim, a middle-distance spatial position which receives light and implies distance beyond. The Rower-fruit color of the spots elongated into oval or erotic evocations.

Of course, in some cases the color is derived from the local land-scape; Ethel Schwabacher has referred to a hill near his house that inspired drawings and a painting, where nature rather than art history dominated.

Gorky frequently suspends shapes from the top of the painting, usually left of center—dangling shapes downward. Most modern painters have a pictorial necessity to make works heavier at the top, that is, a need to weight the top of the canvas; to weight the bottom is traditional. When moving from still life to landscape, the horizon can be controlled by putting the weight above, or controlled by suspending lines from the top. This necessity is sometimes solved at the back of the "box" of the picture space, such as Picasso's little window, or, again, one might have a painting within a painting, something that Gorky does in all periods of his work. Indeed, even a photograph of Willem de Kooning and Gorky together shows a painting behind them on the left and the easel goes out of the photograph at the top left of center, as if the photograph were a painting itself.[17]

The "Exquisite Corpse" game also unfolds from top to bottom downward in elongation of form. (Julien Levy does not know of any composite drawing by Gorky and Matta, but they drew at the same time, an "exchange game," each finding shapes and excitedly showing them to each other.) Schwabacher mentions that a central support column used in the Newark Mural appears in the Uccello, *The Miracle of the Host*, on Gorky's studio wall;[18] of the sacred tree mentioned in the *Garden of Sochi* letter,[19] Seitz says, "One can identify a tree trunk at upper center."

Gorky wrote a description for the Newark Airport about the house of his childhood, where he was born. "In the ceiling was a round aper-ture to permit the emission of smoke. Over it was placed a wooden cross from which was suspended by a string an onion into which seven feathers had been plunged. As each Sunday elapsed, a feather was removed, thus denoting passage of Time. . . . Through these elevated objects-floating feather and onion—was revealed to me, for the first time, the marvel of making from the common—the uncommon."[20]

The ambiguity of possibility, the recurrence of the suspended line, occurs for a thousand reasons.

Gorky emphasized what most painters later in the fifties were admonished to avoid, the finding of multiple images wanted or unwanted in a work, the implication of subject matter. From the fifties to the seventies, the mystique of flat space and nongeometric, nonorganic, nonsubject matter continued to be a dictum around town.

Back to the forties and to ambiguity. The artist finds shapes, chooses, moves the hand; the mind finds ambiguity. It isn't always the same story. Artists play with form as executioners play with death. When painters talk together, we talk about materials and ambiguity of space and form and color, never mind what Degas said.

Gorky's use of light and shadow relates to his color. The shadow often becomes the predominant shape, as in the Gorky drawing that I own, *Untitled*, 1936. It becomes the pull of the other shapes. Harold Rosenberg says of shadow ". . . knitted of myriad cross-hatchings, carefully toned; the manual routine no doubt had a soothing influence."[21] Gorky himself referred to "shadows in constant battle like the lancers of Paolo Uccello . . ."[22] Shadow soon becomes a thing in itself and finally a color. In art history, shadow is usually defined symbolically.

I have just revisited the Gorky painting in the San Francisco Museum of Art. It has many characteristics of the painter. The edge holds the shapes and releases them at the same time. It is unfettered at the bottom; there is the pull of a diagonal line on the right top, a center-to-left window, and the bar on the left side (like the "Chinde" or Shaman's line which in a Navajo design lets out the evil spirits—here it lets the tension run in and out) which implies both edge and other space to which the line is sent.

There is much warm white overpainting, pink, white and lavender-white; there is an important lavender bean middle right, and a green head on the left. Cadmium red emphasizes a winged shape to the left, three red lines in the bean, and some turquoise emphasis in the center.

I have been examining Gorky's work in terms of this exhibition for the last two years and flashes of meaning have occurred very like Gorky's paintings, like color leaps or flows. I have had the pleasure of conversations with Karlen Mooradian, Ethel Schwabacher, Julien Levy, Isobel Grossman, Donald Grossman, and, also, Marcos Grigorian and other Armenian artists in Tehran, Iran. And many others.

When I went to New York City in 1951, everyone seemed to be involved with memories of Gorky. Even today I dare not look at his work too closely. Unlike many artists, Gorky takes over the mind, and those hard-won spectacular forms of Gorky become like a poem that you think you once wrote.

This to me is an electrifying Gorky quote (to his sister Vartoosh): "Had I known that painting was so exhausting I should not have chosen it as a career. But no matter, it must have been my destiny. I must have been born to it."[23]

SONIA DELAUNAY
BY ALICE BABER

"Colors are notes of a poetic language which expresses states of soul."

S onia Terk Delaunay was born November 14, 1885, in the Ukraine, and after adoption at age five by an uncle, she was reared amidst the imperial elegance of St. Petersburg. Rich impressions of the Russian landscape and the vivifying cultural and spiritual currents of an empire nearing collapse fed her childhood and youth.

Before she was fourteen she was reading Goethe, Shakespeare, and Voltaire, each in the original, and, of course, Dostoevski. Her uncle's almost regal dwelling was a virtual museum and conservatory. His cook was second only to the czar's.

In her youth Delaunay showed a gift for painting and was encouraged by her early teachers. At eighteen her family allowed her to leave for Germany, where she studied for two years under Professor Schmidt-Reuter in Karlsruhe. In 1905, having just turned twenty, she went to Paris and enrolled at the Académie de la Palette.

In the apartment below her Left Bank studio lived the German art critic Wilhelm Uhde, whom she married in 1909. He introduced her to the work of Braque, Derain, Vlaminck, and Dufy. But their marriage did not last, for he had also introduced her to the painter Robert Delaunay, whom she married in 1910.

The Delaunays' Paris studio was the frequent meeting place for an expanding circle of young artists. Guillaume Apollinaire lived with them for a while; their other acquaintances included Henri Rousseau and Blaise Cendrars.

From 1912 Sonia's work, which had branched out into tapestries, bookcovers, pastels, collages, lampshades, embroideries, dresses, and waistcoats, took a new direction: the revolutionary treatment of color that has distinguished her career.

The Delaunays spent 1914–20 in Spain and Portugal, where Sonia painted her series of Portuguese Still lifes and her *Market in the Minho*. After World War I, she achieved rapid success in theater costumes with the 1918 Serge de Diaghilev production of the ballet *Cléopâtre*. The next year she designed clothes for Gaby and the decoration of the "Petit Casino" in Madrid where he starred. The opera singer Lahovska was outfitted by her for *Aïda* at the Barcelona Opera House.

After returning to Paris, Sonia received her first commission for fashion designs in 1922. She caused a revolution by putting onto silk the geometrical and abstract patterns of her paintings.

For the 1925 production of the album of her works she won high critical acclaim. In the same year the Delaunays were among those exhibited at the Exhibition of Decorative Arts in Paris. The next year she designed her first film costumes, for Le Somptier's *Le p'tit Parigot* and L'Herbier's *Vertige*.

From 1930–35 Sonia concentrated almost entirely on her painting. She was awarded a gold medal at the 1937 International Exhibition in Paris for her mural, Journeys Far Away, in the Railway pavilion.

The Delaunays participated in several other exhibitions before World War II forced them to flee to the south of France. Robert died at Montpellier in 1941. After his death, Sonia moved to Grasse, where a small circle of artists had gathered, and she did not return to Paris until 1944.

After the Liberation many writers including Maurice Raynal and André Salmon asked her to do covers for their books. Her prolific work has included lithographs, gouaches, colored engravings, catalog covers, invitation cards, posters, playing cards, motifs for ceramics, carpet designs, stained-glass windows, and mosaics.

-Ed.

Tapestries by Sonia Delaunay were exhibited this past year at the Corcoran Gallery of Art, Washington, DC (October 20– November 26, 1972), the New York Cultural Center, New York (April 13–May 20), and the Everson Museum of Art, Syracuse, New York (June 15–August 20).

Ten of the fourteen maquettes for the tapestries were specially designed for weaving; the other four were chosen from paintings. They were all woven by Pinton S.A., Felletin-Aubusson. The show at the New York Cultural Center also introduced the book, Sonia Delaunay: Rhythms and Colours by Jacques Demase with a preface by Michel Hoog (New York Graphic Society Ltd., Greenwich, Connecticut, 1973).

Delaunay's childhood in Russia, her arrival in Paris as an art student, her work as a prime mover in abstract color painting, and her painting of pottery with brilliant color and design, begun in Portugal in 1915, are described and depicted in the book. It also includes the patchwork blanket she made for her son Charles, in 1911, which foreshadows her later tapestries, the fantastic simultane dresses, the incredible woven coats, the costume designs for theater and the Diaghilev ballet, and the 1928 Citroën whose body was painted with one of her textile designs, the precursor of the Rolls Royces of today's rock stars. I wish that more examples of the book covers had been included; happily there is a color reproduction of the six-and-one-half-foot fold out book which she made in collaboration with the poet Blaise Cendrars. Long before the artists of the late fifties felt free to work in all media, Delaunay had been transforming objects by using color and disk shapes. Many of these themes, colors, and forms continue through her lifetime.

On a quiet street near the Boulevard Saint Germain, Delaunay has a two-story living room studio. Stairs lead to a balcony. When I have visited her, she has usually been working with gouache on paper, while sitting at her desk on the balcony. The entire space is immaculately white, as is the rest of the studio. A strong impression of green comes from an enormous plant which grows as high as a tree in front of the double window of the studio. There are touches of blue and red, and the great gray cat, who dominates the upstairs from its basket, suggests the soft grays of a Delaunay painting.

On my most recent visit, Delaunay was, as usual, working. I asked her who had been her early influence, and she replied Gauguin. During an after-dinner drive, she asked the driver to stop at the Trocadéro, where we watched the fountains and lights for some time. Now I read in Demase's book that in the course of their walks through the city, Sonia and Robert Delaunay "loved looking at the multicoloured halos around the street lights . . .; the electric street lighting . . . had caught her imagination . . .; she was fascinated by the coloured shimmer of the street lights on rainy nights." I also read, "The colours of her childhood, of the Ukraine and its colourful peasant weddings, with the red and green beribboned dance dresses . . ., memories of an album of traditional costumes which her uncle had once brought back from Sweden . . . Van Gogh's and Gauguin's influence is still present."

A Russian heritage plus symbolism plus color theories out of Neo-lmpressionism.

One feels the Russian influence very strongly: Russian peasant colors, the Russian Orient, and the high art of Russian icons, red and green. One recalls that by the time Delaunay first arrived in Paris as an art student, the Symbolists had freed color from naturalism; anything could be any color. The Fauves and the Expressionists continued in the use of strong color examining pure planes and primitivism. The Neo-lmpressionists had looked to the color ideas of people like Michel Eugene Chevreul who produced the theory of "simultaneous contrast of colors." The Delaunays called their movement simultane, referring to this simultaneous contrast theory.

"To the Delaunays the term 'simultane' did not imply the adoption of a theory," according to Hoog, "but rather they took the term as a 'banner'." Moreover Robert Delaunay said that simultane referred to the movement of light and simultaneous contrast (Robert Delaunay: Light and Color by Gustav Vriesen and Max lmdahl, Harry N. Abrams, Inc., New York, 1969). "In the movement of colors there are varying values of speed: the slow movement of complementary colors and the fast movement of dissonant colors." At another time he said, "This primitive disc was a painted canvas on which the colors, facing and contrasting with each other, had no other meaning beyond the visible; they were, in fact, contrasting, circularly placed colors . . . but what kind of colors? Red and blue tones in the center . . ., juxtaposed red and blue result in ultrarapid vibrations which can be seen with the naked eye. I once called this experiment a 'blow with a fist'."

Perhaps a clearer picture of what the Delaunays were trying to do can be had by referring to Chevreul's book, *The Principles of Harmony and Contrast of Colors and their Applications to the Arts* (1839). Chevreul, already a great chemist, was named Director of Dyes for the Royal Manufacturers at the Gobelin in 1825, and it is interesting that the man who influenced so many painters, or, rather, summed up many of their perceptions, was a chemist working with color in tapestry. He became involved with the interaction of colors of dyed wools. Why did black wool look gray next to blue wool but maintain its color next to red wool? He developed his color theories with great simplicity, not in the complicated way usually found in secondary sources. His law of "simultaneous contrast" states that contiguous colors affect each other. He discusses six principles for artists:

> "(1) Put a color on the canvas, it not only colors that part of the canvas to which the pencil has been applied, but it also colors the surrounding space with the complementary of the color, (2) To place White beside a color is to heighten its tone, (3) Putting Black beside a color lowers its tone, (4) Putting Gray beside a color renders it more brilliant, and at the same time it tints this Gray with the complementary color which is in juxtaposition, (5) To put a dark color near a different, but lighter color, is to raise the tone of the first, and to lower that of the second, independently of the modification resulting from the mixtures of the complementaries, (6) Put beside each other two flat tints of different tones of the same color, [and] Chiaroscuro is produced . . ."

Sonia Delaunay said in 1926, "Chevreul had discovered these laws scientifically and had checked them experimentally; but in Spain and Portugal, where the radiancy of light is greater and purer than here, my husband and I were able to confirm them in nature itself. The very quality of this light enabled us to go further than he had in analysing harmonies obtained through contrasts, and even to discover dissonances: I mean rapid vibrations caused by the proximity of warm and cold tones which stimulate an intense excitement through color" (from *Rhythms and Colours*).

Delaunay has stated, "Vision of infinite richness, for one who can see the relationship of colors among themselves, the contrasts and the dissonances, and the action of the one on the other . . . Colors are notes of a poetic language which expresses states of soul."

In reading Delaunay's tapestries for color, I find a multiplicity of afterimages, many colored lights flickering around like bits of lightning. There is a general avoidance of gradations of the same color and of contrasting color, often complementary or near complementary. Overlapping and interlocking are used to create space and form. In the changes of color from one pure area to another, the fairly sharp edges of the forms themselves are maintained, but changes occur within the form. Often there is an axis line through a circular vortex or a concentric circle, and all the colors of the wheels within wheels change hue on each side of the axis. Memories of Cubist facets have almost completely disappeared. As one sees a group of the tapestries, the colors sweep out into the room. There are reds everywhere, then blacks, greens, blues, yellows. The colors react on each other; halations dance about the space.

One is struck by the textures created by the weavers. Recent developments in texturing include: double chains, triple and quadruple chains, and a single and double chain combination that creates a basketlike effect. The pepper and salt areas, which resemble crayon over rough paper in Delaunay's gouache, are made with two strands of wool, one black, one white.

MY PAINTINGS ARE MY DIARY
BY ALICE BABER

My paintings are my diary, but I decided recently to keep some written notes. Each day, in the morning, I write my feeling about the sense of that day's color. It is the most important aspect of the day.

The written diary starts. I am in a car on the way to the ocean. I write about the sky. "A yellow and blue day turning brown as film turns color." Or, "a red day filled with purple tongues and soft green shadows." Today I am caught by T. S. Eliot's idea that the first voice of poetry is "the voice of the poet talking to himself or to nobody." The second voice is that of "the poet addressing an audience." My paintings are perhaps the same, like communal keening from an African mountain top. Anyway, the paint answers back so there is always a dialogue.

I want the viewer to create part of the meaning. Ambiguity is important to me. Recently I discussed ambiguity with a painter friend. We discussed the circle, a form that we both use. The circle is a wheel, a wheel is a clock, is an apple, is an eye, is a sun, is a moon, etc.

Another artist said yesterday, "there must be some mystery even for yourself." I liked that and added it to my notes. She is painting the ghost of Spring Street.

I spent the winter in Minnesota about five years ago. In the middle of that time, I went to Santa Barbara for two weeks at the College of Creative Studies. My paintings in Minnesota were all becoming white. The colors were hidden under the snow (one of these is now in the Museum of the University of California at Berkeley). After my two weeks in Santa Barbara, I painted strong color again and the painting that I did when I returned to Minnesota is now in the Ala Story Collection of the Santa Barbara Museum of Art.

Later, I painted the terrible fire in the mountains and the earthquake. I painted grape arbors and rose gardens and quiet pools.

The tangled memories of my travels are like embroidery threads of many colors caught up in a patterned wicker basket, intertwined with two hoops and a large Jost needle. Or like spinning balls of yarn covered by feathers falling from Montezuma's coat.

∞

New York is pocked with rain and tar holes. The rain came following a series of days so clear and so buoyant that everyone suffered from various stages of exhaustion or was reduced to willy-willies of depression. But I work high, High on the prospects of my travels and the thought of work to do. A metaphysical deadline; a compulsive barrier to rest or even to relax combined with a need for torpor. To write the *Odyssey* from a hammock.

In Bundi, there is sand in the omelette. Approaching the town of the great miniatures late at night, fires were still burning around in the marketplace. The oak bungalow was high of ceiling and the air icy cold.

The driver went for omelettes and a hotplate. The former came wrapped in newspapers, warm and slightly sandy like a beach picnic. The hotplate was to heat the room. A modern device, the plate, purchased locally, did not fit the outlet in the bungalow. So the driver took it apart and placed the wires directly in the socket. The hotplate burned brightly and the enormous room became as warm as toast. Later, around three, feeling warm and fearful of a fire from the blazing eye of the plate, I pulled it out and the room immediately returned to its icy cold.

Dawn, still cold and clear, and the town itself revealed as a miniature, a damaged one, of course, on dried paper (it was the dry season), an old aqueduct well, filled to the second elephant's ears, in patterned water with moss was a series of sculptured arches going down into the earth, lost sculpture buried in water. In Bundi, as the dry season prevails, perhaps all the arches rise out of the well of the earth and show themselves.

The town has great reverence for the powers of the water god and in the middle of the lake reservoir is a hulking half-submerged sculpture to Lord Vishnu in his incarnation as the many headed snake of the universe of the waters.

The marketplace in Bundi, five feet above the street, has protection from the floods, but the effect was strange for a marketplace as if the stalls were hermits' niches, slightly inconvenient for the passing parade of customers. Was it in Bundi that we also visited a man who had miniatures? His house was in a suburban area, a cottage separate from his neighbors. He was hospitable and brought out little books wrapped in cloth. They were real, but the art had no magic, nevertheless the books had their own quality. A wrapped book is almost erotic, but we persisted in our search for the perfect Bundi miniature.

∽

I sort through my slides. Should my lecture be done by theme or by time, sequentially or relationally?

The most exquisite animal in the world resides in a temple near Katmandu. He is an ermine or a rat or another creature who holds in his paw a scepter. He faces a crude altar not worthy of his eyes, with wandering, no doubt, holy chickens and ragged white pigeons and the red and black darkness of the sacred hole. The keeper of the temple has an air short of laissez-faire, he smolders a bit at unholy pilgrims walking in his sacred shits. Outside the temple is the great chasm, created by the sword of a Paul Bunyan-like god. They have strung a rope bridge across and the guide ran across and back laughing at my fear to follow. But the rat is on my side of the chasm. He is made of bronze and is about four feet long and rat-proportionally high. The bronzes in Tanjor, Krishna as Mercury, and Donatello's St. John the Baptist, covered with fur, are his peers.

I have made a study of sculpture covered with hair. There is a wall in the old museum in Munich where Mary Magdalene in all her Glory goes to heaven surrounded and transported with her angels. She is covered with carved fur except for her breasts and knees. Last night, I saw a painting from the Casco circle of a Magdalene in the desert, in which her Jong hair covers her. Perhaps it is the other Mary. At one time, I thought that you could separate them and I studied the festivals of the three Marys and found that Mary Magdalene went into the desert for a hundred years or so. We read about it at Henri Dora's house in Santa Barbara on Thanksgiving day.

The Desert Fathers are sometimes covered with hair and sometimes with long strings of beards. There is a saint in a monastery at Meteori. A wild verger tried to prevent the taking of sacred energies through photography. Meteori is approached across a vast plain which as plains go was not exciting, one has left the drama of Thermopylae behind, and few voices of Greek ancestors speak on the plains. The high peaks of Meteor look precisely like the reproductions of them, the sky for once accurately blue. As one gets closer one can see the hermit areas, so high in the peaks, that one wonders how often they come down, if ever. Thoreau went to Boston every Saturday, not less frequently than his neighbors. Perhaps all famous hermits have a back side of the mountain to go down.

That's what we did at Palenque. And, as we went down, I saw a great black snake swallowing a turkey and a poet also going down said no it was the remains of an old fire and I saw that it was, all twisted and charred. And when I got home and told a friend that I felt something soft under my foot and looked down and said, "My God, what is it, a mouse?" And my friend looked and said that it really was a mouse.

The rat of the universe gnaws the roots of the great tree and causes the churning of the sea of milk.

—Alice Baber
Santa Barbara, 1976

MEMOIR OF ALICE BABER
BY DENISE LASSAW

I had many mothers in the art world of the 1950s. Besides my birth mother, Ernestine Lassaw, and my god-mother Elaine de Kooning, there was Alice Baber, a radiant being with very white skin and black hair. She was a person who brought colors to life. Each time she returned from an adventure in India, Central America or Asia she brought armfuls of handmade clothes as gifts. Before I was a teen my "style" was set—wearing Alice's dresses embroidered with feathers, small mirrors, or hand-woven nubby plant-dyed fabric. These delights were not yet sold in New York City. Perhaps this made me look weird but I belonged to a rare tribe and I was proud to wear our colors. Alice and Ernestine were buddies, going to drawing classes, studying French together, roaming galleries or museums, finding magical rocks. Although Alice looked soft her mind was a finely sharpened tool, not to be distracted by foolish things. She could hold her own on any subject. From Alice and my other mothers I learned to be an independent thinking human. We didn't doubt our naturally clever minds, and did not conform to a society that had lesser expectations of our sex. Alice and my other mothers were creators of beauty. If one creates beauty what does it matter what sex you are? But I am glad they are being more fully appreciated now, even if they have to wear the label of "woman" artist.

ACKNOWLEDGMENTS

I wish to first thank Jody Klotz, of Jody Klotz Fine Art, who champions Alice Baber's art. She traveled miles out of her way from Abilene, Texas, to hear me lecture on several other women artists in Williamsburg, Virginia, and asked: "Have you ever thought of writing about Alice Baber?" I responded that I had long been curious about Baber. Jody has offered important encouragement, assisted my research, and facilitated this project in many essential ways. She has also turned up many a lost painting by Alice Baber and shared valuable insights. I wish also to thank Georgia Hickson and Joshua Wright, who worked with Jody to help make this project happen.

With my early interest in abstraction, color, and women artists, I should have met Alice Baber, but I didn't.[1] Instead, long after Baber's death in 1982, I met, interviewed, and wrote about Paul Jenkins, her companion for nearly a decade to whom she was briefly married. He did not speak about Baber. I also knew Baber's close friends, the late Ernestine and Ibram Lassaw and their daughter Denise Lassaw, who has shared with me invaluable firsthand eyewitness accounts of Baber.

Among Baber's other friends, acquaintances, and colleagues in the art world, I have sought out Joellen Bard, Phyllis Braff, Stephanie Brody-Lederman, Arlene Bujese, Ann Chwatsky, Lois Dodd, Roslyn Drexler, Natalie Edgar, Audrey Flack, Mary Frank, Mary Garrard, Betty Gold, Katherine Komaroff Goodman, Lillian Heidenberg, Jamie Jones, Kaylie Jones, Joyce Kozloff, Edvard Lieber, Robert Littman, Ann McCoy, Dennis Masback, Margaret Poser, Archie Rand, Ce Roser, Lucy Freeman Sandler, Joan Semmel, Alice Kates

Shulman, Joan Snyder, Sharon Theobald, and Nina Yankowitz. At the distance of so many years, only some of those who crossed paths with Baber have memories that are still vivid, but I appreciate everyone's efforts to recall Alice Baber.

I appreciate invaluable help from Alice Baber's nephew, John M. Kern, who has been very attentive and engaged with this project. I also thank others of Alice's extended family: Bruce Baber, Geoff Kern, and Shannon Kern. I also benefited from speaking with Hilarie Jenkins, Alice's stepdaughter. I also thank the Paul Jenkins Estate for permission to quote from his unpublished writings and an interview.

I wish to acknowledge the art historian Alexander Nemerov, who shared with me interviews he conducted with the late writer Herbert Gold for a biography of Helen Frankenthaler. Gold, it turns out, was involved with both her and Baber in the same period in the 1950s.

Many others helped or tried to help with various aspects of this project, including Susan B. Anthony, Andrew Bolotowsky, Greta Berman, Suzaan Boettger, Monica Brunelle, Bernadette Bucher, William "Mac" Chambers, Penny Hart Dell, Roz Dimon, Francine Demeulenaere, Rachel Eley, Charles Fick, Eric Fischl, Margaret Fisher, Mary Garrard, Kimberly Goff, Lynn Gumpert, Helen Harrision, Gail A. Hornstein, Paul Huffman, Hayden Hunt, Rick Kelsheimer, Russell Light, Rosanne T. Livingston, Tetsuya Oshima, Margaret Poser, Juan Puntes, Mehrnush Rahimi, Susie Retblatt, Carole Rosenberg, Alla Rosenfeld, Gabriele Selz, Adrienne Sharpe-Wesenan, George Roger Stanley, Louis Stern, Eli Sterngass, Brad Tucker, and Diane Tepfer. I have also benefited here from all those who assisted me with my earlier research on abstract expressionism for my biography of Lee Krasner and on feminist art for my biography of Judy Chicago.

Starting with my days as a young graduate student, I met (at least once) many of those who appear in these pages, but are no longer with us, including John Ashbery, Dore Ashton, Will Barnet, Elaine Benson, Isabel Bishop, Louise Bourgeois, Sonia Delaunay, Sari Dienes, Mary Beth Edelson, Elsa Honig Fine, Connie Fox, Helen Frankenthaler, Betty Friedan, Grace Glueck, Michael Goldberg, Clement Greenberg,

Peggy Guggenheim, Grace Hartigan, Harry Holtzman, Budd Hopkins, Richard Howard, Paul Jenkins, Susan Donnelly Jenkins, Buffie Johnson, Wolf Kahn, April Kingsley, Hilton Kramer, Lee Krasner, Fay Lansner, William S. Lieberman, Marisol Escobar, Mercedes Matter, Thomas M. Messer, Henry Moore, Robert Motherwell, Eleanor Munro, Hans Namuth, Alice Neel, Louise Nevelson, Arnold Newman, Linda Nochlin, Georgia O'Keeffe, Betty Parsons, Philip Pavia, Mimi Poser, Faith Ringgold, Gabriel Rosenberg (aka Gabrielle Roos), Harold Rosenberg, A. M. Sachs, Irving Sandler, Miriam Schapiro, Charles Seliger, Michel Seuphor, Dorothy Sieberling, Jean Siegel, David Slivka, Rose Slivka, May Natalie Tabak (Rosenberg), Esteban Vicente, Andy Warhol, Hannah Wilke, and Jane Wilson. Recalling them makes reconstructing Baber's story more vivid for me.

I am fortunate to have had invaluable help from staff members at the William and Anita Newman Library at Baruch College, CUNY, especially Lisa Ellis and Wilton Yeung; the Archives of American Art, Smithsonian Institution; the Norton T. Dodge Foundation; the Edgar County Genealogy Society and the county clerk's office; the Kansas (Illinois) High School; the Lindenwood University Library; the Indiana State Archives; and the New York Public Library, including the Library for the Performing Arts at Lincoln Center.

Many of Baber's artworks are now in museums, all of which have helped my research by making these works and information about them available to me, especially Andrea Klutzke at the Art Museum of Greater Lafayette, Indiana; Jennifer Seas and Gisela Alvarez at the Tarble Arts Center in Charleston, Illinois; Tiffany Gale at the Link Art Gallery in Paris, Illinois; Mary Helen Miskuly at the Castellani Art Museum of Niagara University, Lewiston, New York; Marshall Price at the Nasher Museum of Art at Duke University, Durham, North Carolina; Cynthia Iavarone at the Metropolitan Museum of Art, New York; David Horowitz at the Solomon R. Guggenheim Museum, New York; and Amy MacLennan at the Sheldon Swope Art Museum in Terre Haute, Indiana.

I wish to thank Jessica Case at Pegasus Books for understanding the significance of publishing a biography of Alice Baber before her story was erased from history; for her sage advice; and her continuing enthusiasm and support of this project. I am also grateful for the suggestions of Jessica LeTourneur Bax, and the care with which she copyedited this book.

My husband, John Van Sickle, has also contributed to this project with his steadfast encouragement, editorial acumen, scholarship, and his enthusiasm for Alice Baber and her story.

Since this is the first scholarly study on Alice Baber, I include extensive source notes, which the casual reader can choose to ignore. I have tried to uncover and preserve the details of Baber's life and career. I am confident that there will be keen interest in Baber's life and work among art historians, biographers, curators, critics, and pop culture writers. Except for articles published or initiated during Baber's lifetime, when I began this project I found only of some cursory information on websites, not all of which is accurate. While this project was underway, however, several new exhibition catalogues appeared, beginning in 2023 with *Alice Baber: Color Hunger*, offering further evidence that the art market has begun its reevaluation of Baber's art.[2] Another two exhibitions with substantial catalogues followed in the spring of 2024: *Alice Baber: Reverse Infinity* and *Alice Baber: Colors of the Rainbow*, which contains my essay.[3] In the fall of 2024, a London gallery published a catalogue to accompany its Baber exhibition, making the new attention truly international.[4] Since some of these published texts convey errors, misinformation, or details that do not agree with my carefully documented research, I try to address most of these discrepancies and my proof in the endnotes of the text that follows.

I am aware that missing documentation and artworks could come to light only after this book goes to press. I have learned from the Baber family about a series of burglaries to a Baber home before they moved all of Alice's art and documents to safer locations. People holding art and documents obtained without clear title may be hesitant to share such objects, which lack proper provenance. Thus, their authenticity will remain uncertain, potentially affecting our understanding of details of Alice Baber's life, her art, and its development.

LIST OF BLACK-AND-WHITE
ILLUSTRATIONS IN THE TEXT

p. 110: Alice Baber's high school yearbook entry, Kansas Community High School, Kansas, Illinois, 1946. "Not all artistic people are Bohemians; Alice proves it." Baber Family Archives.

p. 116: Alice Baber as Nancy Baber's maid-of-honor at her sister's formal wedding, October 17, 1948, at the United Presbyterian Church in Kansas, Illinois, Baber Family Archives.

p. 118: Alton Pickens, Alice Baber's art professor at Indiana University, Bloomington.

p. 130: Alice Baber and the artist Gregory Masurovsky in Amsterdam, ca 1964, photographer unknown, Alice Baber Papers, Archives of American Art, Smithsonian Institution, Washington, DC.

p. 135: Paris, France living room of James and Gloria Jones with their two children (Kaylie and Jamie) playing in front of their painting by Alice Baber, May 1967, *Life Magazine,* photograph by Loomis Dean.

p. 137: Alice Baber and Libby Durgin (right), the wife of the photographer, Walter Silver, who took this photograph in Paul Jenkins's New York studio, ca 1960. ©NYPL.

p. 144: Alice Baber & Ernestine Lassaw wading at Vaux de Vicomte, France, July 2, 1961, photographed by Ibram Lassaw in a stereo slide.

p. 145: Alice Baber on patio at Lassaws' home with Paul Jenkins, who is sketching Denise Lassaw, 1958, The Springs, East Hampton, NY, photographed by Ibram Lassaw in a stereo slide.

p. 149: Alice Baber in her Paris, France studio, 1963, photograph by Marianne Adelmann, Baber Family Archives.

p. 159: Alice Baber featured in the Paris, Illinois *Daily Beacon-News,* November 20, 1963, subtitled: "Article Written by James Jones Pays Tribute to Talent Shown on Canvas," Baber Family Archives. Photograph by Marianne Adelmann.

p. 160: Nancy Hanks, Alice Baber's cousin and friend, who was the second person to head the National Endowment for the Arts (NEA), 1969-1977. She was the first woman to lead the agency, serving under both President Richard Nixon and President Gerald Ford.

p. 174: Alice Baber at a Gutai show in Osaka, Japan, with Jiro Yoshihara, Paul Jenkins, and William S. Lieberman (at the time a curator at the Museum of Modern Art in NYC), November 29, 1964.

p. 178: Alice Baber and Paul Jenkins posing as a Maharaja and his spouse in a tourist photographic studio in India, 1964, Alice Baber Papers, Archives of American Art, Smithsonian Institution, Washington, DC.

p. 201: Alice Baber and Paul Jenkins with their collection of ivories, John D. Schiff photographed them for a November 1967 article by Joanna Eagle on "Artists as Collectors" in *Art in America,* 1967. Courtesy of Leo Baeck Institute.

p. 203: Ethel Fisher, *Alice Baber and Paul Jenkins,* 1967, Oil on canvas, 51 x 40 inches, Courtesy LewAllen Galleries, Santa Fe, NM.

p. 208: Adin Baber, Alice Baber's father, standing before *Phenomena Astral Signal* (1964-65) by Paul Jenkins in his son-in-law's New York studio, ca 1965, photographer unknown, Baber Family Archives.

p. 217: Alice Baber in her studio ca 1967, photographer unknown.

p. 219: Richard Galef, friend and photographer of Alice Baber, while serving in the U.S. Army during World War II, before they met.

p. 227: A Smiling Alice Baber with her canvas, *Seven Green Leagues* (1967, cropped in this photograph) on view at the Santa Barbara Museum of Art at the January 1970 opening of "Trends in 20th Century Art," with its curator, Ala Story and Gerald Nordland, director of the San Francisco Museum of Art, which loaned the works in this show, Alice Baber Papers, Archives of American Art, Smithsonian Institution, Washington, DC. Santa Barbara Newspress Photograph.

p. 237: Alice Baber in her Studio, photographed in 1972 by her friend, Richard Galef, with whom she traveled to Tehran in 1974.

p. 264: Alice Baber at her show at Centro Colombo Americano, Bogotá, Colombia, 1977.

p. 293: Alice Baber photographed painting watercolors in 1981 at her home in Sag Harbor, New York, by Ann Chwatsky, © AnnChwatsky.

p. 302: Alice Baber photographed painting watercolors in 1982 at her home in Sag Harbor, New York, by Hans Namuth, © 1991 Hans Namuth Estate, Courtesy of Center for Creative Photography, University of Arizona.

NOTES

Introduction

1 "Alice Baber, 54, Artist of Lyrical Abstractions," *New York Times*, October 7, 1982, D26. https://www.nytimes.com/1982/10/07/obituaries/alice-baber-54 -artist-of-lyrical-abstractions.html.

2 In his major monograph—Albert Elsen, *Paul Jenkins* (Harry N. Abrams, 1975), 274—lists for 1958 in the "Biographical Outline": "Is given an ivory Eskimo knife by Alice Baber. This and other ivory knives are later used as tools in his painting." And for 1964: "Marries the painter Alice Baber. . . . In Tokyo he meets Jiro Yoshihara, who invites him to Osaka, where he and Alice Baber have a two-artist show with the Gutai Artists." Yet, Elsen, garbling the history of Jenkins's meeting Yoshihara in New York long before he traveled to Japan, also tells the story of Jenkins's development without mentioning, for example (on page 67), that he was with Alice Baber in Spain. See chapters 7 and 9, this volume.

3 See, for example, Gail Levin, "Paul Jenkins: From America's Heartland to an International Journey," and Suzanne Donnelly Jenkins, "Artist Biography," in *Paul Jenkins: From America's Heartland to an International Journey*, ed. Joanna Robotham (Tampa Museum of Art, 2022), and Gail Levin, "Paul Jenkins, Yasuo Kuniyoshi and Asian Affinities," in *Paul Jenkins: Paintings and Works on Paper 1984–2010* (Redfern Gallery, 2018), where the chronology omits his marital history entirely. Before he married Alice Baber, Jenkins was married to Esther Ebenhoe, with whom he had a daughter, Hilarie Paula Jenkins. See https://www.thekimblefuneralhome.com/obituary/5383306.

4 Randy Kennedy, "Paul Jenkins: Painter of Abstract Artwork, Dies at 88," *New York Times*, June 17, 2012, https://www.nytimes.com/2012/06/18/arts /design/paul-jenkins-abstract-expressionist-painter-dies-at-88.html; Michael McNay, "Paul Jenkins Obituary," *Guardian* (UK), June 21, 2012, https://www .theguardian.com/artanddesign/2012/jun/21/paul-jenkins.

5 Julian Machin, "Paul Jenkins: Painter Whose Art Brimmed with the Energy of Life," *Independent* (UK), June 27, 2012, https://www.independent.co.uk /news/obituaries/paul-jenkins-painter-whose-art-brimmed-with-the-energy -of-life-7893598.html. Added as if it were an afterthought or a correction online not identified as such is the following: "Paul Jenkins, painter and writer: born Kansas City 12 July 1923; married firstly Esther Ebenhoe, secondly Alice Baber, thirdly Suzanne Donnelly; one daughter; died New York City 9 June 2012."

6 Natalie Edgar Pavia, who maintained friendships with both Alice and Paul, speculated to Denise Lassaw on April 13, 2025, that Alice might have given Paul a group of her artworks as part of a divorce settlement, which seemed preposterous to me, until I realized that he might have taken them in exchange for his larger financial contribution toward their joint expenses, just as he took paintings from his friend Matsumi Kanemitsu in exchange for his financial support.

7 Albert Elsen, *Paul Jenkins* (Harry N. Abrams, 1975), plate 46.

8   Eliza Gregory, "Alice Baber and Paul Jenkins," in *Alice Baber* (London: Ronchini Gallery, 2024), 7.

9   Fontainebleau is about forty-three miles outside of Paris.

10   Lynn Gumpert and Debra Bricker Balken, eds., *American in Paris: Artists Working in Postwar France, 1946–1962* (Hirmer, 2022), refers to Jenkins on pages 29, 35–38, 61, 72, 82, 100, 107, 114–16, 116, 120–21, 165–67, 194, 202, 207, 224, 266, and 269. At the exhibition's opening at the Grey Art Museum at New York University on March 1, 2024, I asked Balken why she omitted Baber and she mentioned her visit with Suzanne Donnelly Jenkins and not finding any work by Baber, which then existed in Jenkins's estate and elsewhere. Apparently, Jenkins's widow had wanted to obscure Baber's very existence. The Grey Art Museum has works by Baber postdating 1962 in its permanent collection.

11   Gumpert and Balken include some artists who spent only six months in Paris; for example, Sheila Hicks.

12   Sophie Levy and Michel Hilaire, *United States of Abstraction; Artistes Américains en France, 1946–1964* (Musée d'Arts de Nantes, 2021), 133, 141.

13   Enez Whipple, *Guild Hall of East Hampton: An Adventure in the Arts* (Harry N. Abrams, 1993), 56, 253. In today's money, $138,000 in 1983 is $446,246.

14   Doris Meadows, "Four Island Museums Expanding," *New York Times,* January 19, 1986, https://www.nytimes.com/1986/01/19/nyregion/four-island-museums-expanding.html: "Guild Hall has one project in progress and another on the planning boards. Under way is a $10,000 conversion of the former Leidy Gallery to the Alice Baber Memorial Library. The new library will contain books and archival material focusing on Long Island artists."

15   See Ernestine Lassaw to Alice Baber, May 12, 1978, asking if she wants to house-sit in East Hampton while Ernestine and Ibram are away visiting their daughter in Alaska. Baber recalled: "I have known the Lassaws since I first came to New York." Archives of American Art, Washington, DC (hereafter AAA).

16   One of these books, for example, is the large-format *Kangra Paintings of the Gita Govinda* (National Museum, New Delhi, 1963). I first visited India in 1980 and held a Distinguished Fulbright Chair in India in 2015–2016.

17   Among the community of artists who participated in shows at Ashawagh Hall were James Brooks, Elaine de Kooning, Willem de Kooning, Lee Krasner, Ibram Lassaw, and Jackson Pollock.

18   See Gail Levin, "Making Art History in Springs: 1975," *East Hampton Star,* July 26, 2011, https://gaillevin.commons.gc.cuny.edu/wp-content/blogs .dir/1515/files/2023/09/CaroleeSchneemannEHStar.pdf

19   See, for example, Sylvia Moore, "Alice Baber," in *North American Women Artist of the Twentieth Century*, ed. Jules Heller and Nancy C. Heller (Garland Publishing, 1995), 43–44.

Chapter 1. Taking the Plunge: New York City (1951–1954)

1   Alice Baber, interview by Paul Cummings, May 24, 1973, Archives of American Art, Washington, DC (hereafter AAA). See also Alice Baber, undated interview with Elizabeth Roberts [hereafter as E.R.] appears in Baber's papers as an undated transcript with E.R. AAA. For this somewhat obscure gallery, see https://artfacts.net/institution/john-heller-gallery/36390.

2   Among the members who showed at the Argent Gallery, see, for example, a group show that included sculpture by Louise Nevelson among others, reviewed: "Sculpture Shown in Argent Gallery: National Association of Women Artists Represented Here," *New York Times*, February 27, 1953. On the history of the Argent Galleries, see https://rucore.libraries.rutgers.edu /rutgers-lib/68272/ and Ronald G. Pisano, *One Hundred Years; A Centennial Celebration of the National Association of Women Artists* (Nassau County Museum of Fine Art, 1988), 16, 20.

3   Warren Cohen, *East Asian Art and American Culture: A Study in International Relations* (Columbia University Press, 1992), 96 and 111. Alan Reed Priest was curator of "Oriental Art" at the Metropolitan Museum from ca 1928 to 1965.

4   Dylan Thomas, quoted in Ross Wetzsteon, *Republic of Dreams: Greenwich Village: The American Bohemia, 1910–1960* (Simon & Schuster, 2002), 482.

5   Alice Baber, interview by Paul Cummings, May 24, 1973; Alice Baber, interview by E. R., undated transcript. Eliza Gregory, *Alice Baber* (Ronchini Gallery, 2024), 7, claims that "Baber completed a brief stint at the École des Beaux-Arts, having moved to Paris in 1951." Baber did not, however, move to France in 1951; she merely spent a few months there attending a summer program.

6   Wetzsteon, *Republic of Dreams*, xii, 283.

7   Rick Beard and Leslie Cohen Berlowitz, eds. *Greenwich Village: Culture and Counter Culture* (Rutgers University Press, 1993), 167–68.

8   Alice Baber, interview by Karl Fortess, December 2, 1972, New York City, AAA.

9   "Vogue Magazine Looks for Talent," *Indiana Daily Student*, September 22, 1949, 2.

10   Susan W. Cutter, *Alice Baber, Painter* (Women in the Arts, 1975), 7.

11   The examples cited here refer to the iconic curved glass and wood table designed by Isamu Noguchi in 1947, the Lounge chair and ottoman designed in 1956 by the husband and wife team of Charles and Rae Eames, and a sofa with circular foam cushions that was first designed in 1956 by Irving Harper of George Nelson Associates.

12   Baber's father claimed that she worked for Nelson two years; see Adin Baber to Mrs. D. M. Rhodes, March 24, 1962, AAA. Baber, in her undated interview with E. R., 15, claimed that she worked for George Nelson "for a year."

13   Adin Baber to Bonnie Shoot Miller (Alice's aunt, Lois's sister), handwritten note, December 25, 1954, Baber Family Archives.

14   "Beauty in a Busy Place," *Life*, December 13, 1954, 114.

15   "Beauty in a Busy Place," 114.

16   Adin Baber to Mrs. D. M. Rhodes, March 24, 1962.

17   See *McCall's*, for example, for December 1955. Baber is still listed on the masthead for the April 1956 and 1957 issues. By the latter date, she is listed beneath the name of Philip Miller, "the art coordinator." She appears to have worked on obtaining illustrations for editorial content, rather than graphic design of the magazine.

18   Denise Lassaw to the author, April 2025.

19   This particular brochure is marked copyright 1947, suggesting that Alice Baber was not the author, although she might have had it as a prototype. Italics in the original.

20   See Maureen Honey, *Creating Rosie the Riveter: Class, Gender, and Propaganda During World War II* (University of Massachusetts Press, 1984).

21   Alice Baber, interview by E. R., undated transcript.

22   See John Fagg, "Chamber Pots and Gibson Girls: Clutter and Matter in John Sloan's Graphic Art," *American Art* 29, no. 3 (Fall 2015); Barbara Gallati, "Arthur Dove as Illustrator," *Archives of American Art Journal* 21, no. 2 (1981); Gail Levin, *Edward Hopper as Illustrator* (W. W. Norton, 1979); Lewis Browne, *The Graphic Bible* with illustrations by Mark Rothko (still known as Marcus Rothkowitz) (Macmillan, 1928).

23   Alice Baber, interview by Paul Cummings, May 24, 1973.

24   Alice Baber, interview by Paul Cummings, May 24, 1973. *Dream of Saint Ursula* by Vitorre Carpaccio is in the Galleria dell' Accademia, Venice.

25   This canvas is in the Matisse Museum in Nice, France.

26   See "Art to Be Shown in Many Mediums: Exhibition of Work by Matisse," *New York Times*, November 12, 1951, 22. See the catalogue: Alfred H. Barr Jr., *Matisse: The Art and His Public* (Museum of Modern Art, 1951), 441.

27   See Gail Levin, *Lee Krasner: A Biography* (William Morrow, 2011), 122–27.

28   Alice Baber, interview by E. R., undated transcript.

29   Alice Baber, interview by E. R., undated transcript.

30   See Robert Beverly Hale, *Drawing Lessons from the Great Masters* (Watson-Guptill, 1964), 11.

31   This master's degree, which Baber began, but never finished, has sometimes been claimed erroneously; for example, by Lisa N. Peters, "Biography: Alice Baber," in *Alice Baber: Reverse Infinity* (Berry Campbell Gallery, 2024), 59, who cites the University of Indiana, Bloomington, as the institution Baber attended, but which, however, is known as Indiana University. Baber obtained her undergraduate degree there and earned some graduate credits, which fell short of the number required to earn a master's degree.

32   Alice Baber to Adin Baber, undated letter, postmarked 1965, Baber Family Archives.

33   Alice Baber, "Color," in *Color Forum* (University of Texas at Austin, 1972), 8.

34   Alice Baber, "Gorky's Color," in *Arshile Gorky: Drawings to Paintings* (University of Texas Art Gallery, 1975), 77.

35   Ethel Schwabacher, *Arshile Gorky: Memorial Exhibition* (Whitney Museum of American Art, 1951).

36   Howard Devree, "Whitney to Offer Arshile Gorky Art," *New York Times*, January 4, 1951, 27.

37   Schwabacher, *Arshile Gorky*, 17.

38   See Levin, *Lee Krasner*, 296–300.

39   Alice Baber, undated manuscript, Alice Baber Papers, AAA.

40   Alice Baber, interview by Paul Cummings, May 24, 1973.

41   Alice Baber, interview by Paul Cummings, May 24, 1973.

42   Cutter, *Alice Baber, Painter*, 6.

43   Alice Baber, interview by Paul Cummings, May 24, 1973.

44   Baber might also have seen Fragonard's *The Swing* in the Wallace Collection in 1951, when she first visited London.

45   Alice Baber, interview by Paul Cummings, May 24, 1973.

46   Alice Baber, interview by Paul Cummings, May 24, 1973.

47   Alice Baber, interview by E. R. As noted earlier in this chapter, this interview
     by E.R. is an undated transcript.

Chapter 2. The Scene: Cedar Bar to the Club (1953–1958)

1   Alice Baber, interview by Paul Cummings, May 24, 1973, Archives of
     American Art, Washington, DC (hereafter AAA).
2   Alice Baber, interview by Paul Cummings, May 24, 1973.
3   Alice Baber, in *Tenth Street Days: The Co-Ops of the 50's*, ed. Joellen Bard
     (Education, Art & Service, 1977), 32. Baber's oil painting, *Bon Voyage* (1959)
     is reproduced in this catalogue as no. 115.
4   Baber, *Tenth Street Days*, 32.
5   Baber, *Tenth Street Days*, 32.
6   Baber listed this on her application to Yaddo in 1958.
7   Thomas B. Hess, "Younger Artists and the Unforgivable Crime," *Artnews*,
     April 1957, 46–49.
8   Philip Pavia, quoted in *Club Without Walls: Selections from the Journals of Philip
     Pavia*, ed. Natalie Edgar (Midmarch Arts Press, 2007), 104.
9   Alice Baber is still listed as an editor on the masthead of *McCall's* through
     February 1959, after she had left for Paris.
10   Baber, *Tenth Street Days*, 32.
11   Baber, "March Gallery.," unpublished, Alice Baber Papers, AAA.
12   This show included Lenart Anderson, Rocco Armento, Alice Baber,
     Waldemar Baranowski, Robert Beauchamp, June Corwine, Francine
     Felsenthal, William Gambini, Joann Gedney, Burt Hasen, Budd Hopkins,
     Richard Ireland, Lester Johnson, Matsumi Kanemitsu, Elaine de Kooning,
     Boris Lurie, Marcia Marcus, Felix Pasilis, Pat Passlof, Wallace Reiss, Peter
     Stander, Ray Spillenger, Tom Young, and Wilfrid Zogbaum.
13   Natalie Edgar, "Postscript Changing of the Guard," in *Club Without Walls:
     Selections from the Journals of Philip Pavia*, ed. Natalie Edgar (Midmarch Arts
     Press, 2007), 131.
14   Susan W. Cutter, *Alice Baber, Painter* (Women in the Arts, 1975), 5.
15   "Reg Butler—Bruno Cassinari—Jan Cox—Irving Kriesberg—Alton Pickens,"
     Curt Valentin Gallery, New York, May 26–June 19, 1953.
16   Alice Baber, interview by E. R., undated transcript, 3–4, AAA.
17   Wolf Kahn interviewed by Paul Cummings for the Archives of American
     Art, January 16, 1978.
18   Andrew Bolotowsky to the author, telephone interview of July 28, 2025; he
     still has the short film, "Wolf Kahn Paints a Picture." This filming took place
     before Wolf Kahn met his future wife, Emily Mason, in 1956.
19   Alice Baber, interview by E. R., undated transcript, 4.
20   Alice Baber, interview by E. R., undated transcript, 15.
21   The Lassaw daybooks are in the collection of their daughter, Denise Lassaw.
22   In an email to the author, April 30, 2025, Denise Lassaw reports that her
     parents and she stayed with Duchamp in Spain in 1961.
23   Alice Baber, interview by E. R., undated transcript, 4–5.
24   Alice Baber, interview by E. R., undated transcript, 5–6.
25   Jeffrey Potter, *To a Violent Grave: An Oral Biography of Jackson Pollock* (G. P.
     Putnam's Sons, 1985), 121–22.

26 Lucy Freeman Sandler, email to the author, March 9, 2024.

27 Alice Baber, "Footnote on the Club," in *Color Forum* (University of Texas at Austin, 1972), 4.

28 Baber, "Footnote on the Club," 4.

29 Milton Resnick to his students, quoted in Geoffrey Dorfman, *Milton Resnick: Painter in the Age of Painting* (Design Books: 2025), 109.

30 Resnick, quoted in Dorfman, *Milton Resnick*, 109.

31 For Ibram Lassaw, the Club, and Zen, see Ellen Pearlman, *Nothing & Everything: The Influence of Buddhism on the American Avant-Garde, 1942–1962* (Evolver Editions, 2012), 105–9. The author of this biography of Baber, while a curator at the Whitney Museum, conducted a very long interview with Harry Holtzman aboard a Flying Tigers cargo jet to Paris in 1977. See also Natalie Edgar, ed., *Club Without Walls: Selections from the Journals of Philip Pavia* (Midmarch Arts Press, 2007), 176.

32 For the entire reminiscence by Denise Lassaw, see appendixes.

33 This copy of *Just Weeds* remains in the possession of Denise Lassaw.

34 Alice Baber, interview by Paul Cummings, May 24, 1973.

35 William Barrett, ed., *Zen Buddhism: Selected Writings of D. T. Suzuki* (Doubleday, 1956).

36 Alice Baber, interview by Paul Cummings, May 24, 1973.

37 Invaluable documentation of Baber's personal life is contained in the Lassaws' daybooks, which are in the possession of Denise Lassaw.

38 Denise Lassaw, email to the author, December 8, 2023.

39 Calvin Tomkins, *Duchamp: A Biography* (Henry Holt, 1996), 119, reports that Breton moved out of their Village apartment when Hare moved in to live with Jaqueline and Aube, but Salomon Grimberg, *Jacqueline Lamba: In Spite of Everything, Spring* (Pollock-Krasner House, 2001), 23, writes that Lamba and Aube moved into Hare's Greenwich Village apartment at 42 Bleecker Street.

40 Sixty years later, Wilson recalled that Lamba "had not been among those worth saving." Quoted in Grimberg, *Jacqueline Lamba*, 23, 34n50, based on his telephone interview of October 5, 2000, with Susanne Wilson (Coggeshall).

41 André Breton, *How To Protect Young Cherry Trees From Hares* [*Jeunes cerisiers garantis contre les lièvres*], trans. Edouard Roditi (View Editions, 1946); Tomkins, *Duchamp*, 351.

42 Salomon Grimberg, "Dallas Society for Psychoanalytic Psychology and the Dallas Museum of Art presented a lecture, 'Jacqueline Lamba: A Female Surrealist,'" and reported that Lamba and Hare were together ten years from 1941, https://web.archive.org/web/20081010144401/http://www.dspp.com/arts/grimberg.htm.

43 Denise Lassaw, email to the author, December 8, 2023.

44 Lassaw, quoted in Grimberg, *Jacqueline Lamba*, 26.

45 Grimberg, *Jacqueline Lamba*, 28.

46 Quoted in Grimberg, *Jacqueline Lamba*, 28.

47 Lassaw, quoted in Grimberg, *Jacqueline Lamba*, 26.

48 Alice Baber, interview by E. R., undated transcript, 14.

49 Robert Goldwater, "Hare," in *Three American Sculptors*, E. C. Goosen, R. Goldwater, and I. Sandler (Grove Press, 1959), 28.

50   Baber later knew and collaborated with Herb Aach, who, however, was married and living in Mexico, although he returned and lived in Hazleton, Pennsylvania, from 1954 to 1963, but he was unlikely to be Baber's "Herb."

51   Alice Baber Papers, AAA.

52   James Jones, "Alice Baber and the Tragedy of Light," *Studio International*, September 1965, 1; reprinted in many places, including in Arlene Bujese, ed., *25 Artists by Photographer Hans Namuth* (University Publications of America, 1982), 30–31.

53   See, for example, how Herbert Gold and James Jones published together: Arabel J. Porter, ed., *New World Writing 2: Second Mentor Selection* (Mentor Books, 1952), including James Baldwin, Norman Mailer, Shirley Jackson, James Jones, Dylan Thomas, Herbert Gold, W. H Auden, Jean Genet, Calder Willingham, James Merrill, Theodore Roethke, et al. There is also correspondence between the two novelists in the James Jones Papers at the Harry Ransom Center at the University of Texas at Austin.

54   Alix Kates Shulman to the author, June 3, 2024, in person communication followed up with email and phone calls.

55   Albert Goldman, "Most Happy Fellow: *Salt*, by Herbert Gold," *New Republic*, June 8, 1963, 23–24.

56   Goldman, "Most Happy Fellow," 23–24.

57   Alix Kates Shulman, "Women Writers in the Beat Generation," *Village Voice*, 1989; A version of this essay appears in Alix Shulman, *A Marriage Agreement and Other Essays: Four Decades of Feminist Writing* (Open Road, 2012), and was also published in *Moody Street Irregulars* 28 (Fall 1994): 3–9; republished in *Liber* at https://www.liberreview.com/issue-1-2-women-writers/.

58   Herbert Gold, *My Last Two Thousand Years* (Random House, 1972), 84.

59   Gold, *My Last Two Thousand Years*, 176–77.

60   The following quotations from Herb Gold are from his unpublished interviews—September 19 and October 2018—with Alexander Nemerov for his *Fierce Poise: Helen Frankenthaler and 1950s New York* (Penguin, 2022).

61   David Hare, quoted in April Kingsley, *The Turning Point: The Abstract Expressionists and the Transformation of American Art* (Simon & Schuster, 1992), 107.

62   Alice Baber, interview by Paul Cummings, May 24, 1973. See also Marika Herskovic, *New York School: Abstract Expressionists: Artists Choice by Artists: A Complete Documentation of the New York Painting and Sculpture Annuals, 1951–1957* (New School Press, 2000). This book misspells Baber's surname as "Barber."

63   Audrey Flack, *Audrey Flack: With Darkness Came Stars* (University of Pennsylvania Press, 2024), 87.

64   Alice Baber, application for Yaddo, 1958, Yaddo Papers, New York Public Library.

65   Dore Ashton, "Art: Works by Browne," *New York Times*, April 2, 1957, 36, https://timesmachine.nytimes.com/timesmachine/1957/04/02/96950688.pdf.

66   Baber, *Tenth Street Days*, 32.

67   Joan Marter, ed., *Women of Abstract Expressionism* (Denver Art Museum, 2016), 160.

68   Dore Ashton, "Art: A Local Anthology New York Annual, at the Stable Gallery, Offers Many Works of Merit," *New York Times*, May 8, 1957, 58.

69   Alice Baber, interview by Paul Cummings, May 24, 1973.

70 "Alice Baber . . . A Brief Biography," in *Alice Baber, 1928–1982* (Alice Baber Art Trust, 1990), 11.

71 See "5 ACA Artists," November 14–26, 1955, AAA. The other two artists were Gregorio Pestopino and Sarai Sherman. Robert Goldwater to Alton Pickens, August 28, 1955, Alton Pickens Papers, AAA. Goldwater wrote, "I would advise strongly against the A.C.A. This is based partly upon their past (and present?) political bias, but also because I cannot decern aqny [*sic*] over all sense of quality and discrimination in what they have recently been showing." Pickens ignored this warning and had a solo show at ACA from April 13 to May 12, 1956.

72 Alice Baber, interview by E. R., undated transcript, 6–7.

73 The others in this show were William Gambini, Tom Young, Augustus Goertz, Sam Goodman, Rocco Armento, Budd Hopkins, and Ray Spillenger.

74 Cutter, *Alice Baber, Painter*, 5.

75 Jules Olitski, "Appreciation: Clement Greenberg in My Studio," *American Art* (Summer/Fall 1994): 125–26.

76 The press release for this show states, "The Workshop Gallery is under the personal management of the Misses Connie Levene and Anita Janoff." Constance Kane Papers, AAA.

77 Handwritten price list in a ledger, Constance Kane Papers, AAA.

78 See also Alice Baber to Adin Baber, postmarked Paris, May 12, 1959, Baber Family Archives, in which she reminds her father that he had met Greenberg while visiting New York, on 12th Street on the north side of St. Vincent's Hospital.

Chapter 3. Finding a Partner (1958)

1 Alice Baber to Elizabeth Ames, letter requesting an application form dated February 7, 1958. Yaddo Records, New York Public Library.

2 Alice Baber to Elizabeth Ames, letter requesting an application form dated February 7, 1958.

3 Herbert Gold to Elizabeth Ames, February 8, 1958, Yaddo Records, box 226, New York Public Library.

4 Lassaws' daybook, July 1957.

5 I learned that Solomon was gay from one of his distant relatives, but see also https://www.robertbrokl.com/richard-caldwell-brewer---1923-2014 ---overlooked-gay-artist.html.

6 Martica Sawin, "Hyde Solomon," *Arts Magazine*, November 1958, 42. This appears in the same issue that reproduced Alice Baber's *Battle of the Oranges* in a capsule review of her first solo show at the March Gallery.

7 For Alice Baber's application, letters of recommendation, and her dates of residency, see Yaddo Records, box 226, New York Public Library.

8 Matsumi Kanemitsu, interview by Marjorie Rogers, 1976, Los Angeles Art Community: Group Portrait, Oral History Program, University of California, Los Angeles. I have tried to preserve his broken English as per the transcription.

9 Matsumi Kanemitsu, interview by Marjorie Rogers.

10 Matsumi Kanemitsu, interview by Marjorie Rogers.

11 Matsumi Kanemitsu, interview by Marjorie Rogers.

12 Matsumi Kanemitsu, interview by Marjorie Rogers.

13 Archie Rand, email to the author, April 16, 2025.

14 Hilarie Jenkins, interview with the author, March 21, 2024.

15 Paul Jenkins, interview with the author, June 26, 2008.

16 Quoted in Gail Levin, *Lee Krasner: A Biography* (William Morrow, 2011), 305.

17 Evidence is in the dated photographs taken by the Lassaws and shared with the author by Denise Lassaw.

18 See Levin, *Lee Krasner*, 310–11.

19 They signed a separation agreement in 1957. See Paul Jenkins Papers, Archives of American Art, Washington, DC (hereafter AAA). See October 30, 1962, letter from Esther Jenkins to Paul Jenkins, discussing their separation agreement of five years earlier and requesting that the terms of income to support Hilarie be changed to provide $20 per week rather than points toward his paintings.

20 This exchange of residences is also confirmed by Gabrielle Selz, *Light on Fire Book: The Art and Life of Sam Francis* (University of California Press, 2021), 123. She documents that Mitchell was still present in her high-ceiling studio in an old brownstone in early 1957, but by February 1958, Selz documents that Mitchell attended Francis's Paris party: "The stormy Joan Mitchell and Jean-Paul Riopelle arrived. Mitchell was living in France again with Riopelle, even though he was still married and blunting his Catholic guilt with a daily intake of forty Ricards" (132).

21 Alice Baber, interview by E. R., undated transcript, 14, AAA. All italics in quotes replicate the original text (usually an underscored word) unless so indicated.

22 Alice Baber to Paul Jenkins, n.d., 1958, Paul Jenkins Papers.

23 Alice Baber to Paul Jenkins, n.d., 1958, Paul Jenkins Papers. Baber did not seem to save Jenkins letters to her, one of which she recalls in this letter. The following quotations are from this same letter. Baber misspelled the surnames of Petersen and Dreyfus.

24 Alice Baber to Paul Jenkins, undated letter, Paul Jenkins Papers, no. 12452.

25 Alice Baber to Paul Jenkins, undated letter, Paul Jenkins papers, no. 12481.

26 Alice Baber to Paul Jenkins, undated letter, Paul Jenkins papers, no. 12481.

27 Alice Baber to Paul Jenkins, undated letter, Paul Jenkins papers, no. 12481.

28 Alice Baber to Paul Jenkins, undated letter, Paul Jenkins papers, no. 12481.

29 Jennifer Dunning, "Leslie George Katz, 78, Founder of Eakins Press," *New York Times*, May 4, 1997.

30 Alice Baber, interview by E. R., n.d., Alice Baber Papers, AAA.

31 Alice Baber to Paul Jenkins, undated letter, Paul Jenkins papers, no. 12481.

32 Alice Baber to Paul Jenkins, n.d., 1958, Paul Jenkins Papers, no. 12480.

33 Mark Schorer, *William Blake: The Politics of Vision* (Henry Holt, 1946), 403, 421.

34 This drawing inscribed by Baber was auctioned off by someone who claimed to have gotten it from her uncle, who is said to have worked on stretchers for Jenkins. One wonders if Jenkins who was very careful about his public image, would have casually discarded such an intimate work to an employee. Katherine Komaroff, interview with the author, March 23, 2024, recalls Jenkins as being very generous with gifts.

35 Paul Jenkins, in Albert Elsen, *Paul Jenkins* (Harry N. Abrams, 1975), 66, 274.

36 Ann McCoy, "Alice Baber: Light as Subject," *Art International* 24, no. 1–2 (1980): 140.

37 Susan W. Cutter, *Alice Baber, Painter* (Women in the Arts, 1975), 6.

38   Virginia Pitts Rembert, "Where Atlantis Is: Alice Baber's Paintings," *Arts Magazine*, February 1978, 124.

39   Alice Baber, quoted in Rembert, "Where Atlantis Is," 124.

40   Alice Baber, interview by Paul Cummings, May 24, 1973, AAA.

41   For Paul Jenkins's engagement with Asian art and culture, see Gail Levin, "Paul Jenkins, Yasuo Kuniyoshi and Asian Affinities."

42   See Elsen, *Paul Jenkins*, 67, notes Jenkins's interest in Goethe at this time. See also: "Goethean observation as phenomenology," especially Goethe's account of illusory colors and after images that could have been relevant for Jenkins. https://www.lancaster.ac.uk/users/philosophy/awaymave/405/wk8.htm.

43   Paul Jenkins to Albert E. Elsen, quoted in *Paul Jenkins*, 81.

44   Laxmi P. Sihare, "The Interrelation of Sounds and Colors," unidentified inscribed offprint, AAA.

45   Sihare, "Interrelation of Sounds and Colors." Sihare was identified "as a recipient of fellowships from the Rockefeller Foundation and the JDR 3rd fund, and a former Special Research Consultant to the International council of the Museum of Modern, New York" who "received his doctorate on June 1. 1967 from the Institute of Fine Arts, New York University."

46   Paul Jenkins, with Suzanne Donnelly Jenkins, *Anatomy of a Cloud* (Harry N. Abrams, 1983), 194.

47   Alice Baber, interview by Paul Cummings, May 24, 1973. She also referred to this painting: "It has a terrible title by mistake called *Icon Rock*. And it came from an icon. I mean, that was sort of my influence. And I liked the rocks in Cappadocia [in Turkey], which is a place I like to go."

48   Alice Baber, interview by Paul Cummings, May 24, 1973.

49   Alice Baber to Georges F., unpublished interview, 1980, Alice Baber Papers.

50   Lynn Gumpert and Debra Bricker Balken, *Americans in Paris: Artists Working in Postwar France, 1946–1962* (Grey Art Gallery, 2022), 38. See also Eliza Gregory, *Alice Baber* (Ronchini Gallery, 2024), 7.

51   See Paul Jenkins divorce papers from his marriage to Esther Ebenhoe in the Paul Jenkins Papers, and entry for 1957 in the "Biographical Outline," in Elsen, *Paul Jenkins*, 274.

52   Adin Baber to Mrs. D. M. Rhodes, March 24, 1962, AAA.

53   Adin Baber to Nancy Baber, January 5, 1972, Baber Family Archives.

54   Adin Baber to Nancy Baber, January 5, 1972.

55   Sotheby's New York, September 28, 2023, lot no. 1, Alice Baber's painting, *Wind Divided Mist the Darker* (1972), brought her highest record at auction, $698,500.

56   Alice Baber to Mike Bennett, September 5, 1977, AAA. The actual number of years must have been between four and five since she alternatively cited both numbers.

57   Adin Baber to Mrs. D. M. Rhodes, March 24, 1962. The only clue to Baber's interest in murals is her later friendship with Urban Neininger.

Chapter 4. First Solo Show (1958)

1   Alexandra de Lallier, "Alice Baber's Water-Colors: A Dialogue of Media," typescript, early draft of published article, 1, Archives of American Art, Washington, DC (hereafter AAA).

2   Alice Baber, interview by Mary Trasko, undated typescript, Alice Baber Papers, AAA.

3   See Alexander Nemerov, *Fierce Poise: Helen Frankenthaler and 1950s New York* (Penguin, 2021).

4   See Nathan Kernan, *Milton Resnick Paintings, 1937–1987* (Milton Resnick and Pat Passlof Foundation, 2018).

5   Lee Hall, *Elaine and Bill: Portrait of a Marriage: The Lives of Willem and Elaine de Kooning* (HarperCollins, 1993), 244, 254.

6   Paul Jenkins to Anne Alpert, April 4, 1966, Paul Jenkins Papers, AAA, recalls this great party "after Alice's first opening at the March Gallery."

7   See Paul Jenkins and Esther Ebenhoe Jenkins, eds. *Observations of Michel Tapié* (George Wittenborn, 1956).

8   On Sam Francis and Zen, see Gabrielle Selz, *Light on Fire: The Art And Life Of Sam Francis* (University of California Press, 2021), 119.

9   Alice Baber, interview by Paul Cummings, May 24, 1973, AAA.

10   Alice Baber, "Color," in *Color Forum* (University of Texas at Austin, 1972), 8.

11   Alice Baber, interview by E. R., undated transcript, AAA. Actually, there is only one known still life painting by Judith Leyster, but other still life tableaux exist within other paintings.

12   Alice Baber, interview by George F., 1980, Alice Baber Papers, AAA.

13   Alice Baber, interview by Paul Cummings, May 24, 1973.

14   Alice Baber, interview by Paul Cummings, May 24, 1973.

15   Ann McCoy, "Alice Baber: Light as Subject," *Art International* 24, no. 1–2 (1980): 138.

16   For Hartigan's *Oranges* paintings, see Cathy Curtis, *Restless Ambition: Grace Hartigan, Painter* (Oxford University Press, 2015), 108–10.

17   Alice Baber, artist's statement in Feminist Art Program, in *Art: A Woman's Sensibility*, ed. Miriam Schapiro (California Institute of the Arts, 1975), 6.

18   J. R. M. [James R. Mellow], "Alice Baber, *Arts Magazine*, November 1958, 59.

19   Mellow, "Alice Baber," 59.

20   James Schuyler, "Reviews and Previews: New Names This Month," *Artnews*, October 1958, 16.

21   Schuyler, "Reviews and Previews," 16.

22   See James Pete Drexler, *Coronado's Route to Cíbola* (EdVenture Books, 2015).

23   Alice Baber, interview by George F., 1980, AAA.

24   Frederick W. Hodge, ed., *Spanish Explorers in the Southern United States, 1528–1543: The Narrative of Alvar Nuñez Cabeça de Vaca* (Scribner, 1907), 9.

25   Schuyler, "Reviews and Previews," 16.

26   Adin Baber to Nancy Baber, January 5, 1972.

27   See Ellie Whitney, D. Bruce Means, and Anne Rudloe, *Priceless Florida: Natural Ecosystems and Native Species* (Pineapple Press, 2004), 85–86.

28   Adin Baber to Nancy Baber, January 5, 1972.

29   Schuyler, "Reviews and Previews," 16.

30   It was auctioned in Italy on February 23, 2021.

31   James Schuyler, "Reviews and Previews," 16.

32   de Lallier, "Alice Baber's Water-Colors," 44.

33   de Lallier, "Alice Baber's Water-Colors," 44.

34   James Jones, "Alice Baber, quoted by James Jones in 'Alice Baber and the Tragedy of Light,'" *Studio International*, September 1965, 1.

35   James Jones, "Alice Baber," in *25 Artists by Photographer Hans Namuth*, ed. Arlene Bujese (University Publications of America, 1982), 30.

36   James Jones, "Alice Baber and the Tragedy of Light," *Studio International*, September 1965, 1, reprinted in Bujese, *25 Artists by Photographer Hans Namuth*, 30.

37   Lee Krasner, quoted in Gail Levin, *Lee Krasner: A Biography* (William Morrow, 2011), 323–24.

38   James Jones, "Alice Baber," in Bujese, *25 Artists by Photographer Hans Namuth*, 30.

39   Alice Baber to Alexandra de Lallier, interview transcript from broadcast for WBAI-FM Radio, March 21, 1980.

40   Dan Cameron, "Alice Baber: Touching the Sky," in *Alice Baber: Reverse Infinity* (Berry Campbell Gallery, 2024), 7, mistakenly claims that Baber "began spending extended periods of time" in Paris in 1958, when she was clearly still in New York State through her well-documented late spring–early summer visit to Yaddo in Saratoga Springs; her first solo show in November; Fred McDarrah's photograph of her with Jenkins on November 25, 1958; and for Christmas Day 1958.

Chapter 5. Flashback to Child of Tragic Vision (1928–1946)

1   James Jones, "Alice Baber and the Tragedy of Light," *Studio International*, September 1965, 1, reprinted in *25 Artists by Photographer Hans Namuth*, ed. Arlene Bujese (University Publications of America, 1982), 31.

2   Jones, "Alice Baber and the Tragedy of Light," 1.

3   Alice Baber to Adin Baber, postmarked Paris, May 12, 1959, with return address of the home she shared with Paul Jenkins at 15 Rue Decrès in the 12th arrondissement, Baber Family Archives.

4   Baber wrote to her father that James Jones was from Palestine, Illinois, when his biography lists him as coming from Robinson, Illinois, located just seven miles to the west. The population in Palestine was then less than a third as large as Robinson, but it was a farming community with which Adin Baber would have been familiar. Palestine is said to be the oldest town in Illinois.

5   James Jones, "Alice Baber," reprinted in Bujese, *25 Artists by Photographer Hans Namuth*, 30.

6   See Frank McShane, *Into Eternity: The Life of James Jones, American Writer* (Houghton Mifflin, 1985), 8–10.

7   Adin Baber wrote the genealogy of the Hanks family, privately publishing three books: *The Hanks Family of Virginia and Westward*; *Nancy Hanks, of Undistinguished Families*; and *Nancy Hanks: Destined Mother of a President*. See also Carolyn Howk, "Adin Baber and the Hanks Genealogy," *Illinois History* 32, no. 1 (1978): 17–18. Adin Baber's papers are in the Illinois History and Lincoln Collections. https://archon.library.illinois.edu/ihlc/?p=collections/controlcard&id=5035.

8   Lois's father, Tilford Taylor Shoot, was the son of John Sanford Shoot and Mary Louise Harlan, also of Coles, Illinois. Lois's mother, Mary Elizabeth Wilhoit, the child of Orville Wilhoit and Elizabeth Evinger, was born in Westfield, Illinois, another small town in the same region of Charleston, Illinois.

9   Lois Shoot Baber's sisters were Bonnie S. Miller, Esther S. Dudley, Elizabeth
    S. Gannaway, and Gertrude S. Blair. The photo of the five sisters is labeled as
    having been taken at 1443 7th Street, Charleston, Illinois, circa 1934.

10 Adin Baber to Nancy and grandsons, written second and third week August
    1972, Baber Family Archives.

11 Adin Baber kept a diary of this honeymoon trip to Quebec in early October
    1924, which survives in the Baber Family Archives.

12 See obituary for Adin Baber's father, Alice's paternal grandfather, Dexter
    Baber, in "Dexter Baber, Long Prominent Resident of County, Dies at 98,"
    Paris Beacon-News (Paris, IL), November 5, 1965, Archives of American
    Art, Washington, DC (hereafter AAA). This article says that Adin Baber
    resides at the family home in Dudley (a town near Paris in Edgar County,
    Illinois). This obituary states that the Dudley Community Center to benefit
    young people "was financed through the gift of corn gleanings from the Baber
    acreage . . . when young people themselves gathered the corn left in the field
    and sold it to provide funds for the center." Dexter Baber was the son of Adin
    and Mary Ellen Hanks Baber. His mother was a first cousin of Abraham
    Lincoln. See also "Dexter D. Baber Born near Kansas, Passes Away at the
    Age of 98 Years," *Kansas Journal* (Edgar County, IL), November 11, 1965.

13 For Adin Baber's genealogy, see https://ancestors.familysearch.org/en/KK73
    -WM3/adin-baber-1834-1902.

14 The settlement of Dexter's estate was held up in litigation with Adin's first
    cousin. The litigation was on the part of Brian Baber, the son of the late
    Telford Baber, Adin's brother; John M. Kern, multiple conversations with the
    author, 2024.

15 "Sale of Farm Land," January 21, 1967, advertisement of public auction,
    Robert Craig Auctioneer, Indianola, IL, newspaper clipping, Baber Family
    Archives. Adin Baber to Nancy Baber, December 12, 1967, claims that at
    his death she will inherit land that he estimates will be worth "a quarter of a
    million dollars." Letter is in Baber Family Archives.

16 *Jasper Weekly Courier* (Jasper, IN), December 10, 1915, states: "Asa J. Baber, aged
    eighty-four, is dead. He was president of the First National bank for 50 years."

17 This date of 1924 is documented by a clipping from the Paris newspaper
    announcing Adin Baber's engagement to Lois Shoot on September 9, 1924,
    Baber Family Archives. His position is confirmed by a listing in the 1926
    Paris city directory.

18 The First National Bank of Paris, IL appears to have been liquidated on
    March 27, 1931 and gone into receivership on May 4, 1931, before being
    absorbed by the Edgar County National Bank in Paris, IL.

19 Janet Poppendieck and Marion Nestle, "The Plight of the Farmer," in
    Breadlines Knee-Deep in Wheat: Food Assistance in the Great Depression
    (University of California Press, 2014), 1–15, http://www.jstor.org/stable
    /10.1525/j.ctt6wqbmq.7.

20 See Alan Nasser, "The 1930s and the Great Depression," in *Overripe Economy:
    American Capitalism and the Crisis of Democracy* (Pluto Press, 2018), 86.

21 John M. Kern (Alice Baber's nephew), interview by the author, January 25, 2024.

22 Claire Hilton, "90 Years Ago: The Mental Treatment Act 1930," *Royal College
    of Psychiatrists* (blog), September 9, 2020, https://www.rcpsych.ac.uk/news

-and-features/blogs/detail/history-archives-and-library-blog/2020/09/09
/90-years-ago-the-mental-treatment-act-1930-by-dr-claire-hilton.

23   Adin Baber to Dexter Dole Baber, February 23, 1931, on St. Francis Hospital
      stationary, addressed "Dear Dad," and signed with his nickname, "Ben," Baber
      Family Archives. The following quotations are also from this same letter.

24   William Shakespeare, *Macbeth*, act 3, scene 4. See https://www.folger.edu
      /explore/shakespeares-works/macbeth/read/3/4/.

25   Edmund Wilson, "The Jumping-Off Place," *New Republic*, December 23,
      1931, 156–58.

26   John M. Kern, interview by the author, May 21, 2024.

27   Sylvia Moore, "Alice Baber," *Woman's Art Journal* 3, no. 1 (1982): 40. Moore
      interviewed Baber for this article. According to *Alice Baber, 1928–1982* (Alice
      Baber Art Trust, 1990), 11, Baber's mother also had health concerns when the
      family spent winters in Florida.

28   Chester Braningame [?], March 25, 1930, addressed to "My dear Mrs. Baber,"
      private collection.

29   Lois Shoot Baber to Gertrude Shoot Blair, January 15, 1932, Baber Family
      Archives.

30   Christmas card, Aunt Bonnie to Nancy Shirley Baber in Kansas, Illinois,
      postmarked December 22, 1932, private collection.

31   Adin Baber to his daughters, undated letter, from Kansas, Illinois, dated
      only "March," which discusses his storage of Alice's paintings, Baber Family
      Archives.

32   Adin Baber to his daughters, letter to be read posthumously, Baber Family
      Archives.

33   Adin Baber to Nancy Baber and Alice Baber, undated letter found in Alice's
      box in Kansas, Illinois, bank marked to be read posthumously, Baber Family
      Archives.

34   John M. Kern, interview by the author, January 25, 2024.

35   City directory for Miami, Dade County, Miami Beach, Coral Gables, and
      Hialeah, Florida, lists store for 1934–35.

36   Adin Baber to Nancy Baber, undated handwritten letter from Miami, ca
      1932, signed, "I love you DEEDO," private collection.

37   Alice Baber to Gerry Jane, November 12, 1937, Baber Family Archive.

38   Alice Baber to Gerry Jane, November 12, 1937.

39   For Baber's Rug collection, see Jeffrey Weiss, *Rugs* (W. W. Norton, 1979), 115–18.

40   For the 1940 US Census, the Baber family was still living in Miami, Florida
      (Dade County).

41   Alice Baber, telephone interview with Patrick Taylor, August 13, 1981, copy
      of transcript at Art Museum of Greater Lafayette, Indiana.

42   Alice Baber to Alexandra de Lallier, interview transcript from broadcast for
      WBAI-FM Radio, March 21, 1980.

43   Adin Baber, "The Foodstuff of the DeSoto Expedition," *Tequesta: The Journal
      of the Historical Association of Southern Florida* 1, no. 1 (1941): 34–40.

44   Poem page is in the Baber Family Archives.

45   Baber, "Foodstuff of the DeSoto Expedition," 39.

46   "Alice Baber . . . A Brief Biography," in *Alice Baber, 1928–1982* (Alice Baber
      Art Trust, 1990), 11.

47   Eva Effie Parker was the twelfth and last child of Julia Frances Thrift and Dr.
     Montreville Gaston Parker, who were both born in Guilford, NC. This family
     moved to Indiana. See Nancy Baber McNeill and Louis Franklin Hanks,
     comp., *The Hanks Family of Virginia and Westward: A Genealogical Record from
     the Early 1600s*, 2nd ed. (Arthur H. Clark, 2004), 317.

48   Nancy Baber McNeill, notes, April 24, 1999.

49   It is possible that whoever drafted the text published by the Alice Baber Art Trust
     confused the Choctaw and Cherokee Nations. See also the reference to Choctaw
     ancestry in Adin Baber in collaboration with a number of Hanks descendants, in
     McNeill and Hanks, *Hanks Family of Virginia and Westward*, 154.

50   "Alice Baber . . . A Brief Biography," 11.

51   Adin Baber, "Early Trails of Eastern Illinois," *Journal of the Illinois State
     Historical Society (1908–1984)* 25, no. 1–2 (1932), 49–62.

52   Baber, "Early Trails of Eastern Illinois," 53–54.

53   John M. Kern, email to the author, May 4, 2024.

54   John M. Kern, interview with the author, May 4, 2024.

55   Alice Baber, draft essay for an artists' quilt show, *The Artist and the Quilt*
     (Knopf, 1983), organized by Charlotte Robinson, who was arranging for
     quilts to be produced to the designs of twenty recognized women artists, of
     whom Baber was to be one, Archives of American Art, Washington, DC
     (hereafter AAA).

56   Alice Baber, draft of essay for an artists' quilt show.

57   "Alice Baber," in *The Artist and the Quilt*, ed. Charlotte Robinson (Knopf,
     1983), 54.

58   "Alice Baber," 54.

59   "Alice Baber . . . A Brief Biography," 11.

60   Alice Baber, interview by Paul Cummings, May 24, 1973, AAA, https
     ://www.aaa.si.edu/download_pdf_transcript/ajax?record_id=edanmdm
     -AAADCD_oh_212519. Baber, who exhibited not only in the United States
     but extensively abroad, used both spellings of the color *gray*, as here, but
     also in some of her titles, *grey*, the preferred British spelling. The author has
     chosen to preserve the two variants as found in Baber's titles and writing.

61   Adin Baber to Nancy Baber McNeill, May 12, 1954, Baber Family Archives.

62   "Alice Baber," 54.

63   Alice Baber as quoted in Virginia Pitts Rembert, "Alice Baber" in *Alice Baber:
     A Retrospective Exhibition* (Greater Lafayette Museum of Art, 1982), 2.
     Rembert wrote that she interviewed Baber numerous times beginning in
     1975; see 7n2.

64   Adin Baber to Elizabeth Roberts, February 26, 1974, AAA. Adin
     Baber announced this project to his daughter Alice in 1966 and they
     were privately published in 1968 and then republished posthumously as
     Thoughts of a Little Girl, illustrated by Lloyd Ostendorf, for the Swope
     Art Museum in Terre Haute, Indiana, in 2019. See "Lloyd Ostendorf,"
     Chicago Tribune, November 4, 2000, https://www.chicagotribune.com
     /2000/11/04/lloyd-ostendorf/.

65   Adin Baber, in "'Preface,' Adin Baber, Father of the Artist, 1968," reprinted
     in *Alice Baber: Color Hunger* (Swope Art Museum, 1982).

66 Adin Baber, "Preface."

67 See letter from Adin Baber to Alice Baber, August 8, 1967, which includes this poem at the top of a list of poems written when Alice was age five until age eight.

68 Alice Baber, "Beauty," poem, 1935, AAA.

69 Alice Baber, interview by Paul Cummings, May 24, 1973.

70 Alice Baber, interview by Paul Cummings, May 24, 1973.

71 Alice Baber, interview by Paul Cummings, May 24, 1973.

72 The original remains in the Baber Family Archives.

73 "Alice Baber . . . A Brief Biography," 11.

74 Dolores Knippel, comp, and Mary Ellsworth, illustrator, *Poems for the Very Young Child* (Whitman Publishing, 1932).

75 Aunt Bonnie, Lois Shoot's sister, was known by her married name, Bonnie S. Miller.

76 S. A. Oliveria, M. Saraiya, A. C. Geller, M. K. Heneghan, and C. Jorgensen, "Sun Exposure and Risk of Melanoma," *Archives of Disease in Childhood* 91, no. 2 (2005): 131–38. https://www.ncbi.nlm.nih.gov/pmc/articles /PMC2082713/.

77 Alice Baber's jingle, "Busy," said to have been written at age six, predicts the energetic, peripatetic, and dedicated life Baber would lead:
    Busy as a bee
    Busy am I
    Busy all day long
    Till the stars are in the sky.
    Another poem from age six is titled "The Morrow," in which the context suggests that she means "The Mirror," rather than tomorrow:
    Look in the morrow
    What do you see there?
    Why you see your face and hands,
    And your curly
    Locks of hair.
    Related to Alice's poem about the robin is "Birds," written when she was six years old:
    Out of the eggs the little ones come
    Peep out of the nest to the light
    They have no feathers on their bodies
    But there mother's love is tight
    Soon out in the blue air you are flying
    In the sunshine on a swift flight
    Baber follows with yet another avian theme, "Chankens," which seems to be a six-year-old's spelling of *chickens*:
    Fluffy little chankens
    Hopping to and frow
    Whan their mother
    calls them
    they must always go
    This poem about chickens suggests Baber's experience in rural Illinois.

78   By the age of seven, she penned "Alice's Kitten":
         Fluffy is our little cat.
     The next poem in the booklet reverts to Alice's sixth year and is untitled:
         The moon rose over the ocean
         The ripples of silvery moonlight
         Make a path o'er the darkening waters
         Which extended far into the night.

79   The last poem in the volume is untitled, but identified as having been written
     when she was eight years old. Once again she refers to lilies:
         And when the day is done,
         Lady twilight tells the wind
         To break the stems of none
         No night will not mar them
         Not day will she scar them
         Nor dawn will she harm them
         Those lilies that blow
         The reason is Fairies
         Lie hidden away
         In the depths of those
         lilies that blow.

80   Alice Baber, "End of a Day in the Tropics," poem, 1935, AAA.

81   Susan W. Cutter, *Alice Baber, Painter* (Women in the Arts, 1975), 5.

82   John M. Kern, interview by the author, January 25, 2024, recalled that his
     mother like to hang her childhood painting of hollyhocks next to one that
     Alice had painted, pointing out that hers was better than the one by Alice.

83   Nancy Baber McNeill to Norbert Nelson, February 15, 1983, Tarble Arts
     Center, Eastern Illinois University, Charleston.

84   Alice Baber, interview by Paul Cummings, May 24, 1973.

85   Alice Baber, interview by Mary Trasko, undated typescript, Alice Baber
     Papers, AAA.

86   Alice Baber, interview by Paul Cummings, May 24, 1973.

87   "Looking Back in Beacon-News Files: Thirty Years Ago," September 18,
     1971, AAA.

88   For commentary on Vincent van Gogh's mental state, see Dietrich Blumer,
     "The Illness of Vincent van Gogh," *American Journal of Psychiatry* 159, no. 4
     (2002): 519–26, https://pubmed.ncbi.nlm.nih.gov/11925286/.

89   Alice Baber's unpublished and undated notes in AAA. See also many related
     studies such as Alexa A. Albert and Judith R. Porter, "Children's Gender-
     Role Stereotypes: A Sociological Investigation of Psychological Models,"
     Sociological Forum 3, no. 2 (1988): 184–210.

90   Alice Baber, interview by E. R., undated transcript, AAA. See also Rockwell
     Kent's *World Famous Paintings* (Wise & Company, 1939).

91   Alice Baber, quoted in Robinson, *Artist and the Quilt*, 53.

92   Alice Baber, interview by Paul Cummings, May 24, 1973.

93   The Venetian Pool was designed by designed by Phineas Paist with Denman Fink.

94   Alice Baber, interview by Paul Cummings, May 24, 1973. Baber's mention
     of the small town of Kansas, Illinois, was mistranscribed as "Catus," which

doesn't exist in Illinois. The town of Kansas today has a population of just under seven hundred. The Baber homestead was slightly north and east of the town of Kansas.

95 Alice Baber, interview by Mary Trasko, undated typescript, Alice Baber Papers, AAA.

96 Adin Baber to Elizabeth Roberts, February 26, 1974. See also ancestry.com "Lois Shoot Baber died on August 2, 1943, in Kansas, Illinois, at the age of fifty, and was buried in Fairview Cemetery, Kansas Township, Illinois."

97 The Edgar County clerk confirmed Lois Shoot Baber's cause of death.

98 John M. Kern, interview by the author, January 25, 2024.

99 John M. Kern, email to the author, March 29, 2025.

100 Collection of Baber Family Archives.

101 Alice Baber, undated handwritten notes, AAA.

102 Alice Baber, undated handwritten notes, AAA.

103 Despite any negative feelings Alice had held about her sister, she eventually resolved them sufficiently to name her sister and her children as beneficiaries in her last will and testament.

104 John M. Kern, email to the author, May 4, 2024.

105 Alice Baber's high school report cards are in the Baber Family Papers.

106 Alice Baber, telephone interview with Patrick Taylor, August 13, 1981.

107 Alice Baber, quoted in Sylvia Moore, "Alice Baber," *Women's Art Journal* 3, no. 1 (1982): 43.

108 Alice Baber, telephone interview with Patrick Taylor, August 13, 1981.

109 Alice Baber, telephone interview with Patrick Taylor, August 13, 1981.

110 Alice Baber, poem, summer 1940, Alice Baber Papers, AAA.

111 Rembert, "Alice Baber," 2.

112 Rembert, "Alice Baber," 2.

113 Carol Steen and Greta Berman, "Synesthesia and the Artistic Process," in *The Oxford Handbook of Synesthesia*, ed. Julia Simner and Edward M. Hubbard (Oxford University Press, 2013), 673.

114 Steen and Berman, "Synesthesia and the Artistic Process," 673.

115 "Speaking of Psychology: Tasty Words, Colorful Sounds: How People with Synesthesia Experience the World, with Julia Simner, PhD," *Speaking of Psychology* (podcast), July 2021. https://www.apa.org/news/podcasts /speaking-of-psychology/synesthesia: "We found that people with synesthesia, with verified synesthesia, are significantly more likely to experience anxiety disorder than other people. And we were really surprised about this."

116 See American Psychological Association, "Tasty Words, Colorful Sounds: How People with Synesthesia Experience the World," YouTube, July 21, 2021, https://www.youtube.com/watch?v=PYqsF53Bzyg.

117 Alice Baber, "Color," in *Color Forum* (University of Texas at Austin, 1972), 8.

118 Steen and Berman, "Synesthesia and the Artistic Process," 674–75.

119 MoMA lists an incorrect date of 1960 online, although this work was previously published by the Baber Estate with the painting's correct date of 1969. The forms of *The Turning Door* relate to other paintings around 1969, not 1960. See this 1983 document, which was the cover of a brochure for a show held by the Alice Baber Estate at the Elaine Benson Gallery in Bridgehampton, NY, September 30–October 2, 1983. This benefit sale was to establish the Alice

Baber Memorial Fund of Guild Hall Museum, East Hampton, NY; a copy of this document can be found in the Alice Baber Papers, AAA.

120 Alice Baber, undated handwritten essay, in Alice Baber Papers; emphasis added.

121 G. S. Whittet, essay for Alice Baber entry, *Contemporary Artists* (London, 1977).

122 *Merriam-Webster* definition of "bohemian": https://www.merriam-webster .com/dictionary/Bohemian.

123 Alice Baber's height and eye color are listed in her 1951 passport 1951, AAA. See Rembert, "Alice Baber," 2. Many who knew Alice Baber, such as photographer Ann Chwatsky, have commented how attractive Baber was. Edvard Lieber, conversation with the author of August 16, 2025, recalled meeting Alice, whose "complexion was like mother of pearl in moonlight."

Chapter 6. Further Education in Art (1946–1951)

1 *Linden Leaves*, Lindenwood College yearbook for 1946–1947, 134.

2 *Linden Leaves*, 134.

3 Alice Baber, undated handwritten notes on poetry, Archives of American Art, Washington, DC (hereafter AAA).

4 Alice Baber, undated handwritten notes on poetry.

5 Alice Baber, interview by Paul Cummings, May 24, 1973, AAA.

6 See also documentation that Watts studied with Philip Guston at the University of Iowa. See Lindenwood College Bulletin, November 1949, https://digital commons.lindenwood.edu/cgi/viewcontent.cgi?article=1070&context=catalogs.

7 John M. Kern, interview by the author, January 25, 2024.

8 Adin Baber to his daughters, Baber Family Archives. My interpretation of the family religion reflects that of Alice Baber's nephew, John M. Kern.

9 Alice Baber, interview by Paul Cummings, May 24, 1973.

10 Alice Baber, interview by Paul Cummings, May 24, 1973.

11 *40 Masterpieces: A Loan Exhibition of Paintings from American Museums, 6 October to 10 November, Fortieth Anniversary Exhibition* (St. Louis Art Museum, 1947), 22.

12 "Max Beckmann: Excerpts from the Writings of the Artist," in *Max Beckmann* (St. Louis Art Museum, 1948), 43.

13 "Max Beckmann," 43.

14 Hanns Swarzenski, "Prefatory Note," in *Max Beckmann*, 6.

15 Virginia Pitts Rembert, "Alice Baber" in *Alice Baber: A Retrospective Exhibition* (Greater Lafayette Museum of Art, 1982), 2. Rembert wrote that she interviewed Baber numerous times beginning in 1975; see 7n2.

16 Alice Baber, interview by E. R., undated transcript, 11–12, AAA.

17 Alice Baber, interview by Mary Trasko, undated typescript, Alice Baber Papers, AAA.

18 For example, see Pickens featured as one of the "Artists on the Picketline," in *New Masses*, February 5, 1946.

19 Lincoln Kirstein to Alton Pickens, May 31, 1950, Alton Pickens Papers, AAA.

20 "Indiana University Instructor Wins Oil Painting Blue Ribbon," *Indiana Daily Student*, September 3, 1949, 6.

21 The others recognized by *Life* included Franklin Boggs, Aleta Cornelius, Eldzier Cortor, Frank Duncan Jr., Hazard Durfee, Stephen Greene, Edward

Melcarth, Siegfried Reinhardt, Howard Warshaw, Hubert Raczka, Edward Stevens, Bernard Perlin, Honoré Sharrer, Kenneth Nack, Joseph Lasker, and Dean Ellis.

22 "Alton Pickens Gains Honors as one of Best Young Artists," *Indiana Daily Student*, May 9, 1950, 4.

23 See Erika Doss, ed., *Looking at Life Magazine* (Smithsonian Institution Press, 2001), 42. One study claimed that in a given thirteen-week period in 1950, "about half of all Americans, ten years and older, had seen one or more copies" of the magazine.

24 It is noteworthy that the Art Department at *Life* was then headed by Dorothy Seiberling, who managed this story and wrote to Pickens on January 4, 1950, AAA.

25 Alton Pickens, "Outline of Introduction to Art," September 1950, 3, Alton Pickens Papers.

26 Alice Baber to Mimi Posner, "New York Professional Women Artists," 1974, Solomon R. Guggenheim Museum, https://soundcloud.com /guggenheimmuseum/new-york-professional-women.

27 Diane Russell, "Alton Pickens Exhibits Work: Discusses Art with Campus," *Vassar Miscellany News*, October 3, 1956, https://newspaperarchives.vassar. edu/?a=d&d=miscellany19561003-01.2.14&e=-------en-20--1--txt-txtIN--------

28 Alice Baber, interview by Paul Cummings, May 24, 1973.

29 See *Red Man Series Untitled*, ca 1961, oil on canvas, 50 x 66 inches, reproduced in *Alice Baber, 1928–1982* (Alice Baber Trust, 1990), 15.

30 "Edward Hopper Objects," letter to Nathaniel Pousette-Dart, February 1935, in *The Art of Today*, 6, 11, quoted in Gail Levin, *Edward Hopper as Illustrator* (W. W. Norton, 1979), 1.

31 Alice Baber, interview by Mary Trasko, undated typescript, 4, Alice Baber Papers, AAA.

32 Alice Baber, interview by Paul Cummings, May 24, 1973.

33 Alice Baber, interview by Mary Trasko.

34 Alexandra de Lallier, "The Watercolors of Alice Baber," *Women's Art Journal* 3, no. 1 (1982): 46n2. De Lallier interviewed Baber for her article.

35 See Margaret Harvey, "Hiroshige Block Prints Fascinating Oriental Art," *Indiana Daily Student*, November 4, 1949, 2.

36 Alice Baber, interview by Paul Cummings, May 24, 1973.

37 Jerrold Maddox, to Alice Baber, February 2, 1973, informing her that she had earned thirty-five hours of graduate credit at Indiana University and nine hours at Fontainebleau, but that sixty hours were then required for the MFA requirement. He stated that there had been some confusion whether she could have qualified for the thirty-six-hour MAT degree, but that required a "teachers certificate," Alice Baber Papers, AAA.

38 Alice Baber, interview by Paul Cummings, May 24, 1973.

39 See James H. Jones, *Alfred C. Kinsey: Public/Private Behavior* (W. W. Norton, 1997).

40 See letter of recommendation of April 21, 1956, from Samuel Yellen to Agnes Ringe Claflin, Vassar College, AAA.

41 See Samuel Yellen, *In the House and Out and Other Poems* (Indiana University Press, 1952), 55, 61.

42   See Samuel Yellen, "The Say the Last Supper is Badly Damaged," *Antioch Review* 9, no. 3 (1949): 386, or Samuel Yellen, "Nighthawks," *Commentary*, November 1951, 436, which is the first known poem referring to Edward Hopper's 1942 painting, *Nighthawks*, and the only poem about Hopper known by me to be published during the artist's lifetime. See Gail Levin, *The Poetry of Solitude: A Tribute to Edward Hopper* (Universe Books, 1995), which includes and discusses this poem by Yellen: https://webapp1.dlib.indiana.edu/bfc/view?docId=B03-1984

43   Alice Baber, "Twilight Meeting," 1949–1950, Alice Baber Papers, AAA.

44   See W. E. McClain and J. E. Ebinger, "Woody Vegetation of Baber Woods, Edgar County, Illinois," *American Midland Naturalist* 79, no. 2 (1968): 419, cites Adin Baber.

45   See McClain and Ebinger, "Woody Vegetation of Baber Woods," 419.

46   "Baber Woods," https://dnr.illinois.gov/inpc/area.area6edgarbaberwoods.html.

47   Alice Baber, interview by Paul Cummings, May 24, 1973.

48   Alice Baber, unpublished handwritten manuscript, ca 1967, AAA.

Chapter 7. Return to France (1959–1962)

1   "Helen Frankenthaler, A Brief Biography," https://www.frankenthalerfoundation.org/helen/biography.

2   Paul Jenkins, "Jenkins Paints an Opinion," *Artnews*, November 1966, 55.

3   Paul Jenkins and Esther Ebenhoe Jenkins, eds., *Observations of Michel Tapié* (George Wittenborn, 1956).

4   Jenkins and Jenkins, *Observations of Michel Tapié*, 9.

5   See Gail Levin, "The Extraordinary Interventions of Alfonso Ossorio, Patron and Collector of Jackson Pollock and Lee Krasner," *Archives of American Art Journal* 50, no. 1–2 (2011): 4–19.

6   Alice Baber, interview by Paul Cummings, May 24, 1973, Archives of American Art, Washington, DC (hereafter AAA).

7   Alice Baber to Adin Baber, postmarked Paris, May 12, 1959.

8   For *The New American Painting* as shown in eight European countries, 1958–1959, see Frank Spicer, "The New American Painting," Tate Modern, https://www.tate.org.uk/research/publications/modern-american-art-at-tate/essays/new-american-painting.

9   Albert Elsen, *Paul Jenkins* (Harry N. Abrams, 1975), 274, states, "Meets James and Gloria Jones at Dr. Daniel T. Schneider's house in New York. Is given an ivory Eskimo knife by Alice Baber."

10   Alice Baber to Adin Baber, postmarked May 12, 1959. The reference appears to be to Mitchell's 1950 trip to Mexico. See Patricia Albers, *Joan Mitchell: Lady Painter: A Life* (Knopf, 2011), 152. Baber confused the ancient Mayan temples in the Yucatán with the ancient Inca Empire in Peru. She had not yet begun her own extensive travel to Latin America.

11   This photograph is in the Paul Jenkins Papers at the Archives of American Art, Washington, DC, and the verso is incorrectly labeled (but not in Baber's handwriting): "ALICE BABER GREGORY MASUROVSKY PARIS PAUL JENKINS PAPERS."

12   See the Rijksmuseum's website for this statement on Judith Leyster: https://www.rijksmuseum.nl/en/collection/node/Judith-Leyster--6b888886998f333d4310dc396aa02c63.

13 See "Shirley Goldfarb," in *United States of Abstraction; Artistes Américains en France, 1946–1964* (Musée d'Arts de Nantes, 2021), 229.

14 Michel Butor, "Interview with Gregory Masurovsky," in *Gregory Masurovsky: A World in Black and White: Two Essays and an Interview* (Black Mountain Dossiers, 2004), 40.

15 Alice Baber to Adin Baber, postmarked Paris, May 12, 1959, Baber Family Archives.

16 James Jones to Paul Jenkins, November 25, 1959, James Jones Papers, Harry Ransom Center, University of Texas at Austin.

17 James Jones to Paul Jenkins, November 25, 1959.

18 James Jones to Paul Jenkins, November 25, 1959. Henri could be Henri Michaux, a French poet, writer, and painter in this social circle.

19 It appears that one of the two reproductions of an Alice Baber painting named *Bon Voyage* has been accidentally flipped and that the one dated 1958 and reproduced in *It Is: A Magazine for Abstract Art* in the Winter/Spring 1959 issue, 61, is correctly dated. The other reproduction is published later in Joellen Bard, ed., *Tenth Street Days: The Co-Ops of the 50's* (Education, Art & Service, 1977), 42, published in conjunction with five shows held December 20, 1977–January 7, 1978 at Amos Eno Gallery, 14 Sculptors Gallery, Noho Gallery, Pleiades Gallery, and Ward-Nasse Gallery).

20 Paul Jenkins to James and Gloria Jones, postmarked December 21, 1959, James Jones Papers.

21 Paul Jenkins to James and Gloria Jones, postmarked December 21, 1959.

22 Paul Jenkins to James and Gloria Jones, postmarked December 21, 1959.

23 Paul Jenkins, interview by Colette Roberts, January 1968, AAA.

24 Katherine Komaroff Goodman, interview by the author, March 23, 2024; Hilarie Jenkins, interview by the author, March 22, 2024.

25 Kaylie Jones, *Lies My Mother Never Told Me: A Memoir* (William Morrow, 2009), 18.

26 Kaylie Jones, "Memories," in *Alice Baber* (Ronchini Gallery, 2024), 11.

27 Alice Baber to Paul Jenkins, Dukes Hotel, London, postmarked March 8, 1960, Paul Jenkins Papers, AAA; Max Beerbohm, *Zuleika Dobson: Or, an Oxford Love Story* (Heinemann, 1911).

28 Alice Baber to Paul Jenkins, postmarked March 8, 1960.

29 See Silver's photograph of Willem de Kooning at https://digitalcollections.nypl .org/items/a61321a0-e905-0131-335b-3c075448cc4b. Silver served in the Air Force during World War II and worked part of the time as a photo lab technician. His archive is in the Photographic Division of the New York Public Library.

30 For a reproduction of this painting in the Tehran Museum of Contemporary Art, see https://fineartamerica.com/featured/light-in-august-willem-de -kooning-roberto-morgenthaler.html.

31 Alice Baber to Paul Jenkins, postmarked March 8, 1960.

32 Alice Baber to Gloria Jones, undated letter of spring 1960, James Jones Papers.

33 Alice Baber to Gloria Jones, undated letter of spring 1960.

34 Alice Baber to Gloria Jones, undated letter of spring 1960.

35 https://digitalcollections.nypl.org/items/ba1cb5e0-e905-0131-a1be -3c075448cc4b. This photograph was later mislabeled Paris 1957, when neither Alice nor Paul was there, nor were they yet together. The incorrect

label does not even identify Alice, but it is clearly Baber and either in Paul Jenkins's Paris studio after 1959 or in his New York City studio after 1958.

36   Paul Jenkins to Ibram and Ernestine Lassaw, undated postcard from Costa Brava, Spain, signed, "Much love" from both Paul & Alice," in the possession of Denise Lassaw.

37   Alice Baber, unpublished manuscript for a book on Paul Jenkins, ca 1967, Alice Baber Papers, AAA.

38   Elsen, *Paul Jenkins*, 67. On page 274, however, for the "Biographical Outline" (perhaps compiled by someone else), Elsen's book lists the trip to Spain correctly under 1960.

39   Elsen, *Paul Jenkins*, 67.

40   Alice Baber to Elizabeth Roberts, unpublished undated interview (before 1969), Alice Baber Papers. Her comment about her allergy to tobacco smoke contradicts the memory of Herb Gold. Either he misremembers or she developed an allergy to smoke following their encounter.

41   Ernestine Lassaw to Alice Baber, September 16, 1961, Alice Baber Papers.

42   Alice Baber to Irving and Lucy Sandler, undated letter of early 1961, courtesy of Lucy Sandler. Denise Lassaw, email to the author, March 20, 2024, confirms that her mother, Ernestine, was studying French even before planning their 1961 tour of Europe that included seeing Alice and Paul in Paris and their excursion together to Les Vaux.

43   Alice Baber to Irving and Lucy Sandler, undated letter of early 1961.

44   James Fitzsimmons, Kenneth B. Sawyer, and Pierre Restany, *The Paintings of Paul Jenkins* (Editions Two Cities, 1961). At this time, this was a very small publisher that issued some books of poetry in Paris.

45   Fitzsimmons, Sawyer, and Restany, *Paul Jenkins*, 28.

46   Paul Jenkins to James and Gloria Jones, February 9, 1961, James Jones Papers.

47   The Kandinsky show was held February 8–March 4. 1961.

48   Alice Baber to Irving and Lucy Sandler, undated letter of early 1961.

49   Jones, *Lies My Mother Never Told Me*, 18.

50   Alice Baber to Irving and Lucy Sandler, undated letter of early 1961.

51   Ernestine Lassaw to Paul Jenkins, undated letter of 1961, signed, "Love the Lassaws," Alice Baber Papers.

52   Irving Sandler, "Reminiscences," in *Paul Jenkins on Canvas and Paper, 1989–2009* (Redfern Gallery, 2014). Sandler recalled writing for a show in "Luzern," but Jenkins's 1962 show in Switzerland took place in Zurich at Galerie Charles Lienhard and was accompanied by a catalogue with an essay by Irving Sandler.

53   Ernestine Lassaw to Paul Jenkins, undated letter of 1961, Alice Baber Papers.

54   Alice Baber, unpublished handwritten manuscript ca 1967.

55   Alice Baber, unpublished handwritten manuscript ca 1967.

56   Denise Lassaw, typed letter, March 18, 1962, AAA.

57   31st Venice Biennale, 1962, *2 Pittori, 2 Scultori. Stati Uniti d'America: Louise Nevelson, Loren MacIver, Jan Muller, Dimitri Hadzi*. Esposizione Organizatta Sotto Gli Auspici Del L'International Council of the Museum of Modern Art, New York.

58   Alice Baber to "Annely," who appears to be the German-Jewish art dealer Annely Juda, who took refuge in London and settled there, later opening her own gallery, July 9, 1962, Alice Baber Papers.

59 Alice Baber to Annely, July 9, 1962.
60 Denis Bowen to Alice and Paul, 1962, Alice Baber Papers.
61 Denis Bowen to Alice and Paul, 1962.
62 Virginia Pitts Rembert, "Alice Baber," 1982, 6. Rembert got to know Baber over several interviews dating from the mid-1970s.
63 Alice Baber, interview by George F., 1980, Alice Baber Papers.

Chapter 8. Literary Links (1963)

1 See, for example Alice Baber, "Long Island," annotated typescript, January 20, 1979, Archives of American Art, Washington, DC (hereafter AAA), cited later, in which she wrote: "Besides the white paintings, and the green-blue watercolors, I have also worked this year on a series of dark Nocturnes while reading *The [Master] Pipers* by George Sand. Whenever I read more about her, I realize the energy, and the vast amount of work that she did from midnight to morning reminds me of the power of the colors of the night."
2 See Elizabeth Harlan, *George Sand* (Yale University Press, 2004), 141–48.
3 Albert Sonnenfeld, "George Sand: Music and Sexualities," *Nineteenth-Century French Studies* 16, no. 3–4 (1988): 312.
4 George Sand, *The Bagpipers* (Little, Brown and Company, 1890), trans. Katherine Prescott Wormeley, dedication, https://gutenberg.org/cache/epub/66513 /pg66513-images.html.
5 See Virgil, *Eclogue* 2, in John Van Sickle, *Virgil's Book of Bucolics: The Ten Ecologues Translated into English Verse* (Johns Hopkins University Press, 1991).
6 Sand, *Bagpipers*. See also a more recent translation by Rosemary Lloyd long after Baber's death: George Sand, *The Master Pipers* (Oxford University Press, 1994), 40–41.
7 Sand, *Bagpipers*.
8 Sand, *Bagpipers*.
9 Sand, *Bagpipers*, "Fourth Evening."
10 The typescript of this poem reads "it's"—a grammatical error, AAA.
11 Alice Baber, poem of summer 1940, AAA.
12 Kenneth Grahame, *The Wind in the Willows* (Charles Scribner's Sons, 1908).
13 For understanding these poignant themes in Sand's *Les maîtres sonneurs*, see David A. Powell, *While the Music Lasts: The Representation of Music in the Works of George Sand* (Bucknell University Press, 2001), 45.
14 Powell, *While the Music Lasts*, 48.
15 Terence Diggory, "Introduction," in *The Journals of Grace Hartigan, 1951–1955*, ed. William T. La Moy and Joseph P. McCaffrey (Syracuse University Press, 2009), xx.
16 Susan W. Cutter, *Alice Baber, Painter* (Women in the Arts, 1975), 5.
17 *Le Monde* ad for this show can be found in the issue for January 25, 1963, 9, ProQuest Historical Newspapers.
18 Cutter, *Alice Baber, Painter*, 5.
19 Keith Sutton, *Alice Baber*, brochure for La Galerie de la Librairie Anglaise, January 18–February 14, 1963.
20 John Ashbery, *Alice Baber*, brochure for La Galerie de la Librairie Anglaise, January 18–February 14, 1963.
21 J. M., "A Travers Les Galeries: Alice Baber," *Le Monde*, January 25, 1963, 9, author's translation from the French.

22   John Ashbery, "Paris' Biggest Exhibition of Spanish Paintings Since 1848,"
     New York Herald-Tribune, January 30, 1963.

23   *Village Voice*, January 31, 1963, 5.

24   Cutter, *Alice Baber, Painter*, 5.

25   Albert Elsen, *Paul Jenkins* (Harry N. Abrams, 1975), 274. See James Jones,
     Moving Shapes Without Names (Galerie Karl Flinker, 1961). An article by the same
     name was also published by James Jones in *Art International*, March 1961, 22–26.

26   Tom Hess to Paul Jenkins, January 23, 1963, Paul Jenkins Papers, AAA.

27   United States Information Service, London, Press release of February 28,
     1963, Alice Baber Papers, AAA.

28   Keith Sutton in *Alice Baber*, New Vision Center Gallery, London, March
     1963, AAA.

29   Natalie Edgar in *Alice Baber*, New Vision Center Gallery, London, March
     1963, AAA.

30   Conroy Maddox, "Baber & Hurst: New Vision Centre Gallery," *Arts Review*
     (London), March 9–23, 1963, 16.

31   Maddox, "Baber & Hurst," 14.

32   New Vision Centre Gallery card for Galerie Wirth Berlin, August 28–
     September 16, 1964, reprints the list of the group by surname only: Al-Kazi,
     Baber, Bowen, Coutts-Smith, Durham, Feiler, Gummerson, Newcombe,
     Partridge, Ramis, Rothenstein, Stapleton, Van Caillie, Wohl, Woffram, and
     Wynne-Jones.

33   See Aberystwyth Arts Festival, *Modern American Painting*, 1963, brochure
     with checklist, AAA.

34   Canceled checks signed by Alice on her father's account at the Citizens
     National Bank of Paris, Illinois, survive to document his generosity.

35   Alice Baber, interview by Paul Cummings, May 24, 1973, AAA.

36   Alice Baber, interview by Paul Cummings, May 24, 1973.

37   Paul Jenkins to Ernestine Lassaw, September 30, 1963.

38   Mary Ann Morris Tucker, "paintings by alice baber win acclaim at one
     woman show in new york," Paris, Illinois, *Beacon-News*, November 20, 1963.

39   Ernestine Lassaw, datebook for November 1963.

40   Ernestine Lassaw, datebook for November 1963.

41   Transcript of a 1964 audio recording made by Adin Baber recounting this
     unexpected Christmas Day 1963 meeting with Nancy Hanks, transcribed
     by Nancy Baber McNeill in Santa Barbara, California, September 10, 1984,
     Baber Family Archives. At the time of the event, Nancy Baber McNeill was
     living with her family in Germany.

42   Paul Jenkins to Adin Baber, January 27, 1964, Paul Jenkins Papers, AAA.

43   Paul Jenkins to Adin Baber, January 27, 1964.

44   Adin Baber to Paul Jenkins, February 24, 1964, Paul Jenkins Papers.

45   Alice Baber to Paul Jenkins, undated letter of 1964, Paul Jenkins Papers.

46   "Recent Acquisitions—Seven American Paintings," press release, Museum of
     Modern Art, November 5, 1964.

47   Alice Baber to Paul Jenkins, undated letter of early November 1964, Paul
     Jenkins Papers.

48   Alice Baber to Paul Jenkins, undated letter of early November 1964.

49   Alice Baber to Paul Jenkins, undated letter of early November 1964.

50 According to Denise Lassaw, email to the author, April 11, 2025, Ibram Lassaw had studied classical sculpture techniques, including plaster modeling and casting at the Clay Club with Dorothea Denslow, who was one of the foremost authorities in the United States, of facial restorative art and headed the plastic surgery department at the McAllister School of Embalming in New York City. Among the death masks by Ibram Lassaw was one of the Jewish activist Vladimir Jabotinsky, made in 1940.

51 Denise Lassaw, email to the author, April 11, 2025, states that when she spoke to Paul about Ibram's version of this story, she later got an angry email from his wife Suzanne telling her to take down from the internet the story of Ibram and the death mask. Denise added, "Suzanne was very protective of Paul, his work and his reputation. He had lots of Alice's work and they just buried it all."

52 "Paul Jenkins: Painter Whose Art Brimmed with the Energy of Life," *Independent* (UK), June 27, 2012, https://www.independent.co.uk/news/obituaries/paul-jenkins-painter-whose-art-brimmed-with-the-energy-of-life-7893598.html.

53 See reference to this undated manuscript in chapter 2.

54 Dylan Thomas, *The Poems of Dylan Thomas*, (New Directions, 1952), 207–8.

55 It was, according to Irving Sandler's calendar, May 29, 1964; calendar reference courtesy Lucy Sandler. This date is confirmed by Ernestine Lassaw's daybook: "Meet train Irv, Lucy and Alice," which records that they had cocktails "at the Andersons" on May 31. Ibram Lassaw's daybook lists "weekend guests—Alice Baber, Lucy & Irv Sandler; May 30 Beaches. May 31 Cocktail parties dinner at Susan & Bill's [de Kooning].

56 Alice Baber to Paul Jenkins, undated letter of early November 1964.

57 Alice Baber to Paul Jenkins, undated letter of early November 1964.

58 Hilarie Jenkins, interview by the author, March 22, 2024.

59 Hilarie Jenkins, interview by the author, March 22, 2024.

60 Alice Baber to Paul Jenkins, undated letter of early November 1964.

61 Paul Jenkins to Alice Baber, telegram, June 11, 1964, Paul Jenkins Papers.

62 Paul Jenkins seems to have had little to do with his daughter Hilarie Paula Jenkins.

63 A copy is found in the Ethel Fisher Papers, AAA.

64 Adin Baber to Paul Jenkins, June 23, 1964, Paul Jenkins Papers.

65 Alice Baber to Colette Roberts, audio recording of 1969 interview, AAA.

66 Paul Jenkins to Adin Baber, August 11, 1964, Paul Jenkins Papers.

67 Paul Jenkins to Adin Baber, August 11, 1964.

68 Paul Jenkins to Adin Baber, August 11, 1964.

69 Paul Jenkins to Adin Baber, August 11, 1964. It does not appear that the article was ever published.

70 Paul Jenkins to Adin Baber, August 11, 1964.

71 Alice Baber to Adin Baber, ca July 1964, Baber Family Archives.

72 Adin Baber to his daughter Nancy, January 5, 1972, copy to Alice, in Baber Family Archives.

73 Katherine Komaroff Goodman, interview by the author, March 23, 2024.

74 Denise Lassaw, email to the author, December 20, 2023.

75 Clement Greenberg, "After Abstract Expressionism," *Art International* 6, no. 8 (October 25, 1962): 24—32.

76 Michael McNay, Obituary Paul Jenkins, *Guardian* (UK), June 21, 2012, https://www.theguardian.com/artanddesign/2012/jun/21/paul-jenkins.

77 Recorded in Ernestine Lassaw's daybook, arrived July 3, 1964, and left on July 7.

Chapter 9. First Adventures in Asia (1964–1965)

1 Alice Baber, untitled and undated manuscript, 1967, Alice Baber Papers, Archives of American Art, Washington, DC (hereafter AAA).

2 Paul Jenkins and Esther Ebenhoe Jenkins, eds., *Observations of Michel Tapié* (New York: George Wittenborn, 1956).

3 Ming Tiampo, "Under Each Other's Spell," in *Gutai and New York* (Pollock-Krasner House and Study Center, 2009), 7.

4 Tiampo, "Under Each Other's Spell," 8–9.

5 Paul Jenkins, interview by Colette Roberts, January 11, 1968, in his New York studio, AAA.

6 Matsumi Kanemitsu, interview by Marjorie Rogers, 1976, Los Angeles Art Community: Group Portrait, Oral History Program, University of California, Los Angeles.

7 Matsumi Kanemitsu, interview by Marjorie Rogers.

8 Tiampo, "Under Each Other's Spell," 8–9.

9 Matsumi Kanemitsu, interview by Marjorie Rogers.

10 Matsumi Kanemitsu, interview by Marjorie Rogers.

11 Matsumi Kanemitsu, interview by Marjorie Rogers.

12 "History," International House of Japan, https://www.i-house.or.jp/eng/history/index.html. See also Kaimai Jun, *Matsumoto Shigeharu: Bearing Witness* (LTCB International Library Trust and International House of Japan, 2012).

13 Paul Jenkins, interview by Colette Roberts, January 11, 1968.

14 Alice Baber, undated handwritten notes, ca 1967, AAA.

15 Toshio Yoshida to Mr. Paul Jenkins & Mrs. Alice Baber, July 20, 1965, Paul Jenkins Papers, AAA.

16 Paul Jenkins to Tom Hess, undated letter of 1964, Paul Jenkins Papers.

17 See "Secret Obsession: Paul Jenkins, Artist and Collector of Japanese Art," Nippon Club Web Gallery, January 12, 2024, https://nippongallery.nipponclub.org/NewsEvents/Details/52.

18 Reproduced in *Gutai and New York*.

19 Paul Jenkins, interview by Colette Roberts, January 11, 1968.

20 The name of the photographer is unknown. From left: Jiro Yoshihara, Paul Jenkins, William S. Lieberman (identified by the author who knew him years later). Alice Baber, *Document Gutai, 1954–1972* (Ashiya City Culture Foundation, 1993), 51. See also "The Beauty of Tricky Structures Created by Gutai Member Yuko Nasaka," *Gutai: Still Alive 2015*, vol. 1 (Whitestone Gallery): "On Nov. 29, William S. Lieberman, a curator at the Museum of Modern Art, visited the show for research." https://www.whitestone-gallery.com/blogs/articles-post/gutai-still-alive-yuko-nasaka-1.

21 Among galleries where Alice Baber works from the Paul Jenkins Estate can be found are Jody Klotz Fine Art, Abilene, Texas; Berry Campbell Gallery, New York City; and Ronchini Gallery in London and New York. See the

introduction to this book for further details of how Baber's artworks became
hidden by Paul Jenkins and his widow.

22   Alice Baber, untitled and undated essay, 1967, Alice Baber Papers.

23   Alice Baber, interview by Paul Cummings, May 24, 1973, AAA.

24   Alice Baber, untitled and undated essay, 1967.

25   Alice Baber, untitled and undated essay, 1967.

26   Alice Baber, artist's statement in Feminist Art Program, in *Art: A Woman's
     Sensibility*, ed. Miriam Schapiro (California Institute of the Arts, 1975), 6.

27   See André Van Lysebeth, *Tantra: The Cult of the Feminine* (Weiser Books,
     1995), 17.

28   Katherine Anne Harper and Robert L. Brown, *The Roots of Tantra* (SUNY
     Press, 2012), 48, 117, 40–53.

29   Alice Baber, interview by George F., 1980, Alice Baber Papers.

30   Alice Baber to Ernestine Lassaw, handwritten undated letter ca mid-January 1965,
     on stationery from the International House of Japan, Paul Jenkins Papers, AAA.

31   Alice Baber to Ernestine Lassaw, handwritten undated letter ca mid-January 1965.

32   Alice Baber to Ernestine Lassaw, handwritten undated letter ca mid-January 1965.

33   Alice Baber, undated handwritten notes, AAA.

34   Alice Baber, interview by Paul Cummings, May 24, 1973.

35   Alice Baber, interview by Karl Fortess, December 2, 1972, AAA.

36   Alice Baber, untitled and undated essay, 1967.

37   Paul Jenkins to Jiro Yoshihara, January 1965, Paul Jenkins Papers.

38   Alice Baber, undated writings, typed essay labeled "Section 2," 5.

39   Alice Baber, interview by Paul Cummings, May 24, 1973.

40   Paul Jenkins to Jiro Yoshihara, January 1965.

41   For Paul Jenkins's engagement with Asian art and culture, see Gail Levin,
     "Paul Jenkins, Yasuo Kuniyoshi and Asian Affinities," in *Paul Jenkins:
     Paintings and Works on Paper 1984–2010* (Redfern Gallery, 2018).

42   The rare first edition was published in 1963 in Bombay by the Board of
     Trustees of the Prince of Wales Museum.

43   Alice Baber, handwritten manuscript, undated notes, AAA.

44   Alice Baber, interview by Mary Trasko, undated typescript, Alice Baber Papers.

45   The invitation was kept by Baber's friend Ethel Fisher, in her papers, AAA.

46   William Grimes, "Jacques Kaplan, 83, Bold Furrier Dies," *New York
     Times*, July 22, 2008, https://www.nytimes.com/2008/07/22/nyregion
     /22kaplan.html.

47   Grimes, "Jacques Kaplan, 83, Bold Furrier Dies."

48   Ce Roser, interview by the author, May 27, 2024.

49   Ce Roser, interview by the author, May 27, 2024.

50   "Desert Color Changes Artist's Mind About Staying," *Arizona Republic*,
     November 19, 1965, 35.

51   "Desert Color Changes Artist's Mind About Staying."

52   "Desert Color Changes Artist's Mind About Staying."

53   Adin Baber to Alice Baber, December 20, 1965, AAA.

54   Wolfgang Saxon, "Nancy Hanks Dead at 55; Headed National Arts Group,"
     New York Times, January 8, 1983.

55   Irving and Suzanne Sarnoff, *Intimate Creativity: Partners in Love and Art*
     (University of Wisconsin Press, 2002), 33.

56   Alice Baber, undated [she was still working on it throughout 1968] writings, typed essay labeled "Section 1: Introduction: Paul Jenkins: The Painter," AAA.

57   Alice Baber, unpublished manuscript about Paul Jenkins, Alice Baber Papers.

58   Alice Baber, interview by Paul Cummings, May 24, 1973.

59   Alice Baber, interview by Paul Cummings, May 24, 1973.

60   Alice Baber, interview by Paul Cummings, May 24, 1973.

Chapter 10. Finding a New York Dealer (1965–1966)

1   Shows at A. M. Sachs were in 1965, 1966, 1969, 1971, 1973, 1975, 1977 and 1978. Baber's first show at Sachs was October 26–November 13, 1965, card at Archives of American Art, Washington, DC (hereafter AAA).

2   A. M. Sachs, "History of the A. M. Sachs Gallery," brochure, ca 1976, AAA.

3   Sachs, "History of the A. M. Sachs Gallery." The author recalls seeing, as a young graduate student, a John Ferren show at the Sachs Gallery. Abe Sachs stands out as unusually welcoming.

4   Alice Baber to Abe Sachs, July 24, 1965, Paul Jenkins Papers, no. 6554, AAA.

5   Alice Baber to Abe Sachs, July 24, 1965.

6   Alice Baber to Jack Mayer, August 10, 1965, Alice Baber Papers, AAA.

7   Alice Baber to Jack Mayer, August 10, 1965.

8   Alice Baber to Jack Mayer, August 10, 1965.

9   "Alice Baber," *Artnews*, November 1965, 12.

10   Alice Baber, interview by Paul Cummings, May 24, 1973, AAA.

11   Alice Baber, "Color," in *Color Forum* (University of Texas at Austin, 1972), 8.

12   Plato, *Timaeus*, trans. R. G. Bury (Loeb Classical Library, 1929), sec. 24e–25a.

13   Adin Baber to Alice Baber, December 20, 1965, AAA.

14   N. E. [Natalie Edgar], "Alice Baber," *Artnews*, November 1966, 12.

15   "Art: A Many-Sided Bernini | Alice Baber," *New York Times*, November 19, 1966, page 28, https://timesmachine.nytimes.com/timesmachine/1966/11/19/issue.html.

16   "Art: A Many-Sided Bernini: Alice Baber," calls this work *Axe in the Groove*, when it should be *Axe in the Grove*.

17   T. Edgar Lyon, "How Authentic Are Mormon Historic Sites in Vermont and New York?" *BYU Studies Quarterly* 9, no. 3 (1969): 343.

18   Lyon, "How Authentic Are Mormon Historic Sites," 344. Italics are the author's.

19   See the website of its descendant, Lindenwood University: https://www.lindenwood.edu/.

20   Alice Baber, interview by E. R., undated transcript, AAA.

21   Alexandra de Lallier, "The Watercolors of Alice Baber," *Women's Art Journal* 3, no. 1 (1982): 45–46.

22   Genesis 28:10–19.

23   Susan W. Cutter, *Alice Baber, Painter* (Women in the Arts, 1975), 6.

24   Genesis 28:12. For various versions of this passage, see biblehub.com/genesis/28-12.htm

25   Alice Baber, interview by E. R., undated transcript.

26   Alice Baber, annotated typescript, undated, AAA. Baber began this statement, "Lavender Ladder to the Sun which is here in the San Francisco

Museum," which suggests this was written for a lecture that she gave there. It could be dated to her lecture in January 1970, when San Francisco loaned a show of works from its collection to the show *Trends in 20th Century Art*, held at the Santa Barbara Art Museum.

27   See Iqtidar Alam Khan, "The Nobility Under Akbar and the Development of His Religious Policy, 1560–80," *Journal of the Royal Asiatic Society of Great Britain and Ireland*, no. 1/2 (1968): 29–36

28   Alice Baber, unpublished notes, Alice Baber Papers. Emphasis in the original.

29   Robert F. Olson (with Masao Ichishima in 1979) translated the *Bhāvanākrama*, a set of three Buddhist texts written in Sanskrit by the Indian Buddhist scholar yogi Kamalaśīla (c. ninth century CE). These works are the principal texts for mental development in Tibetan Buddhism.

30   Columbia University General Studies catalogue listing, 1968.

31   Alice Baber, interview by Paul Cummings, May 24, 1973.

32   Ramakrishna-Vivekananda Center at 17 East 94th Street in New York, Alice Baber Papers, AAA.

33   Gail Levin, "Japanese Cultural Influence in American: The Boston-New York Exchange," *Source Notes in the History of Art* 31, no. 3 (2012): 13–22. https ://gaillevin.commons.gc.cuny.edu/files/2014/03/SOURCE_Notes_in_the _History_of_Art_Vol._XXXI_No._3_Spring_2012-libre.pdf.

34   Alice Baber, undated handwritten manuscript, AAA.

35   Alice Baber to Lore and Andreas Becker, typescript letter from New York, n.d. They were in Moscow July 12–17; in Leningrad July 17–21; in Kiev July 21–23. Receipt from Lewis and Duveen Travel Service, Inc., June 10, 1966, Paul Jenkins Papers.

36   Joanna Eagle, "Artists as Collectors," *Art in America*, November 1967, 57.

37   *Alice Baber Paris Gemälde* [Paris Paintings], Kölnischer Kunstverein, September 13–October 9, 1966, AAA.

38   Alice Baber to Lore and Andreas Becker, n.d., 1966, Paul Jenkins Papers.

39   Alice Baber to Lore and Andreas Becker, n.d., 1966.

40   Paul Jenkins, *Strike the Puma* (Èditions Gonthier, 1966).

41   G. I. Gurdjieff, *The Herald of Coming Good: First Appeal to Contemporary Humanity* (Samuel Weiser, 1971).

42   A. M. Sachs Gallery, press release for her show of November 15–December 3, 1966, AAA.

Chapter 11. Questions of Identity (1966–1968)

1   Karl Flinker to Alice Baber, June 27, 1966. Actually, Michel Seuphor was the pseudonym of the Belgian artist Fernand Berckelaers, who wrote and edited three books—*A Dictionary of Abstract Painting* (Tudor Publishing Co., 1958), *Abstract Painting: 50 Years of Accomplishment* (Dell Laurel Edition, 1964), and *The Sculpture of this Century* (George Braziller, 1960), so this promised book on American art appears not to have been published. The 1964 Dell volume does not include Baber's work.

2   Michel Seuphor, *Dictionary of Abstract Painting* (Tudor Publishing Company, 1957), 194.

3   "The Americans Among Us," *Tatler*, July 2, 1966, 28.

4   "Women's International Art Club," *Tatler*, September 3, 1966, 46.

5   Alice Baber to Paul's aunt Louise, April 26, 1966, Paul Jenkins Papers, no.
     12351, Archives of American Art, Washington, DC (hereafter AAA).
6   Alice Baber to Diane and Irvin Shapiro, April 12, 1966, AAA.
7   Paul Jenkins to Adin Baber, September 22, 1966, Paul Jenkins Papers.
8   Paul Jenkins to Adin Baber, September 22, 1966.
9   Grace Glueck, The Club Creeps Back," *New York Times*, December 25, 1966, 175.
10   Glueck, Club Creeps Back," 175. Italics are in the original.
11   Paul Jenkins to Adin Baber, February 2, 1967, Paul Jenkins Papers.
12   Paul Jenkins to Adin Baber, February 2, 1967.
13   Paul Jenkins to Adin Baber, February 2, 1967.
14   Paul Jenkins to Adin Baber, February 2, 1967.
15   Paul Jenkins to Adin Baber, February 2, 1967.
16   Adin Baber to Paul Jenkins, March 8, 1967, Paul Jenkins Papers.
17   Pierre Schneider, "Zuka ou la nouvelle fidélité," *L'Expresse*, January 25–31,
     1965, 37.
18   Zuka (Zenaida Gourievna Booyakovitch) to Alice Baber, February 18, 1968,
     Alice Baber Papers, AAA.
19   Ann McCoy, interview by the author, December 26, 2023.
20   See Robert N. Raskin, "Narcissism and Creativity: Are They Related?"
     Psychological Reports 46, no. 1 (1980), https://doi.org/10.2466/pr0.1980.46.1.55.
21   This note about Esther, Paul's first wife, is on the same page that she records
     her sister's jealousy, AAA.
22   These handwritten notes by Alice Baber appear on a typescript labeled "All of
     my mystical experiences have had to do with," AAA.
23   These handwritten notes by Alice Baber appear on a typescript labeled "All of
     my mystical experiences have had to do with."
24   Undated, unlabeled notes by Alice Baber, AAA.
25   These and all other notes are from Alice Baber's undated handwritten
     manuscripts now in the Archives of American Art.
26   Alice Baber, handwritten, undated notes, AAA.
27   Joanna Eagle, "Artists as Collectors," *Art in America*, November 1967, 57.
28   Eagle, "Artists as Collectors," 57.
29   Ethel Fisher, handwritten note on her copy of Alice Baber's catalogue, *Color
     Forum*, Ethel Fisher Papers, AAA. See also A. M. Sachs Gallery note from
     Abe Sachs to the Museum of Modern Art about his artist Ethel Fisher,
     February 19, 1966, Ethel Fisher Papers.
30   Betty Gold, interview by the author, December 30, 2023.
31   Katherine Komaroff Goodman, interview by the author, March 23, 2024;
     Hilarie Jenkins, interview by the author, March 22, 2024.
32   Paul Jenkins to Mr. and Mrs. Wiseman, July 19, 1967, Paul Jenkins Papers.
     This visit might have been in Los Angeles, not in New York.
33   Paul Jenkins, typed note to Doctor Schmied, August 1967, Paul Jenkins Papers.
34   Esther Jenkins to Paul Jenkins, July 24, 1969, AAA.
35   Katherine Komaroff Goodman, interview by the author, March 23, 2024.
36   Katherine Komaroff Goodman, interview by the author, March 23, 2024.
37   Natalie Edgar, interview by the author, May 11, 2024, East Hampton, NY.
38   Alice Baber, interview by Mary Trasko, undated typescript, Alice Baber Papers.
39   Susan W. Cutter, *Alice Baber, Painter* (Women in the Arts, 1975), 5.

40 Ce Roser, interview by the author, February 16, 2025.

41 Alice Baber, unpublished notes on a Howard Wise Gallery mailing postmarked May 3, 1968, AAA. Another note in a different direction on this mailing notes "Philip Pavia, May 3 Fri. 12:25," followed by a phone number, which suggests that she was in New York by the day of this postmark.

42 Alice Baber, undated notes of dreams, AAA.

43 "Jack Delaney, Restaurateur and Breeder of Horses, 65," *New York Times*, January 16, 1966. https://www.nytimes.com/1966/01/16/archives/jack -delaney-restaurateur-and-breeder-of-horses-65.html.

44 Paul Jenkins, with Suzanne Donnelly Jenkins, *Anatomy of a Cloud* (Harry N. Abrams, 1983), 261.

45 Alice Baber, undated notes of dreams, AAA.

46 A lode is a geological term for a deposit of metalliferous ore that fills or is embedded in a fracture (or crack) in a rock formation or a vein of ore that is deposited or embedded between layers of rock.

47 Albert Elsen to Paul Jenkins, April 12, 1969, Paul Jenkins Papers.

48 Paul Jenkins to Al Elsen, May 26, 1969, Paul Jenkins Papers.

49 Paul Jenkins to Jim and Gloria Jones, April 19, 1969, Paul Jenkins Papers.

50 Paul Jenkins to Jim and Gloria Jones, April 19, 1969.

51 Paul Jenkins to Jim and Gloria Jones, April 19, 1969.

52 Paul Jenkins to Jim and Gloria Jones, April 19, 1969.

53 Paul Jenkins to Jim and Gloria Jones, April 19, 1969.

54 Sam Kaner to Paul Jenkins, note of May 29, 1969; Harry and Rose to Paul Jenkins, June 25, 1969, AAA, wishes them a great summer in Paris and wishes "that Kathy will be able to manage with her cast."

55 Adin Baber to Alice Baber, July 15, 1969, Baber Family Archives.

56 Adin Baber to Alice Baber, July 15, 1969.

57 Adin Baber to Alice Baber, July 15, 1969.

58 See Craig Bailey, *John Ferren* (CUNY Graduate Center, 1979), and Irving Sandler, *The Abstract Spirit: John Ferren (1905–1970)* (Pollock-Krasner House and Study Center, 1993).

Chapter 12. Feminist Imagery and Activism (1969–1973)

1 Peter Schjeldahl, "New York Letter," *Art International*, September 1969, 73.

2 Schjeldahl, "New York Letter," 73.

3 For examples of "central core imagery" from this era, see https://www.brooklyn museum.org/eascfa/dinner_party/core_imagery.

4 Rebecca Allan, "Icons of Female Power: Early Works of Miriam Schapiro," *Artcritical*, February 19, 2016, https://artcritical.com/2016/02/19/rebecca -allan-on-miriam-schapiro/.

5 Susan W. Cutter, *Alice Baber, Painter* (Women in the Arts, 1975), 6.

6 Cutter, *Alice Baber, Painter*, 6.

7 Lucy Lippard, "The Pains and Pleasures of Rebirth: European and American Women's Body Art," *Art in America*, 64, no. 3 (1976), reprinted in Lucy Lippard, *From the Center: Feminist Essays on Women's Art* (E. P. Dutton, 1976), 124.

8 Lippard, "Pains and Pleasures of Rebirth," 124.

9 See the Blanton Museum of Art's website: https://blanton.emuseum.com /objects/13946/lavender-high.

10 Linda Napikoski, "Lavender Menace: the Phrase, the Group, the Controversy," ThoughtCo, February 16, 2021, thoughtco.com/lavender -menace-feminism-definition-3528970.

11 Baber acknowledges this in one of her bibliographies in her papers. See Alice Baber Papers, Archives of American Art, Washington, DC (hereafter AAA).

12 N. E. [Natalie Edgar], "Alice Baber," *Artnews*, May 1969; The italicized "him" is by the biographer for emphasis.

13 Edgar, "Alice Baber."

14 Thomas Victor to Nancy Baber McNeill, June 3, 1985, responding to her letter to him of May 15, 1985, in which she appears to have inquired if his photograph of "Bob" [Shacochis], published in *Time* magazine on February 18, 1985, was taken in front of one of Alice's paintings. Letters in Baber Family Archives.

15 Thomas Victor to Nancy Baber McNeill, June 3, 1985.

16 John Ashbery, quoted on press release from the A. M. Sachs Gallery, 29 West 57th Street, undated, but post-January 1975.

17 G. B., "A Travers Les Galeries: Alice Baber," *Le Monde*, July 2, 1970, 17, author's translation. The show took place June 4–August 1, 1970.

18 Galerie Lambert, June 4–August 1, 1970, Paris, AAA.

19 Adin Baber to Chuck MacNeill, April 23, 1970, Baber Family Archives.

20 Adin Baber to Chuck MacNeill, April 23, 1970.

21 Adin Baber to Chuck MacNeill, April 23, 1970.

22 Archie Rand to Gail Levin, email, April 16, 2025.

23 Denise Lassaw was already living on her own in Alaska and does not recall Richard Galef. Initially, she did not share with me these entries in her parents' daybooks.

24 James R. Mellow, "Today's Series Line-Up: Baber and Baer," *New York Times*, April 11, 1971. The near pun became a real pun in the typo made years later on the paper's website. See https://www.nytimes.com/1971/04/11/archives /todays-series-lineup-baber-and-baer-.html.

25 Mellow, "Today's Series Line-Up."

26 Mellow, "Today's Series Line-Up"; Italics are the biographer's emphasis.

27 Mellow, "Today's Series Line-Up."

28 Mellow, "Today's Series Line-Up"; Italics are the biographer's emphasis.

29 A few months later, Mellow again revealed his sexist attitude—for example, when he dismissed the art of Edward Hopper's wife, Josephine N. Hopper, in her 1968 bequest to the Whitney Museum of American Art as "generally pleasant, lightweight works: flowers, sweet-faced children, gaily colored scenic views." See James R. Mellow, "The World of Edward Is Hopper—The Drama of Light, the Artificiality of Nature, the Remorseless Human Comedy," *New York Times*, September 5, 1971, sec. SM, 14, https://www.nytimes.com/1971/09/05/archives /the-world-of-edward-hopper-the-drama-of-light-the-artificiality-of.html. A close study of Mellow's papers, which are in the Beinecke Rare Book and Manuscript Library, Yale University, a gift of his companion, Augie Capaccio, might shed light on the writer's bias against women painters, even as he was the biographer of Gertrude Stein, who herself usually focused on male artists like Henri Matisse and Pablo Picasso, a close friend.

30 *Arts Magazine*, April 1971, 80.

31 "Alice Baber at A. M. Sachs," *Arts Magazine*, April 1971, 80.

32 "Industry: Art on the Line," *Newsweek*, April 12, 1971, 80–83.

33 The Turmac Tobacco Company went out of business in 2008 and the collection was sold at auction between 2010 and 2012. See Arnold Witte, "The Myth of Corporate Art: The Start of the Peter Stuyvesant Collection and Its Alignment with Public Arts Policy in the Netherlands, 1950–1960," *International Journal of Cultural Policy* 27, no. 3 (2021), https://www.tandf online.com/doi/full/10.1080/10286632.2020.1746291.

34 "The Americans Among Us," *Tatler*, July 2, 1966, 28.

35 "Americans Among Us," 28.

36 "Alice Baber, 54, Artist of Lyrical Abstractions," *New York Times*, October 7, 1982. https://www.nytimes.com/1982/10/07/obituaries/alice-baber-54-artist -of-lyrical-abstractions.html.

37 Jacqueline Moss to Alice Baber, October 18, 1975, Alice Baber Papers, AAA.

38 David L. Shirey, "Lyrical Abstraction Show at Whitney," *New York Times*, May 29, 1971, https://timesmachine.nytimes.com/timesmachine/1971/05/29 /81948358.html?pageNumber=24.

39 Shirey, "Lyrical Abstraction."

40 Shirey, "Lyrical Abstraction."

41 Natalie Adamson, *Painting, Politics and the Struggle for the École de Paris, 1944–1964* (Routledge, 2009), 181.

42 *Charles Estienne & L'art à Paris 1945–1966* (Fondation Nationale des Arts Graphiques et Plastiques, 1984).

43 "Lyrical Abstraction, (c. 1945–1960)," http://www.visual-arts-cork.com /history-of-art/lyrical-abstraction.htm.

44 "Lyrical Abstraction, (c. 1945–1960)."

45 Alice Baber, interview by Paul Cummings, May 24, 1973, AAA.

46 Alice Baber untitled and undated poem, AAA.

47 Alice Baber, interview by Paul Cummings, May 24, 1973.

48 Alice Baber, interview by Mary Trasko, undated typescript, Alice Baber Papers, AAA.

49 Beverley Jackson, "By the Way," *Santa Barbara News Press*, January 6, 1970.

50 Jackson, "By the Way." See also the show's catalogue, *Trends in 20 Century Art*, Santa Barbara Museum of Art, January 6–February 1, 1970. Baber's painting is number forty in the catalogue listing, which can be found in the AAA.

51 Alice Baber, annotated and undated typescript, written for a talk in California, possibly in either 1970 or 1976.

52 See this French fairy tale recorded in Charles Perrault, *Histoires ou Contes du temps passé* (1697; Larrouse, 1923), https://literature.fandom.com/wiki /Hop-o%27-My-Thumb.

53 John M. Kern related this story to me by phone on June 30, 2024, after speaking with Geoff Kern, his younger brother.

54 Betty Gold, interview by the author, December 30, 2023.

55 Ann McCoy, conversation with the author, April 29, 2024; Stephanie Simon, "$5-Million Art Collection Offered to Small Museum: Philanthropy: But Gift from Santa Barbara Man Would Require an Expensive Move by Conejo Valley Facility," *Los Angeles Times*, January 14, 1994, https://www.latimes .com/archives/la-xpm-1994-01-14-mn-11702-story.html.

56 Invitation is in Baber Family Archives.

57 Alice Baber, Santa Barbara Museum of Art, May 1976. Ernest and Robin S, Jones, were longtime Santa Barbara residents; she was an antiques and fine arts collector, dealer, appraiser and patron of the arts.

58 "The 1971 San Fernando Earthquake," California Department of Conservation, https://www.conservation.ca.gov/cgs/earthquakes/san-fernando.

59 "The Club (Fine Arts)," Wikipedia, https://en.wikipedia.org/wiki/The_Club _(fine_arts).

60 *Color Forum* (University of Texas at Austin, 1972).

61 Robert Slutzky married Gabriele Rosenberg in 1963 on license no. 28658, issued in Manhattan, New York City, New York.

62 Gabriele Roos died in 2022. I learned from her friend that she was bitter that Slutzky, her husband, had a mistress for four years. Her name change was related to cutting off that part of her life as well as her history as a Jewish refugee from Nazi Germany.

63 *Color Forum*, 53. Rosenberg's mother was Dr. Med. Margarethe Rosenberg, née Levinson, pathologist and part-time photographer. Her father was Dr. Jur. Kurt Rosenberg, born in Hamburg, Germany, in 1900. He worked as a lawyer and married in 1927. In 1937 he went on an exploratory trip to the United States and emigrated in 1938 with his wife and their daughters, Thekla-Maria and Gabriele. They settled in Mount Vernon, NY. He worked in an export business until 1956, when he was readmitted to the bar in Germany and took on restitution cases. He died in 1977. His papers, The Margaret and Kurt Rosenberg Family Collection, are at the Leo Baeck Institute of the Center for Jewish History in New York: https://archives.cjh .org/repositories/5/resources/13388.

64 Gabriele Rosenberg, "On Color," in *Color Forum*, 10.

65 Alice Baber, interview by Karl Fortess, December 2, 1972, AAA.

66 Alice Baber, "Curator's Notes," in *Color Forum*, 2–3. See Baber's full essays in this catalogue in the appendixes of this book.

67 Baber, "Curator's Notes," 3.

68 Baber, "Curator's Notes," 3.

69 Alice Baber, interview by Paul Cummings, May 24, 1973.

70 Alice Baber, "Color," in *Color Forum*, 9.

71 Baber, "Color," 9.

72 Alice Baber, untitled and undated typed manuscript on metaphor from the 1970s, probably intended for a session at a conference, Alice Baber Papers, AAA. On page 6 of this manuscript, a handwritten notation states, "When I first suggested the topic for this panel to Herb Aach he responded with his usual brilliance and quickness to create this panel and select the participants."

73 Alice Baber, untitled and undated manuscript on metaphor from the early 1970s.

74 Alice Baber, untitled and undated manuscript on metaphor from the early 1970s.

75 Alice Baber, untitled and undated manuscript on metaphor from the early 1970s.

76 Alice Baber, untitled and undated manuscript on metaphor from the early 1970s.

77 See a headline that ran on page one of the *Indiana Daily Student* for October 20, 1949, that read "make your choice: mark your 'x' polls to open."

78 Alice Baber, untitled and undated manuscript on metaphor from the early 1970s.

79 Alice Baber, untitled and undated manuscript on metaphor from the early 1970s.

80 See James P. Choca and Edward D. Rossini, *Assessment Using the Rorschach Inkblot Test*, (American Psychological Association, 2018), https://www.apa.org/pubs/books/4311033.

81 Alice Baber to Paul Cummings, interview of May 24, 1973, AAA.

82 Alice Baber, interview by Paul Cummings, May 24, 1973.

83 Alexandra de Lallier, "The Watercolors of Alice Baber," *Women's Art Journal* 3, no. 1 (1982): 45.

84 Alice Baber to Alexandra de Lallier, interview transcript from broadcast for WBAI-FM Radio, March 21, 1980.

85 Alice Baber to Alexandra de Lallier.

86 Baber's saved program for the Corcoran Conference is in the Alice Baber Papers, AAA.

87 Joseph Mascheck, "IX Painters Fordham University," *Artforum*, April 1973,

88 *Women Choose Women*, January 12–February 18, 1973. Catalogue text by Lucy R. Lippard and Women in the Arts. Artists in the show are listed in the catalogue.

89 Lucy R. Lippard, "Women Choose Women," New York Cultural Center, 1973. This essay is reprinted in Lucy R. Lippard, *From the Center: Feminist Essays on Women's Art* (E. P. Dutton, 1976), 44.

90 James R. Mellow, "Art: Focusing on Works by Women," *New York Times*, January 14, 1973, https://timesmachine.nytimes.com/timesmachine/1973/01/14/91429475.html?pageNumber=57.

91 Roslyn Drexler, "Women on Their Own," *New York Times*, January 28, 1973, 129. https://timesmachine.nytimes.com/timesmachine/1973/01/28/103217228.pdf.

92 April Kingsley, "Women Choose Women, *Artforum*, March 1973, https://www.artforum.com/features/women-choose-women-212969/.

93 Alice Baber, "Sonia Delaunay," *Craft Horizons*, December 1973, 39.

Chapter 13. Nomadic Challenges (1973–1975)

1   See letters of February 2, 1973, from Alice Baber to Dean Michael Hammond, and to Dean Dr. Gibson Danes, both at the College at Purchase, Alice Baber Papers, Archives of American Art, Washington, DC (hereafter AAA).

2   Bates Lowry, *The Visual Experience: An Introduction to Art* (Prentice-Hall, 1967).

3   See Rudolf Arnheim, *Art and Visual Perception*, 2nd ed. (University of California Press, 1974), 303–29.

4   See printed announcement in AAA. The uptown show took place January 13–February 1, 1973. See also *Village Voice*, January 18, 1973, 28, which lists the show at 141 Prince Street as taking place January 20–February 10, 1973.

5   Roberta Pancoast Smith, "Alice Baber: A. M. Sachs," *Artforum*, April 1973, https://www.artforum.com/events/alice-baber-235354/.

6   Smith, "Alice Baber: A.M. Sachs," describes this triptych as one of Baber's most recent works. Although this triptych has since been misdated, it appears in her 1982 retrospective as having been painted in 1972.

7   Alice Baber, undated typescript manuscript, AAA.

8   Alice Baber to Georges F., unpublished interview, 1980, Alice Baber Papers, AAA.

9   Carol Steen and Greta Berman, "Synesthesia and the Artistic Process," in *The Oxford Handbook of Synesthesia*, ed. Julia Simner and Edward M. Hubbard (Oxford University Press, 2013), 674–75.

10   Alice Baber, undated typescript manuscript.

11   Alice Baber, draft of an undated letter to her friend [Paul] Georges, Alice
     Baber Papers, AAA. Baber and Georges showed together in at least one
     group show, *Looking Back: Exhibition of Older and Present Work by 13 Artists*,
     held May 2–21, 1958, at the Marino Art Galleries in New York. It
     included Dorothy G. Voss, Paul Georges, Boris Lurie, William Gambini,
     Tom Young, Lester Johnson, Augustus Goertz, Sam Goodman, Rocco
     Amento, Alice Baber, Budd Hopkins, Ray Spillenger, Felix Pasilis, and
     Matsumi Kanemitsu. See the catalogue: https://www.iberlibro.com/servlet
     /BookDetailsPL?bi=30918500114.

12   "Alice Baber," obituary, *East Hampton Star*, October 14, 1982, 2. https://
     nyshistoricnewspapers.org/?a=d&d=teh19821014-01.1.2&srpos=2&e
     =-------en-20-teh-1--txt-txIN-%22Alice+Baber%22---------.

13   Alice Baber, interview by E. R., undated transcript, 18, AAA.

14   Alice Baber, interview by E. R., undated transcript, AAA.

15   See May Tabak Rosenberg's poem "Viva la Difference" about Baber with a
     French title, but translated into Spanish, dated January 6, 1975, Alice Baber
     Papers.

16   May Natalie Tabak, January 6, 1975, quoted in in *Alice Baber: Color, Light, and
     Image* (St. Mary's College of Maryland Gallery, 1977).

17   Alice Baber, text on announcement card for two shows at the A. M.
     Sachs Gallery locations in New York City, January–February 1973, AAA;
     Biographer added the italic emphasis.

18   Joanna Eagle, "Artists as Collectors," *Art in America*, November 1967, 59.

19   Alice Baber, "Color," in *Color Forum* (University of Texas at Austin, 1972), 8.

20   Alice Baber, interview by Karl Fortess, December 2, 1972, AAA.

21   Baber saved the programs for these lectures in her papers at the AAA. See
     also Jorge Luis Borges, *Qué es el Budismo?* (Editorial Columba Coleccion
     Esquemas, 1976).

22   Alan Watts, *The Way of Zen* (Pantheon, 1957), and Alan Watts, *Psychotherapy
     East and West* (Pantheon, 1961).

23   Her show took place at Chanakya Gallery from January 18 to 28, 1974.

24   "Visions of Light and Colour," *Statesman*, January 22, 1974.

25   "Colours Inspire Alice," *Hindustan Times*, January 26, 1974.

26   Anna Quindlen, "Three Sides to Every Painting," *New York Post*, August 31,
     1974; "Charging Our Cultural Batteries," *New York Daily News*, September 6,
     1974; "Strolling in Park, Through 12 Triangles," *New York Times*, September
     5, 1974; "Walk thru Triangles," *Today's Art*, n.d., 16, stamped January 1, 1975.

27   Course announcement, "Women Artists Past to Present," Fall 1974, AAA.

28   John M. Kern, email to the author, May 5, 2024.

29   James Jones, reprinted in *Alice Baber, Exhibition of Paintings*, December 5–31,
     1974, Gallery Ala, Iran America Society Cultural Center.

30   Gordon Winkler to Alice Baber, July 24, 1974, Alice Baber Papers.

31   Eliza Gregory, "Alice Baber and Paul Jenkins," in *Alice Baber* (London:
     Ronchini Gallery, 2024), 7, wrote erroneously that Baber and Jenkins
     "traveled together to India, Korea, Iran," Baber's only trip to Iran was in 1974,
     years after the marriage to Jenkins ended in 1968. Their trip together to Japan
     and India is discussed in chapter 9 of this volume.

32   Alice Baber panel discussion took place on May 11, 2024, at the Berry
     Campbell Gallery with Dan Cameron, Gail Levin, and Ann McCoy on the
     occasion of a show of Alice Baber's art.

33   Margaret Poser, email to the author, May 10, 2024.

34   A typed text on a postcard from the mural painter Urban Neininger to
     Alice Baber at her New York studio at 597 Broadway from Chilmark,
     Massachusetts, on Martha's Vineyard dated August 11, 1977, Alice
     Baber Papers, states that he imagines that she had heard news of recent
     developments in East Hampton "Galef and Gabby (No, not together!). If you
     don't know, write and we'll relay the earthshaking news." Thus, Baber appears
     to have maintained some interest in Galef.

35   James Jones, quoted in Herbert Mitgang, "James Jones, Novelist, 55, Dies;
     Best Known for 'Here to Eternity,'" *New York Times*, May 10, 1977. https
     ://www.nytimes.com/1977/05/10/archives/james-jones-novelist-55-dies-best
     -known-for-here-to-eternity.html.

36   Kaylie Joncs, "Memories," in *Alice Baber* (Ronchini Gallery, 2024), 11.

37   Kaylie Jones, interview by the author, April 17, 2025.

38   Kaylie Jones, interview by the author, April 17, 2025.

39   "Sotheby's Has Struck Oil Selling Art to Iranians," *New York Times*, May 18,
     1975, 52.

40   At least two American curators worked in Tehran collecting American
     contemporary abstract art: Donna Stein and Robert C. Hobbs.

41   Joan Mitchell to Alice Baber, undated letter of late 1974–early 1975, Alice
     Baber Papers.

42   See Richard E. Cytowic, *Synesthesia: A Union of the Senses* (Springer, 1989), 14–16.

43   Patricia Albers, *Joan Mitchell: Lady Painter* (Knopf, 2011), 55–56. This book
     discusses Mitchell's synesthesia, but does not even mention Alice Baber,
     although ample documentation of the two women's friendship survives.
     Albers does discuss Paul Jenkins.

44   Al Brunelle, "Alice Baber at Sachs," *Art in America*, July/August 1975, 106.

45   Alice Baber, interview by Paul Cummings, May 24, 1973, AAA.

46   Robert Littman, email to the author, June 5, 2024. Littman recalls that he
     worked at the A. M. Sachs Gallery ca 1967.

47   Phyllis Braff, email to the author, December 11, 2023.

48   Miriam Schapiro, ed. *Art: A Woman's Sensibility* (California Institute of the
     Arts, 1975), 2.

49   Alice Baber quoted in Schapiro, *Art: A Woman's Sensibility*, 6, 82. Galef's
     name appears misspelled in the photo credits.

50   Kaylie Jones, interview by the author, April 17, 2025.

51   Author's interview with Susan B. Anthony, Richard Galef's widow, who
     confirmed that he traveled with Baber to Iran. Galef had two sons from his
     previous marriage, which ended in divorce.

52   The checklist is in the feminist archives at Rutgers University.

53   See advertisement for the course in the *Village Voice*, August 21, 1978, 41.
     See also George Bolge, *Woman's Art Journal* 3, no. 2 (Autumn 1982–Winter,
     1983): 54n1, and Pamela H. Simpson, "Review of Richard Martin, *Dorothy
     Gillespie*," *Woman's Art Journal* 20, no. 2 (Autumn, 1999–Winter, 2000): 60.
     See also Dorothy Gillespie, "Professionalism and the Woman Artist," in

Feminist Collage: Educating Women in the Visual Arts, ed. Judy Loeb (Teachers College Press, 1979), 215, who mentions Baber and gives some detail about the course they started together.

54 "Functioning in the Art World," as listed as course 5905-3 in "Human Relations Work-Study Center," *New School Bulletin*, January 6, 1976, 12.

55 "Functioning in the Art World."

56 A notable exception was the course that Paul Sachs taught at Harvard's Fogg Museum. See "Portrait of the Artist as a Director," *Harvard Magazine*, September–October 2002, https://www.harvardmagazine.com/2002/09 /portrait-of-the-artist-a-html.

57 "Roanoke Native Dorothy Gillespie, Who Died at 92, Devoted Much Her Life to Art," *Roanoke Times*, September 30, 2012; Ben Steelman, "Artist Dorothy Gillespie Dies," *Wilmington Star-News*, October 1, 2012, https://www.starnewsonline.com/story/news/2012/10/01/ artist-dorothy-gillespie-dies/30925409007/.

58 "The 1975 Art World/The Women In It, Panel Discussion Moderated by Alice Baber, May 7, 1975 Part 1," Radford University Digital Collections, https://monk .radford.edu/records/item/27147-the-1975-art-world-the-women-in-it-panel -discussion-moderated-by-alice-baber-may-7-1975-part-1?offset=3.

59 See Gail Levin, *Edward Hopper: An Intimate Biography* (Knopf, 1995), 457–63.

60 MaryAnn Tucker, "Artist in Residence: Alice Baber of Kansas," *Paris Beacon-News* (Paris, IL), June 27, 1975.

61 Brad Tucker, interview by the author, June 29, 2025. Brad is the son of Mary Ann Morris Tucker, who earned a degree in journalism at the University of Illinois Urbana–Champaign.

62 "Women's Exhibit at Springs," *East Hampton Star*, August 21, 1975. https ://nyshistoricnewspapers.org/?a=d&d=teh19750821-01.1.10&srpos=15&e =-------en-20-teh-1--txt-txIN-%22Alice+Baber%22---------.

63 See Gail Levin, "Making Art History in Springs, 1975," *East Hampton Star*, July 26, 2011, https://gaillevin.commons.gc.cuny.edu/wp-content/blogs. dir/1515/files/2023/09/CaroleeSchneemannEHStar.pdf. This may be the first time that the author made a published mention of Alice Baber, who had until now remained an enigma to me.

64 Phyllis Derfner, "Color, Light, and Image," *Art International*, March/April 1976, 13.

65 *Alice Baber*, Women's Interart Center, New York, 1975.

66 Rose Slivka, "Song to the Color in the Paintings of Alice Baber," in *Alice Baber* (Women's Interart Center, 1975).

67 Alice Baber, *Isfahan Remembered* (1975) is now in the Alice Baber Memorial Collection, Art Museum of Greater Lafayette, Indiana.

68 Visual Artists Coalition Inc., *Women Painters and Poets*, organized for the Visual Artists Coalition Inc. for a show at New York University's Loeb Student Center, 1977.

69 See Gail Levin, *Lee Krasner: A Biography* (William Morrow, 2011), and Richard Howard, "Lee Listening: Lee Krasner Pollock," *Grand Street* 4, no. 1 (Autumn 1984): 183–86.

70 Richard Howard, "Alice and the Beautiful," January 1975, quoted in undated press release, "Excerpts from Articles & Reviews of Alice Baber's Paintings," AAA.

71 "First Exhibit at Art Center," *Paris Beacon-News* (Paris, IL), October 16, 1975.
72 "First Exhibit at Art Center."

Chapter 14. Color Hunger: Appetite for Latin America (1975–1977)

1   Susan W. Cutter, *Alice Baber, Painter* (Women in the Arts, 1975), 6.
2   Cutter, *Alice Baber, Painter*, 6.
3   Alice Baber, "Gorky's Color," in *Arshile Gorky: Drawings to Paintings* (University of Texas Art Gallery, 1975), 76.
4   Alice Baber, "Gorky's Color," 76.
5   Alice Baber, "Gorky's Color," 76.
6   Elaine Benson to Alice Baber, January 1976, Archives of American Art, Washington, DC (hereafter AAA). The artists shown together were Mary Abbott, Alice Baber, Elaine de Kooning, Fay Lansner, Buffie Johnson, Ce Roser, and Margot Stewart.
7   Letter of September 27, 1978, from Leonar Vielbig, Esq. to Leonard, outlining the purchase price and details around the property sale, AAA.
8   Alice Baber filled in forms for *Who's Who in America* on February 14, 1979, and May 20, 1981, Alice Baber Papers, AAA. See also Alice Baber to Landlord, August 16, 1978, in which she complains of the "dangerous falling plaster" in her apartment at 73 Bedford Street Mews, AAA.
9   Ann McCoy, interview by the author, December 26, 2023. Alice Baber's nephew, John M. Kern, recalls the studio, where he stayed for several months, as a third-floor walk-up, but that the floors were very far apart with high ceilings. John M. Kern, interview by the author, May 24, 2024.
10 Thomas Albright, "Alice Baber," *San Francisco Chronicle*, June 17, 1976.
11 Albright, "Alice Baber."
12 See, for example, Jane (Mrs. Llewellyn) Thompson, director of the Art in Embassies program, to Alice Baber, August 1, 1978, October 2, 1978, and November 1, 1978, AAA. The USIA was called USIS overseas until the two were merged in 1999.
13 William M. Chodkowski, "The United States Information Agency, American Security Project, November 2012, http://www.jstor.com/stable/resrep06059.
14 Chodkowski, "United States Information Agency," 2.
15 J. Mae, "What's on in Art," *Colony Reporter* (Guadalajara, Mexico), December 25, 1976, 4.
16 Alice Baber to Donald B. Goodall, director of the Blanton Museum of Art at the University of Texas at Austin, L975, September 29, 1975, Alice Baber Papers, AAA. Baber proposed to participate in the symposium on contemporary art and literature in Latin America, which he was planning.
17 Noted in a letter from Alice Baber to Mr. Heseler in Munich, Germany, April 15, 1976, Alice Baber Papers.
18 Dennis Masback, interview with the author, April 28, 2025.
19 Grace Glueck, "Art: An Impressionist Re-emerges," *New York Times*, February 11, 1977, C-17, https://www.nytimes.com/1977/02/11/archives/art-an-impressionist-reemerges.html.
20 Alice Baber, quoted in Ann McCoy, "Alice Baber A. M. Sachs," *Art/World*, February 1977.

21 McCoy, "Alice Baber A. M. Sachs."

22 Lawrence Goldsmith, *Watercolor Bold and Free* (Watson-Guptill, 1980), 19, 78.

23 Goldsmith, *Watercolor Bold and Free*, 19.

24 Goldsmith, *Watercolor Bold and Free*, 78.

25 Alice Baber, quoted in Goldsmith, *Watercolor Bold and Free*, 78.

26 List is in typescript by Joellen Bard, labeled "Alice Baber: Mission to Latin America," handwritten at top of the manuscript is "edited by J. Siegel (WAN)," which is Jean Siegel for Women Artists News, AAA.

27 Alice Baber to Helen Hughes, director of the Instituto Cultural Dominico Americano, Santo Domingo, Dominican Republic, February 7, 1977, AAA.

28 A. M. Sachs Gallery press release for Alice Baber, February 5–24, 1977, AAA.

29 Rose S. Berstein to Alice Baber, January 4, 1977, AAA.

30 Cyro Fernandes, president of the Instituto Cultural Brasileiro Norte-Americano, to Alice Baber, August 10, 1976.

31 Joellen Bard, "Alice Baber: Mission to Latin America," AAA.

32 Bard, "Alice Baber: Mission to Latin America." A version of this manuscript was published as Joellen Bard, "Alice Baber: Mission to Latin America," *Women Artists Newsletter* 2, no. 10 (April 1977): 6, https://www.jstor.org/stable/pdf/community.28046880.pdf.

33 Baber, quoted in Bard, "Alice Baber: Mission to Latin America," *Women Artists Newsletter*, 6d.

34 Untitled biography of Alice Baber, ca 1979, Alice Baber Papers.

35 Alice Baber, quoted in "Baber Show Ready," at time of her November 1976 show at the Arvil Gallery at Hamburgo 241, Mexico City, undated clipping in Alice Baber Papers; card, also in AAA, states that the show was "on el patrocinio de la Embajada de Los Estados Unidos de NorteAmerica [under the patronage of the embassy of the United States of North America]."

36 Bard, "Alice Baber: Mission in Latin America."

37 Alice Baber, quoted in "Baber Show Ready," undated unidentified clipping from Mexico City, Alice Baber Papers.

38 Denise Lassaw, email to the author, December 27, 2023.

39 Alice Baber, interview by Mary Trasko, undated typescript, Alice Baber Papers. See her triptych in the Guggenheim Museum in New York.

40 Alice Baber to Ms. Asta Rose Alcaide, January 5, 1977, Alice Baber Papers.

41 Alice Baber to Ms. Asta Rose Alcaide, January 5, 1977.

42 Alice Baber to Ms. Asta Rose Alcaide, January 5, 1977.

43 Alice Baber, quoted in Sylvia Moore, "Alice Baber," *Women's Art Journal* 3, no. 1 (1982): 40.

44 Bard, "Alice Baber: Mission to Latin America."

45 Alice Baber, interview by E. R., undated transcript, AAA.

46 Alice Baber, "Curator's Notes," and "Color," in *Color Forum* (University of Texas at Austin, 1972).

47 Baber, "Color," 9.

48 Giovanni G. Bellani, *Felines of the World: Discoveries in Taxonomic Classification and History* (Elsevier, 2020).

49 Alice Baber, unpublished and undated manuscript, typed with handwritten annotations and corrections, AAA. This can be dated ca 1981 since she writes, "At the moment a symbolist show is on at MoMA."

50 Alice Baber to Dr. Herman Kruger in San Isidro, Lima, Peru, draft of January 23, 1979, letter.

51 Alice Baber, page 2 of annotated typescript, headed, "I attended the panel on semiotics this afternoon and was grateful to hear the word metaphor used." AAA.

52 Paul Jenkins, *Strike the Puma: A Play* (Éditions Gonthier, 1966). For a reference to a jaguar by Borges, see his short story "The Writing of the God," in *Labrinths* (New Directions, 1962). In the story, a Mayan priest is imprisoned by the Spanish and kept in a cell next to a jaguar. The priest can only see the jaguar through a small window.

53 "Casting Bits," *Backstage*, January 19, 1968, 18.

54 G. I. Gurdjieff, *The Herald of Coming Good: First Appeal to Contemporary Humanity* (Samuel Weiser, 1971.

55 Paul Jenkins, interview by Colette Roberts, January 11, 1968, in his New York studio, AAA.

56 G. I. Gurdjieff, *The Herald of Coming Good: First Appeal to Contemporary Humanity* (Samuel Weiser, 1971.

57 Jenkins, *Strike the Puma*.

58 Jenkins, *Strike the Puma*, 15–16.

59 See, for example, Stefan Pociask, "How Often Do Jaguars and Pumas Meet in the Wild?" *Forbes*, December 10, 2018, https://www.forbes.com/sites /quora/2018/12/19/how-often-do-jaguars-and-pumas-meet-in-the-wild /#2741853a3d43.

Chapter 15. Recognition, Then Becoming Very Gray (1977–1982)

1 Lee Krasner's first American retrospective opened at the Houston Museum of Fine Arts and did not reach MoMA until after Krasner's death on June 19, 1984.

2 Norton T. Dodge, *Women in the Soviet Economy: Their Role in Economic, Scientific, and Technical Development* (Johns Hopkins University Press, 1966).

3 See John McPhee, *The Ransom of Russian Art* (Macmillan, 1994). The Norton and Nancy Dodge Collection of Soviet Nonconformist Art, which contains roughly twenty thousand works of art, was donated to Rutgers University in the mid-1990s, where it is on permanent display at the Jane Voorhees Zimmerli Art Museum.

4 Andrew Russeth, "Storied Collection of Soviet Nonconformist Art Heads to Zimmerli Art Museum at Rutgers," *Artnews*, November 2017.

5 For the Cremona Farm, see https://en.wikipedia.org/wiki/Cremona_Farm. Other sponsors of Baber's show were the Maryland Arts Council and the St. Mary's College of Maryland Visiting Artists program.

6 The foundation of Norton T. Dodge has been very helpful, but has not been able to answer this question.

7 Wolfgang Saxon, "Nancy Hanks Dead at 55; Headed National Arts Group," *New York Times*, January 8, 1983.

8 Jonathan Ingersoll, in *Alice Baber: Color, Light, and Image* (St. Mary's College of Maryland Gallery, 1977). See also "Abstract Artist to Exhibit at SMC,"

Enterprise, February 24, 1977, Archives of American Art, Washington, DC (hereafter AAA).

9 The works in this show from public collections were *Lavender Ladder Turning-Akbar's Hunt* (1972, Whitney Museum of American Art); *Open Staircase* (1964–65, The Corcoran Gallery of Art); *Sun Ladder* (1965, The Herbert F. Johnson Museum, Cornell University); *The Key of Sound and Light* (1976, American Institute of Architects); *Wheel of Day* (1975, Santa Barbara Museum of Art); *Noble Numbers* (1970, National Collection of Fine Arts, [Smithsonian Institution]); *Akbar's Dream* (1973, Kresge Art Gallery, Michigan State University).

10 In addition, the St. Mary's College catalogue reproduced Baber's *Sacred Space Series V* (1975), *Sounds of the Piper's Ladder* (1975), *The Bridge of Sounds* (1974), *Swirl of Sounds: The Ghosts in the Banyan Tree* (1975), as well as three 1975 oils constituting a large triptych (*Ganish-Lord of the Four Corners, Feather Mask Dance, Wind Feather Dance*) on loan from Palm Beach Galleries and one canvas from Baber's own collection. Nancy Hanks's loan is now part of her bequest to the Nasher Museum of Art at Duke University. The lender of one painting, the Henri Gallery in Washington, DC, located at 1500 21st Street NW, gave Baber a solo show in April 1977.

11 See these essays reproduced in this book's appendixes.

12 Alice Baber, "My Paintings Are My Diary," in *Alice Baber: Color, Light, and Image*.

13 Baber, "My Paintings Are My Diary." She refers to the Aztec emperor of Mexico, who was overthrown and killed by the Spanish conquistador Hernán Cortés. This text was originally part of Baber's lecture in Santa Barbara, California, in 1976.

14 Alice Baber's *Bon Voyage* is reproduced in the show's catalogue. See Joellen Bard, *Tenth Street Days: The Co-Ops of the 50's* (Education, Art & Service, 1977), 42, no. 115. Despite this reproduction, Joellen Bard recalled that Dore Ashton had tried to exclude Baber's art from this show. The catalogue notes that work was selected for travel by Ashton and Bard for a show circulated by the Gallery Association of New York State, so Ashton probably succeeded in excluding Baber from the touring show.

15 Jean Cohen, "1978," "Sidney Janis Reads the Future," "More About Tenth Street Days—and Beyond," in *Mutiny and the Mainstream: Talk That Changed Art, 1975–1990*, ed. Judy Seigel (Midmarch Arts Press, 1992), 81.

16 Joellen Bard, telephone interview by the author, June 7, 2024.

17 See Joellen Bard, "Alice Baber: Mission to Latin America," *Women Artists Newsletter*, April 1977, 6, https://www.jstor.org/stable/pdf/community.28046880.pdf.

18 Joellen Bard, conversation with the author, June 7, 2024; Joellen Bard, email to the author, June 10, 2024.

19 On the personal aspect of this relationship with Nelson Rockefeller, see Michael Whitney Straight, *Nancy Hanks, An Intimate Portrait: The Creation of a National Commitment to the Arts* (Duke University Press, 1988), 50–52.

20 Leigh Markopolos, "Dore Ashton, 'Response to Crisis in American Art, (1969),'" *e-flux*, February 23, 2017, https://www.e-flux.com/criticism/239837/dore-ashton-response-to-crisis-in-american-art-1969.

21   Straight, *Nancy Hanks*, 21.

22   Alice Baber to Clara Diament Sujo, June 29, 1977, Alice Baber Papers, AAA.

23   First Lady Rosalynn Carter visited Bogotá, Colombia, during her diplomatic
     tour of seven Latin American nations and Caribbean Islands in June 1977.

24   Alice Baber to Clara Diament Sujo, June 29, 1977.

25   Alice Baber to Alexandra de Lallier, interview transcript from broadcast for
     WBAI-FM Radio, March 21, 1980.

26   Alice Baber to Alexandra de Lallier, March 21, 1980.

27   Frances Aronson Gallery, press release, May 12, 1978, AAA.

28   Kaylie Jones, "Memories," in *Alice Baber* (Ronchini Gallery, 2024), 11.

29   October 1978, press release, "the art package ltd., eva h cohon decor,"
     Highland Park, Illinois, AAA.

30   See October 16, 1978, letter from Cornelia Riewald to Alice Baber, making
     arrangements for this program at the American Cultural Center in Paris. See
     also "pour la presse," October 24, 1978, Alice Baber Papers.

31   "Pour la presse," October 24, 1978.

32   "Pour la presse," October 24, 1978. Baber was in Paris from 1959 to 1968.

33   Alice Baber to Fran Switt, just after July 11, 1978, since it mentions Harold
     Rosenberg's recent death. Switt worked for the USIA, from about 1970
     to 1995, mostly as a cultural affairs officer, AAA. Maggie Tripp was also
     involved in organizing this conference on women; see Maggie Tripp to Fran
     Swift, April 11, 1978, AAA.

34   Susan Sontag, "Illness as Metaphor" first appeared, in an earlier version, in *New
     York Review of Books*, January 26, 1978; February 9, 1978; and February 23, 1978.

35   John M. Kern, interview by the author, January 25, 2024.

36   Susan W. Cutter, *Alice Baber, Painter* (Women in the Arts, 1975), 6.

37   Virginia Pitts Rembert, "Alice Baber," in *Alice Baber: A Retrospective Exhibition*
     (Greater Lafayette Museum of Art, 1982), 6. Rembert does not seem to have
     known of the connection of the Isenheim Altarpiece to skin afflictions.

38   For the Isenheim Altarpiece, see Ann Stieglitz, "The Reproduction of Agony:
     Toward a Reception-History of Grünewald's Isenheim Altar After the First
     World War," *Oxford Art Journal* 12, no. 2 (1989): 87–103, https://onlinelibrary
     .wiley.com/doi/10.1111/jdv.19024. See also Nicholas Kluger and Giuliano
     Brandozzi, "Digital Necrosis in the Isenheim Altarpiece (1512–1516)," *Journal
     of the European Academy of Dermatology and Venereology* 31, no. 7 (2023),
     https://onlinelibrary.wiley.com/doi/10.1111/jdv.19024.

39   Henry B. Wheatley, ed., *The Diary of Samuel Pepys* (George Bell and Sons, Ltd.,
     Macmillan, 1893.), 9 vols. These volumes appear to be from different editions. It
     is not clear if Alice read Pepys, but she had access to her father's library.

40   Vivien Raynor, "Art: A 50-Year Camera's-Eye View of Mexico," *New York
     Times*, December 29, 1978, https://www.nytimes.com/1978/12/29/archives
     /art-a-50year-cameraseye-view-of-mexico.html.

41   Margaret Betz, "Alice Baber," *Artnews*, December 1978, vol. 77, 155–56.

42   Leticia Kent, "Mazursky: 'It's O.K. Not to Be Married,'" *New York Times*, March 5,
     1978, https://www.nytimes.com/1978/03/05/archives/mazursky-its-ok-not-to-be
     -married-paul-mazursky-its-ok-not-to-be.html; *People*, June 19, 1978.

43   Alice Baber to Ann [McCoy], undated letter of ca 1978, begins, "I think
     that it a great idea for you to do the article for Art International. Thank you

for thinking of it." Alice Baber Papers, AAA. Ann McCoy, interview by the author, May 25, 2024, confirming that this letter was written by Baber to her, when she was on her way to visit Berlin.

44 Alice Baber, "Long Island," annotated typescript, January 20, 1979, AAA.

45 Baber, "Long Island."

46 Alice Baber to David Galloway, February 14, 1979, Alice Baber Papers.

47 Melody Cooke, "Baber's Work Complex," *Niagara Gazette* (Niagara Falls, NY), February 16, 1979.

48 Cooke, Baber's Work Complex."

49 Enez Whipple, *Guild Hall of East Hampton: An Adventure in the Arts* (Harry N. Abrams, 1993), 39.

50 Guild Hall printed invitation to Alice Baber to participate in Women Artists of Eastern Long Island, January 12, 1979, signed by Rae Ferren, the exhibition coordinator, Alice Baber Papers, Guild Hall.

51 Baber, "Long Island."

52 Baber, "Long Island."

53 These prints are listed in the catalogue for Baber's March 1983 show, *Alice Baber: Walter Colors and Lithographs*, held at the National Gallery of Jamaica, AAA. The third and fifth on the list were each 22 x 30 inches and the others were 19 x 25 inches.

54 "Alice Baber, Untitled (Abstract)," Santa Fe Art Auction, March 15, 2023, https://www.santafeartauction.com/auction-lot/alice-baber-untitled -abstract_1A74901B55.

55 Juan de Muga of Ediciones Polígrafa to Alice Baber, March 29, 1979, AAA.

56 See the list dated January 17, 1983, Alice Baber Papers, AAA, for her 1983 show for USIA in Santo Domingo. Most were 22 x 30 or 32 x 26 inches. Other titles were loaned to her shows in Haiti and Jamaica in 1983. Each edition in Barcelona was for eighty-five prints. The titles for the 1974 lithographs are listed on the checklist for the show, *Alice Baber: Color, Light and Image*, Amerika Haus, Frankfurt, 1980. AAA.

57 Constance Kane, "A Journey of Light and Color," *Alice Baber: Watercolours and Lithographs*, April 26–May 10, 1983, American Center, Port of Spain [Capital of Trinidad and Tobago], AAA.

58 Eleanor Munro, *Originals: American Women Artists* (Simon & Schuster, 1979), 313.

59 See notice of Brandeis University's 12th Annual Regional Art Tour to benefit its library, in which Alice Baber agreed to participate, October 31, 1972. A Brandeis program for a related visit to meet Alice Baber at the home of one of her collectors is dated April 28, 1973, AAA. See February 20, 1973, letter from Smithsonian Associates Resident Program, AAA.

60 See photographs of Baber's loft in Jeffrey Weiss, *Rugs* (New York: W. W. Norton & Co., 1979), 115-118 and Jeffrey Weiss, *Lofts* (New York: W. W. Norton & Co., 1979), 62-66.

61 Virginia Pitts Rembert, "Where Atlantis Is: Alice Baber's Paintings," *Arts Magazine*, February 1978, 125.

62 Brenda Price, "Who's Got What? A Survey of Collectors and their Relationship to Women Artists," *Feminist Art Journal* (Summer 1977): 15–20.

63 Price, "Who's Got What?," 16–17.

64 Alice Baber, interview by E. R., undated transcript, AAA.

65   Alice Baber, interview by E. R.

66   "King Korokī Dies; Māori Leader, 59," *New York Times*, May 20, 1966.
     https://timesmachine.nytimes.com/timesmachine/1966/05/20/90219942.pdf.

67   "King Koroki Dies."

68   Vaughan Yarwood, "Falcon of the Dawn: Maoridom Gains a Queen," *New
     Zealand Geographic*, March–April 2013, https://www.nzgeo.com/stories
     /falcon-of-the-dawn/.

69   Richard Hakluyt, *The Principal Navigations, Voyages, Traffiques and Discoveries
     of the English Nation*, 16 vols. (James MacLehose and Sons, 1589).

70   See Grace Glueck, "2 Museums Are Given $13 Million in Art," *New York
     Times*, February 10, 1979, 23, https://timesmachine.nytimes.com
     /timesmachine/1979/02/10/111072164.html?pageNumber=23. See also
     "House Post Figure (Amo)," Metropolitan Museum of Art, https://www
     .metmuseum.org/art/collection/search/313697.

71   This Māori House Post Figure was shown at the Metropolitan Museum of Art in
     the exhibitions *Art of Oceania, Africa and the Americas from The Museum of Primitive
     Art*, May 10–August 17, 1969; *Sculpture of Oceania*, April 4–September 5, 1972;
     and in *Art of Oceania, Africa and the Americas*, September 22, 1972–1974.

72   Alice Baber, "Gorky's Color," in *Arshile Gorky: Drawings to Paintings*
     (University of Texas Art Gallery, 1975), 76.

73   Rebecca Allan, "Icons of Female Power: Early Works of Miriam Schapiro,"
     Artcritical, February 19, 2016, https://artcritical.com/2016/02/19/rebecca
     -allan-on-miriam-schapiro/.

74   See also several undated works by Alice Baber that include the word *path*: *The
     Jaguar Finds the Red Path to the Mountains*, oil on canvas, 48 x 90 inches; *The
     Path of the Sun Leads to the Piper*, oil on canvas, 91 ½ x 49 ½ x 1 ½ inches; Art
     in Embassies, Washington, DC, gift of the Alice Baber Estate.

75   Alice Baber, interview by Paul Cummings, May 24, 1973, AAA.

76   Alice Baber, interview by Paul Cummings, May 24, 1973.

77   Alice Baber, interview by Paul Cummings, May 24, 1973.

78   In the 1950s, Ernestine Lassaw gave a party to which Rothko and his wife
     came and Baber recalled meeting them. Alice Baber, unpublished interview
     by E. R., before 1969, Alice Baber Papers.

79   Alice Baber, "Night," typescript of unpublished poem, Alice Baber Papers, 23.
     Hand annotated, read at the Lindenwood Poetry Society, which implies that
     she wrote this in her first two years as a college student.

80   Alice Baber to Alexandra de Lallier, March 21, 1980.

81   John Russell, "Louise Reinhardt Smith, 91, Patron of the Modern, Is Dead,"
     New York Times, July 15, 1995, https://www.nytimes.com/1995/07/15
     /obituaries/louise-reinhardt-smith-91-patron-of-the-modern-is-dead.html.
     She bequeathed her collection to the Museum of Modern Art, but gave at
     least two paintings to the Metropolitan Museum—one in 1983 by Claude
     Monet, the other by Georges Braque, which she gave in 1979, in honor of the
     curator William S. Lieberman, who had moved to the Met from MoMA in
     1979 to become chair of the Twentieth-Century Art Department.

82   Since the Met is set to start major construction for its wing devoted to
     contemporary art, it could easily sequester this Baber painting until the
     opening of the new wing, set for 2030.

83 Alice Baber to Alexandra de Lallier, March 21, 1980.

84 Jones, "Memories," 11.

85 Edwin P. "Ted" Kennedy to Alice Baber, November 4, 1980, Alice Baber Papers.

86 Telegram from Frances Aronson Gallery to Alice Baber c/o Betty Gold, March 25, 1980.

87 Ann McCoy, interview by the author, May 25, 2024; Dan Cameron (who was working next door at Tibor de Nagy) to the author, May 6, 2024.

88 Phyllis Braff, "From the Studio," *East Hampton Star*, March 5, 1981. https ://nyshistoricnewspapers.org/?a=d&d=teh19810305-01&e=-------en-20-teh -1--txt-txIN-%22Alice+Baber%22---------. For synchromism, see Gail Levin, *Synchromism and American Abstraction, 1910–1925* (George Braziller, 1978).

89 Braff, "From the Studio."

90 Dr. Donald Arnush to Alice Baber, June 26, 1981; Betty Gold to Alice Baber, get well note postmarked June 1981, AAA.

91 Ann McCoy recalls that Baber's cancer began as a melanoma (interview with the author, December 26, 2023). Baber's nephew John M. Kern (interview with the author, January 25, 2024), who confirms the melanoma, recalls that Baber had an earlier diagnosis, thought that she had beat the disease, only to have it return.

92 Pat Fisher, quoted in Straight, *Nancy Hanks*, 397; Wolfgang Saxon, "Nancy Hanks Is Dead at 55: Headed National Arts Group," *New York Times*, January 8, 1983, 17, https://timesmachine.nytimes.com/timesmachine/1983 /01/08/150904.html?pageNumber=17.

93 Norbert Nelson would also die from melanoma eleven years after Baber. See "Norbert N. Nelson, '50," *Princeton Alumni Weekly*, December 4, 2013, https ://paw.princeton.edu/memorial/norbert-n-nelson-%E2%80%9950.

94 Ce Roser, interview by the author, May 28, 2024.

95 Elsa Honig Fine, *Woman's Art Journal* (Spring/Summer 1982).

96 Sylvia Moore, "Alice Baber," *Women's Art Journal* 3, no. 1 (1982); Alexandra de Lallier, "The Watercolors of Alice Baber," *Woman's Art Journal* 3, no. 1 (1982): 44–46.

97 Ernestine Lassaw, daybook for 1982, in the possession of Denise Lassaw.

98 Jones, "Memories," 11.

99 Margot Wittkower and Rudolf Wittkower, *Born Under Saturn: The Character and Conduct of Artists* (W. W. Norton, 1964).

100 Susan B. Anthony (Richard Galef's widow), interview by the author, July 23, 2024.

101 Arlene Bujese (art dealer), interview by the author, November 23, 2023. Nancy Hanks would donate this and other paintings she owned by Baber to the Nasher Museum of Art at her alma mater, Duke University.

102 Ernestine Lassaw, daybook for 1982.

103 Dorothy Seiberling, "A New Kind of Quilt," *New York Times*, October 3, 1982, https://www.nytimes.com/1982/10/03/magazine/a-new-kind-of-quilt.html.

104 Dorothy Gillespie and Charlotte Robinson to Alice Baber, July 20, 1978, AAA.

105 "Artist to Display Exhibit at University," *Tuscaloosa News*, October 3, 1982, 12C.

106 "Alice Baber," *Paris Beacon-News* (Paris, IL), October 7, 1982.

107 Alice Baber's funeral book, Baber family archives.

108 Fran Switt to Norton Dodge, October 21, 1982, Cremona Foundation.

109 Kathy Matter, "Marquee: Spotlighting the Arts; Alice Baber: A Tribute Sculpture to Salute Artist," *Journal and Courier* (Lafayette, IN), December 6, 1982, 19.

110 Matter, "Marquee."

111 Virginia Pitts Rembert, "Alice Baber," in *Alice Baber: A Retrospective Exhibition* (Greater Lafayette Museum of Art, 1982), 2.

112 Matter, "Marquee."

113 Audrey Flack to Sharon Theobald (executive director of the Greater Lafayette Museum of Art, March 31, 1983.

114 "About the Art Museum," Art Museum of Greater Lafayette, https://www.art lafayette.org/about.

115 Sharon Theobald, interview by the author, February 5, 2024.

116 "A Baber Memorial," *East Hampton Star*, September 22, 1983, https://nys historicnewspapers.org/?a=d&d=teh19830922-01.1.29&srpos=1&e =-------en-20-teh-1--txt-txIN-%22Alice+Baber%22---------.

117 "Baber Memorial."

118 The painting's accession number is 1967.052.

119 "Artistry in Sound: A Musical Experience of Paul Jenkins' 'Phenomena near Baber Woods,'" Terre Haute Symphony Orchestra, April 24, 2024, https://www .thso.org/events/2024/4/14/artistry-in-sound-baber-woods.

120 Annabelle Hebert (director of Guild Hall) to Ernestine Lassaw, October 20, 1983.

121 Handwritten list is in the possession of Denise Lassaw.

122 Denise Lassaw, email to the author, December 27, 2023.

123 Denise Lassaw, email to the author, December 27, 2023.

124 Denise Lassaw, email to the author, December 27, 2023.

125 Norbert N. Nelson to Ernestine and Ibram Lassaw, July 7, 1983, in the possession of Denise Lassaw.

126 Arlene Bujese, ed., *25 Artists by Photographer Hans Namuth* (University Publications of America, 1982), 30–31, 91.

127 Hans Namuth, "Interview," in Bujese, ed., *25 Artists by Photographer Hans Namuth*, 3.

128 Thomas M. Messer, "Foreword," in Bujese, ed., *25 Artists Photographer by Hans Namuth*, ix.

129 Phyllis Braff, email to the author, December 11, 2023.

130 Phyllis Braffto author, December 11, 2023.

131 See Jody Klotz Fine Art, Abilene, Texas, *Alice Baber: Colors of the Rainbow*, May 7–June 21, 2024, the catalogue of which features my essay. See also Berry Campbell Gallery, New York, *Alice Baber: Reverse Infinity*, April 18–May 18, 2024, with an essay by Dan Cameron.

Curator's Notes by Alice Baber

1   Jeanne Siegel used some of our tapes over WBAI, New York City, and it is to her that we owe the name "Color forum."

Gorky's Color by Alice Baber

1   Julien Levy, *Arshile Gorky*, Harry N. Abrams, Inc., New York, p. 34.

2   Karlen Mooradian, "The Unknown Gorky," Art News, 66:52-3+, September 1967.

3   Harold Rosenberg, *Arshile Gorky, the Man, the Time, the Idea*, Horizon Press, Inc., 1962.

4   Levy, *op. cit.*, p. 26.

5   Levy, *op. cit.*, quoting Ethel Schwabacher, p. 30.

6   Ethel K. Schwabacher, *Arshile Gorky*, Whitney Museum of American Art, Macmillan Company, 1957, p. 66.

7   William Seitz, *Arshile Gorky Painting, Drawing, Studies*, Doubleday and Company, Museum of Modern Art, 1962, fold between pp. 31 and 33.

8   Mooradian, *op. cit.*, p. 53.

9   Sandra Ley conversations.

10 Brooks Joyner, *The Drawings of Arshile Gorky*, University of Maryland Art Department and Art Gallery, 1969, p. 7, quoting Ethel Schwabacher, *Arshile Gorky Memorial Exhibition Catalogue*, Whitney Museum of American Art.

11 Stuart Davis, "Arshile Gorky in the 1930s: A Personal Recollection by Stuart Davis," *Magazine of Art*, February 1951, p. 57.

12 For color, Gorky would have seen exhibitions at the Museum of Modern Art, Pierre Matisse, Julien Levy, and others.

13 Joyner, *op. cit.*, p. 12.

14 Schwabacher, *op. cit.*, pp. 73–74.

15 Seitz, *op. cit.*, p. 28.

16 Gustav Vriesen and Max Imdahl, *Robert Delaunay, Light and Color*, Henry N. Abrams, Inc., New York, 1967, p. 61.

17 Rosenberg, *op. cit.*, p. 43.

18 Joyner, *op. cit.*, p. 10, quoting Ethel Schwabacher, *Arshile Gorky Memorial Exhibition Catalogue*, Whitney Museum of American Art.

19 Seitz, *op. cit.*, p. 26.

20 Joyner, *op. cit.*, "My Murals for the Newark Airport—an Interpretation," p. 12; Schwabacher, p. 73.

21 Rosenberg, *op. cit.*, p. 71.

22 Schwabacher, *op. cit.*, p. 66.

23 Schwabacher, *op. cit.*, p. 114.

Acknowledgments

1   After my doctoral dissertation at Rutgers University, "Wassily Kandinsky and the American Avant-Garde, 1912–1950," my first book was *Synchromism and American Color Abstraction, 1910–1925* (George Braziller, 1978). My work on women artists includes trying to inscribe Josephine (Mrs. Edward) Hopper into art history, on whom I first began publishing in 1980; biographies of Judy Chicago (2007), Lee Krasner (2011), and a book and exhibition project on Theresa Bernstein (2013); studies of Sonia Delaunay (2016 and 2024), Frida Kahlo (2021), Connie Fox (2016), and Lynne Drexler (2022); as well as articles on many other contemporary women artists.

2   *Alice Baber: Color Hunger* (Luxembourg & Co., 2023) with an extra essay by Lydia Yee.

3   See Jody Klotz Fine Art, *Alice Baber: Colors of the Rainbow*, exhibition, May 7–June 21, 2024, the catalogue of which features my essay. See also Berry Campbell Gallery, *Alice Baber: Reverse Infinity*, exhibition, April 18–May 18, 2024, with essay by Dan Cameron.

4   See Ronchini Gallery, *Alice Baber* (Ronchini, 2024) with texts by Eliza Gregory, Kaylie Jones, and Piero Tomassoni.

INDEX